Unintended consequences of peacekeeping operations

Unintended consequences of peacekeeping operations

Edited by Chiyuki Aoi, Cedric de Coning and Ramesh Thakur

United Nations
University Press

TOKYO · NEW YORK · PARIS

United Nations University Press
United Nations University, 53-70, Jingumae 5-chome,
Shibuya-ku, Tokyo 150-8925, Japan
Tel: +81-3-5467-1212   Fax: +81-3-3406-7345
E-mail: sales@hq.unu.edu   general enquiries: press@hq.unu.edu
http://www.unu.edu

United Nations University Office at the United Nations, New York
2 United Nations Plaza, Room DC2-2062, New York, NY 10017, USA
Tel: +1-212-963-6387   Fax: +1-212-371-9454
E-mail: unuona@ony.unu.edu

United Nations University Press is the publishing division of the United Nations University.

Cover design by Mea Rhee

Printed in the United States of America

ISBN 978-92-808-1142-1

Library of Congress Cataloging-in-Publication Data

Unintended consequences of peacekeeping operations / edited by Chiyuki Aoi,
Cedric de Coning, and Ramesh Thakur.
   p.   cm.
  Includes index.
  ISBN 978-9280811421 (pbk.)
  1. United Nations—Peacekeeping forces. 2. United Nations—Armed Forces.
I. Aoi, Chiyuki. II. De Coning, Cedric. III. Thakur, Ramesh Chandra, 1948–
JZ6374.U53   2007
341.5′84—dc22   2007003294

Contents

Tables

Contributors

Katarina Ammitzboell, from
Denmark, has more than 10 years
of experience with governance,
conflict resolution and post-conflict
situations, including Afghanistan,
Timor Leste, Burundi, Mozambique,
South Africa, Egypt, Lebanon,
Senegal and Chile. She has worked
for the United Nations, non-
governmental organizations,
research institutions and
government. She holds an MSc in
International Development and
Public Sector Economics and an
LLM in International Human
Rights Law and Islamic Law from
England. Her area of specialization
is state-building and political
institutional development with a
focus on democratic governance,
constitutional processes, justice,
human rights, Islamic law and legal
pluralism. She has been working
both in and with Afghanistan for
over three years with the United
Nations Development Programme
as assistant country director for
governance, which included
programmes in support of the Bonn
process. She was a consultant for
the multi-donor evaluation on
state-building, disarmament,
demobilization and reintegration,
and provincial reconstruction teams
that has just been released.
Currently she works as a
Democratisation Expert for
the European Commission and
is finalizing research on
democratization in Afghanistan.

Kwesi Aning attended the University
of Ghana, Legon, and subsequently
earned a PhD in Political Science
from the University of Copenhagen,
Denmark. He has taught at several
universities in Denmark, Austria,
the United Kingdom, Nigeria, Sierra
Leone and Ghana, where he was
attached to the Legon Centre for
International Affairs (LECIA). Dr
Aning serves on and reviews articles
for several international journals
and has published extensively in

scholarly journals and contributed several book chapters. His most recent publications have appeared in *Asian and African Studies*, *Encyclopedia of African History*, *Review of African Political Economy*, *Conflict, Security and Development* and *African Security Review*. Dr Aning presently works with the African Union Commission in Addis Ababa, Ethiopia, where he occupies the position of Expert, Common African Defence and Security Policy (CADSP) and Counter-terrorism.

Chiyuki Aoi is an Associate Professor of International Politics at Aoyama Gakuin University in Tokyo. She was previously an Academic Programme Officer at the United Nations University and a Junior Professional Officer at the United Nations High Commissioner for Refugees. She was educated in Japan at Sophia University (BA) and the University of Tokyo, and in the United States at the Massachusetts Institute of Technology (MS) and Columbia University (PhD).

Cedric de Coning is a Research Fellow with the African Centre for the Constructive Resolution of Disputes (ACCORD) and the Norwegian Institute of International Affairs (NUPI). He started his career with the South African Department of Foreign Affairs and served in Washington DC and Addis Ababa (1988–1997). While in Addis Ababa he was deployed on election observer missions for the Organization of African Unity to Ethiopia, Algeria and Sudan. On his return to South Africa he joined ACCORD as Programme

Manager of the Training for Peace Programme and later as Assistant Director (1997–2000). He served with the United Nations Transitional Administration in East Timor in 2001 and with the UN Department of Peacekeeping Operations in New York in 2002. He holds a Master's degree (Cum Laude) in Conflict Management and Peace Studies from the University of KwaZulu-Natal, South Africa, and is a DPhil candidate with the Department of Political Studies of the University of Stellenbosch, South Africa. He is the Secretary General of the United Nations Association of South Africa and a Senior Research Associate with the Centre for International Political Studies at the University of Pretoria.

Stuart Gordon is a Senior Lecturer in the Department of Defence and International Affairs at the Royal Military Academy, UK. During 2003 he was Operations Director for the US/UK Iraq Humanitarian Operations Centre (Baghdad). Recent publications include *Alms and Armour* (Manchester University Press, forthcoming); "Development, Democracy and Counter Insurgency: Evaluating Nepal's Integrated 'Security' and 'Development' Policy", *Asian Survey*, Vol. 45, No. 4, July/August 2005; "Military–Humanitarian Relationships and the Invasion of Iraq: Reforging Certainties?", *Journal of Humanitarian Assistance*, 2003.

Françoise J. Hampson taught at the University of Dundee, Scotland, before moving to the Department of Law and Human Rights Centre at the University of Essex, UK, where she is currently a Professor.

Her principal areas of interest are the law of armed conflict and international/regional human rights law, in which fields she has published and lectured widely. She was on the Steering Committee and Panel of Experts of the International Committee of the Red Cross for the study on customary international humanitarian law. She has been the applicants' legal representative in many cases before the European Court of Human Rights, in connection with which she was awarded the Liberty Human Rights Lawyer of the Year award in 1998, with her colleague Professor Kevin Boyle. She has been a member of the UN Sub-Commission on the Promotion and Protection of Human Rights since 1998. She is a Governor of the British Institute of Human Rights.

Florian F. Hoffmann currently teaches international law and human rights in the Law Department at the Catholic University of Rio de Janeiro (PUC-Rio, Brazil). He is also the Deputy Director of that department's human rights centre, the Núcleo de Direitos Humanos. He did his undergraduate studies in law and government at the London School of Economics and Political Science, and holds a Master's degree (*Mestrado em Ciências Jurídicas*) from the PUC-Rio. He gained his PhD in Law at the European University Institute (Florence, Italy) with a thesis entitled "Can Human Rights Be Transplanted: Reflections on a Pragmatic Theory of Human Rights under Conditions of Globalization". His research interests include human rights in theory and practice,

international accountability, international legal theory and general legal philosophy. Within the Núcleo de Direitos Humanos he is, *inter alia*, co-coordinating a research project on "International Trade, Development, and Human Rights", which seeks to work on the interface between these three issue areas from the perspective of the global South, and a study on "Rights Consciousness, Access to Justice, and Alternative Means to Realise Human Rights", conducted jointly with the NGO VivaRio. He is, *inter alia*, a member of the Executive Board of *Sur – Human Rights University Network*, a book review editor for the *Leiden Journal of International Law*, a European and International Law editor for the *German Law Journal*, and a member of the editing team of the incipient *CPOG-J – Journal of Critical Perspectives on Global Governance*.

Vanessa Kent is a Senior Researcher and Training Co-ordinator for the Training for Peace Programme at the Institute for Security Studies (ISS) in Pretoria, South Africa. She joined the ISS after working for the Canadian Department of Foreign Affairs, where she was responsible for issues related to United Nations peace operations, and before that coordinated the work of the G8 Political Director. Prior to joining Foreign Affairs, she worked as international project and development co-ordinator for the Palestinian Legislative Council in the West Bank (Palestinian territories) and political research officer for the League of Arab States (London Mission). She holds an MA in War Studies from King's College, London (UK).

Ai Kihara-Hunt, a Japanese national brought up in Japan and Germany and educated in the United Kingdom, has worked in the field with different peacekeeping operations, intergovernmental organizations and non-governmental organizations in human rights. These include the Organization for Security and Co-operation in Europe in Bosnia and Herzegovina; the United Nations Mission in East Timor, the United Nations Transitional Administration in East Timor and the Commission for Reception, Truth and Reconciliation (CAVR) in Timor Leste; and the United Nations High Commissioner for Refugees in Sri Lanka. She has obtained an MA in Rural Development from the University of Sussex, UK, and an LLM in International Human Rights Law from the University of Essex, UK. Her main professional area of interest is the interpretation and application of international human rights law in different contexts, chiefly in post-conflict situations. She is currently working in the Office of the High Commissioner for Human Rights.

Shukuko Koyama is a PhD candidate at the University of Bradford, UK. Shukuko has worked as a Project Officer at the United Nations Institute for Disarmament Research, Geneva, Switzerland, and a Disarmament, Demobilization and Reintegration Officer with the United Nations Organization Mission in the Democratic Republic of Congo (MONUC).

Shin-wha Lee is an Associate Professor in the Department of Political Science and International Relations at Korea University and is Research Director of Ilmin International Relations Institute at Korea University. She received her PhD (International Relations) from the University of Maryland at College Park, USA, and held a Post-Doctoral Fellowship at the Center for International Affairs, Harvard University, USA (1994–1997). Among her previous positions were Researcher at the World Bank (1992); Co-ordinator of Minorities at Risk Project (1993–1994); Special Advisor to "the Rwandan Independent Enquiry" appointed by UN Secretary-General Kofi Annan (1999); Chair's Advisor of ASEAN+3 East Asian Vision Group (2000–2001); Korean Delegate of the Korea-China-Japan Future Leaders Forum (2004); and Visiting Scholar at the East Asian Studies Programme, Princeton University, USA (2005). Professor Lee has published more than 60 books and articles (in English and Korean) covering the fields of non-traditional security issues, East Asian cooperation and regionalism, and the role of the United Nations and international organizations in global peace and security.

Frédéric Mégret, PhD (Université de Paris I, Graduate Institute of International Studies of the University of Geneva), is an Assistant Professor of Law and the Canada Research Chair on the Law of Human Rights and Legal Pluralism at the University of McGill, Canada. Before joining the University of McGill, he was an

Assistant Professor in the Faculty of Law of the University of Toronto, Canada, and a research associate at the European University Institute in Florence, Italy. In the past, Professor Mégret has worked for the International Committee of the Red Cross and assisted the defence counsel of one of the accused before the International Criminal Tribunal for Rwanda, and he was a member of the French delegation at the Rome conference that created the International Criminal Court. As part of his military service in France, he was a Peacekeeper with the United Nations Protection Force (UNPROFOR) in Sarajevo in 1995. Professor Mégret is currently co-editing the second edition of *The United Nations and Human Rights: A Critical Appraisal* (Oxford University Press, 2006) with Professor Philip Alston. Most recently, Professor Mégret has been advising the Liberian government on the design of a vetting procedure to screen out applicants to the Liberian armed forces who may have been involved in war crimes or grave human rights abuses.

C. S. R. Murthy is a Professor in International Organization at the Centre for International Politics, Organization and Disarmament, School of International Studies, Jawaharlal Nehru University, New Delhi, India. He was Chairperson of that Centre from 2003 to 2005. He has authored one book, *India's Diplomacy in the United Nations: Problems and Perspectives* (Lancers Books, 1993) and edited three books, including *India and UNESCO: Five Decades of Cooperation* (Indian National Commission for Cooperation with UNESCO, 1997). He has contributed some 40 papers in reputed journals and books touching upon international conflicts and security, peacekeeping, the United Nations, including Security Council reform, the third world, human rights and India's foreign policy. He is also Editor-in-Chief for *International Studies*, a premier academic journal published in India. He was Fulbright Scholar at the Institute of War and Peace Studies, Columbia University, New York, USA, from 1993 to 1994. From 1983 to 1984 he was Leverhulme Commonwealth Visiting Fellow at the Department of International Relations, University of Keele, UK.

Henri Myrttinen, MSc, is a Researcher with the Indonesian Society for Social Transformation (INSIST) in Yogyakarta, Indonesia. One of his focal areas is researching issues linked to gender and violence. He has worked extensively on these issues in Southeast Asia and is currently writing his PhD on masculinity and violence in Timor Leste for the University of KwaZulu-Natal, South Africa.

Arturo C. Sotomayor is an Assistant Professor of international relations and Latin American comparative politics in the Division of International Studies of the Centro de Investigación y Docencia Económicas (CIDE) in Mexico City. His areas of interest include civil–military relations in Latin America, UN peacekeeping participation by South American countries and Latin American comparative foreign policy, especially vis-à-vis the United

Nations. He is the current coordinator of the Academic Workshop on National and International Security in Mexico. He received his PhD in political science from Columbia University, USA. His publications have appeared in the *Journal of Latin American Politics and Society, Revista Mexicana de Política Exterior* and edited volumes. He is currently working on a book on Latin American engagement in UN-sponsored peace operations.

Ramesh Thakur is a Distinguished Fellow at the Centre for International Governance Innovation and Professor of Political Science at the University of Waterloo in Canada. He was Vice Rector and Senior Vice Rector of the United Nations University (and Assistant Secretary-General of the United Nations) from 1998 to 2007. Born in India, Professor Thakur was educated in India and Canada and has held full-time academic appointments in Fiji, New Zealand and Australia and visiting appointments elsewhere. He was Professor of International Relations and Director of Asian Studies at the University of Otago in New Zealand and Professor and Head of the Peace Research Centre at the Australian National University in Canberra before joining UNU in 1998. He was a Commissioner on the International Commission on Intervention and State Sovereignty and one of the principal authors of its report *The Responsibility to Protect*. He was Senior Adviser on Reforms and Principal Writer of the UN Secretary-General's second reform report. He is the author/editor of some 30 books, the most recent being *From Sovereign Impunity to International Accountability: The Search for Justice in a World of States* (United Nations University Press, 2004), *Making States Work: State Failure and the Crisis of Governance* (United Nations University Press, 2005), *International Commissions and the Power of Ideas* (United Nations University Press, 2005), and *The United Nations, Peace and Security: From Collective Security to the Responsibility to Protect* (Cambridge University Press, 2006). He also writes regularly for the national and international quality press, including the *Australian, Daily Yomiuri, Die Tageszeitung, Globe and Mail, Hindu, International Herald Tribune* and *Japan Times*.

Preface

This book was produced through a joint project by the United Nations University (UNU) in Tokyo, the African Centre for the Constructive Resolution of Disputes (ACCORD) in Durban, and the Training for Peace (TfP) Programme. The TfP Programme is a partnership between the Norwegian Institute of International Affairs (NUPI), the Institute for Security Studies (ISS) and ACCORD, and is funded by the Royal Norwegian Ministry of Foreign Affairs. The co-editors were drawn from the UNU and the TfP Programme at ACCORD, and the development process and research were funded by UNU and Norway through the TfP Programme.

This book project has, from the outset, consciously striven to add gender, multicultural and global perspectives to its research through the choice of the examples and geographical cases covered, and, most importantly, through the choice of the editors and contributing authors. Among the three editors and thirteen contributing authors there are seven women. All the inhabited continents are represented, and the countries of origin of the authors include: Australia, Canada, France, Finland, Denmark, Germany, Ghana, India, Japan, Korea, South Africa, the United Kingdom and Uruguay. A special effort was made to incorporate researchers from as wide a range of disciplines as possible, and the different disciplines represented include: conflict resolution, human rights, international law, international relations, peace studies, political science and security studies.

Chiyuki Aoi
Cedric de Coning
Ramesh Thakur

Abbreviations

ACCORD	African Centre for the Constructive Resolution of Disputes
ACOTA	African Contingency Operations Training Assistance
AU	African Union
BOI	Board of Inquiry
CA	civil affairs
CARE	Co-operative for Assistance and Relief Everywhere
CEDAW	Convention to Eliminate all Forms of Discrimination Against Women
CIMIC	civil–military cooperation
CIVPOL	Civilian Police
CMCoord	humanitarian civil–military coordination
CMOCs	Civil–Military Operations Centres
CUNPK	Centre for United Nations Peacekeeping
DDR	disarmament, demobilization and reintegration
DPKO	Department of Peacekeeping Operations
DRC	Democratic Republic of Congo
ECOMOG	ECOWAS cease-fire monitoring group
ECOWAS	Economic Community of West African States
GAF	Ghana Armed Forces
GoG	Government of Ghana
GPS	Ghana Police Service
HIV/AIDS	human immunodeficiency virus/acquired immune deficiency syndrome
HPD	Housing and Property Directorate
ICRC	International Committee of the Red Cross
IGO	intergovernmental organization
ILA	International Law Association

INGO	international non-governmental organization
Interfet	International Force for East Timor
IO	international organization
ISAF	International Security Assistance Force [Afghanistan]
ISS	Institute for Security Studies
KFOR	Kosovo Force
KPC	Kosovo Protection Corps
MONUC	Mission des Nations Unies en République Démocratique du Congo (United Nations Organization Mission in the Democratic Republic of Congo)
MOs	Military Observers
MOU	Memorandum of Understanding
NATO	North Atlantic Treaty Organization
NGO	non-governmental organization
OCHA	Office for the Coordination of Humanitarian Affairs
OEF	Operation Enduring Freedom
OHCHR	Office of the UN High Commissioner for Human Rights
OIK	Ombudsperson Institution in Kosovo
OIOS	Office of Internal Oversight Services
ONUB	United Nations Operation in Burundi
OSCE	Organization for Security and Co-operation in Europe
PISGs	Provisional Institutions of Self-Government
PKF	peacekeeping force
PNTL	Policia Nacional de Timor Leste
PRTs	Provincial Reconstruction Teams
PSOs	peace support operations
RDTL	Republica Democrática de Timor Leste
RPF	Rwandan Patriotic Front
SEA	sexual exploitation and abuse
SGBV	sexual and gender-based violence
SNA	Somali National Alliance
SOFA	Status-of-Forces Agreement
SRSG	Special Representative of the Secretary-General
STDs	sexually transmitted diseases
TCC	troop-contributing country
TfP	Training for Peace Programme
UÇK	Ushtria Çlirimtare e Kosovës
UK	United Kingdom
UN	United Nations
UNAMA	United Nations Assistance Mission in Afghanistan
UNAMIR	United Nations Assistance Mission for Rwanda
UNAMSIL	United Nations Mission in Sierra Leone
UNDP	United Nations Development Programme
UNHCR	United Nations High Commissioner for Refugees
UNICEF	United Nations Children's Fund [previously the United Nations International Children's Emergency Fund]
UNIFEM	United Nations Development Fund for Women

UNMIK	United Nations Interim Administration Mission in Kosovo
UNMIL	United Nations Mission in Liberia
UNMISET	United Nations Mission of Support in East Timor
UNMOGIP	United Nations Military Observer Group in India and Pakistan
UNOSOM	United Nations Operation in Somalia
UNPKO	United Nations Peacekeeping Operation
UNPOL	UN police
UNPROFOR	United Nations Protection Force for the former Yugoslavia
UNTAC	United Nations Transitional Authority in Cambodia
UNTAET	United Nations Transitional Administration in East Timor
UNU	United Nations University
US	United States

Part I

Introduction

1

Unintended consequences, complex peace operations and peacebuilding systems

Chiyuki Aoi, Cedric de Coning and Ramesh Thakur

This book deals with the simple but rather stark reality – that peace operations do not generate only positive and beneficial outcomes. Peace operations can also have negative consequences – an increase in corruption and criminal activities such as trafficking for example. Peace operations tend to distort the host economy, may cause an increase in sexual violence against women and children and may add to the spread of HIV/AIDS.

No intervention in a complex system such as a human society can have only one effect. Whenever there is an attempt to bring about change in a complex system, the system reacts in a variety of ways. Some of these reactions are *intended*, in the sense that the intervention was designed to bring about these changes. Others are *unintended*, in that those planning the intervention did not mean for these reactions to come about at all.

The traditional focus on peace operations has been on their intended consequences. Researchers and practitioners are typically concerned with improving the ability of peace operations to achieve their intended objectives. We have studied peace operations to find out whether they have been successful, and in measuring their success our focus has usually been on whether they have achieved the mandate they were tasked with. However, various incidents over the last decade have drawn our attention to the fact that peace operations can also generate unintended consequences. In the months leading up to the UN World Summit in 2005, the two examples that were the most frequently used to criticize and ridicule the United Nations, and its Secretary-General, were the

Unintended consequences of peacekeeping operations, Aoi, de Coning and Thakur (eds), United Nations University Press, 2007, ISBN 978-92-808-1142-1

Iraq "oil-for-food scandal" and the sexual abuses perpetrated by UN peacekeepers in the Democratic Republic of Congo (DRC). Both of these examples were especially shocking precisely because of their unintended and counterintuitive nature.

This book is an attempt to shed light on these unintended consequences, not to further de-legitimize peace operations but to encourage lessons learned aimed at improving our ability to undertake peace operations in a more effective and less damaging way in future. In order to do so, we have to understand how unintended consequences come about and explore ways in which we can improve our ability to anticipate and counter potential negative unintended consequences.

Unpacking the terminology

In an edited volume of this nature, it is necessary to start by clarifying what we mean by the terms "unintended consequences" and "peace operations". The varied contributors to this volume have been selected to bring a range of different insights into peace operations and their unintended consequences. Some associate peace operations with United Nations peacekeeping operations in the Democratic Republic of Congo or Timor Leste. Others think of NATO-style peace support operations in Kosovo or stability operations undertaken by coalitions of the willing such as the International Security Assistance Force (ISAF) in Afghanistan. And there are examples of unintended consequences from all these missions in this volume. However, in the end the contributors agreed to use the UN collective term for its range of interventions, namely "peace operations".

Peace operations

"Peace operations", the term used in this book, refers to a whole range of multidimensional, multifunctional and complex peace operations, authorized by the UN Security Council, that involve not only military but also various civilian and police components. Although the primary focus is naturally on the United Nations, various chapters in this book incorporate the reality that contemporary peace operations are undertaken not only by the United Nations, but by a variety of other actors, including coalitions of the willing such as ISAF, security alliances such as the North Atlantic Treaty Organization, regional organizations such as the European Union and the African Union and subregional organizations such as the Economic Community of West African States.[1] We exclude military interventions or actions that fall outside the peacekeeping to peace enforcement spectrum, such as counter-insurgency operations, anti-terrorism operations, war and occupation.

The mandates of peace operations vary considerably, but in general they are international interventions undertaken in support of a peace process. In the short term they are designed to monitor cease-fire agreements, provide an enabling secure environment for humanitarian action and prevent a relapse into conflict. In the medium to long term, their purpose is to address the root causes of a conflict and to lay the foundations for social justice and sustainable peace. However, peace operations cannot achieve such a broad mandate on their own and need to be understood as an integral part of a larger peacebuilding system that consists of security; political, governance and participation; humanitarian; socio-economic; and justice and reconciliation dimensions. In this context, peace operations are embedded in a larger post-conflict peacebuilding project that simultaneously pursues a broad range of programmes that collectively and cumulatively address both the causes and consequences of a conflict, with the aim of achieving a system-wide impact across the conflict spectrum.

Peacebuilding systems facilitate several simultaneous short-, medium- and longer-term programmes at multiple levels, with a broad range of partners and from a wide range of disciplines, to prevent disputes from escalating, to avoid a relapse into violent conflict and to build and consolidate sustainable peace. In this complex multi-agency environment, peacebuilding requires coordination with a wide range of internal and external actors, including government, civil society, the private sector and a multitude of international organizations, agencies and non-governmental organizations, so that the total overall effect of their various initiatives has a coherent impact on the peace process.

Unintended consequences

As peace operation activities have grown in complexity, so have their side-effects. Traditional peacekeeping rested on the assumption that it had no impact on the future direction of the peace process other than to offer a neutral third-party service that would objectively monitor a cease-fire; i.e. the assumption was that the peacekeeping operation was neutral in its effect.[2] In the post–Cold War era, however, the focus of international conflict management has increasingly shifted from peacekeeping, which was intended to maintain the status quo, to peace operations, which are intended to manage change.[3]

As stated earlier, and as will be explored in more detail below, it is not possible to intervene in a complex system such as a human community and have only one effect. Whenever we attempt to change something in a complex system, the system responds to our intervention in a number of ways. We can anticipate that the system will respond in some of these ways, and some of these responses will have been the intended response that we wanted to elicit. However, the system is likely also to respond in other ways that we did not anticipate. All those reactions that fall outside the scope of the response we wanted to elicit are the unintended consequences of our intervention.

The peace operations that are the subjects of our research in this book have mandates that are formulated in the form of a United Nations Security Council resolution. The intended consequences of these operations can be assessed by analysing these mandates. The unintended consequences generated by these operations refer to acts that were not intended when these mandates were adopted or when they were executed.

Some unintended consequences could be foreseen or anticipated, especially if they have occurred in similar circumstances in the past, whereas others may be totally unexpected. These nuances may have important implications and will be discussed in more detail below. It is also important to note that not all side-effects are necessarily negative; some may be neutral and others may actually be positive. This volume will describe and give examples of all three types of unintended consequences, although our primary focus will be on negative unintended consequences because they are potentially the most harmful to the society peacekeepers are intended to serve, as well as to peace operations themselves.

A few qualifications need to be made. Unintended consequences need to be distinguished from a failure to achieve the intended consequences. For example, we exclude from our understanding of unintended consequences failures in achieving economic growth, where economic recovery was mandated, in addressing public crimes, where the maintenance of public security was intended, or in keeping the peace, where peacekeepers were mandated to contain conflicts.

Secondly, unintended consequences need to be distinguished from the "mixed motive" phenomenon in intervention decisions. We accept that states participating in peace operations may have motives for supporting operations other than those stated in the formal mandate of the operation. These motives typically include national interests, such as fear that the territory of the state in conflict may be used by international terrorists, or that armed groups opposing the government of a neighbouring country may use the chaos of the conflict to launch attacks against it. Or they may relate to a country's policy to limit the flow of refugees into its territory. Our definition of unintended consequences does not consider these mixed motives themselves as unintended consequences of peace operations, although they may cause or aggravate unintended consequences and will then be addressed in that context.

Thirdly, the fact that this book is devoted to unintended consequences is not meant to suggest that peace operations are doomed to failure or that unintended consequences will always impede the ability of a mission to achieve its intended outcome. It is difficult to make a general assessment of the overall scale and impact of unintended consequences on peace operations. From the cases studied in this book there are few, if any, missions that have failed as a direct result of the unintended consequences they have generated.[4] There are many, however, whose effectiveness has been hindered by some of the unintended consequences that have come about as a result of its actions.

This book will conclude that, in general, the success of peace operations has been qualified by negative consequences. But to assess the scope and scale of the degree to which this has been the case one would need to focus on each particular mission. This volume contains a number of country-specific studies[5] that provide us with a wide array of mission-specific examples. We will see that in some countries the unintended consequences may be of such a scale that they have a minimal impact on the ability of the peace operation to fulfil its mandate. In others, potentially damaging unintended consequences may be identified at an early stage and managed. In some cases, however, for instance the sexual exploitation and abuse by peacekeepers in the DRC, the unintended consequences may have a severe impact far beyond the mission itself. The various examples of unintended consequences studied in this book suggest that some unintended consequences are overestimated,[6] whereas other consequences may be only remotely connected to the peace operation itself,[7] for there are many variables that influence the outcomes of these complex processes. The book makes the point that unintended consequences come about as part of the dynamic character of complex systems and cannot be avoided. However, we can improve our ability to anticipate, mitigate and discount potential negative unintended consequences and, if we do so, this should result in the improvement of the overall effectiveness of peace operations.

Objective

This brings us to the purpose of this book, which in the first place is to contribute to the improvement of peace operations. The book considers peace operations to be an important instrument in the range of options available to the international community when it attempts to prevent conflict, contain its consequences or manage peace processes. It is therefore in our collective interest to learn lessons from both our successes and our failures, so as to continuously refine and enhance our capacity to undertake more effective peace operations.

This book is an attempt to focus on one aspect of peace operations that needs to be better understood, namely their unintended consequences. We now know from recent literature, public criticism and international debate that some of these unintended consequences can be extremely damaging to individuals and communities where peacekeepers are deployed. Unintended consequences can weaken the ability of the peace operation to achieve its intended objectives. Some can be harmful to the very concept of peaceful interventions, and may even undermine the legitimacy of the organizations that are responsible for the deployment and supervision of peacekeepers. In order to avoid these potentially negative unintended consequences, we need to understand how they come about and explore ways in which we can improve our ability to anticipate and counter such potential negative unintended consequences. The objective of this book is to make a modest contribution towards enhancing our understanding of the unintended consequences of peace operations.

The editors and contributing authors were struck by the absence of literature on, or even remotely related to, the phenomenon of unintended consequences. Most of the references that were available are anecdotal. The failure to take unintended consequences into account probably stems from the fact that researchers and practitioners have been preoccupied with the intended consequences of peace operations – whether a certain mission has achieved its original intended mandate. The only notable exception to this trend has been the focus given within the realist school of international relations to unintended strategic consequences of limited military intervention, including peace operations.[8]

This lack of attention to and awareness of the unintended consequences of peace operations is probably also due to the deeply embedded and uncritical liberal assumptions about peace operations. Not only are peace operations expected to serve largely liberal-internationalist purposes of creating stable, market-oriented democratic polities,[9] which are regarded as inherently "good", but they are at the same time expected to be successful. Decision-makers, practitioners in the field and analysts operate according to the belief that peace operations authorized by the UN Security Council reflect the will of the international community and therefore are inherently "good". Peace operations are therefore expected to produce positive outcomes such as promoting stability and durable peace; they are expected to rebuild and develop; and they are expected to generate respect for the rule of law, human rights and democracy. Participation in peace operations by troop-contributing countries is thus a contribution to the global good and the risks involved, including casualties, are regarded as a noble sacrifice for the greater good.[10] After the failures of the missions in Somalia, Bosnia and Rwanda in the early 1990s, the liberal assumption has been tempered to accept that peace operations may, for a variety of reasons, fail to produce these *intended* results. However, the liberal assumption has not yet matured to the extent where it is commonly recognized that peace operations also generate *unintended consequences* – especially negative economic, social or political side-effects that are contrary to the liberal intent.

The fact that peace operations will generate a variety of unintended consequences, some of which may be negative and even pathological to the mandate or the intended consequences of the mission, is thus counter-intuitive to many observers under the influence of the liberal assumption that peace operations are inherently "good". This book hopes to contribute to breaking down that outdated myth, and to stimulate an awareness that "unintended consequences" are a natural characteristic of complex systems, so that it becomes common practice for decision-makers, practitioners and researchers to anticipate, mitigate and discount, as far as it is possible, potential unintended consequences in their planning, execution and evaluation of peace operations.

Methodology

This edited volume is a collection of studies into various aspects and examples of unintended consequences. Its aim is to improve our understanding of the phenomenon by comparing some of the forms unintended consequences may take, by analysing their causes and impact and by assessing some of the ways in which the international community has tried to manage unintended consequences in the past. The specific examples are complemented by a couple of chapters that analyse the broader phenomenon and, through the introductory and concluding chapters, we hope to shed some light on the different ways in which unintended consequences have been manifested in the past, as well as suggest ways in which unintended consequences can be categorized and offer some recommendations as to how they can be anticipated and countered in future.

Over the last decade, various unintended consequences were identified or hinted at in various types of literature, by international organizations like the United Nations and in public debate. From these, we have selected a couple of examples as being representative of unintended consequences in general, and that could be meaningfully explored in more depth in order to gain deeper insight into the phenomenon. In Part II, the book deals with unintended consequences that have an impact on individuals and groups. In Chapter 2, Henri Myrttinen and Shukuko Koyama look at the unintended consequences of peace operations on Timor Leste from a gender perspective, and, in Chapter 3, Vanessa Kent deals with the sexual exploitation and abuse of civilians by UN peacekeepers and humanitarian workers, with specific reference to Liberia.

In Part III, Katarina Ammitzboell looks into the impact of peace operations on the host economy, with reference to Afghanistan and Kosovo (Chapter 4). Shin-wha Lee focuses on the unintended consequences of peace operations on humanitarian action in Chapter 5. In Chapter 6, Stuart Gordon looks at the unintended consequences of civil–military coordination on peace operations.

In Part IV, the book focuses on the unintended consequences of peace operations for troop-contributing countries. Chapters 7, 8 and 9 look at the phenomenon from the perspective of three prominent troop-contributing countries and regions. Kwesi Aning deals with the case of Ghana in West Africa, C. S. R. Murthy looks into the case of India and South Asia and Arturo C. Sotomayor studies Argentina and Uruguay in the southern cone of South America.

In Part V, the book looks at how the international community can, and has, dealt with unintended consequences. In Chapter 10, Françoise J. Hampson and Ai Kihara-Hunt consider the ways in which the international community deals with violations by international personnel. Florian F. Hoffmann studies the case of the Ombudsman in Kosovo, as one example of how to manage potential unintended consequences, in Chapter 11. And, in Chapter 12, Frédéric Mégret deals with the vicarious responsibility of the United Nations when faced with unintended consequences.

We would have liked to have included some additional chapters. We wanted one on HIV/AIDS but could not find an author willing or able to address this topic, owing to a lack of comparative data. We would have liked to add a chapter on corruption, but again were unable to find an author able to address this topic. Although various chapters in this volume deal with the way in which the United Nations and others have responded to specific unintended consequences, the editors would have liked to add a chapter on the contemporary policies and procedures that the United Nations, at the headquarters level, has in place to deal with some of these unintended consequences. The United Nations was itself, however, dealing with the fallout of the "sex for aid" scandal in West Africa and the sexual exploitation and abuse by peacekeepers in the DRC and other peace operations at the time this book was researched, and was therefore preoccupied with reassessing its own policies and procedures. In this context, the United Nations declined to contribute such a chapter and, because most of this information was not in the public domain, we were unable to find an author who had sufficient knowledge of the internal procedures and policies of the United Nations system to do justice to this topic.

Theoretical explanations for unintended consequences

It may be of use to consider whether and how unintended consequences have been dealt with by others in the past. This section touches on a couple of theoretical approaches to unintended consequences or related topics with a view to shedding light on the different theoretical explanations that have been put forward in the past to explain unintended consequences and how to manage them.

Complex systems theory

In his book *System Effects: Complexity in Political and Social Life*, Robert Jervis[11] argues that, although it is widely known that social life and politics constitute systems, we do not seem to recognize that many outcomes are the unintended consequences of complex interactions. According to Jervis, we are dealing with a system when (a) a set of units or elements is interconnected so that changes in some elements or their relations produce changes in other parts of the system, and (b) the entire system exhibits properties and behaviours that are different from those of the parts.[12] Jervis argues that, as a result, systems often display non-linear relationships, which means that outcomes cannot be understood by adding together the units or their relations, and many of the results of actions are unintended. Many others, such as Cilliers,[13] regard non-linearity as a key defining element of complex systems. According to these theorists, unintended consequences should thus be understood within the context of a dynamic, non-linear, complex system that is constantly self-regulating through multiple feedback mechanisms. You do not need a complex system to have unintended consequences but, when you are dealing with complex systems, unintended consequences should be understood as a natural outcome of the dynamics of such a system and the phenomenon should therefore not come as a surprise.

Jervis goes on to point out that, in a system, the chains of consequences extend over time and over many areas and they are always multiple. He uses the example of doctors, who refer to the undesired impacts of medication as "side-effects". Although there is no criterion other than our intent to determine which effects are the intended effects and which effects are "side" effects, the point is that disturbing a system will produce several changes.[14] Hardin agrees with Jervis when he argues that, as result of the interconnectedness of systems, one can never merely do one thing. He argues that in a complex system it is not possible to develop "a highly specific agent which will do only one thing".[15]

Charles Perrow studied "error-inducing" systems whose problems cannot be traced to faults in any particular element or to the relationship between any of them. He found that when interconnections are dense it may be difficult to trace the impact of any change even after the fact, let alone predict it ahead of time, making the system complex and hard to control.[16]

Interconnections are highlighted when a system is disturbed by the introduction of a new element,[17] for instance the impact of the presence of a peace operation on the host economy. Because most systems either have been designed to cope with adversity or have evolved in the face of it, breakage or overload at one point rarely destroys them. It will, however, produce disturbances at other points.[18] Extensive interconnections in a system make it flexible, but they also mean that disruptions can spread easily throughout a system.[19]

Jervis argues that, in a system, actions have unintended effects on the actor, on others and on the system as a whole, which means that one cannot infer results from intent and expectations and vice versa.[20] He concludes that the phenomenon – namely that consequences are unintended – is a basic product of complex interconnections. In some cases the results can be the reverse of the intention, in others they can be orthogonal to it, as with the side-effects of medications.[21]

Problems are created when the effects of incentives cannot be limited to the target population,[22] for instance when the level of assistance to a refugee camp or a camp for internally displaced people creates tension with the surrounding host community because the availability of food inside the camp is better than outside, or when ex-combatants are perceived to benefit more from the international community, through a disarmament, demobilization and reintegration (DDR) programme, than those who did not participate in the violence. Assisting some categories of beneficiaries may make it worthwhile for others to assume that status, for instance in times of famine when parents may abandon some of their children because a specific aid agency caters only for abandoned children. Supply creates its own demand in what economists call the "moral hazard" problem: people who know that they will be helped if they are in need may not struggle hard to avoid this outcome.[23]

This does not mean that we are powerless in the face of unpredictable and unstable system effects. Jervis argues that system effects change as actors learn about them and about others' beliefs about them.[24] Jervis suggests three general methods of acting when system effects may be prevalent and powerful. First, people can constrain other actors and reduce if not eliminate the extent to which their environment is highly systemic and characterized by unintended consequences. Second, the appreciation that people operate in a system may enable them to compensate for the results that would otherwise occur. Third, people may be able to proceed toward their goals indirectly and can apply multiple policies, either simultaneously or sequentially, in order to correct or take advantage of the fact that, in a system, consequences are multiple. None of this guarantees success, but human action can be effective in the face of complex interconnections, and a systems approach need not induce paralysis.[25]

While complex interactions in a system mean that some of the consequences will be unintended and undesired, it is hard to measure their frequency. Albert Hirschman points out that straightforward effects are common and often dominate perverse ones.[26] If this were not the case, it would be hard to see how societies make progress or how any stable human interaction could develop.[27]

The double effect theory

The traditional philosophical debate about the ethical problems caused by unintended consequences has become known as the "double effect" debate. Gregory Reichberg and Henrik Syse[28] argue that we enter the terrain of "side-effect harm" when moral, legitimate acts have undesired effects. "Double effect" refers to the two different kinds of effect that our interventions tend to have. On the one hand, there is the intended outcome that our actions were meant to produce. On the other hand, there are the side-effects, or unintended consequences, that result from our intervention. The idea that we are answerable for these unintended consequences, yet in a manner that is different from the accountability that is associated with our intentional projects, has been dubbed the "principle of double effect".

The phenomenon of double effect becomes a moral problem when the side-effects are not desirable, and especially when they are harmful for those affected. Actors are responsible for such side-effects when these are foreseeable and they still choose to proceed. Actors are blameworthy for harmful side-effects when they allow them to happen if they could have been prevented, or when they make no, or only an insignificant, attempt to minimize them.[29] The principle of double effect can serve as a valuable tool when applying ethical considerations to the unintended consequences of peace operations.

The principle of double effect is a moral principle for assessing actions that produce side-effect harm. In short, it states that, although actors are responsible for the harmful side-effects that ensue from their actions, actions that produce harmful side-effects are nevertheless permissible provided that:

(1) the primary goal of the action is legitimate;
(2) the side-effects are not part of the actor's intended goal;
(3) the side-effects are not a means to this goal;
(4) the actor aims to prevent or minimize the side-effects; and
(5) no alternative courses of action could have been taken that would have led to fewer or no side-effects.[30]

The principle of double effect can be used both as a tool for analysing actions that have already taken place, and as a guide for action in obligating actors to consider in advance what side-effects might result from their actions and, if presumed harmful, how these effects can be prevented or minimized.

Just War theory

Just War theory holds that, in certain circumstances, war can be justified and is thus not always immoral. Just War theory builds on double effect theory, but is focused on decisions about going to war or undertaking military interventions. In the process, Just War theorists have articulated a set of conditions for war and interventions that can be useful when considering the ethical aspects of the unintended consequences of peace operations. In this context we will consider two elements of Just War theory, namely competent authority and intention, and we will address the issue of inclusive moral deliberation.

Competent authority

One aspect of Just War theory argues that only specially designated public officials, paying due attention to legal constraints, have the authority to engage a nation in a course of armed conflict.[31] Put differently, the task of the competent authority is to oversee the social impacts of the intervention, with due attention to national and international law. The competent authority has a responsibility to identify and anticipate unintended consequences. Just War theory argues that, when negative impacts are the result of an exercise of authority, even if purely incidental and unintended, those in positions of authority have a responsibility to take measures to eliminate or mitigate these impacts.[32]

An additional reason competent authority is important is that it must be possible, both during the decision-making process and after the fact, to see clearly who made what decision. Thus, procedural transparency is crucial, so that those affected by the decision can have some trust that the right people are making the decisions. Or, put alternatively, the actual decision-making process must be able to be revealed at some later stage, so that it is open to criticism and assignment of responsibility.[33]

Intention

A very important notion in Just War theory is the criterion of intention. The criterion takes note of the fact that an agent may have just cause but nevertheless act from a wrongful intention,[34] for example, delivering humanitarian assistance to a particular beneficiary population for the sake of attracting media attention instead of on the basis of need. This criterion focuses attention on the goals or aims of the intervention and the way in which those goals should influence the actions performed and the strategies followed. This is an important part of the "right intention" idea: it seeks to direct our attention to the actual good we seek to attain through our actions.[35] We would not describe the purpose of medicine in terms of what is good for the physician,[36] yet in peace operations you often hear arguments such as those made stating that the United Nations should educate peacekeepers to follow the code of conduct because their poor behaviour is harmful to the image of the United Nations, rather than focusing on the harm their behaviour may be causing.

Inclusive moral deliberation

Deon Rossouw suggests caution in transferring Just War theory and the principle of double effect from their traditional contexts.[37] He identifies three key "dis-analogies" between the context of international business (which is his focus) and war, one of which is of particular importance to our context. Rossouw argues that the nature of war is such that decisions about military engagement and the moral implications thereof have to be made unilaterally. He argues that international business differs from war because business has the possibility of engaging with those who might be affected by the foreseeable negative consequences of its actions. This is true in the peace operations context as well, or at least in those missions where consensus is understood to be a prerequisite for the deployment of a peace operation, which is the norm in United Nations peace operations.

Dwight Furrow argues that ethical principles, despite their pretension to be objective, tend to be parochial. We tend to universalize our own ethical standards and to impose our ethical preferences and ethical interpretations upon others.[38] Consequently, unilateral ethical deliberations, despite the best intentions, contribute to ethical blind spots. In peace operations, however, the possibility to engage the stakeholders, both internal and external, about the impact of negative consequences on them creates the opportunity for bilateral and multilateral moral deliberation that does not exist in the Just War tradition.

To paraphrase Rossouw, peacekeepers or humanitarian agencies do not have to deliberate on their own about the possible foreseeable unintended consequences of their actions, but can engage directly with those they suspect might be affected negatively to find out how they perceive the intended actions. Through such proactive stakeholder engagement the peacekeepers and aid workers might learn of more side-effects, both positive and negative, that they had not initially foreseen given their lack of knowledge of host country realities.[39] The latter is implicit in various humanitarian and development codes of conduct and initiatives, such as "The Code of Conduct for The International Red Cross and Red Crescent Movement and NGOs in Disaster Relief",[40] the Rome Declaration on Harmonization[41] and the Good Humanitarian Donorship Initiative,[42] and has been addressed by some of the initiatives on peacebuilding,[43] but more can be done to integrate this approach into the planning and management of peace operations.

The "do no harm" approach

Another approach, perhaps more contemporary and thus better known among the peace and aid practitioner community, is Mary Anderson's "do no harm" approach to international humanitarian and development assistance.[44] The "do no harm" approach has come about as a result of the work of the Local Capacities for Peace Project, which is aimed at improving the ability of humanitarian or development assistance programmes to operate in conflict situations in ways that assist local people without feeding into or exacerbating the conflict.

The "do no harm" initiative confirms and recognizes complex system effects and argues from the outset that, when international assistance is given in the context of a violent conflict, it becomes part of that context and thus also of the conflict.[45] The research of the Local Capacities for Peace Project has shown that the interaction between external aid and local communities produces relatively predictable outcomes. Anderson argues that, when one can start to anticipate aid's impact, it becomes possible to avoid negative effects and enhance positive ones.

Although acknowledging that international aid has done harm in certain cases, Anderson argues that it is a moral and logical fallacy to conclude that, because aid can do harm, a decision not to give aid would do no harm. In reality, a decision to withhold aid from people in need would have unconscionable negative ramifications. She argues instead that the challenge for aid workers, and their donors, is to figure out how to do the good they mean to do without inadvertently undermining local strengths, promoting dependency and allowing aid resources to be misused in the pursuit of war.[46]

The "do no harm" project is a very practical attempt at improving aid by proposing a framework that aid workers can use when planning, monitoring and evaluating their programmes to ensure that these programmes are implemented in such a way as to avoid negative effects and enhance positive ones. We will return to the potential of the "do no harm" project to be applied beyond the humanitarian and development assistance sphere in the concluding chapter.

Conclusion

The purpose of this book is to contribute to the improvement of peace operations. It is an attempt to focus on one aspect of peace operations that needs to be better understood, namely their unintended consequences. Unintended consequences can be negative, neutral or positive, but our focus will mainly be on the negative unintended consequences, because they are the most harmful to the communities that peace operations are intended to serve, to the very notion of peace operations and to the organizations that mandate and deploy peacekeepers. In order to avoid these potentially negative unintended consequences, this book intends shedding light on how they come about and it explores ways in which we can improve our ability to anticipate and counter such potential negative unintended consequences. The objective of this book is thus to make a modest contribution towards enhancing our understanding of the unintended consequences of peace operations.

Notes

1. On the transformation of peacekeeping there is an abundance of literature. See, for instance, Ramesh Thakur and Albrecht Schnabel (eds), *United Nations Peacekeeping Operations: Ad Hoc Missions, Permanent Engagement*, Tokyo: United Nations University Press, 2002.
2. See Lester B. Pearson quoted in Brian Urquhart, *Hammarskjold*, New York: Norton, 1994, p. 176.
3. Espen Barth Eide, presentation delivered at the "DDR from a Peacebuilding Perspective" Course, Norwegian Defence International Centre (NODEFIC), 19–24 January 2004.
4. Somalia would come to mind but, as per the delineation used in this book, the collapse of that mission was due to its failure to achieve its intended objective, not due to unintended consequences.
5. See Henri Myrttinen and Shukuko Koyama (Chapter 2) for a case study on Timor Leste, Vanessa Kent (Chapter 3) for a case study of Liberia, Katarina Ammitzboell (Chapter 4) for case studies on Afghanistan and Kosovo, and Kwesi Aning (Chapter 7), C. S. R. Murthy (Chapter 8) and Arturo C. Sotomayor (Chapter 9) for case studies of Ghana, India, Argentina and Uruguay.

6. See Murthy (Chapter 8), referring to the number of cases of HIV/AIDS in the Indian Army.
7. See Sotomayor (Chapter 9), referring to the civilizing effect on the military.
8. For a critical view of the strategic effectiveness of peacekeeping deployments, see Richard Betts, "Delusion of Impartial Intervention", *Foreign Affairs*, November/December 1994. Fortna also tests realist as well as institutionalist propositions about the impact of peace processes accompanied by peacekeeping deployments. See Page Fortna, *Peace Time: Cease-fire Agreement and the Durability of Peace*, Princeton, NJ: Princeton University Press, 2004.
9. On the liberal-internationalist agenda of peacebuilding missions, see Roland Paris, "Peacebuilding and the Limits of Liberal Internationalism", *International Security*, 22(2), Fall 1997, pp. 54–89, and *At War's End: Building Peace after Civil Conflict*, Cambridge: Cambridge University Press, 2004. As for the classic critique of the liberal agenda of modernization, see Samuel Huntington, *Political Order in Changing Societies*, Boston: Yale University Press, 1968.
10. See Sotomayor (Chapter 9). See also Charles Moskos, *Peace Soldiers: The Sociology of a United Nations Military Force*, Chicago: University of Chicago Press, 1976.
11. R. Jervis, *System Effects: Complexity in Political and Social Life*, Princeton, NJ: Princeton University Press, 1997.
12. Ibid., p. 6. For more definitions of systems, see Anatol Rapoport, "Systems Analysis: General Systems Theory", *International Encyclopaedia of the Social Sciences*, Vol. 15, New York: Free Press, 1968, p. 453; and Ludwig von Bertalanffy, *General Systems Theory: Foundations, Development, Applications*, New York: Braziller, 1986, p. 55.
13. Paul Cilliers, *Complexity and Postmodernism: Understanding Complex Systems*, London: Routledge, 1998, p. 3.
14. Jervis, *System Effects*, p. 10.
15. G. Hardin, "The Cybernetics of Competition", *Perspectives in Biology and Medicine*, 7, Autumn 1963, pp. 79–80.
16. Charles Perrow, *Normal Accidents*, New York: Basic Books, 1984, p. 172, quoted in Jervis, *System Effects*, p. 16.
17. Jervis, *System Effects*, p. 18.
18. Ibid., p. 19.
19. Ibid., p. 19.
20. Ibid., p. 61.
21. Ibid., p. 62.
22. Ibid., p. 63.
23. Ibid., p. 64.
24. Ibid., p. 253.
25. Ibid., p. 261.
26. Albert Hirschman, *The Rhetoric of Reaction*, Cambridge, MA: Harvard University Press, 1991, quoted in Jervis, *System Effects*, p. 68.
27. Jervis, *System Effects*, p. 68.
28. G. Reichberg and H. Syse, "The Idea of Double Effect – in War and Business", in L. Bomann-Larsen and O. Wiggen, eds, *Responsibility in World Business: Managing Harmful Side-effects of Corporate Activity*, Tokyo: United Nations University Press, 2004, p. 17.
29. Bomann-Larsen and Wiggen, *Responsibility in World Business*, p. 4.
30. Ibid., p. 5.
31. Reichberg and Syse, "The Idea of Double Effect – in War and Business", p. 31.
32. Ibid., p. 31.
33. Ibid., p. 32.

34. Ibid., p. 32.
35. Ibid., p. 33.
36. Ibid., p. 33.
37. G. J. (Deon) Rossouw, "Business Is Not Just War: Implications for Applying the Principle of Double Effect to Business", in Bomann-Larsen and Wiggen, eds, *Responsibility in World Business*, pp. 39–49.
38. D. Furrow, *Against Theory: Continental and Analytical Challenges in Moral Philosophy*, London: Routledge, 1995.
39. Rossouw, "Business Is Not Just War", p. 45.
40. See ⟨http://www.ifrc.org/publicat/conduct/index.asp⟩ (accessed 31 October 2006).
41. Note the February 2003 Rome Declaration on Harmonization signed by 28 developing countries and 49 donor organizations. The four main principles highlighted in the Declaration are: recipient countries coordinate development assistance; donors align their aid with recipient countries' priorities and systems; donors streamline aid delivery; and donors adopt policies, procedures and incentives that foster harmonization. For the full declaration see ⟨http://www1.worldbank.org/harmonization/romehlf/Documents/RomeDeclaration.pdf⟩ (accessed 31 October 2006), and, for more information on the overall initiative, see ⟨http://www.aidharmonization.org⟩ (accessed 31 October 2006).
42. "The Principles and Good Practice of Humanitarian Donorship", *Humanitarian Exchange*, No. 29, March 2005, p. 7.
43. See the report of the Peacebuilding Forum 2004 Conference "Building Effective Partnerships: Improving the Relationship between Internal and External Actors in Post-Conflict Countries", New York, 7 October 2004, available at ⟨http://www.ipacademy.org/PDF_Reports/PBF_Conference_Report_NY_Oct.pdf⟩ (accessed 31 October 2006).
44. M. B. Anderson, *Do No Harm: How Aid Can Support Peace or War*, London: Lynne Rienner, 1999.
45. Ibid., p. 1.
46. Ibid., p. 2.

Part II

Unintended consequences for individuals and groups

2

Unintended consequences of peace operations on Timor Leste from a gender perspective

Shukuko Koyama and Henri Myrttinen

Gender mainstreaming has been one of the major policy goals within United Nations (UN) agencies that have specialized in peace and security over the last decade. However, the gender perspective has traditionally not been a starting point for planning peace operations. It has, in fact, been more or less invisible, even in cases in which there is, at least on paper, a relatively strong commitment to taking the gender perspective into account.[1] Hence, one can expect this to be one of the areas in which one finds a range of unintended consequences. On the ground, anecdotal examples of sexual abuse and gendered exploitation by peace operation personnel have been reported, be it in books written by former UN staff[2] or in the media. This is especially true for negative impacts, such as prostitution and trafficking linked to peace operations, which are considered to be – literally – "sexy" topics. The problems surrounding the UN mission in the Democratic Republic of Congo (Mission des Nations Unies en République Démocratique du Congo – MONUC) which arose in 2004/2005 with respect to prostitution and sexual abuse have once again highlighted these issues. However, assessments of these missions from a gender perspective have not been carried out systematically and have often suffered from sensationalism. While focusing on the headline-grabbing negative impacts, more subtle impacts, both negative and positive, have been neglected in these accounts.

In order to partially fill the gap in the body of the study of the UN peace operations, this chapter aims to analyse some of the short-, medium- and longer-term unintended consequences of peace operations

Unintended consequences of peacekeeping operations, Aoi, de Coning and Thakur (eds), United Nations University Press, 2007, ISBN 978-92-808-1142-1

conducted by the United Nations as seen from a gender perspective, taking the UN missions in what is now the Democratic Republic of Timor Leste (Republica Democrática de Timor Leste – RDTL) as the case study to be examined.

Gender analysis in the security field often focuses on the sexual aspects of gender. However, we take a wider view of the issue, looking at the aspects of both sexuality and social roles in gender. Thus, key questions that will be addressed include the impact of the UN missions on prostitution, the spread of sexually transmitted diseases (STDs), and more specifically of HIV/AIDS, and the temporary local partners of UN staff and children left behind by UN personnel, as well as more intangible effects such as the social empowerment of women and changes in gender attitudes. Some important gendered effects of the missions, such as a gendered analysis of the disarmament, demobilization and reintegration processes carried out under UN auspices and, linked to this, the issue of small arms and light weapons, are not considered in this chapter but are discussed elsewhere.[3]

Rationale

This chapter examines the cases of the two UN missions in Timor Leste – the United Nations Transitional Administration in East Timor (UNTAET) and the follow-up mission, the United Nations Mission of Support in East Timor (UNMISET). We analyse a range of unintended gendered impacts of the missions and weigh up whether, and to what extent, the lessons learned from earlier peace operations had any effects on the missions in Timor Leste from a gender perspective.

From late 1999 to May 2002, UNTAET was in charge of running the country in a post-conflict situation and the United Nations maintained a sizeable presence for another three years afterwards, still wielding considerable influence in the post-independence period. The missions led to a massive influx of foreigners – very wealthy foreigners, when compared with the local population – into a society that had been very much closed off from the outside world for a long time and was still very conservative in terms of its gender norms.

Though much of the study will highlight negative impacts of the UN missions, this is by no means intended to diminish the work carried out by the local and international staff of the missions, the considerable risks they often took and the many positive results, tangible and intangible, of the missions. The issues we discuss are easily "emotionalized": some interviewees indulged in a kind of mischievous glee and moral indignation in recounting episodes of misconduct and, at the other end of the spectrum, others reacted angrily to what they saw as an attempt by outsiders to unduly criticize the positive work they had accomplished. Some reacted very positively to the endeavour and saw it as asking relevant questions, whereas others, notably those in charge of information work for peacekeeping force (PKF) contingents, seemed at times to be in a state of denial – or perhaps naivety – about the impact of their presence and actions.

Given that UNTAET/UNMISET had an explicit "gender mandate", two questions lie at the heart of this analysis. What did the UN system intend to do in terms of gender issues? What were the unintended consequences of the missions, in terms of the consequences both of activities not specifically seen as having a gendered impact, and of those that were specifically designed to have a gendered impact?

Methodology

After briefly summarizing the historical background to the peace operations in Timor Leste, this study will look at both the negative and the positive unintended, long-term impacts of the peace operations, specifically from a gender perspective.

We examine the following impacts:
- prostitution and trafficking,
- sexualized violence and sexual harassment by UN staff,
- the spread of STDs, most specifically HIV/AIDS,
- local women and children left behind by UN staff,
- the gendered employment patterns of locals hired for the UN missions, and
- changes in the gender dynamics brought about by the UN missions.

One of the difficulties of gendered studies on peace operations is the rarity of quantitative data disaggregated by gender. Because no comprehensive, quantitative surveys covering these issues exist and because it was not possible to carry out these surveys in Timor Leste, the findings will be more of a qualitative nature. This lack of quantitative data disaggregated by gender demonstrates the need for more gender mainstreamed policy awareness among policy-makers and academics in the field of peace operations.

A further difficulty is that much of the information gathered, especially on issues of sexual harassment and prostitution, is, by necessity, based on hearsay and often comes from informants who wish to remain anonymous. The study visits carried out as part of this study, the literature review and our previous study visits to other regions with a UN PKF presence (Bosnia-Herzegovina, Cambodia and Kosovo) reveal a pattern linking the presence of UN personnel to sexual harassment, prostitution and trafficking. At the same time, the missions have catalysed a range of other gendered effects that are less scandalous but perhaps more profound.

The research is based on a review of the literature available on the missions, on background interviews, and on observations and interviews during visits to Timor Leste in 1999, 2002, 2004 (twice) and 2005. A total of 35 interviews were carried out, some formal and some informal, with representatives of the Timor Leste government, the UN administration, the PKF and UN police (UNPOL) officers, representatives of other UN agencies, representatives of Timorese and international civil society organizations, media representatives, sex workers and their clients.

Given the delicate nature of the topic, a majority of the interviewees asked to remain anonymous and thus we decided to keep all sources anonymous. The fact that anonymity was requested, especially by those within the missions, can also be seen as an indication of the lack of openness in dealing with problematic issues within the UN system. The report also draws upon our work with Timorese civil society actors between 1998 and 2005.

Historical background

The deployment of the UNTAET mission in late 1999 was a direct reaction to the international outcry over the wave of violence carried out by pro-Indonesia militias following the UN-organized referendum on independence for the territory. Internal and external pressure forced the Indonesian government to agree to the deployment of an international peacekeeping force, the International Force for East Timor (Interfet), and the establishment of a transitional UN administration, UNTAET, which would run the country until full independence on 20 May 2002. Following independence, the United Nations maintained its presence in the country in the form of UNMISET, which lasted until May 2005. This has since been followed by two more missions, the United Nations Office in Timor-Leste (UNOTIL) and the United Nations Integrated Mission in Timor-Leste (UNMIT).

The Timor Leste missions were somewhat different with respect to gender awareness in comparison with previous such missions. The Timor Leste missions were influenced by the debates on gender, peace and conflict of the 1990s, the Beijing Women's Summit, and UN Security Council Resolution 1325, which was passed during these missions, as well as by debates within and outside of the UN system following cases of sexual misconduct and assault during UN missions in the Balkans,

Table 2.1 Comparison of UNTAET and UNMISET personnel strengths

	UNTAET	UNMISET
Duration	October 1999– May 2002	May 2002– May 2005
Maximum deployed personnel[a]	13,272	7,023
Foreign	737	796
Civilian	0	0
PKF and Military Observers	9,150	5,000
CIVPOL	1,640	250
Locally hired staff	1,745	977
% women, foreign contingent	n/a	31.8%
% women, locally hired	n/a	12.9%

[a] inclusive of UN Volunteers.
Sources: UNDPKO, "East Timor – UNMISET – Facts and Figures", ⟨http://
www.un.org/Depts/dpko/missions/unmiset/facts.html⟩ (accessed 20 November
2006); e-mail communication with UNMISET office, 19 November 2004.

Cambodia and Somalia. The Timor Leste missions have been regarded,
at least within the UN system, as some of the most gender aware to
date.

The intended gendered consequences of the UN missions

The peace operations in Timor Leste had a clear intention to mainstream
gender in the missions and promote women's advancement in Timorese
society. The UNTAET mission was, together with the United Nations
Interim Administration in Kosovo mission, which commenced a few
months earlier in Kosovo, one of the first to have a specially designated
Gender Affairs Unit. However, as the UNTAET Special Representative
of the Secretary-General (SRSG), the late Sergio Vieira de Mello, stated,
the establishment of this unit was not a given:

> I was against the creation of a Gender Affairs Unit for the UN's Transitional
> Authority [*sic*] in Timor Leste. I did not think a Gender Unit would help re-
> build institutions from the ashes of what the militia left. I was wrong. The first
> regulation I passed guaranteed human rights, including CEDAW [Convention
> to Eliminate all Forms of Discrimination Against Women] as a foundation of
> all new government institutions we created. The Unit brought this to life by
> reaching out to East Timorese women, and, together with UNIFEM [the United
> Nations Development Fund for Women], provided support that resulted in a
> higher percentage of women in the Constituent Assembly than in many coun-
> tries. The Unit worked with East Timorese women to create what is now the
> East Timorese Government Office for the Advancement of Women.[4]

The key document outlining what the UN missions intended to do in terms of gender issues is the UNTAET Gender Equality Promotion Fact Sheet.[5] The main points of action outlined are:
- gender mainstreaming within the mission,
- the establishment of the Gender Affairs Unit,
- support for East Timorese women in decision-making,
- incorporation of gender issues into the constitution, and
- campaigns against domestic violence.

Gender mainstreaming within the mission

Gender mainstreaming of both the UNTAET and UNMISET missions has taken place, at least on paper, with gender issues taken into account at all levels of decision-making. Interviews with mission staff indicate, however, that implementation in practice has occasionally been a struggle.

Gender-sensitivity training was carried out for mission staff (including PKFs and UNPOL) and the newly established East Timorese police force (Policia Nacional de Timor Leste – PNTL), as well as for RDTL government staff.[6] In spite of the push for gender equality and gender mainstreaming, both UNTAET and UNMISET had mainly men in the top positions and, for example, only 9 per cent of UNPOL were women – although this is still above the UN peace operations' average of 4 per cent.[7]

Sustainability of the gender mainstreaming initiative at the level of the UN system remains an issue. With the drawdown of UNMISET, other UN agencies such as UNIFEM or the United Nations Development Programme (UNDP) have taken over the work to support Timor Leste. Though all UN agencies take gender issues into account in theory, their work in Timor Leste has at times been criticized for a lack of gender sensitivity, as was the case with the UNDP's RESPECT programme.[8] Others have pointed out that much of the implementation of the pronounced gender mainstreaming measures had to be pushed through by Timorese civil society representatives against an initially reluctant or sluggish UN administration.[9]

The work of the Gender Affairs Unit

The Gender Affairs Unit focused on the following core functions:
- capacity-building and awareness-raising,
- gender situational analysis and data collection,
- policy analysis,
- implementation and evaluation,
- rule of law and legislative analysis, and
- networking and outreach.[10]

Following the end of the UNTAET mission and the proclamation of independence on 20 May 2002, the Gender Affairs Unit became integrated into the RDTL government. In UNMISET, the post of a Gender Advisor was located in the office of the SRSG. The role of the Gender Advisor consisted of disseminating public information on gender issues and coordinating the UNMISET Inter-Agency Group on Gender, which was tasked with gender mainstreaming in the mission and gender rights work.[11] In addition to the installation of the Gender Advisor, the second UNMISET SRSG, Sukehiro Hasegawa, established a commission to investigate reports of sexual misconduct by UN staff.

Despite the institutional effort, actual implementation of gender mainstreaming faced some challenges. For example, the post of the Gender Advisor remained vacant for some time during the mission. The activities of the Gender Affairs Unit were partially carried out by the Human Rights Unit, which left some issues that demanded gender-specific investigation unattended to.

Support for East Timorese women in decision-making

UNTAET support for the political participation of East Timorese women concentrated mainly on the elections to the Constituent Assembly and local elections. Training was given by UNTAET and UNIFEM to female candidates. The results of the elections demonstrate the advancement of women politicians to some degree. On the other hand, it also became clear that female politicians struggle to obtain positions at a higher decision-making level.

Although no quota was established, public discussions about a set ratio of female candidates raised awareness of the issue among the political parties and the general public. Of the candidates to the Assembly, 27 per cent were women and the final representation of women in the Assembly was 26 per cent, one of the highest proportions in the Asia-Pacific region. Of the female candidates, however, only a quarter were in the top 15 positions on the respective party lists.[12] In the cabinet that was formed following the elections, two ministerial posts were given to women, one woman was appointed vice-minister and two women were appointed as advisers to the prime minister, for gender affairs and human rights, respectively.[13]

The incorporation of gender issues into the constitution

The incorporation of gender issues into the constitution was the most successful of the mission's gender mainstreaming activities. During the process of drafting the future constitution of the Democratic Republic of

Timor Leste, constitutional commissions were set up across the territory; 40 per cent of the commissioners were women and special efforts were made to ensure women's participation in the process. A working group on women and the constitution was established by the Gender Affairs Unit. Civil society organizations drew up a Women's Charter of Rights, which was signed by 8,000 people and presented to the SRSG. As a result of this work, gender equality is enshrined as one of the Timorese constitution's fundamental principles.[14]

Campaigns against gender-based violence

Gender-based violence is a major problem in post-conflict Timor Leste. There has been a dramatic increase in reported sexualized and domestic violence. In statistics collected during the UNTAET administration, up to 40 per cent of recorded crimes fell into this category.[15] However, this figure needs to be treated with some caution. It may actually indicate not an increased level of violence but an increased level of reporting of violent crimes, because East Timorese women would have been very reluctant to report these crimes to the Indonesian occupation forces. On the other hand, the crime statistics may involve serious underreporting, because both UN and Timorese police staff may have recorded cases of, say, intimate homicide under "murder" and not sexualized violence. Furthermore, East Timorese women may still be very reluctant to report sexualized violence to the authorities for fear of being socially stigmatized, because of a lack of interest and concern by the law enforcement officials and for fear of losing their livelihood – the husband is still overwhelmingly the breadwinner, especially in rural areas. UNTAET statistics estimated that the reports accounted for only 15 per cent of all cases of gender-based violence.[16] Therefore, the actual figures for domestic violence in Timor Leste are much higher than the reported figures.

Efforts by UNTAET and UNMISET to counter the problem included public awareness campaigns. The Gender Affairs Unit was involved in helping to draft legislation on the issue. Training has been given to both UNPOL and the PNTL on how to deal with gender-based violence. UN CIVPOL (Civilian Police) established a Vulnerable Persons Unit (VPU) with female officers, translators and counsellors, who worked together closely with local women's organizations. Each of the districts had a UN CIVPOL assigned to be a focal point for gender-based violence.

The results of the gender-sensitivity training given to the PNTL have been somewhat underwhelming. The work of the VPU was hampered by a lack of female UN CIVPOL, translators and specialists in general and ones with expertise in the field in particular.[17] Based on interviews carried out during our field visits, it would appear that both the police and the judiciary remain insensitive to cases of gender-based violence brought to them, especially in rural areas. PNTL officers have been accused of sexual misconduct and sexual harassment of sex workers.[18] These examples show that gender awareness needs to be raised among the policy-planners as well as among the implementers of such a training campaign.

A further disturbing case was the rape of a minor by six PNTL officers in the summer of 2004. Investigation of the case was obstructed by the PNTL and, when the accused officers stood trial, a crowd of PNTL officers surrounded the courthouse in Dili to show their support to the defendants and to intimidate witnesses.

Unintended consequences, from a viewpoint of sexuality

The impact of the UN mission on the sex industry

Sex and the United Nations have caught international media attention in the last few years. Cases of sexual misconduct and assault involving UN personnel have made the media headlines but, apart from journalistic and the United Nations' internal investigations, this field has attracted little systematic research.

It is useful to provide working definitions of "prostitution" and "sex work". First, prostitution, which is the selling of sexual services in exchange for money or material benefits, takes on a number of forms. The women and men, boys and girls involved might not themselves see what they do as prostitution and might reject the labels "prostitute" or "sex worker" owing to the social and moral stigmas linked to these terms.[19] For the sake of this chapter and for lack of better terminology, however, both terms will be used, with prostitution referring to the explicit selling of sexual services and sex work covering the broader field of explicit and implicit sale of sexual services (e.g. in karaoke bars or massage parlours).

In order to be able to put the Timor Leste missions in perspective, it may be helpful to look at the case of Cambodia during the UN Transitional Authority in Cambodia (UNTAC) in 1992–1993. Because there is almost a decade between the missions in Timor Leste and in Cambodia, the comparison allows us to see some of the developments both within the UN system and regarding the legacy of a complex peace operation. Similarly to the UNTAET mission, UNTAC was in charge of transitionally running the country, though the mandate in Cambodia was somewhat narrower. One of the most visible impacts of the UNTAC mission from the gender perspective was its effect on the Cambodian sex industry.

Flashback: UN presence and prostitution in Cambodia

Links between the military and prostitution are by no means a new phenomenon,[20] and are also visible in other UN peace operations, for example in Bosnia-Herzegovina, Cambodia, the Democratic Republic of Congo, Kosovo or Sierra Leone. Responses have varied from mission to mission and from contingent to contingent, with some taking very much a laissez-faire attitude towards the issue whereas others have been much more stringent.

The UNTAC mission was anecdotally infamous for its impact on prostitution in Cambodia. An indication of this is that the only display in the Siem Reap Museum of National History covering the UNTAC period in Cambodia is a wax figure of a peacekeeper with his arm around a sex worker. In addition to the interviews we conducted in Cambodia, several studies give evidence of the links between the presence of UNTAC and the "boom" in the Cambodian sex industry.[21] All respondents who were interviewed as part of this study, as well as the vast majority of written accounts of the UNTAC period, confirm the impression that UN staff – peacekeepers, police and civilian staff – used the services of sex workers regularly and in a highly visible manner, ranging from visiting striptease bars or massage parlours to having sex with prostitutes.

Relatively more stable relationships between the comparatively affluent internationals and economically dependent citizens were also formed, with local women becoming "part-time wives" of the expatriates. Interestingly enough, cases of expatriate women having "part-time husbands" are not mentioned, but these cannot be ruled out. Given the extreme power imbalances inherent in these relationships, as well as the intricacies of human relationships in general, it is often difficult for an outside observer to see whether it is a case of "grey area" prostitution or a *bona fide* relationship between two lovers.

In some cases, UN staff reportedly engaged in sexual relationships with minors, be it with under-age sex workers or with local children. An international staffer who worked for UNTAC recalls catching a Pakistani CIVPOL sleeping with a local teenage boy in a field bed in a CIVPOL office. These offices were located in the provinces.

Members of the UN mission not only appear to have been notorious for buying services from sex workers, but in some cases were actively involved in facilitating prostitution. The French PKF contingent is reported to have had its own "field brothel", and the Bulgarian PKF contingent, in part drafted straight from military prisons, is reported to have set up its own prostitution ring in north-eastern Cambodia.[22]

However, it is difficult to support the anecdotal accounts with hard data. No precise data are available on the number of sex workers active in Cambodia before, during and after UNTAC. Estimates put the number of pre-UNTAC sex workers at around 6,000, which then increased to 20,000. Other sources speak more generally of a three-fold increase.[23] Thus, as also noted by several of the Cambodian women's organizations interviewed, prostitution did exist in pre-UNTAC Cambodian society and the customers included locals as well as expatriates.

Despite the reports of sexual misconduct, to our knowledge no UN staff were punished for using the services of sex workers. The permissive attitude of the UNTAC leadership is perhaps best illustrated by the comment made by the SRSG, Yasushi Akashi, when he was challenged by Cambodian civil society representatives on the issue. His reply was to state simply that "boys will be boys", and no effective action was taken by UNTAC to address the issue.

Prostitution and sex work in Timor Leste

Prostitution has historically existed in Timor Leste, at least since Portuguese times and definitely during the Indonesian occupation.[24] The current form of the internationalized sex industry, which emerged in Timor Leste after the arrival of UNTAET, is, however, traceable to the sex industry that emerged in Thailand during the Vietnam War. The sex industry in Thailand was created for the "rest and recreation" of US troops, and spread throughout Southeast Asia with the spread of tourism.[25] Out of this, the Thai sex industry evolved to cater both to locals and, increasingly, to foreign tourists. The pattern was replicated in other countries in the region, such as Indonesia, and the sex industry became increasingly transnational. In Timor Leste, there are in fact direct links to the Thai sex industry, with sex workers being recruited in Bangkok and Pattaya to work in Timor Leste.

In today's Timor Leste, sex work occurs in the following contexts: in illicit brothels; on the streets; in massage parlours; in karaoke clubs; in bars, nightclubs and discos; or in hotels and guesthouses, which actively or passively facilitate prostitution. Most of the sex work is concentrated in the capital city, Dili.

Sex work is a lot less conspicuous in Dili than in Bali, Jakarta or Bangkok. Much of it is facilitated through massage parlours, karaoke bars and "health clubs". "Grey area" prostitution takes place in restaurants, bars and nightclubs. Prostitution is not illegal in Timor Leste, which currently still uses Indonesian legislation on this issue. Under this legislation, providing or buying sexual services is not a criminal act but third-party facilitation is. The sanctions for UN staff caught buying the services of sex workers vary, ranging from no sanctions, to reprimands, repatriation and possible discharge. This reflects the lack of a unified policy on the issue and the variations in how seriously these cases are taken by the mission staff and national contingents.

There are also "ripple" effects in the region, with prostitution occurring in "rest and recreation" places for UN mission staff, such as in Bali. According to interviewed customers, the drawdown of the UN missions also led to a reduction in the presence of sex workers – and a shift in the nationalities of the international sex workers. Some of the establishments have apparently closed, with some of the owners rumoured to have moved on to other UN peace operation staging areas, such as Sierra Leone.

Besides "professional" sex workers, there are also cases where locals – especially minors – are offered money or material benefits in exchange for sex more or less at random, i.e. where the person would not have had any prior intention of offering sexual services for money or goods. Paedophilia is also an issue in Timor Leste: of the 110 male sex workers surveyed in Dili by the Alola Foundation, 75 per cent were under 18.[26]

Sex workers

Sex workers include locals and foreigners. Trafficking, especially of women, for work in the sex industry is also an issue in Timor Leste, though it seems to be confined to trafficking into and not out of the country, at least for now. According to a baseline study on prostitution and trafficking, approximately 370 sex workers were active in Dili, a city of approximately 150,000 inhabitants, towards the end of UNMISET.[27] Of these, 260 were female (110 East Timorese, 150 foreign) and 110 male (100 local, 10 Indonesian). The foreign sex workers tend to be from East and Southeast Asia, mainly from neighbouring Indonesia, Thailand, the Philippines and the People's Republic of China. Individual cases of Australian and Vietnamese sex workers were also reported.

Customers

According to the data gathered by the Alola Foundation study and corroborated by the interviews carried out as part of this study, the customers of the sex workers included both locals and internationals. No detailed data are available on the numbers and background of customers during the UNTAET/UNMISET missions. Based on a comprehensive study carried out by the Alola Foundation on sex work and trafficking in Timor Leste, oral information and our field experiences during the UNTAET/ UNMISET missions, the vast majority of customers were men. Interviews with sex workers and customers were carried out as part of the field studies. They revealed that both foreign and local men were the most common customers, the majority being civilians (e.g. civilian UN staff, contractors, journalists, workers with non-governmental organizations, businesspeople and other internationals) and not members of the security forces. Both local and international military and police were, however, also mentioned as being customers. One non-Timorese sex worker interviewed claimed to have had up to ten customers a day during "peak" times but was down to one or none a day towards the end of UNMISET.

The most "eye-catching" cases are those of foreign UN staff, especially members of the PKF or CIVPOL components. In one of our interviews in April 2004 with a Thai sex worker in Dili, it became evident that her clientele consisted mostly of expatriates.

Quantifying the correlation between the existence of UNMISET and the scale of prostitution is difficult. However, according to our interviews with both sex workers and clients, "business" had reduced dramatically with the drawing down of the UNMISET staff. Expatriates also use the services of part-time or "grey area" sex workers in the bars and night-clubs of Dili. We observed UN staff – including a Russian CIVPOL – negotiating prices for sexual services in a Dili nightclub in April 2004. The CIVPOL even offered – possibly in jest, but perhaps not – to help one of us in similar "negotiations" in order to gain a lower rate. In comparison with Cambodia, however, UN personnel have not been so actively involved in prostitution in Timor Leste.

Actions taken by UNMISET

The UNTAET/UNMISET missions did not lead to such a highly visible increase in prostitution as was the case with UNTAC in Cambodia. Nevertheless, the presence of UN staff, contractors, the press and international non-governmental organizations (NGOs) has led to a marked increase in prostitution. This has been mainly concentrated in Dili.

The change in approach and attitude has not, however, always been consistent, nor has progress been linear. For example, the Portuguese peacekeepers in Bosnia-Herzegovina were subject to much stricter controls than those involved in the subsequent UNMISET mission. There seems to have been a change in the "rules of engagement" in this respect, with Portuguese UNTAET PKFs adhering to stricter regulations than under UNMISET. With Australian PKFs, the opposite could be observed, with a corresponding change in the attitude of the local population vis-à-vis the respective PKF contingents. Although there has been progress between UNTAC and UNTAET/UNMISET, missions that have commenced since the Timor missions have had much graver problems in terms of prostitution, the spread of HIV/AIDS and gender insensitivity.

In a sense, the PKFs are easier to control because it is possible to place them under curfew and sanctioning is easier. Controlling the activities of CIVPOL, civilian UN staff and even other foreigners (contractors, humanitarian aid workers, media personnel) is much more difficult, because they are not under a military regimen and they do not live in barracks. It is also debatable whether confining UN staff to their quarters, leading to an increased gap between the "internationals" and the local population, would be desirable. The key to changing the undesirable behaviour is therefore a change in attitude amongst UN staff. One of the interviewees put it in somewhat drastic terms: "If someone cannot keep their libido in check for six months, they should not be deployed on a mission."

The use of sexual services by peacekeepers has been severely restricted, especially during UNMISET, by the imposition of an early curfew on peacekeeping contingents. Some contingents, such as the Australian one, have limited the number of alcoholic drinks per day that the soldiers can drink. The only exception in terms of curfews was the Portuguese Battalion (PorBatt), which had a laissez-faire attitude towards the nocturnal activities of its soldiers and hence gained a certain notoriety in Dili. Its soldiers were known to visit massage parlours regularly, they got involved in bar brawls and there were several reported cases of children fathered by PorBatt soldiers. As noted above, the rules applying to the Portuguese peacekeepers in Timor Leste were much less strict than in the other missions they have participated in.

Although a circular was put out by the SRSG in 2003 barring UN staff from visiting places where prostitution takes place, there was, unlike for example in Bosnia-Herzegovina or Kosovo, no specific "blacklist" of bars or nightclubs for the mission. However, individual contingents did bar their members from entering certain bars, although this was owing to the high probability of bar brawls there, not to concerns about the possibility of prostitution. The police contingent of the mission, UNPOL, undertook several raids together with the Timorese police force, PNTL, against suspected brothels employing trafficked women, with somewhat mixed results.[28] In one "sting", several Singaporean CIVPOL in UNMISET were caught in a massage parlour and were repatriated, as was a CIVPOL officer of undisclosed nationality in another PNTL/UNPOL raid.

Sexual assault and misconduct by UN personnel in Timor Leste

In Timor Leste, the Jordanian contingent gained a particularly notorious reputation for sexual assault. The first case of rape occurred before their arrival in Timor Leste, during a 45 minute stopover at Darwin Airport in

northern Australia. Further cases of rape and of bestiality followed. According to a UN source interviewed by us, several members of the contingent were court-martialled and executed upon their return to Jordan. We
were not able to access any written documentation of these cases but
they were mentioned repeatedly in discussions and interviews with both
Timorese and international respondents. The identity and rank of those
executed were not known to the source. In 2000, several Australian
peacekeepers who were part of the Interfet forces were accused of sexually harassing Timorese women. They were repatriated and dishonour-
ably discharged. According to an UNTAET worker based in the area at
the time, several of the engineers in the Japanese PKF contingent were
accused of harassing adolescents at a local orphanage in the exclave of
Oecussi, and were reportedly confined to their barracks when not on
duty following several incidents.

The spread of HIV/AIDS

HIV/AIDS has not as yet reached epidemic proportions in Timor Leste,
although the potential for explosive growth exists and is linked to the sex
trade. A survey carried out in 2003/2004 among sex workers revealed 3
per cent of them to be HIV positive. Given that 40 per cent of the sex
workers interviewed had never even seen a condom, let alone practised
safe sex on a regular basis, this figure could easily increase very rapidly.[29]
Unfortunately, no reliable national HIV/AIDS statistics are available for
Timor Leste to date, because there is no national testing programme nor
is the healthcare sector in a state to implement such a programme. A
handful of HIV/AIDS cases were reported amongst UNTAET staff and
possibly in one to two cases the virus was transmitted by UN personnel
to local sexual partners in Darwin, Australia, according to the local press.
This has prompted calls by the local authorities for mandatory HIV/
AIDS testing of UN personnel.

Local women and children left behind by UN staff

A further unintended legacy of the UN missions has been the "widows"
and "orphans" left behind by expatriate UN staff. We were not able to
gain any information on the numbers involved because no thorough assessment of this situation has been carried out. Based on our interviews,
we would estimate that the number of children left behind would be in
the dozens and the number of women in the range of tens to a maximum
of one hundred. Undoubtedly, male partners were also left behind, by
both male and female expatriates. As previously noted, these relationships have been much more inconspicuous and have attracted much less

attention than the use of sex workers, both in the public eye and in terms of research. Thus, the figures are even vaguer for these groups, but in general would seem to be smaller than those for the prevalence of the use of sex workers.

Some particularly disturbing individual cases came up in the interviews. For example, a Portuguese peacekeeper in Ainaro, Timor Leste, fathered a child to a mute and deaf Timorese woman (raising questions about how consensual the sexual acts were) and refused to support the child that she bore him.

The local partners left behind by their foreign partners are in a very precarious position. Given the traditional concepts in Timorese society, which look down on pre-marital sex, the women are viewed as "damaged goods" and often face ostracization by the community. Former male partners tend not to be ostracized, unless they are openly homosexual. The children born of these relationships may or may not be in a slightly better situation if the community is ready to accept them in spite of – or in some cases even because of – their "foreign" origin. According to some of the interviewees, both Timorese and international, children of Fijian peacekeepers have been especially warmly welcomed. Some of the local partners and offspring have been lucky enough to receive support from their erstwhile partners, but oral information indicates that many have not. The local partners have no means of legal recourse to ensure that they will indeed receive support from the other parent of the child.

The intended social consequences of the UN missions

Gendered employment patterns of locals hired for the UN missions

UN missions, especially those on the scale of the Timorese missions, with their large civilian components, create a range of job opportunities for locally hired staff. These can be short term (e.g. election staff) or longer term, unskilled or highly skilled, within the formal UN administration or outside of it, e.g. as personal drivers or domestic workers for UN staff.

The UNTAET/UNMISET missions created an unprecedented range of job opportunities, especially for women, who had previously been marginalized in the labour markets. In a sense, whole new sectors of labour market were created – such as the NGO sector and the newly established national public administration. These opportunities were open to both men and women, but for women this represented an especially novel situation. Often, however, the job openings follow traditional concepts of gender roles. UNMISET, for example, did not hire any female drivers or security guards. Women were mostly offered administrative posts or jobs involving tasks similar to domestic work.

Using the Cambodian case as a comparison again, we can gain a view of what kind of future might exist for Timorese staff previously employed with the United Nations. The most highly skilled openings have been within the UN system or in international NGOs. Many of the women, especially in the Cambodian case, have gone on to work for international NGOs, drawing on their language skills and expertise gained during the UN mission, because their advancement in the civil service or in commercial fields had previously been blocked by men. It is still too early to say whether or not this will also be the case in Timor Leste, though there is undoubtedly a clear trend for NGOs to employ women.

Changes in gender dynamics brought about by the UN missions

The UN missions have had a more intangible, but nonetheless significant, effect in terms of changing local gender dynamics. Timor Leste experienced an influx of new concepts, new attitudes and new behavioural patterns with regard to gender roles being displayed by the expatriates, be they UN staff, NGO workers, contractors or media personnel. Some of these imported enactments and conceptualizations of gender roles were more conservative than those prevalent in the local society, but by and large they were more liberal.

Though the phenomenon is difficult to quantify, our interviews and observations made during the visits to Timor Leste do point to a "gender revolution" that has taken place and is taking place in society. The UN missions played a role in catalysing these processes. The impact was sometimes direct and intentional, i.e. through specific UN policies such as the gender awareness training given to the Timor Leste police force. Sometimes the impact was more indirect and was communicated through the actions and attitudes displayed by the UN staff. In addition, opening up these previously relatively closed regions to the influences of the outside world led to a change in concepts linked to gender.

As mentioned previously, the UNTAET mission was one of the first UN missions to incorporate a gender unit, though not without having to overcome some internal reluctance. Those working with gender issues for the UN missions were quite circumspect about the scale of the difference they had made, contending that they had at best been able to "sow seeds" or create initial spaces for debate.

If the Cambodian experience is any guide to things to come, the longterm impact on gender dynamics in Timor Leste may be very significant. For, even without a specific gender unit and with an underrepresentation of women in the UNTAC administration,[30] the mission was able to initiate a slow redefinition of gender roles. As one Cambodian interviewee put it, the UNTAC presence "introduced, for the first time, concepts such as democracy, human rights and gender equality – but also helped create an atmosphere in which young couples could openly walk hand in hand in public".

The gender revolution is visible in a number of ways, such as an increased participation of women in civil society, in both politics and administration, in the security forces and in public life in general. Sexualized and domestic violence have become political issues instead of taboo, though the debate has yet to lead to a substantial reduction in the occurrence of either. Gender-based sexualized violence and domestic violence remain an enormous problem. An encouraging sign, however, is that both women and men are campaigning against violence, thus opening up spaces for more non-violent manifestations of masculinity.

In Timor Leste, the new social atmosphere has also led to a tentative opening of social spaces for the gay and transsexual communities in Dili, and to a lesser extent for the lesbian and bisexual communities. The situation is, however, very different in the rural areas of the country where these social spaces do not exist.

Unintended consequences of UN gender policies

The intended effects on gender relations that the UN missions sought to bring about have also had unforeseen impacts. According to a number of Timorese respondents, there has been a feeling among some men in Timorese society that women were being given preferential treatment by the United Nations and other international actors. Though this is not corroborated by the figures (e.g. 74 per cent of parliament members and 87 per cent of local UNMISET staff were men), the fact that social spaces for women were opened up where none existed before has led to this impression.

Measures seeking to empower women have also often led to their being burdened with even more work. In addition to the training or the work given by the United Nations, the women also often had to take care of their domestic chores as well. Many had to ask their husbands for permission to join training courses or to apply for jobs and this was not always forthcoming.

For women with young children, attending training or having a job meant having to ask an older female sibling or member of the extended family to take care of the children. This then meant that the older sibling or cousin would not be able to attend school full time.

Conclusions

It is impossible *ex post facto* to quantify the impact of the UN missions compared with what would have happened had the missions not taken place. Other factors such as Timor Leste's increasing exposure to the outside world would have had, for better and/or for worse, its impacts on gender relations in Timor Leste even without the UN missions. Although these processes might or might not have taken place without a UN presence, they were clearly catalysed by the massive outside interventions that these missions represented.

These processes included certain negative impacts that could have been prevented or reduced by outside actors such as the United Nations. Comparing the Cambodian and Timorese missions, the debates around gender issues and peace operations over the course of the 1990s have had an impact within the UN system. The international interviewees tended to see Cambodia – as far as the issue of the missions' negative, gendered impacts goes – as a negative benchmark. Local interviewees tended to be more generous and stressed the longer-term positive impacts in terms of gender. However, there does not appear to have been any systematic transfer of "lessons learned" from Cambodia to Timor Leste. Rather, there seems to have been a change of perceptions and attitudes within the UN system. Several of the UN mission interviewees in Timor Leste mentioned that they would have liked to have seen a more systematic approach to critiquing past missions – as well as their own mission – and a more structured process of disseminating this information to those preparing for the new mission.

Whereas the more visible and blatant unintended effects such as prostitution, the spread of STDs or sexual misconduct can be dealt with through relatively simple measures, the more subtle impacts are much more difficult to address. The more intangible results, such as the empowerment of women and sexual minorities, are difficult to gauge but they are important in the long term. Thus, they should not be overlooked but rather investigated in more detail.

One point that became very clear during the research is that, despite pronouncements to the contrary, the term "gender" as it is and was used by the United Nations and others in Timor Leste is still by and large equated with "women" or "women and children". Issues of masculinity or of sexual minorities were scarcely raised.

Another obvious issue raised as a consequence of this research is that reliable data are not available. Much information had to be gained from interviews and personal recollections, often second or third hand. The research community in the field of peace operation studies is only slowly becoming aware of the relevance of gender analysis. Because of the lack of data, the gender analysis has not been able to advance far yet. There is still much to do, not only for organizations such as the United Nations but also for the research community.

The Timor missions were, as Whittington put it, a "unique experiment" in bringing gender issues into a complex peace operation.[31] Although the missions were not as complete a success in this respect as they are sometimes portrayed, a lot of good work has been done and lessons have been learned. For the UN system, the missions were a beginning for the process of truly integrating gender issues into peace operations in reality and not just in speeches and position papers. For Timorese society, the missions meant the sowing of a whole range of different seeds in terms of gender issues, many of them controversial.

Notes

1. See, for example, Elisabeth Rehn and Ellen Johnson Sirleaf, *Women, War, Peace: The Independent Experts' Assessment on the Impact of Armed Conflict on Women and Women's Role in Peacebuilding*, New York: UNIFEM, 2002.
2. K. Cain, H. Postlewait and A. Thomson, *Emergency Sex and Other Desperate Measures: A True Story from Hell on Earth*, New York: Hyperion, 2004; P. Edwards, "Imagining the Other in Cambodian Nationalist Discourse before and during the UNTAC Period", in S. Heder and J. Ledgerwood, *Propaganda, Politics and Violence in Cambodia: Democratic Transition under United Nations Peacekeeping*, Armonk, NY: M. E. Sharpe Publishing, 1996, pp. 50–72; T. Riddle, *Cambodian Interlude: Inside the United Nations' 1993 Election*, Bangkok: Orchid Press, 1997.
3. See, for example, for Timor Leste, Saleh Abdullah and Henri Myrttinen, "Gender, Violence and Small Arms and Light Weapons (SALW) in East and West Timor", in Vanessa Farr and Albrecht Schnabel (eds), *Gender Perspectives on Small Arms and Light Weapons*, forthcoming.
4. Quoted in Rehn and Sirleaf, *Women, War, Peace*.
5. UNTAET, *Gender Equality Programme*, UNTAET Fact Sheet 11, Dili: United Nations Transitional Administration in East Timor, 2002.
6. Ibid.
7. UNIFEM, Timor Leste Country Page on Women Waging Peace Portal, 2005, available at ⟨http://www.womenwarpeace.org/timor_leste/timor_leste.htm⟩ (accessed 31 October 2006); UNIFEM, *Disarmament, Demobilisation and Reintegration (DDR) – The Key to Keeping the Peace*, UNIFEM Issue Brief, 2005.
8. H. La'o, "Observations Regarding the RESPECT Programme in East Timor", *La'o Hamutuk Bulletin*, 5(5–6), 2004, pp. 1–3.
9. C. Scott, *Are Women Included or Excluded in Post-Conflict Reconstruction? A Case Study from East Timor*, London: Catholic Institute for International Relations, 2003.
10. S. Whittington, "Peacekeeping Operations and Gender Equality in Post-Conflict Reconstruction", paper presented at the EU-LAC Conference on "The Role of Women in Peacekeeping Operations", Chile, 4–5 November 2002.
11. Ibid.
12. UNIFEM, *Support for Women in 2001 Elections in East Timor*, Bangkok: UNIFEM East and Southeast Asia Regional Office, 2002.

13. UNTAET, *Gender Equality Programme*.
14. Ibid.
15. Ibid.
16. Ibid.
17. Ibid.; Whittington, "Peacekeeping Operations and Gender Equality in Post-Conflict Reconstruction".
18. Alola Foundation, *Trafficking in East Timor – A Look into the Sex Industry of the Newest Nation*, Dili: Alola Foundation. 2004.
19. S. Thorbek and B. Pattanaik, *Transnational Prostitution: Changing Patterns in a Global Context*, London: Zed Books, 2002.
20. C. Eifler and R. Seifert, eds, *Soziale Konstruktionen – Militär und Geschlechterverhältnis. Forum Frauenforschung, Band 11*, Münster: Westfälisches Dampfboot, 1999; C. Eifler and R. Seifert, *Gender und Militär – Internationale Erfahrungen mit Frauen und Männern in Streitkräften*, Königstein: Ulrike Helmer Verlag, 2003; C. Enloe, *Bananas, Beaches and Bases: Making Feminist Sense of International Politics*, Berkeley: University of California Press, 1989; C. Enloe, *Maneuvers – The International Politics of Militarising Women's Lives*, Berkeley: University of California Press, 2000; J. Goldstein, *War and Gender*, Cambridge: Cambridge University Press, 2001.
21. Cain et al., *Emergency Sex and Other Desperate Measures*; Edwards, "Imagining the Other in Cambodian Nationalist Discourse before and during the UNTAC Period"; J. Jordens, "Persecution of Cambodia's Ethnic Vietnamese Communities during and since the UNTAC Period", in Heder and Ledgerwood, *Propaganda, Politics and Violence in Cambodia*, pp. 134–157; Riddle, *Cambodian Interlude*.
22. Riddle, *Cambodian Interlude*.
23. Jordens, "Persecution of Cambodia's Ethnic Vietnamese Communities during and since the UNTAC Period".
24. Alola Foundation, *Trafficking in East Timor*.
25. Thorbek and Pattanaik, *Transnational Prostitution*.
26. Alola Foundation, *Trafficking in East Timor*.
27. Ibid.
28. Ibid.
29. Ibid; Elizabeth Pasani, "The Dili STI Study 2003", Dili: Family Health International/IMPACT, 2004.
30. Riddle, *Cambodian Interlude*.
31. S. Whittington, "The UN Transitional Administration in East Timor: Gender Affairs", *Development Bulletin*, 53, 2000, pp. 74–76.

3

Protecting civilians from UN peacekeepers and humanitarian workers: Sexual exploitation and abuse

Vanessa Kent

As of January 2005, United Nations (UN) peacekeepers were deployed in near record numbers, with some 73,000 military, police and civilian peacekeepers worldwide.[1] Liberia is host to one of the largest UN missions, with approximately 17,000 military, civilian and civilian police personnel, as well as additional humanitarian representatives from UN agencies and other international organizations, including international non-governmental organizations (INGOs). As in other modern war contexts, the Liberian conflict has had a devastating effect on civilian populations, particularly women and children. The statement that "[w]arfare is no longer fought in remote battlefields between armies but is fought in our homes, our schools, our communities and increasingly on women's bodies" accurately characterizes this.[2] Assessments undertaken by INGOs in Liberia observe that, during the 14 years of conflict, pervasive, systematic and widespread rape and sexual violence occurred, affecting anywhere between 60 per cent and 75 per cent of Liberian women.[3]

It is unfortunate that the general public is no longer as shocked as it once was by reports of belligerents engaging in systematic and widespread rape in times of war. But when UN peacekeepers – including military, police and civilian personnel – and humanitarian workers, mandated to safeguard local populations in conflict zones, are accused of similar behaviour, we are looking not only at gross violations of human rights but at the perversion of an international system intended to prevent crimes against humanity, including sexual and gender-based violence.

Unintended consequences of peacekeeping operations, Aoi, de Coning and Thakur (eds), United Nations University Press, 2007, ISBN 978-92-808-1142-1

At the policy level, the United Nations has promulgated a comprehensive set of guidelines to deter UN peace operations personnel from committing acts of sexual exploitation and abuse (SEA), including the 2005 strategy to eliminate future sexual exploitation and abuse.[4] UN peacekeepers are expected to abide by the highest standards of conduct at all times. However, cases of sexual abuse, exploitation and violence committed by UN personnel are reported with predictable regularity. As far back as the 1992 UN peace operation in Somalia, peacekeepers were recognized as vectors in the increase in the number of women and children resorting to commercial sex work in post-conflict settings.[5] Lessons from past missions, including those in Haiti, Mozambique, East Timor, Bosnia, Kosovo and Cambodia, inform us that the arrival of peacekeepers increases the demand for prostitutes substantially: "rape, trafficking in women and children, sexual enslavement and child abuse often coexist alongside peace operations".[6] More recently, and in response to the increasing number of reports filed from peace missions that UN personnel as well as aid workers are soliciting prostitutes and, in some cases, sexually violating women and children, the Secretary-General appointed his special adviser on sexual exploitation and abuse, Prince Zeid Ra'ad Zeid Al-Hussein of Jordan, to report on the efforts undertaken by the organization to prevent, identify and respond to violations. Although these violations are met with an outcry from local communities and international agencies, the latter have also been found complicit in exploitative activities. Moreover, reports of peacekeepers' involvement with trafficked women and prostitution rings have drawn worldwide attention.[7] Even where acts of misconduct are not as shocking, they are no less deserving of attention and remedial action. Incidents of sexual harassment by international staff towards locally engaged personnel, for example, have been called "pervasive" and "tolerated" by many civilians working within missions. The United Nations' rhetoric about a "zero-tolerance policy" regarding cases of sexual exploitation and abuse must be matched by decisive and accountable action.

Recently, the United Nations' Department of Peacekeeping Operations (DPKO) has taken a strong and visible stance against sexual misconduct by implementing preventative measures, including the enhancement of in-mission training and the deployment of in-mission code of conduct/personnel officers. It has also established responsive measures, such as the implementation of procedures for proper and rapid investigations and the identification of SEA focal points for reporting incidents and coordinating investigations. Encouraging inter-agency coordination will also serve as an important mechanism, both to prevent incidents and to respond to allegations in a coherent and coordinated manner. Peace operation environments, created by the large influx of peacekeepers, socially and economically affect women and girls. Therefore, educating local populations on their rights is also an essential component of the United Nations' strategy as it can promote an environment that supports human rights, rather than one that undermines them.

This chapter examines the unintended – though real and predictable – impact that thousands of personnel – civilian, police and military – have on levels of local prostitution and, in some cases, on the increase in the number of trafficked women and children. I will also highlight the current strategies in place in the United Nations Mission in Liberia (UNMIL) to investigate allegations of abuse committed by UN personnel. Research findings affirm that only a plan of action within a broader framework of protection from all forms of abuse and exploitation can be successful. Thus, the United Nations must implement and enforce existing preventive and responsive mechanisms within the United Nations, the UN agency systems and INGOs, as well as work to strengthen local institutions that promote women's human rights and equality. I also suggest that, even as it strives to eliminate such practices, the United Nations must predict the potential negative consequences that acts of sexual misconduct can have on the mission, and immediately and visibly put in place mechanisms to prevent such acts from occurring. In cases where acts of misconduct do occur, a weak response will undermine confidence in the organization and encourage perpetrators to continue without fear of prosecution or punishment. Protection is a central and indispensable component of humanitarian action, and only a multi-pronged approach can lead to a mutually reinforcing strategy. The United Nations must therefore visibly and credibly implement existing policies by holding individuals accountable for the reputation of the organization. A list of key recommendations is provided as a way forward at the end of the chapter.

Background

That humanitarian aid workers and UN peacekeepers are the perpetrators of sexual exploitation and abuse (SEA) is not news. Among the first reports of violence against local populations – including murder, torture, rape and other sexual violence – were recorded in Cambodia and Somalia in the early 1990s. Further to this, the 1995 United Nations High Commissioner for Refugees (UNHCR) guidelines on prevention and response made reference to the fact that refugee women and girls were being approached for sexual favours in exchange for goods during aid distribution.[8] Graça Machel's 1996 study on the impact of conflict on children also noted that the arrival of peace operations troops has been associated with the rapid rise in child prostitution.[9] However, it was not until the 2002 Save the Children-UK (SCUK) and UNHCR report on sexual exploitation of refugees by UN peacekeepers and aid workers in West Africa[10] that global attention was alerted to the fact that peacekeepers and humanitarian workers were coercing young girls to barter sex for food, money or shelter.

The UN Office of Internal Oversight Services (OIOS) responded to the 2002 SCUK/UNHCR report by setting up an investigation. The OIOS findings could not confirm allegations of extensive sexual exploitation of refugees because many of the stories reported could not be verified. Of the initial 12 cases reported, "no allegation against any United Nations staff member could be substantiated".[11] Of an additional 43 cases, only 10 were substantiated by evidence. Two years later, a memorandum written by the UN Organization Mission in the Democratic Republic of Congo (MONUC) recorded a total of 150 allegations against soldiers, including involvement in a prostitution ring and the rape of minors, some as young as 13. The memorandum prompted another OIOS investigation. The ensuing report confirmed that sexual contact with peacekeepers occurred regularly, usually in exchange for food or small sums of money.[12] The report also noted that the problem was "serious and on-going [and] equally disturbing was the lack of a protection and deterrence programme even at the present time".[13] Of great concern is the implication that peace operations personnel could be motivated by the opportunity to engage in sex tourism, because it was reported that the investigation was "considering the possibility that MONUC has been infiltrated by 'organised pedophiles who recruit their friends'".[14]

The UN mission in Burundi is no exception to scandals involving misconduct. In 2004, one soldier was arrested for rape and murder, and two other soldiers were accused of sexual misconduct.[15] Carolyn McAskie, the Special Representative of the Secretary-General (SRSG) in Burundi, noted that the sheer increase in numbers of soldiers on the ground created an added burden, that of prostitution: "With more soldiers in the area, 'sex workers' are gathering at the borders. This is not the kind of income producing activity that we have envisioned for local women."[16] She added, "[w]ith over 5000 young male soldiers in the peacekeeping mission there, the challenge to the UN to maintain acceptable codes of behaviour among the soldiers was formidable".[17] The UN Mission in Liberia (UNMIL) has also admitted to probing allegations of SEA by its peacekeepers in Liberia, a situation unsurprising to some INGOs, which warned that the lack of a clear and transparent process for reporting sexual exploitation incidents and the delay in identifying community focal points left the country "ripe for another scandal".[18]

Evidently, the UN resolutions, codes of conduct and other directives that call for the implementation of preventative and responsive mechanisms, including full prosecution of crimes against women and children and accountability measures, either are not being implemented or are not effective. The Secretary-General's bulletin on Special Measures for Protection from Sexual Exploitation and Sexual Abuse in October 2003 defines SEA as the "exchange of money, employment, goods or services for sex, including sexual favours",[19] leaving no room for misunderstanding; the United Nations strictly prohibits acts that could be deemed exploitative.[20] The United Nations also strongly discourages "sexual relationships between UN staff and beneficiaries of assistance, since they are based on unequal power dynamics, [and] undermine the integrity and credibility of the UN".[21] Mission-specific codes also stress the UN rules that forbid sex with anyone under the age of 18. A mistaken assumption about the age of the child is not considered a legitimate excuse. The United Nations thus recognizes that the vast disparity and inherent power differential between locals and peace operations personnel, including their perceived position of wealth, status, privilege and authority, are significant factors in incidences of SEA. "Many people don't think it's wrong", said one UN agency representative in Liberia, and noted the need to improve the quality of people hired, as well as to establish stronger accountability mechanisms among personnel.[22]

As cultures, gender relations and traditions vary from country to country, UN peacekeepers must be seen to reinforce, rather than undermine, existing human rights and other international standards. The Secretary-General's special adviser on SEA, Prince Zeid, noted that, despite the United Nations' stance of zero tolerance regarding SEA, "the situation appears to be one of 'zero compliance with zero tolerance'".[23] Jane Holle Lute, Assistant Secretary-General in the DPKO, noted that: "We recognize that sexual exploitation and abuse is a problem in some missions and we're working for a systematic and coordinated approach to strengthen the measures we have in place.... It's obvious that the measures we have had in place have not been adequate to deal with the changing circumstances found in some missions."[24]

In a 2005 report to the General Assembly, the Secretary-General noted that the number of allegations of SEA made by and about United Nations personnel in 2004 was more than double the number reported in 2003.[25] A total of 121 new cases were registered, 105 from the DPKO: "Forty-five per cent of those allegations involved sex with minors and 15 per cent involved rape or sexual assault. Over one third (31 per cent) involved prostitution with adult women and the remaining 6 per cent involved other forms of sexual exploitation and abuse".[26] However, the Secretary-General noted that the data gathered on cases of sexual exploitation and abuse perpetrated by personnel affiliated with the United Nations "may still not reflect the true extent of these deplorable incidents".[27] The United Nations claims that, in cases where misconduct was found to have occurred, appropriate action was taken. As this chapter will examine below, one can only assume that this implies that perpetrators were repatriated, but not necessarily prosecuted.

The legal aspects

The legal status of UN personnel is a complex and delicate issue. Military members of national contingents remain under the exclusive criminal jurisdiction of their own national authorities, and therefore have immunity from local prosecution. The United Nations is bound by Status-of-Forces Agreements (SOFAs) between the United Nations and the host country for the peace operation, and Contribution Agreements, or a Memorandum of Understanding (MOU), between the United Nations and countries sending personnel to the peace operation. This agreement assumes that the troop-contributing country (TCC) will meet its responsibility to exercise criminal jurisdiction over national personnel in return for immunity from local prosecution. However, as countries are not legally bound to undertake this responsibility, few meet this requirement. Repatriation is often the United Nations' only disciplinary option and, once suspects are repatriated, the United Nations loses any influence to ensure the troop- and police-contributing countries (TCCs/PCCs) report back on the issue. Thus, additional disciplinary action depends upon the will and capacity of the country of origin. Most are reluctant to bring charges against their own troops and police for alleged actions that took place in foreign lands. In many cases, contributing countries do not have the requisite legislation to prosecute their peacekeepers upon repatriation. Some countries do not even criminalize many forms of rape and other sexual offences. For example, marital rape is not an offence in many countries. "In light of the fact that 'forced marriages' have been reported in different UN missions, this gap can result in impunity for serious and severe violations of women's human rights if so-called husbands are allowed to sexually assault their 'wives' with impunity."[28]

Military personnel

As recommended in the 2005 report by the Secretary-General's Special Adviser on sexual exploitation and abuse, all future agreements include a legal obligation for member states to take appropriate action, including punitive sanctions, against those who commit acts of SEA. The MOU should, therefore, contain a clause that indicates that, after an investigation concludes that the allegation is well founded and that there is a *prima facie* case of misconduct, the national contingent commander of the TCC in question is responsible for forwarding the case to its national authorities. The SRSG is also responsible for informing the Secretariat, which in turn informs the TCC's Permanent Mission to the United Nations in New York. The decision to repatriate can be made by the TCC, and the UN Secretary-General can also recommend dismissal or repatriation. Although the decision on whether or not to prosecute is a national responsibility, the agreement to follow this procedure should be an essential condition for acceptance of an offer from a TCC to provide troops for UN peace operations. The Secretary-General must therefore receive formal assurances that TCCs will implement their legal obligation to exercise criminal jurisdiction over their troops in return for immunity. Moreover, it is recommended that a reporting procedure be established whereby a TCC must inform on the actions taken as a result of a mission's investigation. Failure to comply with this obligation would result in a "name and shame" of the country (not the individual) in a report by the Secretary-General to the Special Committee on Peacekeeping.[29]

"Experts on mission" and civilian personnel

Military Observers and Civilian Police hold the status of "experts on mission", affording them immunity in their official functions. Similarly, UN civilian staff benefit from "functional immunity" and are further bound to observe the standards of conduct expected of international civil servants.[30] All are obliged to respect local laws and customs. In cases where personnel commit illegal acts in the host country that do not form part of their official functions, they can be subject to local civil and criminal jurisdiction.[31] However, because peacekeepers are usually deployed in areas that do not have functioning legal systems, initiating local prosecution is extremely difficult. Moreover, host countries may be "reluctant to be seen as 'going against' those who are there to help them".[32] Peacekeepers seem aware of the United Nations' limited jurisdiction over them: the OIOS report from the DRC notes:

> despite knowledge that the investigation was ongoing, sexual activities between the military and the local population apparently continued.... It was clear that the investigation did not act as a deterrent for some of the troops, perhaps because they had not been made aware of the severe penalties for engaging in such conduct, nor had they seen any evidence of a negative impact on individual peacekeepers for such behaviour. Without strong reinforcement of the legal requirements and prompt sanctions for violations, they may well continue this behaviour.[33]

Currently, many missions lack sufficient capacity to monitor personnel, and weak coordination between civilian and military police allows for incomplete reporting and follow-up. Thus, there is a need to implement transparent procedures to ensure accountability to victims balanced with a fair judicial review to properly manage the investigation. This may require that the United Nations appoint investigators with specialized expertise to investigate and monitor cases pending before a Board of Inquiry, and to ensure that the proper process required to prepare a case is met. As recommended in the report, the establishment of a permanent professional investigative mechanism to investigate cases of serious misconduct could provide capacity to appropriately undertake investigations, afford witness protection and ensure due process is met. In addition, to ensure that procedures followed during investigations satisfy the requirements of national laws of the TCC, the report suggests that an expert in military law, such as a prosecutor from the TCC concerned, participate in the investigation. Meeting national standards of evidence may propel the TCC to undertake further action, such as prosecution. The report further suggests the organization consider allowing for on-site courts martial in order to gain access to witnesses and evidence and to demonstrate a transparent, accountable and remedial procedure to the local population.[34]

Thus, for now, the United Nations' room for remedial action is severely restricted. Ensuring action is taken will require a combination of efforts including: the establishment of a professional investigative capacity, the implementation of lines of accountability and standards of conduct for UN, UN agency and other humanitarian personnel and the standardization of disciplinary measures. This will further serve to impart a very clear threat of repatriation and prosecution. As long as national authorities retain exclusive jurisdiction to repatriate and prosecute military and police peacekeepers, and humanitarian agencies are negligent in implementing and enforcing their codes of conduct, the pursuit of breaches will be ad hoc. The United Nations, its agencies and member states must all improve their response mechanisms and work in coordination to strengthen the resolve to prevent, as well as enable it effectively to respond to allegations of, SEA, rather than undermine the process in the name of sovereignty or self-protection.

Post-conflict societies: An enabling environment for abuse?

UN peacekeepers arrive in the aftermath of conflict in which sexual and gender-based violence (SGBV) has been used as a deliberate war strategy or features significantly in the daily lives of women and girls. In fact, different forms of SGBV can become institutionalized as many of the conditions that created the violence remain unchanged: women and children in post-conflict settings can be particularly vulnerable to exploitation and abuse. Poverty, weak economic structures, the lack of employment opportunities and the loss of family and community support networks leave them susceptible to prostitution and at risk of recruitment by human traffickers.

Human trafficking is a form of serious exploitation and abuse that is increasingly present in the UN peace operation environments. Trafficking exploits human beings for revenue through sex, forced labour and the trade in human organs. For peace operations (UN and other) there is a crisis of perception in relation to trafficking and the linked issue of SEA, which sees peace operations branded as more part of the problem than the solution, along with criticisms that the issue is not taken seriously by peace operation institutions. Allegations and incidences of peacekeeper involvement with trafficking can be extremely damaging to missions by undermining implementation of police reform and rule of law mandates, perpetuating linkages to organized crime and providing material for anti-UN elements, obstructionists and negative media campaigns. DPKO policy addresses the reality of conflict and post-conflict environments and acknowledges that the arrival of even the initial personnel in preparation for a mission can create a new demand for human trafficking.[35] Although data remain anecdotal, the people involved in mission leadership should presume that elements of organized crime can be expected, because they view the mission as a lucrative business opportunity.

Thus, with limited economic opportunities, many women in UN peace operation environments are sometimes obliged to engage in transactional sex as a means of livelihood for themselves and their families; the opportunity for peacekeepers to engage in seemingly consensual relations is without question. The organization therefore faces the challenge of maintaining ethical standards and codes of behaviour among its disparate troops. UN officials already have a difficult task in recruiting troops and worry that "naming and shaming" the countries of the soldiers involved in sexual abuse cases will make it even harder. In October 2004, UN Deputy Secretary-General Louise Fréchette appealed to international parliamentarians for help with UN peace operations, stating that the United Nations required an additional 30,000 military as well as civilians to satisfy the current demand.[36]

Different nationalities, levels of training and cultures can impose negative perceptions on how men and women should relate in society. Some peacekeepers are insensitive to local cultures and customs and behavioural boundaries, and their presence can be seen as a continuation of the assault and harassment inflicted during the conflict. In an environment where peacekeepers are deployed alongside local populations, it is incumbent upon the United Nations to ensure it creates and maintains an environment that supports the equal application of human rights. Clearly, gender, cultural and human rights training is only a means to an end, and does not necessarily engender a change in behaviour; what is really key will be identifying a way to affect mindsets and attitudes. Many countries have, for instance, a clear and enforced "no sex" policy on mission, but others do not impose such constraints. The countries that have successfully implemented strict non-fraternization policies have succeeded through a variety of measures such as enhanced pre-deployment training, paid leave (especially for those in-mission for over six months), the provision of adequate recreational facilities and a clear chain of command that, from the highest levels, creates an environment that does not tolerate SEA and immediately repatriates a member alleged to have committed any such action. Countries that do not have "no sex" policies should consider investing some of the monies they receive from peace operations into similar activities and facilities. Troop- or police-contributing countries receive over US$1,000 per person per month. This money gets paid to governments, not to individual peacekeepers. Rewarding good behaviour and punishing bad could be seen as an incentive for those who do not want to jeopardize their opportunity to deploy on a UN mission, and a deterrent to those who may be forced to pay compensation to victims. Harsher disciplinary measures combined with incentives for good behaviour may make clear to troops that misconduct carries significant benefits as well as serious consequences.

The abundance of international military, police, civilian, humanitarian and other INGO personnel of a sexually active age, with relative wealth and power, living in difficult conditions far from their homes, suggests that sexual liaisons should be expected. In particular, security forces (military and police personnel) are considered key vectors in the spread of HIV/AIDS. Soldiers have been called a "'bridging' group, acting as a conduit for the spread of HIV into the wider population".[37] As local women barter or sell sex for survival, they are increasingly exposed and vulnerable to contracting HIV/AIDS and other sexually transmitted infections. The possibility of putting host communities at risk of increased levels of HIV/AIDS and sexually transmitted infections is only part of DPKO's concern; it has also been suggested that "HIV/AIDS levels in host nations may soon be a key variable in the calculations of member states considering whether to contribute troops to a particular mission",[38] thus potentially limiting the already small pool of troop- and police-contributing countries.

To curb the spread of HIV/AIDS in mission areas, the United Nations provides in-mission training and distributes condoms (five condoms per officer per week). This, however, has been called a mixed message: on the one hand the United Nations promulgates abstinence and faithfulness to family or partner, and on the other distributes condoms, which is perceived as encouraging sex. The United Nations must work diligently to ensure personnel are clear on the United Nations' rule that strongly discourages relationships between UN personnel and local populations, while acknowledging the practical realities related to condom distribution, training and awareness-raising. Furthermore, it is essential that senior UN management do not appear apathetic towards misconduct: not only must they combat SEA through visible action and implementation of strategies, but they must enforce UN codes of conduct by disciplining those who are guilty of breaching them. In reality, however, many are aware that such acts are rarely punished owing to weak and/or inconsistent policies and mechanisms, regular troop rotation and a lack of coherent and coordinated systems for investigating and following up on allegations made against UN personnel. The lack of accountability for peace operations personnel is a serious problem: experts contend that what little punishment the United Nations can impose does not adequately address the crime and does not provide a deterrent to other people who may be tempted to commit similar acts. The United Nations should be provided with adequate resources to establish units dedicated to minimize and effectively manage acts of misconduct and enforce UN standards of conduct.[39] The monitoring of exploitation and abuse of local populations can be achieved by recording and publishing the licence plates of UN vehicles picking up under-age girls for sex in mission, and regular circulation and monitoring of off-limits location lists.

UN missions must also work to uphold international norms relating to the prevention, investigation, prosecution and punishment of crimes conducted by its personnel. The United Nations must be prepared to conduct investigations in a manner that meets national evidentiary standards to ensure proper process is followed to prepare a case, as well as implement transparent procedures to ensure accountability to, and protection of, the victim. Currently, however, the absence of a responsible and responsive system gives rise to the perception that the United Nations is not concerned about the welfare of those abused. For example, a complaint lodged by an NGO in Liberia accused UN peacekeepers of videotaping young refugee girls in the shower. According to the complainant, the subsequent interview conducted by the United Nations as part of the investigation was undertaken in full view of the alleged perpetrators, thereby intimidating and compromising the rights of the victims.[40]

The opportunity to strengthen local awareness of women's civil, political, economic and social rights is another essential component of any strategy aimed at reducing vulnerability. For example, the Gender and

Human Rights Sections in UNMIL work with civil society groups, including national NGOs, churches, the transitional government and other service providers on, *inter alia*, "training of trainers" workshops on issues related to international human rights standards (for example, the Convention to Eliminate all Forms of Discrimination Against Women, the Convention on the Rights of the Child, the Convention Against Torture and the International Covenant on Civil and Political Rights) and sexual and gender-based violence. Liberia has a large number of national NGOs working to empower local communities and community groups to collectively advocate for their welfare and speak against human rights violations, particularly those committed against women and children, the elderly and other vulnerable groups. These NGOs include the Concerned Christian Community, the Centre for Democratic Empowerment, the Association of Female Lawyers of Liberia, the Women in Peacebuilding Network, the Liberian Women's Initiative and Mano River Women Peace Network. Supporting the community's capacity to inform, educate and respond to cases of SGBV should thus be regarded as a UN responsibility aimed at protecting communities from exploitation and abuse committed by peace operations personnel, and could further support and strengthen their rights on a national level writ large.

The importance of gender balance in peace operations

Until recently, the United Nations has been a male-dominated organization. Ten years ago, women occupied only 13 per cent of decision-making positions within the Secretariat, and 4 per cent within the DPKO. These figures have risen within the system and as of June 2004, with regard to international civilian staff administered by the DPKO, women constituted 27.5 per cent overall, and 12.0 per cent at the director level and above, up from 24.0 per cent and 4.2 per cent, respectively, in 2002.[41] Currently, out of 27 peace operations, 2 are headed by women: the UN missions in Burundi and Georgia. Three women serve as deputy Special Representatives (the United Nations Verification Mission in Guatemala, the United Nations Assistance Mission in Afghanistan, and the United Nations Observer Mission in Georgia). However, these figures do not accurately represent at what levels. According to the Office of the Special Adviser to the Secretary-General on Gender Issues and Advancement of Women, women were represented as follows at 31 December 2005: GS 61 per cent, P-2 49 per cent, P-3 42 per cent, P-4 35 per cent, P-5 31 per cent, D-1 27 per cent, D-2 28 per cent, USG 15 per cent, ASG 20 per cent.[42] As of August 2004, none of the 18 humanitarian coordinators within humanitarian entities in the United Nations system was a woman.

At UNHCR and the World Food Programme, women constitute 40 per cent of professional staff, with approximately 25 per cent of them at the senior level.[43] There also remain many challenges related to the recruitment of female military and police personnel: between 1989 and 1993 only 1.7 per cent were women. Today, these figures remain very low: as of June 2004, women constituted 1 per cent of military personnel and 5 per cent of civilian police personnel assigned by member states to serve in UN peace operations. The Memorandum of Understanding (MOU) between the United Nations and TCCs cannot make requests based on sex for the composition of contingents. Often, the composition of women is directly related to their representation in national armed forces.

Although the United Nations strives to achieve the equal representation of men and women in its organization, this is not only to support efforts aimed at gender equality; in practice, the presence of women amongst military personnel is very important. Professor Gerard J. DeGroot argues that militaries, often conventionally trained, are unable to channel their male capacity for violence. A peacekeeper must combine the qualities of a soldier with those of a social worker: "Because peacekeeping can be violent, combat training is essential. But the peacekeeper must also be conciliatory, patient and peaceful."[44] Because few soldiers combine these qualities, peace operations have been shamed by aggressive behaviour: "Soldiers win wars, but they also occasionally commit atrocities when aggression rages out of control";[45] in particular, the inability to control sexual violence can undermine the United Nations' credibility writ large. Other benefits to deploying increased numbers of women include their capacity to calm stressful situations and their disinclination towards violence.[46]

Moreover, because peacekeepers are deployed alongside civilians, who comprise primarily women and children, victims of SGBV often prefer to report cases of abuse to other women, and men cannot always speak to unmarried women without the latter having a relative present. The UN DPKO notes that:

[W]omen's presence improves access and support for local women; it makes male peacekeepers more reflective and responsible; and it broadens the repertoire of skills and styles available within the mission, often with the effect of reducing conflict and confrontation.[47]

A 1995 study undertaken by the UN Division for the Advancement of Women found that incidents of rape and prostitution fall significantly with just a token female presence, signifying that "men behave when in the presence of women from their own culture ... as it more closely resembles civilian society. Its members are therefore more likely to observe social conventions and define civilised behaviour."[48] DeGroot adds that "[t]here is no evidence that women make better peacekeepers, but a great deal of evidence to suggest that the presence of women improves an operation's chances of success".[49]

Standardizing mechanisms: The case of Liberia

UNMIL

To address allegations of SEA in mission, former SRSG and UNMIL Coordinator Jacques Paul Klein made numerous statements regarding UNMIL's zero-tolerance policy on sexual exploitation and reminded his senior staff that any breach of conduct would result in "serious consequences".[50] However, an internal UN document states that, despite circulation of memoranda on the zero-tolerance policy, "direct opposition to the current 'zero-tolerance policy' [has been] strongly voiced by members of senior management".[51] The note further warns that open and strong disregard for the Department's policy, particularly on the prohibition against prostitution, is sending a strong message to mission personnel that they can behave with impunity. Often, senior managers fail to draw the line and establish clear standards of behaviour.

Managers play an important role in creating an environment that discourages sexual exploitation and abuse by taking action against alleged perpetrators and serving as role models. Thus, managers must be at the forefront of efforts to combat all forms of sexual exploitation and abuse and be held accountable for discharging that role. To ensure compliance, the Special Adviser on sexual exploitation and abuse recommends that senior staff (including national contingent commanders and senior managers) be evaluated, for example as part of their performance goals, on the basis of implementing measures aimed at eliminating SEA. The United Nations urgently requires increased capacity to enforce UN standards of conduct relating to SEA, including the monitoring of off-limit locations.[52] To prevent incidents and address allegations of SEA in mission, UNMIL has identified SEA focal points (located in the trafficking, human rights and human resource offices) to receive reports, monitor incidents and identify patterns. All newly arrived personnel receive induction training on, among other topics, HIV/AIDS, gender and SEA.

UNMIL's mechanism to investigate allegations of abuse is the following: once a report has been filed, the focal points decide on whether or not to investigate. The investigation team comprises a UN legal adviser, a UN security representative, a military police officer (of a nationality other than the alleged perpetrator's) and one of the UN SEA focal points ("a female"). However, this system was widely called "biased" by IN-GOs ("UN security are often found in bars" and have "no investigatory experience"), and focal points admitted being "too busy to assist with investigations, and neither is it part of our TORs [terms of reference]".[53] Following the investigation, the focal points will make a recommendation to the SRSG, who will then follow up with the DPKO in New York. Once a decision has been made, UN Headquarters will report back to the SRSG, who will task the focal points to take further action. To date, only a handful of UNMIL personnel have been repatriated based on incidents of SEA.

UN agencies and INGOs

Allegations against humanitarian personnel are dealt with on an ad hoc basis, from agency to agency, which can limit the effectiveness of a common strategy. Thus, despite recommending that "accountability needs to be addressed at individual agency level and collectively ... to ensure a common approach to protecting against sexual exploitation and abuse and to foster a concept of collective responsibility",[54] there exists no common system of accountability for the humanitarian community. At the time of research, not one humanitarian worker had been repatriated on grounds of sexual misconduct, although one was allegedly identified by trafficked women as a client.[55]

   In order to better respond to allegations of SEA, coordinate investigations and streamline policies, a Task Force of UNMIL, UN agencies and INGO representatives has been established in Liberia. They will coordinate preventive and responsive mechanisms to SEA: the United Nations Children's Fund has taken a lead role amongst UN and associated personnel, and the International Rescue Committee has taken the lead for INGOs. In July 2004, SEA focal points were identified, trained and tasked with implementing policies and procedures within their own organizations, as well as coordinating information between organizations. At the time of the research, these focal points had only just been nominated and trained, and as a result regular coordination between UNMIL, UN agencies and NGOs had yet to be systematically implemented. Moreover, whether the NGOs and UN agencies actually intend to follow up on allegations of abuse is unclear because "there is still a lot of confusion within agencies on what to do ... and anyway, there remains no effective procedural mechanism to pursue allegations of abuse".[56] Many interviewed in the mission area,[57] however, felt that UN agencies and NGOs were more concerned with providing a "culture of protection" for their staff members rather than holding staff accountable for their actions.

Nevertheless, the monthly convening of focal points is an important first step in the recognition of the severity of the issue and the need to exchange and coordinate information, best practices and lessons learned, establish investigatory mechanisms, set up a blacklist of those whose contracts have been terminated on grounds of misconduct and provide in-house training. The group must eventually move beyond coordination to create a list of gaps that remain to be addressed in areas such as training, empowerment, procedures and community reporting.

Despite statements declaring UNMIL's zero-tolerance policy, and the establishment of the Task Force in Liberia, the mission still lacks appropriate "responses from a broad range of actors and a shift in the organisational culture and approach [among] ... agencies".[58] Within mission areas, a standardized code, i.e. one set of guidelines, for all UN and associated staff should be prioritized. This should include a common code of conduct and standards governing individual behaviour of peacekeepers and humanitarian workers. Clearly, all agencies must work together in a coherent and complementary manner to both prevent and respond to cases of SEA. One agency cannot be perceived as more or less lenient than another. Best practices or lessons learned should be disseminated as widely as possible. All prevention and response initiatives must be balanced; providing for prevention mechanisms without providing for response methods for recourse and support systems is as harmful as providing no systems at all.[59] Implementing mechanisms that monitor and evaluate the success or failure of preventive and reactive strategies and policies will assist in developing longer-term measures required to prevent acts of misconduct from occurring in the first place.

The challenge of reporting and identifying perpetrators lies not only in the absence of weak responsive mechanisms; victims are often reluctant to come forward because most often they – and their families – depend largely upon the income generated by UN peacekeepers and associated personnel. Moreover, the stigma attached to rape and prostitution means that sexual assault or exploitation is the single most underreported crime in most societies.[60]

Perhaps it is time for the United Nations to take bold steps and empower an authority to investigate allegations of abuse independently and to mete out swift and visible justice in the countries where the missions are based. This will enable witnesses to testify and communities can see action taken. If applied, this would remove national jurisdiction from contributing countries. This is not inconceivable: the NATO agreements allow host states to exercise secondary jurisdiction over nationals of a contributing state in cases where the contributing country, awarded with primary jurisdiction, is "unwilling" or "unable" to prosecute its own nationals. In 2005, the UN Secretary-General requested additional funding to hire extra employees to staff Personnel Conduct Units in the DPKO as well as seven existing missions to ensure compliance with tightened regulations for conduct.[61] In the field, the units would "establish mechanisms to receive complaints of misconduct, review and verify facts, forward allegations of misconduct and liaise with Headquarters on the follow-up to investigations".[62] Unless paper policies are matched by a commitment from the international community to protect those they purport to assist, mechanisms and strategies, while well intentioned, serve to perpetuate the rhetoric of "prohibiting" acts of SEA, rather than the reality of merely "discouraging" these acts.

Way forward

In order to prevent negative consequences from occurring with the deployment of peace operations personnel, the following is a list of suggestions that could be taken into consideration when planning future peace operations.

Troop- and police-contributing countries (TCCs/PCCs) must enhance pre-deployment training. The main focus should be on human rights, and issues related to gender, culture and SEA should take a rights-based approach; a common understanding must be developed on the values the United Nations is deployed to uphold, such as the principles of equality and non-discrimination.[63]

All personnel should receive standardized in-mission training. Although pre-deployment training is a national responsibility, the United Nations can reinforce certain issues and provide for an understanding of the repercussions of misconduct. Training is important but not a "cure-all": it is a means to an end and not an end in itself. Solving the problem will require a multifaceted approach: the United Nations must ensure it has very clear, enforceable codes of conduct, widely disseminated, visible and reinforced through a clear chain of command.[64] The quality and professionalism of *all* personnel serving in UN peace operations must continually be improved through the application of more rigorous standards, better training and responsive leadership. Senior leadership must set standards by actively supporting the UN policy of zero tolerance; any perception of apathy can encourage misconduct and demoralize staff. Managers in particular must be responsible for creating an environment that discourages SEA and should be held accountable for discharging that role. A recommendation is to evaluate their performance on the basis of implementing measures aimed at eliminating SEA.

TCCs/PCCs must be more accountable to the United Nations by prosecuting repatriated personnel and informing the United Nations of results. Immunity from local prosecution should not imply impunity. The United Nations' MOU must make contributions from countries contingent upon this. TCCs/PCCs must provide better conditions for personnel serving abroad in UN peace operations, including paid leave and recreational facilities. TCCs/PCCs must ensure deployment is based on merit and that only the most qualified personnel are deployed in UN missions. TCCs/PCCs should consider withholding any additional pay granted while serving in a UN mission until the personnel return home with a clean record.

The United Nations should provide some form of assistance and rehabilitation to victims. This can be achieved through the establishment of a voluntary trust fund or by imposing financial penalties on peacekeepers found guilty of serious misconduct (or a combination of the two).

TCCs/PCCs and all agencies should aim to examine policies in place that may prevent women from joining peace operations, and identify strategies and mechanisms to encourage them to do so, with the effect of increasing the number of women participating in peace and humanitarian operations.

All missions and agencies should have policies and procedures for the protection of women and children. All missions and agencies should have confidential systems for directly and indirectly receiving reports about possible SEA. The development of appropriate and common disciplinary procedures for violations should be considered.

UN agencies and international NGOs should identify a qualified member to conduct an analysis of internal response exercises undertaken by the various players. Recommendations should be implemented to standardize response mechanisms.

Member states should support the Secretariat's efforts by supporting the budgetary request to establish Personnel Conduct Units in the DPKO, as well as in the field. UN civilian and/or military police and/or UN security should be used to identify and monitor establishments and well-known corners or streets where prostitution is known to take place and UN vehicles are repeatedly seen stopping to pick up girls.

A database of all personnel whose contracts have been terminated or who have been repatriated because of misconduct should be developed in order to bar them from future employment in mission areas.

There must be similar lines of accountability for military, civilian/ humanitarian and police personnel. Common approaches and collective responsibility, matched with accountability to beneficiaries, are necessary steps towards creating an environment that discourages sexual exploitation and abuse.

The Task Force concept should be replicated, if it has not been already, at the country level in all missions. The Task Force terms of reference include: the establishment of a common information and dissemination strategy, the coordination of efforts and the promotion of a consistent approach. UN mission gender offices must be provided with funds to continue to support local community empowerment and civil society training. SEA focal points should be identified in mission. Focal points should preferably not be in the gender affairs office as this would reinforce the perception that SEA and gender issues are one and the same thing.

Self-reliance opportunities should be a critical aspect of the UN intervention to support local communities and ensure those most vulnerable to SEA are provided with alternatives. Gender-sensitive skills training, income-generating activities and access to credit are recognized to greatly diminish women's vulnerability to sexual exploitation. The United Nations and its agencies must invest more in such activities in the field in order to provide women with opportunities other than commercial sex work.

Conclusion

Incidents of SEA are often pervasive in countries characterized by vast wealth disparities, such as those existing in peace operation environments. Most peacekeepers are aware of the power differentials and do their job with integrity and honour. The frequent reporting of instances of SEA, however, suggests that, unless more aggressive measures are put in place to mitigate or prevent cases of exploitation and abuse, the presence of a large number of male peacekeepers may become the driving force of the local sex industry. Unchecked, this peace operations economy spurs the establishment of brothels, bars and sex clubs, which further contributes to a demand for women. The female victims of this trade are not the key: they suffer disproportionately during and after war and are often forced to barter their bodies simply to survive. Additionally, the absence of the rule of law in most post-conflict settings, including an effective and properly functioning police force, judiciary and penal system, allows transnational criminal networks, official corruption and weak immigration policies to flourish. Human trafficking takes place undeterred by the authorities, and traffickers thrive on the presence of a large number of UN peace operations personnel.

This chapter has argued that there is not one solution to the problem, but rather a multifaceted approach, focusing on both prevention and response, with a particular focus required on the former. No matter the actual extent of the problem, the United Nations' lack of response to this phenomenon creates the impression that it fails to take the issue seriously. There is much the United Nations and other organizations can do to guarantee the rights of women and children: they can actively ensure that employees, whether civilian experts, police or military, uphold the "do no harm" principle and respect the beneficiaries they intend to serve. If the United Nations is to regain credibility in the eyes of the international community, it must bridge the gap between rhetoric and reaction. The lack of accountability and effective response mechanisms within peace missions should compel reform. The United Nations should consider revoking immunity and prosecuting perpetrators in circumstances where countries are unable or unwilling to do so. As the guarantor of international peace and security, the United Nations and its representatives in the field must uphold human rights values and give local populations a reason to trust in the system. It is essential that those mandated to protect and assist use their power for good, and do not violate those who look to them for protection.

Notes

1. United Nations, *Monthly Summary of Military and Civilian Police Contribution to United Nations Operations*, 2005, available at ⟨http://www.un.org/Depts/dpko/dpko/contributors/⟩ (accessed 2 November 2006). In 17 UN missions, this figure includes: CIVPOL 6,765, Troops 56,197, Observers 2,088. The total number of international civilian personnel deployed is approximately 4,530. This does not include locally engaged staff (approximately 8,468) or UN Volunteers (approximately 1,775). (The number of UN missions was correct at the time of writing. The number at September 2006 was 16.)
2. N. Heyzer, "Women, War and Peace: Mobilizing for Security and Justice in the 21st Century", The Dag Hammarskjold Lecture 2004, Uppsala, Sweden, 22 September 2004, available at ⟨http://www.unifem.org⟩ (accessed 2 November 2006).
3. See Amnesty International, *Liberia: No Impunity for Rape – A Crime against Humanity and a War Crime*, AFR 34/017/2004, 14 December 2004, available at ⟨http://www.web.amnesty.org⟩ (accessed 2 November 2006).
4. *A Comprehensive Strategy to Eliminate Future Sexual Exploitation and Abuse in United Nations Peacekeeping Operations*, Report of the Secretary-General's Adviser on sexual exploitation and abuse by UN peacekeeping personnel, H.R.H. Prince Zeid Ra'ad Zeid Al-Hussein, Permanent Representative from Jordan, UN Doc. A/59/710, 24 March 2005.
5. United Nations and UNICEF, *Impact of Armed Conflict on Children. Report of Graça Machel, Expert of the Secretary-General of the United Nations*, 1996, available at ⟨http://www.unicef.org/graca/⟩ (accessed 2 November 2006).
6. E. Rehn, and E. J. Sirleaf, *Women, War, Peace: The Independent Experts' Assessment on the Impact of Armed Conflict on Women and Women's Role in Peace-building*, Progress of the World's Women 2002, Vol. 1, UNIFEM, 2002, available from ⟨http://www.unifem.org/resources/item_detail.php?ProductID=17⟩ (accessed 2 November 2006).
7. K. Holt and S. Hughes, "Will Congo's Women Ever Have Justice?", *The Independent*, 12 July 2004. See also K. Holt and S. Hughes, "SA Troops 'Raped Kids in DRC'", *Pretoria News*, 12 July 2004; IRIN, *Great Lakes: Focus on Sexual Misconduct by UN Personnel*, 23 July 2004, available at ⟨http://www.irinnews.org⟩ (accessed 2 November 2006).

8. United Nations High Commissioner for Refugees, *Guidelines for Prevention and Response: Sexual and Gender-Based Violence against Refugees, Returnees and Internally Displaced Persons*, Geneva, 1995.

9. United Nations and UNICEF, *Impact of Armed Conflict on Children*.

10. UNHCR and Save the Children-UK, *Sexual Violence and Exploitation: The Experience of Refugee Children in Guinea, Liberia and Sierra Leone Based on Initial Findings and Recommendations from Assessment Mission, 22 October–30 November 2001*, available at ⟨http://www.unhcr.org/⟩ (accessed 2 November 2006).

11. UN General Assembly, *Investigation into Sexual Exploitation of Refugees by Aid Workers in West Africa*, UN Doc. A/57/465, 11 October 2002, available at ⟨http://www.un.org⟩ (accessed 2 November 2006).

12. United Nations, *Investigation by the Office of Internal Oversight Services into Allegations of Sexual Exploitation and Abuse in the United Nations Organization Mission in the Democratic Republic of the Congo*, UN Doc. A/59/661, 5 January 2005. See also M. Lacey, "In Congo War, Even Peacekeepers Add to Horror", *Peace Women*, 18 December 2004, available at ⟨http://www.peacewomen.org⟩ (accessed 2 November 2006).

13. United Nations, *Investigation by the Office of Internal Oversight Services into Allegations of Sexual Exploitation and Abuse in the United Nations Organization Mission in the Democratic Republic of the Congo*, p. 10.

14. J. Laconte, "The U.N. Sex Scandal", *The Weekly Standard*, 10(16), 3–10 January 2005.

15. P. Heinlein, "Sex Abuse Charges Mar UN Peacekeeping", *Voice of America*, 17 December 2005, available at ⟨http://www.voanews.com⟩ (accessed 2 November 2006), and E. Gibson, "SA Soldier Held for Murder", *News 24.com*, 4 October 2004, available at ⟨http://www.news24.com⟩ (accessed 2 November 2006).

16. *IRIN Web Special on Violence against Women and Girls during and after Conflict: UN Peacekeeping – Working towards a No-tolerance Environment*, 2004, available at ⟨http://www.irinnews.org/webspecials/gbv/feaUNp.asp⟩ (accessed 2 November 2006).

17. Ibid.

18. Refugees International, *Sexual Exploitation in Liberia: Are the Conditions Ripe for Another Scandal?*, 20 April 2004, available at ⟨http://www.refugeesinternational.org⟩ (accessed 2 November 2006).

19. *Secretary General's Bulletin: Special Measures for Protection from Sexual Exploitation and Sexual Abuse*, UN Doc. ST/SGB/2003/13, New York, 9 October 2003.

20. Ibid., rule 3.2 (c).

21. Ibid.

22. Interview in Liberia, 17 October 2004.

23. World Net Daily, "U.N. 'Peacekeepers' Rape Women, Children", 24 December 2004, available at ⟨http://www.worldnetdaily.com⟩ (accessed 2 November 2006).

24. UN News Centre, "UN Probing Charges of Sex Abuse in DR of Congo, Peacekeeping Official Says", 23 November 2004, available at ⟨http://www.un.org/apps/news/story.asp?NewsID=12623&Cr=democratic&Cr1=congo⟩ (accessed 21 November 2006).

25. UN General Assembly, *Special Measures for Protection from Sexual Exploitation and Sexual Abuse. Report of the Secretary-General*, UN Doc. A/59/782, 15 April 2005, available at ⟨http://daccessdds.un.org/doc/UNDOC/GEN/N05/310/98/PDF/N0531098.pdf?OpenElement⟩ (accessed 21 November 2006).

26. Ibid., para. 10.

27. Ibid., para. 11.

28. Pam Spees, *Gender Justice and Accountability in Peace Support Operations: Closing the Gaps*, A Policy Briefing Paper by International Alert, February 2004, p. 32, n54, available at ⟨http://www.reliefweb.int⟩ (accessed 2 November 2006).

29. *A Comprehensive Strategy to Eliminate Future Sexual Exploitation and Abuse in United Nations Peacekeeping Operations, Section V, Individual Disciplinary, Financial and Criminal Accountability.*

30. United Nations, *Status, Basic Rights and Duties of United Nations Staff Members*, UN Doc. ST/SGB/2002/13, New York, 1 November 2002.

31. United Nations, *Directives for Disciplinary Matters Involving Civilian Police Officers and Military Observers*, DPKO/DDCPO/2003/001, New York, 2003.

32. Spees, *Gender Justice and Accountability in Peace Support Operations*, p. 23.

33. *Investigation by the Office of Internal Oversight Services into Allegations of Sexual Exploitation and Abuse in the United Nations Organization Mission in the Democratic Republic of the Congo*, para. 44.

34. This paragraph is taken from V. Kent, "Peacekeepers as Perpetrators of Abuse: Examining the UN's Plans to Eliminate and Address Cases of Sexual Exploitation and Abuse in Peacekeeping Operations", *African Security Review*, 14(2), 2005, pp. 85–92.

35. United Nations Peacekeeping, *Human Trafficking and United Nations Peacekeeping*, DPKO Policy Paper, New York, March 2004, available at ⟨http://www.un.org/womenwatch/news/documents/DPKOHumanTraffickingPolicy03-2004.pdf⟩ (accessed 2 November 2006).

36. UN News Centre, "Deputy Secretary-General Appeals to Parliamentarians for Peacekeeping Help", 19 October 2004, available at ⟨http://www.un.org⟩ (accessed 2 November 2006).

37. R. Bazergan, "HIV/AIDS: Policies and Programmes for Blue Helmets", Institute for Security Studies, Occasional Paper 96, Pretoria, South Africa, November 2004, available at ⟨http://www.iss.org.za⟩ (accessed 2 November 2006).

38. Ibid.

39. UN General Assembly, *Comprehensive Review on a Strategy to Eliminate Future Sexual Exploitation and Abuse in United Nations Peacekeeping Operations. Programme Budget Implications of Draft Resolution A/C.4/59/L.20*, UN Doc. A/C.5/59/28, New York, 2005.

40. Interview with NGO in Liberia.

41. UN Security Council, *Women and Peace and Security. Report of the Secretary-General*, UN Doc. S/2004/814, 13 October 2004.

42. Office of the Special Adviser to the Secretary-General on Gender Issues and Advancement of Women, "Gender Balance Statistics", available at ⟨http://www.un.org/womenwatch/osagi/fpgenderbalancestats.htm⟩ (accessed 20 November 2006).

43. UN Security Council, *Women and Peace and Security.*

44. G. J. DeGroot, "Is the United Nations Seriously Considering Military Women ... as Peacekeepers?", available at ⟨http://userpages.aug.com/captbarb/degroot.html⟩ (accessed 2 November 2006).

45. G. J. DeGroot, "'Wanted: A Few Good Women': Gender Stereotypes and Their Implications for Peacekeeping", paper presented at the 26th Annual Meeting Women in Uniform in NATO, Brussels, 26–31 May 2002, available at ⟨http://www.nato.int/ims/2002/cwinf2002/cwinf-01.htm⟩ (accessed 20 November 2006).

46. Ibid.

47. Cited in Rehn and Sirleaf, *Women, War, Peace*, p. 63.

48. DeGroot, "'Wanted: A Few Good Women'".

49. Ibid.

50. United Nations letter to UNMIL Force Commander Lt Gen Opande, CIVPOL Commissioner Mr Mark Kroeker and Director of Administration Ms. Savitri Butchey dated 1 October 2003, with a reminder sent on 1 October 2004.

51. United Nations, Internal Confidential Note.

52. United Nations, *A Comprehensive Strategy to Eliminate Future Sexual Exploitation and Abuse in United Nations Peacekeeping Operations*.
53. Confidential interview conducted in UNMIL.
54. Inter-Agency Standing Committee (IASC), *Report of the Task Force on Protection from Sexual Exploitation and Abuse in Humanitarian Crises*, 13 June 2002, para. 10(e).
55. Confidential interview, UNMIL.
56. Interview in Liberia, 17 October 2004.
57. Interviews with UNMIL, UN agencies, NGOs and local community groups took place in Monrovia between 11 and 21 October 2004.
58. IASC, *Report of the Task Force on Protection from Sexual Exploitation and Abuse in Humanitarian Crises*, para. 2.
59. C. Galenkamp, "Protection from Sexual Exploitation and Abuse: Lessons Learned from Sierra Leone", United Nations Office for the Co-ordination of Humanitarian Affairs, 2002, unpublished.
60. International Rescue Committee, *Liberia: Situation Analysis of Gender-Based Violence*, p. 3.
61. UN News Centre, "Additional Staff Needed to Stop Sexual Exploitation and Abuse in Peacekeeping – UN Report", 10 May 2005, available at ⟨http://www.un.org⟩ (accessed 2 November 2006). The seven peacekeeping missions are: UN Organization Mission in the Democratic Republic of Congo (MONUC), UN Operation in Côte d'Ivoire (UN-OCI), UN Operation in Burundi (UNOB), UN Mission in Liberia (UNMIL), UN Stabilization Mission in Haiti (MINUSTAH), UN Mission in Sierra Leone (UNAMSIL) and UN Mission in Sudan (UNMIS).
62. Ibid.
63. United Nations, *Gender Resource Package for Peacekeeping Operations*, New York, Peacekeeping Best Practices Unit, Department of Peacekeeping Operations, 2004, available at ⟨http://pbpu.unlb.org/pbpu/genderpack.aspx⟩ (accessed 2 November 2006).
64. A. Mackay, "Sex and the Peacekeeping Soldier: The New UN Resolution", *Peace News*, No. 2443, June–August 2001, available at ⟨http://www.peacenews.info/issues/2443/mackay.html⟩ (accessed 2 November 2006).

Part III

Host economies, humanitarian action and civil–military coordination

4

Unintended consequences of peace operations on the host economy from a people's perspective

Katarina Ammitzboell

From peacekeeping to complex peace operations

Peacekeeping missions have existed for over 50 years and evolved over time in terms of mandate, focus and scope.[1] Traditional peacekeeping operations focus on maintaining an ending to fighting and hostilities such as observation of cease-fire agreements and separation of the fighting parties. The process can be described as a state of negative peace. Today, the definition of peacekeeping has been expanded in most cases to encompass complex peace operations as the military component has been coupled with large and comprehensive nation-building tasks. Peacebuilding deals with the underlying causes of conflict, including structural problems, and aims to rebuild the nation and state, political stability, economic recovery and social transition towards a more equal distribution of wealth and resources to prevent the eruption of open hostilities.[2] This thinking has been translated into the multifaceted mandate and operation of the UN peacekeeping missions, which in this book are referred to as peace operations. (See Chapter 1 for more detail on the terminology used in this book.)

Thus, peace operations are rather comprehensive missions as experienced in Kosovo, Sierra Leone, East Timor and Afghanistan. Although their mandates and set-up differ in several aspects, they all share a growing emphasis on state-building. The missions in East Timor (Timor Leste) and Sierra Leone, for instance, are complete UN missions with blue helmets and UN leadership over civilian affairs, but in Afghanistan and

Unintended consequences of peacekeeping operations, Aoi, de Coning and Thakur (eds), United Nations University Press, 2007, ISBN 978-92-808-1142-1

Kosovo the international forces are under the command of NATO. The United Nations Interim Administration Mission in Kosovo (UNMIK) involved multiple actors, including the European Union (reconstruction), the Organization for Security and Co-operation in Europe (institution-building), and the United Nations High Commissioner for Refugees (humanitarian issues).[3] Peace operations are increasingly being carried out jointly by multilateral, regional and bilateral actors.

Complex peace operations require larger budgets and more non-military personnel than traditional military peacekeeping operations. For instance, the total cost of the United Nations Transitional Administration in East Timor (UNTAET) for the first seven months (until June 1999) was US$386 million, divided almost equally between the civilian component (the establishment of an entirely new public administration) and the military component. The proportions for the next 12 months were the same. The Security Council was thus fully aware that the cost of UNTAET was running at about US$500,000 per day.[4] The cost of international assistance can exceed – many times over – the GDP of the country it is aimed to assist. The GDP of East Timor was $US80 million in 2001 and the cost of UNTAET amounted to $US547 million annually.[5]

As the mandate of UN operations has become more comprehensive and complex, local expectations continue to rise, which can be a challenge to manage. It is generally known that the perceptions of the local population tend to change from a state of optimism with the arrival of a peace operation and international support to a general sense of frustration as time passes and the livelihoods and living conditions of the local people do not improve as expected or perhaps even deteriorate. Disappointment is aggravated when local people compare their situation with that of the internationals. The negative perceptions of the international assistance and presence may be based on only a few issues and situations, but these may have a disproportionate effect and create widespread resentment among the local population, damaging collaboration and effective institutional development and capacity-building.

Unintended consequences for the host economy can be addressed and measured in different ways. Impact assessments are complicated by the fact that most war-torn societies lack statistics and baseline indicators. There is significant documentation on lessons learned concerning peacekeeping, the economy of war and the impact of aid flow by researchers, by institutions and also by the United Nations.[6] Woodward has examined key lessons learned on economic issues and policy recommendations in particular, which can be summarized as follows: "A need for broad-based impact assessment of peace operations, early emphasis on employment, investment in building institutional and social capital, conscious donor decisions about who to finance and how lending assistance shall be provided."[7] Anderson's concept of "do no harm" was a first attempt to address how negative effects can be prevented or mitigated.[8] Limited documentation exists about the different kinds of unintended economic consequences or side-effects, and how these may harm local people's attitudes, trust and faith in the peace operation's effectiveness in transforming the conflict-prone country. Most views emerge from anecdotal experiences.

This chapter aims to provide an analysis of local people's perceptions of the unintended economic consequences of peace operations. The objective is to shed light on how and why peace operations can have adverse effects on people's standard of living and economic opportunities, in spite of peace operations' benign ambitions (conflict transformation, reconstruction and recovery). On the other hand, there is growing recognition that there is great scope for better utilization of the economic resources and technical expertise that are brought into a war-torn society, because peace operations may also create unintended positive economic consequences.[9] This study will also try to identify the positive side-effects of peace operations that can improve local people's economic prospects. The field of research is vast, and a careful selection of topics was made based on experience, consultation with local researchers and feedback from pilot surveys.

Methodology

The analysis is based primarily on two case studies: Afghanistan and Kosovo. The United Nations Interim Administration Mission in Kosovo (UNMIK) was established in 1999 as the first comprehensive peace operation with both a large civilian component and a military component.[10] A year later, in August 2000, the Brahimi High-level Panel report was published. The report presented a critical review of past peace operations and provided new considerations and approaches for peace operations based on lessons learned.[11] It received immediate prominence, and its recommendations provided a new strategy for the establishment of peace operations. Brahimi himself was appointed as Special Representative of the Secretary-General for the United Nations Assistance Mission in Afghanistan (UNAMA), which was established in March 2002. This provided an opportunity to apply the recommendations in practice, which makes Afghanistan an interesting case study. Brahimi's approach was better known as the "light footprint", and he cautioned against a heavy influx of international assistance to try to avoid adverse economic effects on the host economy. According to this approach, in order to foster national ownership very early on, the local government should be in the "driver's seat" and be part of the decision-making. The role of the United Nations was to guide and advise but not to govern or manage government, as was the case in Kosovo and East Timor.

The planning of UNAMA followed the recommendations for a new "integrated mission" concept, which implied that all relevant UN bodies and agencies should be involved in order to optimize the United Nations' resources and synergy. The United Nations was also to pay attention to the local economy to procure and use local resources as far as possible. In addition, planning was to be done carefully and the agencies were encouraged to use a minimum of international staff and resources to run their operations. However, the integrated planning of UNAMA took more time than usual and, owing to a need to "be on the ground", the UN agencies and other aid organizations went ahead and established their operations in a more or less conventional manner.[12] UNAMA was established as a simple two-pillar structure (Political and Recovery, Rehabilitation and Relief) with eight lightly staffed regional offices.

In East Timor, in the absence of state institutions and government management capacity, the United Nations was granted executive and legislative power and acted as the government.[13] Compared with other transitional administrations, such as Eastern Slavonia (UNTAES) and Kosovo (UNMIK), UNTAET was the most extreme form of transitional administration. It was a rather unusual situation and is more the exception than the *modus operandi* of complex peace operations and therefore was not included as a case study. Some of the missions in Africa, such as the United Nations Mission in Sierra Leone, could have been relevant to get another regional perspective. However, given the framework of this research, two case studies were considered sufficient and manageable. Therefore, the choice was made to focus on Kosovo and Afghanistan. Kosovo was the first comprehensive operation where the planning process did not aim to mitigate the possible adverse effects of the United Nations' presence in the country. In contrast, Afghanistan actively took the "light footprint approach", which was deliberately developed to minimize the adverse effects as much as possible.

My assessment applies a broad definition of peace operations, including bilateral support or support from international organizations other than the United Nations. The research would result in a skewed picture if the analysis was confined to the unintended consequences of only the United Nations, because it operates in a context that comprises various UN agencies, the Bretton Woods institutions, multilateral and bilateral agencies and non-governmental organizations (NGOs).

One criterion when selecting the case studies was that it was possible to identify competent national research teams to undertake surveys and local research. In Kosovo, local researchers were identified through the university in Prishtina. University students carried out the study and the research team leader was a former businessman and academic. In Afghanistan, a local NGO that specialized in conducting surveys undertook the research. Interviews were used as the main method of data collection based on qualitative research techniques.[14] A comprehensive questionnaire was developed and pilot tested. Interviews were undertaken in person to ensure understanding of the questions and to obtain explanations of the answers. Another 13 interviews were conducted with internationals with experience of the peace operations. These interviews were conducted on-line by the author. In Afghanistan, interviews were conducted with 204 people (131 men and 73 women) in Kabul and the neighbouring provinces of Nangarhar, Wardak and Logar. In Kosovo, 30 local people were interviewed from all parts of the country. The survey teams interviewed different kinds of local people, including business representatives, government officials, women, police, nationals employed by international organizations and local NGOs, to get as broad a representation as possible. A second category of interviewees comprised internationals, including UN staff, members of the diplomatic corps, multilateral and bilateral aid representatives and representatives from international assistance forces. It was relatively difficult for the Afghan national researchers to approach representatives from the International Security Assistance Force and diplomatic missions and an international survey adviser was required to facilitate appointments. The surveys in Kosovo and Afghanistan were conducted between September and December 2004.[15] The case studies are not exhaustive or fully comparable, because of the differences in location and number of interviewees. The findings are aimed to underpin assumptions and to identify critical unintended economic consequences that it is recommended should be mitigated.

An overview of complex peace operation assistance and matters of the economy

A post-conflict country is faced with major recovery programmes. These include the rebuilding of a public administration and the establishment of state bodies that can provide basic social services, rebuild infrastructure (including roads, power supply, and water and sanitation), demobilize ex-combatants, conduct reintegration and recovery, return refugees and facilitate economic recovery.

The post-war developmental stage has a significant impact on a country's ability to recover and its capacity to absorb foreign assistance. For instance, the Balkan countries (including Kosovo and Croatia), El Salvador and Namibia are middle-income countries with GDP per capita of $US1,000–2,000. These countries had a greater capacity to absorb peace operation assistance for recovery and development in comparison with poor countries such as Afghanistan, East Timor, Sierra Leone, Burundi, Sudan and Liberia.[16] Although the poorer countries are often in greater need, they may also be more vulnerable to the possible implications of a massive influx of peace operation assistance resulting in distortions and other unintended negative economic consequences. In East Timor, for instance, about 70 per cent of the infrastructure was destroyed, including public buildings, power and water supplies, roads and private houses. A rapid reconstruction programme was deemed critical for recovery and peacebuilding, but foreign contractors did most of the reconstruction because East Timor could not provide a sufficient number of skilled labourers, and the potential for training and the transfer of knowledge and skills was not utilized.

The capacity and infrastructure of the central and local government are obviously fundamental for the administrative and managerial capacity and ability to absorb assistance. Funding of a newly established government's recurrent costs and core budget is critical to transform war-torn political structures into sound institutions, such as responsible public administration and efficient provision of public services.[17] Often donors prefer to fund concrete programmes with relatively quick results, or programmes with high visibility, transparency and financial control. Anxiety about seeing a donor "label" on the result and the difficulty of demonstrating results and impact from funds invested in recurrent costs lead to a reluctance to directly fund operational costs such as salaries and administrative support.

Afghanistan has just come out of 23 years of war. The country is assessed as ranking 173rd out of 178 countries according to the United Nations Development Programme (UNDP) Human Development Index.[18] Afghanistan has limited water and food supplies, and the need for reconstruction is enormous, of both physical and human capital. The government's options are limited to general local revenue from taxes. In 2004 the annual revenue of the Afghan state was US$256 million, and in 2005 it was expected to reach some US$377 million. The bill for civil servants' salaries is approximately US$480 million.[19] National expenditures amounted to about US$1.5 billion in 2004. A target growth rate of 9 per cent is assessed to be necessary for generating economic growth and employment. However, the real growth rate in 2004 was about 4.5 per cent.[20] Some 24 donors finance the deficit. Hence, the country is heavily dependent on foreign support and assistance. Credits obtained from the Bretton Woods institutions pose a potential risk that Afghanistan may find itself in a debt trap from 2012.[21] It is vital to stimulate economic growth and job creation as an integrated part of the reconstruction process. In fact, the Afghan president Hamid Karzai has said that the "economy is key to beating Taliban".[22]

Wrong policies or unintended consequences

It is difficult to make a clear distinction between wrong polices or a lack of policies and unintended consequences. A lack of coordination in design and planning leaves little margin for flexibility regarding the coordination of projects and programmes. Hence, a duplication of efforts readily occurs. Speed seems to be a major concern for peacebuilding projects in post-conflict situations, but the need for speed has trade-offs. More costly solutions are often applied in such instances. Local partners do not get substantively involved in the project cycle, and learning opportunities and experience are missed. Local partners believe that they have several competitive advantages in terms of local knowledge and insight into local power structures and informal institutions. This knowledge can be used for implementation in a less costly way and can be more effective than what international organizations can manage.[23]

"Unintentional policies"

The most predominant frustrations with regard to unintentional policies are found to be as follows:
- promises made but not kept (defined by the number of announced projects that never started, even though they are funded, the number of projects excessively delayed before implementation, and the number of projects remaining incomplete or behind schedule);
- higher costs and extended project duration;
- lack of comprehensive and coordinated tracking and reporting systems (defined by a lack of verification of the accuracy of individual reports by intergovernmental organizations and NGOs to donors or taxpayers, duplication of efforts, over-saturated areas and neglected areas, repetition of unsuccessful methods, and the "loss" of knowledge of lessons learned and best practices);
- high turnover of expatriate staff (defined by short-term contracts and no proper handover, unaddressed stress resulting from unrealistic work expectations, dissatisfaction with the working environment);
- excessive use of international consultants (defined by high costs of travel, high fees and a failure to share expensive experts with local NGOs, other local actors or even among themselves);
- insufficient efforts to identify and hire qualified nationals for major programmes because of a lack of people who can speak English, a lack of

trust, or a lack of pre-job training programmes (defined by a failure to include existing capacity and local knowledge, also, particularly for Kosovo, patronage of Kosovar inputs in international programmes and projects, and local suggestions being discounted and ignored);

- the creation of economic and social problems (examples given include paying drivers monthly salaries that are more than what doctors, teachers, professors and other professionals earn in a year, so that students leave university, in particular in Kosovo, to be drivers, guards or translators, and doctors and other professionals leave to work in administrative roles in NGOs or other internationally supported programmes).

Unintended economic consequences

At an aggravate level, the survey from Kosovo indicates that the majority of Kosovars are critical of the economic consequences of the peace operation. With the passage of time and as Kosovo has faded from the international community's memory, financial assistance has also receded, making the locals discontented with the international effort. It was indicated that international assistance has not trickled down to remote villages and that the locals feel that Serbs received better treatment from international helpers compared with the Albanians.[24] The situation is more balanced in Afghanistan, although the general optimism that prevailed in the wake of the Bonn Agreement in December 2001 is declining, but not to as low a level as in Kosovo. The Afghans emphasize the importance of the international community's role in ensuring security and single out stability as the engine of economic growth that is a positive side-effect of the presence of the peacekeeping forces. A majority of the Afghans are of the view that their economic situation has turned for the better since the arrival of the international community. There is some hope and people have higher expectations as a consequence of the international presence. The Afghans are generally in agreement that, if the international community left Afghanistan, this would adversely affect their businesses and job opportunities because it would disrupt the stability of the country.

Salary disparities

In general, national salary levels become inflated by international assistance. In Kosovo, locals who work with international organizations earn four to five times more than their local colleagues who stay within local institutions. This can cause tremendous problems, when a cleaning lady working for the United Nations in Prishtina earns three to four times more than a government minister (official income).

In Afghanistan, reform of the public sector did not begin until more than two years after the signing of the Bonn Agreement in 2001. There was no certain information about the total number of people on the government payroll. The overall estimation was 700,000 in security and about 300,000 civil servants. If all these people had been offered a competitive salary, none of them would have had an incentive to leave the public administration. It was not economically feasible or sustainable to maintain such a large number of civil servants. The salary for civil servants was set at approximately US$30 per month, which is below the poverty line of US$2 per day. The assumption was that the low salary would lead to an exodus of civil servants and, hence, the public sector would automatically be downsized to reach an economically sustainable level.[25] There was automatic redundancy. Talented and skilled civil servants left their government jobs immediately in favour of international NGOs, the United Nations, embassies and other employment opportunities that materialized when the international community arrived. The new jobs paid salaries from 10 to 50 times more per month.

"Unfortunately the brain drain damaged the state system. First the skilful men left the country for abroad and the remaining skilful employees in the government left jobs for work with international and non-governmental organizations for high salaries. Due to this situation, most of the governmental administration is managed by unskilled persons, bureaucracy and corruption are largely prevailing and badly affect the function of the state."[26]

"Unfortunately, it seems that (with Afghanistan as an example) there appears to be a brain drain with government employees shifting to NGOs, and from there, shifting to UN or bilateral organizations. Certainly, the salary structure of international organizations prevents the desired effect, which should be that the best and brightest from their national cadres should shift into senior government positions. There have been many efforts to alleviate this through offering people substituted positions to the government. Some localized, individual successes have been achieved from this but are unlikely to have a broad impact."[27]

In Kosovo, the international staff agree that the presence of UN personnel and institutions (the European Union, the OSCE and diplomatic missions) affected the local population because the salaries of international staff in UN bodies were at least three to four times higher than those of the local staff. The local staff working for internationals receive significantly higher salaries than any other locals, resulting in a price rise for standard commodities. So the locals are often forced to take more than one job to be able to support their family. This phenomenon is also widespread in Afghanistan.

The average salary for national staff with the United Nations for temporary support staff is US$400–500 per month and for national programme officers is US$700–1100. This is about 300 per cent higher than government salaries. Attempts have been made to establish a code of conduct and ceilings for pay and grading, but this has not prevented the inflation of salary levels or the brain drain. This is a critical issue that requires further research. The short-term and massive need for skilled labour versus the implications for state-building must be addressed. It is important to keep in mind that there is a lack of incentive for qualified nationals to seek employment with the government, let alone the effect of the diaspora, which can bring new and necessary skills and competencies.

The disparity in wage levels made most of the interviewees suspicious of UNMIK. They are under the impression that some of the government employees "have" to take bribes on account of their inadequate remuneration. In Afghanistan, corruption existed prior to the arrival of the international peace operation, but all findings indicate:

- an increase in corruption because of very low salaries, forcing civil servants to look for alternative incomes;
- poor financial management capacity in government;
- the penetration of the drug economy giving people an alternative source of income;
- the continuation of politicized appointments rather than a merit-based and competitive process.

The significant wage differences create antagonism between the different kinds of contracted staff working in the public sector. These include international advisers, national staff hired by international projects, international NGOs for service delivery, and civil servants. In Afghanistan, it was noticeable that the patriotic and loyal civil servants, who had been there through the "hard times" of war, developed resentment towards national staff working for international organizations within the public sector. They are perceived to be capitalizing on the distorted labour market and move from one internationally paid contract to another, with a vacillating loyalty to the state administration.[28]

A new job area is the private security sector, which offers highly lucrative employment. This industry is poaching personnel from all institutions, including the international assistance community, but also newly trained national police and national army personnel. The emerging privatization of what once were military functions to civilian contractors is a new but growing phenomenon in Afghanistan. It is worth mentioning that hundreds of people carrying guns are employed by private companies. This obscures who is in control of security – the international forces or the new private security companies. Who out of these groups holds liability?

As already mentioned, the government is not able to retain qualified staff, leading to continued weak management, which hinders efficient government output and delivery of services. Ineffective bureaucracies continue to operate. It adds to the level of disappointment that the local populations feel as time passes and development has no visible results.

> "A large amount of donations were pledged for the rehabilitation of the health sector, which was not used by the government because of the inefficiency of the health ministry. The health services in Afghanistan are near to zero for the common people. Meanwhile the health ministry of Afghanistan has announced that they have saved international donations!"[29]

Inflation in the wage structure, in combination with rigid concerns about the premature economic sustainability of the peace operation's budget, continues to depress civil service salaries, resulting in continued loss of competent staff from government. The attempt at attaining economic sustainability is also half-hearted in Afghanistan, where an army is being created for US$7 billion and the cost of maintaining this army is estimated at approximately US$800 million per year. This is about twice the amount of government revenues per year.

The "dual public sector syndrome"

To overcome the shortage of capacity to spend and administer funds within the government, internationally managed trust funds have become conventional for post-conflict reconstruction. An international agency, often the UNDP or the World Bank, is in charge of disbursements, but rarely, if ever, are any accountability mechanisms or requirements to report to the national government put in place. International assistance tends to be centralized and biased towards control and accountability that allows only limited trust in the national governmental management capacity. The funding mechanisms make use of their own implementation arrangements and operate on an intrinsic assumption of trickle-down and limited flexibility to fund subnational administration directly.

As an unintended economic consequence, two public sectors are emerging. In Afghanistan, public sector assistance and services are provided by both the new Afghan Transitional Administration and the international assistance programmes supplied by development agencies and NGOs. They are both working for the reconstruction and recovery of Afghanistan, but the national administration, which should be in charge, is under-resourced in terms of capacity resources. Government assets are not adequately protected, risking a depletion of state resources. In Kosovo, the presence of UNMIK has created a dichotomy within the public administration such that the local government possesses hardly any authority, resulting in low morale among local employees. This predominance of UN control has thwarted the ability of the local Kosovar government to build capacity for exercising authority and public management.

The question is whether it is economically efficient and effective to invest in capacity-building because of sustainability problems? Newly trained civil servants will most likely leave for jobs with the international assistance community because of the attractive salaries. The regularity of this happening was discussed earlier in this chapter. When civil service reform is slow and partial, as it is in Afghanistan, international advisers tend to find that it is not worth investing in the national colleagues – who are the "lost generation", because they may become redundant. In general, the priority of international technical advisers has been to "get the job done" because of the need to "deliver", outpacing the time and resources for transfer of knowledge and skills.[30] In addition, there is generally a relatively high turnover of international advisers, resulting in abrupt capacity-building and institutional development. Proper needs assessment should be a precondition. Comprehensive capacity-building plans should be developed through consultation and reflect mutually agreed goals and performance measures and be based on mutual contractual arrangements, such as a compact, between the international donor and the host government. Conditionalities are controversial and difficult to enforce because there may be a variety of reasons why, for instance, a ministry would fail to meet all the set targets. It is important to ensure that the ministry or department is provided with sufficient and proper technical guidance. Experience from the requirements and support as part of the accession process for new members of the European Union could be relevant in exploring post-conflict situations further.[31]

Balance between delivery and sustainability

Because many post-conflict countries receiving aid from peacekeeping forces are developing countries, these countries are obliged in many cases to launch short-term economic stabilization programmes. These programmes are aimed at regulating balance of payments and improving the efficiency of the local economy. Medium- to longer-term adjustment programmes will include downsizing of government, public sector reform, ceiling on salaries and wages and overall a decrease in government spending and an improvement in conditions facilitating the growth of a

market economy.[32] The adjustment programmes are criticized for not being applicable to post-conflict situations. This survey points clearly to the
negative implications of maintaining an unacceptably low salary level for
civil servants in order to achieve economic sustainability. A transitional
administration or newly elected government walks a fine line between
becoming a credible government if it is able to perform or becoming an
unwanted government that might be overturned or set the peacebuilding
process back.

Macroeconomic stabilization policies, including efforts to reduce the
size of the public administration, can counteract the need for public expenditure for recovery job creation and to support development country-
wide. In Afghanistan, the potential for a market economy is fading owing
to a lack of infrastructure, including financial resources, a lack of proper
legislation to secure investors, a lack of defined property rights and a lack
of investment in human capital such as tertiary education, public and private sector management courses, and accounting. A balance is needed
between, on the one hand, creating incentives and enabling an environment for private sector development and, on the other hand, maintaining
a level of public expenditure that supports the building of a credible and
effective public administration and the creation of jobs until private sector growth begins to generate work and services.

In Kosovo, government workers are dissatisfied and dejected about the
state of affairs. They feel a loss of dignity. A large number of civil servants in both countries have extra jobs in order to support their families,
and they spend as little time as possible on their government job. Such a
work attitude is obviously detrimental to the efficiency and performance
of the public administration. The legitimacy and stability of the new government are further challenged by this low staff morale.

Economic opportunities or illusions

In Afghanistan, the survey found that there is an overwhelming belief in
the international community supporting the government in running a
good economy through training and restoring administrative structures.
The respondents are of the opinion that the general economy has improved. However, progress should be viewed in the context of a baseline
of almost zero. In pre-war Afghanistan, the economic growth rate was
about 2–3 per cent per year; in 2004 it was 4.5 per cent, which is less
than that of its regional neighbours.

Complex peace operations require services, goods and facilities. The
impact of this demand on the host economy is mixed. Many of the requirements of international organizations have little to do with the development of sustainable economies in post-conflict societies. On the other

hand, the establishment of UN peacekeeping operations in conflict areas sends important signals both to local entrepreneurs and to international entrepreneurs who have a particular affinity with the conflict area (through language, culture, family ties, etc.). In Kosovo, the general feeling is that the presence of international personnel has led to an increase in demand for goods and services, which has benefited the local economy. It has stimulated business growth and entrepreneurship among the locals. Housing, food, clothing, entertainment, restaurants, transportation and prostitution have gained momentum on account of the presence of these personnel.

The closure of inefficient industries and mines in the new reality under UNMIK is regarded as a setback to the local economy. Particularly in the area of basic commodities and services, local company owners and entrepreneurs are quick to grasp opportunities and rapidly expand their operations to enable them to offer more complex services. This appears to characterize the general situation in Kosovo. However, even for local people who have benefited from the presence of international staff, for example in Prishtina (capital of Kosovo), the difference made to the local landscape in terms of infrastructure and capacity enhancement has been minimal. Some stated that the policy of procuring imported goods and services through international contractors, though essential at times, needs to be reconsidered because procurement at a local level, though risky, could have had a far greater impact in benefiting the local economy. It is perceived that the withdrawal of international staff would affect the service industry, because there would not then be enough affluent clients among the locals to support the services that sprang up as a consequence of the presence of the internationals.

The Afghans are of the opinion that the international presence has benefited the transport, business and construction sectors of the economy as well as being helpful to the hotel and restaurant industry, food stores and retail stores. There is, however, criticism that major purchases of goods are made overseas because these purchases have no beneficial impact on the local economy. Some even regard these choices as a deliberate ploy by the international community to keep the local economy weak. The survey found that, in both Kosovo and Afghanistan, the international presence has resulted in an unprecedented rise in prostitution – a profession that is strongly condemned in traditional and conservative religious societies.

The expatriate community is mostly in charge of entrepreneurship. In Timor Leste, Australians, Portuguese, Chinese Timorese and certain elements of the local expatriate community carried out most of the reconstruction work. Only local shops and restaurants boomed during the time of the UN Transitional Administration in East Timor in Dili. The situation is similar in Liberia, where the Lebanese control business to a large extent. In Afghanistan, international private entrepreneurs took on large-scale reconstruction projects (Turkish), electrical goods (Lebanese) and catering. Road-building, refurbishment works, public sector developments and restaurants contribute very little to furthering a sustainable economy, so restaurants, works projects and, in particular, capital-intensive infrastructure projects close down once the international organizations leave the area, because there is no self-sustaining economic base in place.

There was an opinion that donors do not encourage local contractors involved in trades such as plumbing, carpentry and catering, which could be handed over to local contractors with minimal effort. Local innovation and entrepreneurship are required to sustain an economy in the long term. However, this aspect is usually not given much priority by international donors. They tend to focus on political roadmaps, good governance, human rights, education and health. Foreign investments do not always pay off owing to a lack of stability, financial predictability and the necessary infrastructure, including financial management systems such as banks and enabling legislation. The lack of clarity about the future status of Kosovo is seen to be a major impediment to foreign investment and economic growth.

The NGO community tends to boom in the wake of peace operations. Before the armed intervention in Afghanistan in October 2001, there were about 250 national NGOs; today there are more than 1,000. Some are dedicated and tireless and work for the right reasons. The largest employer of national staff in Afghanistan is the Swedish Committee, which employs some 8,000 nationals. Others are simply local business NGOs that consist of a couple of people trying to capitalize on international assistance for private reasons. In general, there is a lack of transparency and information about how NGO funding is prioritized and spent. The NGOs are not properly involved in the overall state-building and reconstruction through, *inter alia*, the preparation of national budgets. The government has so far neglected to adopt proper regulations that would ensure that genuine NGOs are not mixed with commercial organizations and that their obligations are clarified. In Afghanistan, the NGOs have become the scapegoat for the lack of development and progress.

Job creation is generally the most pressing problem after security in post-conflict situations. Other issues include the reintegration of ex-combatants, returnees, economic growth and development, and transformation of a culture of war to a culture of peace. The international community creates and contracts national experts for government positions to attract competent nationals, often from other countries as a consequence of diasporas, who would not apply for a job on a national civil service pay scale. Before 11 September 2001, and before the bombing of Afghanistan, the UNDP employed 47 staff in total. By the end of 2002,

UNDP employed 427 national staff, and by the end of 2003 it employed 1,915 people.[33] Most of the jobs are with its own programmes and other UN agencies, but some positions in government are also financed through this agency (93 UNDP government-sponsored jobs and 117 other UN agency jobs with the government). Most of the respondents, both nationals and internationals, are of the opinion that employment with the international assistance community provides training and capacity-building, which can help to secure assured employment in the future.

The international assistance forces – NATO or UN Peacekeeping – provide hardly any job opportunities at the onset of peace operations. They use mainly a limited number of translators and bring in all their equipment and goods to ensure that required standards are met. According to the survey, there is unanimity that the presence of peacekeeping forces does not lead to a growth in goods and services. Yet, three and a half years after the peace operation was established, the NATO headquarters of the International Security Assistance Force in Afghanistan was proactively trying to use local labour for construction, catering and cleaning and to procure locally. "Procuring locally can save a lot of money. For example it costs US$300,000 to fly in 120,000 litres of fuel to Afghanistan and we are looking into how we can purchase fuel locally instead."[34]

In a post-conflict situation, the massive influx of billions of dollars into a country with a weak administrative infrastructure and limited democratic and managerial governmental capacity clearly increases the risk of corruption. About 20 per cent of the national respondents in Afghanistan are of the opinion that international assistance has increased corruption. A businessman from Pakistan said, after more than three years of operating in Afghanistan, "I am on my way to close my business in Afghanistan. Before, there was one element of corruption per project but today there is at least nine".[35] The challenge is how to prevent the escalation of corruption. This would require further research on relevant wage levels, management capacity priorities, public awareness, a strong media and accountability requirements both to the host government and also to international agencies, bilateral donors and NGOs. Enforcement measures need to be created in an unorthodox way in a context where law and order are weak and also prone to corruption.

Inflation, skewed markets and social disturbance

The growth in business does not help all nationals: prices seem to increase significantly because the post-conflict assistance tends to overheat parts of the local economy. In Kosovo, the international presence has led to increased prices for goods and services for nationals, taking prices beyond the reach of the local population. The cost of living increased in general by about 50 per cent in Afghanistan, and for some goods the increase was much greater. For example, 1 kg of meat (mutton) was 80 Afghanis (US$1.7/kg) in late 2002 and increased to 180 Afghanis (US$3.9/kg) in 2004. The same applies to other food commodities.

The need for housing and premises has led to a chronic bottleneck in the housing sector, since demand far exceeds supply. The national respondents are especially critical of the excessive rise in rental costs in areas inhabited by foreigners, pushing rents beyond the reach of the locals. The monthly rent of a three-room apartment in Kabul in an area where many nationals live who are employed by international organizations was approximately US$80–100 per month in early 2002 and had increased to almost US$250–300 per month by 2004. Salaries did not increase over this same period. When the Taliban were in power, market prices for apartments were US$5,000–7,000. Now apartments cost more than US$60,000. Many nationals are losing their houses because property rights are not regulated and, since the war, documentation proving ownership is missing. People are evicted from their homes by local, powerful people who either take ownership of the property for themselves or simply want to rent houses out to foreigners. This creates resentment among the nationals, who feel that they are unfairly treated in comparison with expatriates who earn 10 times as much as them or more. Houses in certain areas in Kabul cost US$4,000–8,000 per month.

The Afghans are unanimous in their view that price levels have risen, causing rampant inflation. The Kosovars feel that the presence of the international staff has led to inflation and contributes to a large degree towards the failure of local businesses and to the high rental costs and low profit margins forced upon retailers. Some people have had to abandon living in Prishtina, because they can no longer pay the inflated rental costs in the city (rental costs for houses for internationals are about €2,000 per month). The switch to the euro from the German Mark is regarded as the catalyst of the inflation. However, the increased prices have led to the availability of luxury goods in the local market. The majority of Kosovars say that it is by flagrantly spending the aid money that the international staff maintain a lifestyle completely incongruous with that of the locals. They feel that social strife is created when locals working as drivers with these agencies earn more than university professors. The presence of the international staff results in higher wages for semi-skilled and unskilled workers, whereas skilled workers have been left in a difficult financial position.

The international organizations have shown a visible preference for recruiting women rather than men. In societies where women normally do not have jobs, if 25–50 per cent of women are employed this can fuel social tensions. There have also been cases of abuse of women translators by international peacekeepers, which has led to a lowering of the prestige of the international community in local eyes. In Afghanistan, where the international presence has allowed women to work, although this is a welcome change it has affected the cultural spectrum in Afghanistan, a traditional society. The new jobs that emerge with the international community can have unintended implications for the local power structure and the hierarchy in socio-cultural institutions such as the family. Suddenly young graduates and also skilled women become new breadwinners or perhaps the only breadwinner and the husband and former resistance fighter is unemployed.

According to the survey, the Kosovars view the presence of UNMIK as providing opportunities for them to work and earn a living, whereas under Serbia's rule they were forced out of their jobs. It is the economic impact of the presence of the internationals that the locals are critical of, because it has led to the development of fissures in society; a majority claim to be worse off financially under UNMIK. The financial conditions have led people to commit suicide, being unable to provide for their families. There are also allegations of bias towards the Serb minorities in contrast to the Kosovar Albanian majority, with money being spent in Serb-dominated areas such as Mitrovica. The hyperinflation is blamed on the presence of internationals, which has led to an artificial rise in rental costs and property prices, bringing misery on the locals. As already mentioned, in Afghanistan prices have skyrocketed, but most feel they have stabilized, even though they are still high.

Sustainability is critical, and peace operations are criticized for creating a "balloon" economy. In Kosovo, massive unemployment has resulted in people leaving school or university early, finding no reason to pursue their studies and instead taking up jobs as drivers, etc., with UNMIK. They choose a salary over completing their education. In spite of the "light footprint approach" in Afghanistan, the local people are very sceptical about job security. When local people were asked what they think will happen when international agencies withdraw, all respondents indicated that their businesses will suffer seriously and jobs will be lost. Worst of all, factional fighting would start again and war could break out. Job creation is critical to redirect behaviour and normative change. It is fundamental for the successful reintegration of ex-combatants, the integration of returned refugees and internally displaced persons, and to maintain peace[36] – peace by satisfaction.

Concluding discussion and preliminary recommendations

There is often a debate about the importance of bridging relief to development. The debate seems to have less importance if the focus is on whether the relief and recovery assistance support the implementation of peace accords and address the underlying causes of the conflict.[37] As the situation stabilizes during a complex peace operation, it is critical to value considered planning, implementation modalities and benchmarks above speed. Humanitarian assistance, for example wheat distribution, should be ended if it distorts local production or offers incentives to grow alternative but undesirable crops such as poppies.

Benchmarks should be a combination of comprehensive peacebuilding goals, financial planning and targets and include an examination of the implications of a lack of accomplishments and potential counterfactual implications including costs. There is probably no disagreement that there is an inter-linkage between economic development and peacebuilding, yet there is a lack of comprehensive impact assessments. Comprehensive research and assessment are vitally important for more effective peacebuilding assistance and to prevent the creation of two parallel and almost competing public sectors and two separate economies. It is crucial to identify sound solutions for maximizing job creation and preventing distortions within the host economy, leading to increased resentment. Technical assistance should be organized and delivered within a framework of comprehensive capacity-building strategies that are carefully prepared on the basis of a vision and thorough needs assessments that clearly spell out goals and performance indicators.

There are excellent studies about the economic implications of war and the loss of life, about destroyed infrastructure and production apparatus and about the loss of productive labour that remind us of the horrific costs of conflicts. Research on post-conflict situations should be as comprehensive.

It is recommended that a framework and tools for a conflict-sensitive cost–benefit analysis be developed. Risk assessments, with a focus on potential unintended consequences, need to be carried out during the planning and design phase, as well as regular comprehensive impact assessments during implementation. Furthermore, accountability to the host government should be a requirement and assistance could be based on partnerships and mutual commitments such as a compact. Public information strategies are important to balance expectations and to keep people informed about progress, obstacles and plans.

Acknowledgements

Several people are behind this study and I especially wish to thank Burim Thaci, team leader for the research in Kosovo, Omara Khan, team leader for the research in Afghanistan, Marianne Tychsen, research adviser, Afghanistan, and Akhtar Ayat, who provided valuable assistance for the data processing. I also wish to thank former international peacekeeping mission staff, from various organizations, who took the time to complete long and comprehensive questionnaires. Their frank and insightful views have made an enormous contribution to this study.

Notes

1. At the time of writing (November 2006) there are 18 peace missions and peacekeeping operations.
2. G. Harris and N. Lewis, "Structural Violence, Positive Peace and Peace Building", in Geoff Harris, ed., *Recovery from Armed Conflicts*, London: Routledge, 1999.
3. Richard Caplan, *International Governance in War-Torn Territories*, Oxford: Oxford University Press, 2006, p. 38.
4. Astri Surkhe, "Peacekeepers as Nation-builders: Dilemmas of the UN in East Timor", *International Peacekeeping*, 8(4), 2001, pp. 1–11.
5. Ibid.
6. See, for example, the Peacekeeping Best Practices Unit of the UN Department of Peacekeeping Operations (DPKO), at ⟨http://www.un.org/Depts/dpko/lessons/⟩ (accessed 22 November 2006), and the comprehensive analysis of four country cases in King's College, *A Review of Peace Operations: A Case for Change*, London: King's College, 2003.
7. S. Woodward, "Economic Priorities for Peace Implementation", International Peace Academy Policy Paper Series on Peace Implementation, New York: International Peace Academy, 2002.
8. Mary B. Anderson, *Do No Harm: How Aid Can Support Peace – or War*, Boulder, CO: Lynne Rienner, 1999.
9. During the time of this present research a new and related research project on the economic impact of peacekeeping and, more specifically, "how much money leaks into the local economy and what this does to inflation, the labour market, and economic growth" was launched by the DPKO's Peacekeeping Best Practices Unit and the Peace Dividend Trust. The interim report, based on findings from Timor Leste, was published in 2005. Its useful recommendations will feed into planning of DPKO peace operations. See M. Carnahan, S. Gilmore and M. Rahman, *Interim Report Phase I: Economic Impact of Peacekeeping*, United Nations Peacekeeping, April 2005, available at ⟨http://pbpu.unlb. org/pbpu/library/ECONO%20IMPACT%20OF%20PK%20Interim%20Report.pdf⟩ (accessed 27 November 2006).
10. UN Security Council Resolution 1244, Adopted by the Security Council at its 4011th meeting, 10 June 1999, UN Doc. S/RES/1244 (1999).
11. United Nations, *Report of the Panel on United Nations Peace Operations*, presented before the General Assembly, 21 August 2000, UN Doc. A/55/305-S/2000/809. The report is named after its chairperson, HE Lakhdar Brahimi, who was a former minister of foreign affairs of Algeria and has most recently worked as Special Representative of the Secretary-General in Haiti.
12. King's College, *Afghanistan – A Snapshot Study*, London: King's College, 2003.
13. Anthony Goldstone, "UNTAET with Hindsight", *Global Governance*, 10, 2004, pp. 84–85.
14. J. Mason, *Qualitative Researching*, London: Sage Publications, 2003.

15. The surveys were conducted in Afghanistan by Omara Khan, survey team leader, and Marianne Tychsen, research adviser, and in Kosovo by Burim Thaci, survey team leader. The information was analysed by Akhtar Hayat.
16. A. Suhrke, A. Ofstad and A. Knudsen, *A Decade of Peacebuilding: Lessons for Afghanistan*, Bergen, Norway: Christian Michelsen Institute, 2002.
17. Woodward, "Economic Priorities for Peace Implementation".
18. UNDP, *Afghanistan National Human Development Report 2004 – Security with a Human Face. Challenges and Responsibilities*, United Nations Development Programme, Afghanistan, 2005, available at ⟨http://www.undp.org.af/nhdr_04/NHDR04.htm⟩ (accessed 27 November 2006).
19. Interview with Ministry of Finance, August 2005.
20. B. Rubin, with H. Hamidzada and A. Stoddard, *Afghanistan 2005 and Beyond: Prospects for Improved Stability Reference Document*, New York: New York University, Center on International Cooperation, for the Clingendael Institute, the Royal Government of the Netherlands, 2005, pp. 12–22.
21. Interview with a former adviser at the Ministry of Finance, Afghanistan, February 2005.
22. *Moby Capital Updates*, ⟨http://www.mobycapital.com⟩ (accessed 20 November 2006).
23. S. Mamound, D. Poplack, A. Wakil Sediqi, H. Natiq, and K. Ammitzboell, "Building Effective Partnerships – External and Internal Actors: Afghanistan Case Study", paper presented at the WSP-International Peacebuilding Forum, Geneva, Switzerland, 2004.
24. The surveyors were Kosovar Albanians and they felt, in general, that they were less favoured in comparison with the Serbian population.
25. Interview with senior Afghan officials, Kabul, 2004.
26. Head of a national NGO, Kabul.
27. Former senior UN staff member, Afghanistan.
28. DANIDA (Danish International Development Agency), *Humanitarian and Reconstruction Assistance to Afghanistan 2001–05. A Joint Evaluation from Denmark, Ireland, The Netherlands, Sweden and the United Kingdom*, Ministry of Foreign Affairs of Denmark, Copenhagen, 2005, available at ⟨http://www.um.dk/da/menu/Udviklingspolitik/MaalOgResultatstyring/Evaluering/Evalueringsrapporter/2005/2005.05+Humanitarian+and+Reconstruction+Assistance+to+Afghanistan.htm⟩ (accessed 27 November 2006).
29. National researcher and head of a national NGO, Kabul, September 2004.
30. DANIDA, *Humanitarian and Reconstruction Assistance to Afghanistan 2001–05*.
31. Interview with Ashraf Ghani, former minister of finance, Afghanistan, September 2005.
32. Harris and Lewis, "Structural Violence, Positive Peace and Peace Building".
33. Interview with Human Resources, UNDP Afghanistan, November 2004.
34. Interview with the International Security Assistance Force in Kabul, 11 August 2005.
35. Interview, 1 August 2005.
36. Woodward, "Economic Priorities for Peace Implementation".
37. Suhrke, Ofstad and Knudsen, *A Decade of Peacebuilding: Lessons for Afghanistan*, p. 34.

5

Unintended consequences of peace operations on humanitarian action

Shin-wha Lee

The issue

The primary purpose of the United Nations, as enunciated in its Charter, is to maintain global peace and security. Accordingly, United Nations peace operations are one of the unique activities of the United Nations and also serve as the organization's *raison d'être* in that they aim to establish peace and security in conflict areas. Although the term "peace-keeping" does not appear in the Charter, peacekeeping through peace operations has evolved into a mechanism for maintaining peace in conflict areas around the world.[1] With authorization from the UN Security Council, peace operations are carried out by UN forces and multinational troops serving under UN operational command. Each UN peace operation is given a specific mandate to implement and achieve certain peace-keeping, peacebuilding or peace enforcement functions. However, in the process of carrying out such functions, there have been situations in which results have been different from what was originally intended. These results, in turn, have influenced – both positively and negatively – all the actors involved, including the conflicting parties, civilians and the peacekeepers themselves.

This problem has become more serious in the post–Cold War era. Whereas peace operations in the Cold War era were mostly "traditional" unidimensional military actions that were established in order to monitor cease-fire agreements, post–Cold War peacekeeping missions have often been referred to as complex and multidimensional operations and have

Unintended consequences of peacekeeping operations, Aoi, de Coning and Thakur (eds), United Nations University Press, 2007, ISBN 978-92-808-1142-1

often involved non-military elements such as humanitarian relief assistance and state rebuilding efforts in areas of internal conflict. This departure from traditional peacekeeping coincides with the precipitation of "new" types of post–Cold War crises in which civilians have become the primary target of hostility and assault, thus increasing the impact of the "unintended humanitarian consequences" that arise in the process of carrying out peacekeeping missions.

Because of this, the United Nations would be unable to achieve its task of maintaining global peace and security in the twenty-first century if it did not provide protection to individual citizens in the process of carrying out its peacekeeping activities. If the United Nations does not place "human security" concerns (including the respect for human rights and humanitarian law) at the crux of its peacekeeping missions, unintended (negative) consequences of peace operations on humanitarian action could work towards weakening the credibility of UN peacekeeping efforts, and eventually undermine the *raison d'être* of the United Nations as an organization for maintaining global peace and security.

In this context, this chapter will discuss the concepts and causes of unintended consequences with special reference to the humanitarian aspects. Since it is difficult clearly to define unintended consequences, explanations and analysis will be based on observations that illustrate the inadvertent outcomes of peace operations. Therefore, this chapter will examine changes in the global security environment since the end of the Cold War and proceed to examine specific cases studies, some of which can be sorted into similar categories.

Unintended consequences of peacekeeping: Concepts and causes

There are no clear definitions of the parameters or scope of the unintended consequences of peacekeeping. However, they could be simply referred to as the unintended effects – both positive and negative – of peace operations. Unintended consequences can be observed in various aspects, including the following: the status of women and children (e.g. an increase in prostitution and sexual violence against women and children), the economic structure (e.g. distortions in the local economy owing to inflation and illegal economic activities), civil–military relations (e.g. relations between peacekeepers and international humanitarian aid groups, the impact of peacekeepers on local people), political institutionalization (e.g. the effects of newly established democratic institutions on the local community) and the culture and society (e.g. the impact of new cultures and values on traditional values and lifestyles) of a country, as well as the humanitarian consequences of peace operations and their impact on troop-contributing countries. In some cases, these aspects could overlap. Nevertheless, such consequences occur regardless of whether or not the peacekeeping job was successful in achieving its assigned mission.[2]

The causes of all these consequences can be largely ascribed to changes in the nature of post–Cold War conflicts. There have been a total of 61 operations (16 ongoing) since the United Nations Truce Supervision Organization was established as the first United Nations Peacekeeping Operation (UNPKO) in June 1948 to monitor the Arab–Israeli conflict, 15 of which were carried out during the Cold War era.[3] The majority of Cold War peacekeeping missions were traditional, unidimensional military operations, deployed with the objective to monitor ceasefire agreements and troop withdrawals, and thus acted as a buffer zone between the belligerent forces. Most importantly, they remained impartial and neutral to the conflict. These operations were conducted under the following five principles: (i) consent of the parties involved, (ii) impartiality of the United Nations, (iii) non-use of force except in self-defence, (iv) voluntary contributions from neutral states and (v) command and control of UN forces by the UN Secretary-General. These were all based on fundamental principles stated in the UN Charter including the principle of national sovereignty.[4]

However, the advent of the post–Cold War era required peace operations to take on a broader range of responsibilities in order to respond to newly emerging types of crises.[5] That is, whereas conflicts during the Cold War were mostly waged between states, post–Cold War conflicts were more complex in that they had to deal with many domestic factors (e.g. ethnic rivalries, struggles for self-determination and armed conflict over political control of the government). Out of a total of 57 major armed conflicts during the period 1990–2004, 53 were fought within states. All the 19 active conflicts observed in 2004 were intra-state.[6] According to *SIPRI Yearbook*, major armed conflicts refer to those causing over 1,000 battle-related deaths in any one year. Indeed, "new" conflicts were often based on ethnic, racial and religious differences within a state, and often became intractable when factors such as political power and core economic resources came into play. In such cases, a national government was often unable (or unwilling) to protect its citizens, thus increasing the risk of state failure. The most serious crisis situations that emerged in the midst of intra-state conflict or state failure were often defined along humanitarian lines. In fact, more than 90 per cent of casualties in such conflicts were civilian, most of them women and children, who were often the target of hostility and assault in the course of violence and war.

At this point, it was increasingly difficult for the United Nations to address these new conflicts through its traditional peacekeeping operations. Contemporary peace operations were often deployed to establish peace in areas of conflict, where there was no peace to keep, and where neither cease-fires nor peace agreements, not to mention agreement within the UN Security Council, had been secured.[7] In response to the increased demand for effective peace operations in the post–Cold War era, the United Nations and the international community have made an attempt to develop "complex, multi-dimensional or second generation peacekeeping operations" in order to incorporate a variety of new elements in peace operations, which would encompass observer, peacekeeping, peacebuilding and peace enforcement functions rather than just the traditional peacekeeping role.[8] These new tasks include the settlement of ethnic and civil conflicts, post-conflict state-building activities (e.g. demobilization, disarmament, reintegration, election assistance and economic recovery) and the provision of support to humanitarian relief (e.g. assisting the return of refugees, restoring education and medical facilities, and monitoring human rights violations). However, these multidimensional missions have not been so clear-cut in defining their activities, thus increasing the possibility for unintended consequences to arise during and/or in the wake of peacekeeping missions.

Unintended consequences have increased the level of uncertainty of peace operations because such results remain as obstacles to implementing UN peacekeeping plans, and have thus weakened UN control on the ground. They have also undermined the credibility of UN operations in general, as well as the legitimacy of UN intervention itself as a means for conflict management. Therefore, it is important to understand the various aspects, especially the humanitarian aspects, of unintended consequences of peace operations and to develop corresponding mechanisms that would increase the United Nations' capacity in managing and preventing such occurrences.

Humanitarian aspects of unintended consequences

One of the most serious challenges to peace operations has to do with clarifying the relationship between peacekeeping activities and parallel humanitarian relief efforts. According to the United Nations Office for the Coordination of Humanitarian Affairs (OCHA), today's armed conflicts are coupled with the "active and deliberate targeting of civilians, including humanitarian aid workers, widespread human rights violations, the use of rape and other crimes of sexual violence as brutal weapons of war, particularly against women and children, and the forced displacement of hundreds of thousands of people".[9] Denial of civilian access to basic needs such as food, water and shelter and limited international humanitarian access to crisis zones are also the main causes of human suffering, while ethnic cleansing or genocide is the worst form of humanitarian crisis situation in an area of conflict.

In addition, the safety of humanitarian aid workers in conflict zones has been increasingly jeopardized because warring parties often deliberately attack humanitarian aid missions to disrupt international relief aid activities and also to attract media attention. In recent years, particularly after the events of 11 September 2001, international humanitarian efforts in Afghanistan, Indonesia, Iraq, Sudan, etc., seem to have been caught between two recalcitrant contenders, i.e. the West (represented by the American-led coalition in Iraq) and Islamic insurgents. In particular, with the US-led war on terrorism, aid workers argue that "[b]y sending U.S. troops to conduct what would ordinarily be seen as development work, or by requiring aid workers to coordinate their activities with those of the Western coalition, it becomes easier to identify aid workers – however falsely – as pro-Western and therefore justifiable targets for violence".[10] For example, the truck-bomb attack on the UN office in Baghdad that killed 15 people including UN Special Representative Sergio Vieira de Mello in August 2003, confirmed apprehensions about the likelihood that the United Nations could be designated by Islamic terrorists or the Iraqi resistance as an instrument in realizing US interests in Iraq. It is also believed that radical Islamic groups in Indonesia, the world's largest Islamic nation, are suspicious of Western aid workers, who are mainly held responsible for spreading Christian doctrines, which will consequently have negative connotations for impartial humanitarian operations.[11] Although the United Nations has strongly condemned attacks on humanitarian workers in conflict zones as war crimes, aid workers are increasingly becoming a target in areas of conflict.

In response to growing humanitarian concerns in conflict zones, the United Nations has seriously re-examined its approach to security in carrying out complex peace operations. One distinct example is the *Report of the Panel on United Nations Peace Operations* (August 2000), or the "Brahimi Report", which recommends that the Secretary-General substantially restructure the UN Department of Peacekeeping Operations and promote an integrated task force at the UN Headquarters to plan and support each UNPKO from its inception. It also emphasizes the need to enhance the field operation planning and preparation capacities of UN humanitarian agencies such as the Office of the UN High Commissioner for Human Rights (OHCHR).[12] One of the primary objectives of the OHCHR is to promote the human rights aspect of complex UN missions, whether they are carried out in the form of peacekeeping, peacemaking or peacebuilding activities, by closely collaborating with the DPKO and the UN Department of Political Affairs. Yet, factors in conflicts that often involve humanitarian crisis situations are not fully accommodated when a decision is made to establish a peacekeeping mission in a conflict area since the United Nations is continually preoccupied with how to secure financial and material contributions necessary for carrying out effective peace operations.

The United Nations also has to consider the humanitarian consequences (whether they be positive or negative) of its intervention, most of which are unintended. Such consequences are ascribed not only to the wrongdoings of individual peacekeepers but also to the fact that, when international humanitarian and development assistance is provided in the context of violent conflict, "it becomes a part of that context and thus also of the conflict".[13] Although peacekeeping missions in complex crisis situations seek to be neutral toward all the parties involved in the conflict and to "do good" by helping to reduce tensions and rebuild the country, they can "do harm" since the impact of their operations, like that of other international assistance given in conflict situations, is not neutral and could aggravate, protract or abate the conflict.[14]

How do peace operations generate the unintended consequences on humanitarian action?

First, unintended consequences occur in humanitarian aspects when the initial mandate of a peace operation is expanded by the UN Security Council to include not only a military mission but also humanitarian assistance. The core principles for peacekeepers (i.e. consent, impartiality and the minimum use of force) have proven to be inadequate in coping with new forms of conflicts.[15] Peacekeepers' neutrality between warring factions could instead result in "inaction" in crisis situations that could arise because their use of force is limited to self-defence purposes. Since the use of force is also dependent upon international law and regulations (because of its obligation to obey the principle of "the rule of law"), this limitation could result in avoiding any kind of reaction or intervention in situations of humanitarian crisis.[16]

The military capacities and objectives of peace operations are also limited. Many peacekeepers do not have the proper training needed to provide appropriate support to humanitarian aid organizations. Therefore, because soldiers are often unprepared and lack the discipline to handle crisis situations that could arise, reaction to such situations is at the discretion of the force commanders. Yet, most of the force commanders who are newly assigned to a mission do not have the guidelines on the changes of mission objectives and mandates, nor do the military components of the mission have the proper training needed for carrying out humanitarian aid operations. Peacekeepers are often left with no authority to respond to extreme situations such as ethnic genocide.[17] Eventually, the situation would worsen and in turn force peacekeepers to withdraw, thus creating an additional humanitarian crisis situation, as seen in the case of the 1994 Rwandan genocide.

In addition to the problems associated with the limited nature of mission objectives, different positions and attitudes of member states concerning the mission itself could also create further problems, as analysed by the Brahimi Report. As discussed below, problems with peacekeeping strategies could also be the cause of unintended consequences when the "blue helmets" are unable to act effectively in a situation where the institution or legislative system does not function properly owing to a weakened or failed government, as well as when peacekeepers avoid intervention in conflicts between the major warring factions.

Second, there are situations where the principles of humanitarian organizations are violated with an encroachment by the military component through their undertaking humanitarian-type activities. The objectives of humanitarian organizations are to provide relief aid without discriminating between warring factions, based on the principle of impartiality and neutrality. However, the expansion of humanitarian action carried out by military personnel has increased the suspicion of partiality. For instance, the partiality of humanitarian assistance in the Kosovo crisis was raised when NATO forces provided humanitarian services in the refugee camps.[18] This could, in turn, threaten the safety of aid workers of humanitarian organizations such as the International Federation of Red Cross and Red Crescent Societies and could eventually lead to the refusal to receive international aid by major domestic political parties. The outcome would be increased civilian suffering.[19]

The issue also applies to conflict states that are under embargoes or economic sanctions. The issue of providing humanitarian aid to the people of these countries becomes a matter of concern when it has been decided by the UN Security Council to impose economic sanctions as a means to resolve a conflict. The question of whether humanitarian aid should be restricted because of a "larger mission" is a controversial and thorny question that is still under debate.

Third, human rights violations of civilians by UN peacekeepers are not an old issue. The composition of peacekeeping forces is usually a mixture of soldiers from both developed and developing nations. In the case of many developing countries, forces are sent because of the high salaries paid to troops for service in UN peacekeeping operations. Thus, there are cases where peacekeepers lack the proper training and commitment or the military discipline to carry out peacekeeping activities. Human rights violations by undisciplined peacekeepers, such as sexual misconduct and human trafficking of local civilians and refugees, are a notable example of the unintended humanitarian consequences of peacekeeping operations.[20] There are also several documented cases of abuses committed by peacekeepers from the developed world, e.g. the whole contingent of Italian peacekeepers repatriated from Mozambique, the repatriation of a French civilian peacekeeper from the Democratic Republic of Congo (DRC) and the American police officers linked to human trafficking in Kosovo.

Case analysis of unintended humanitarian consequences

There are several cases of UN peacekeeping operations that have resulted in unintended humanitarian consequences. First, a UN peace operation acting beyond its original mandate of providing humanitarian assistance is often regarded by domestic political parties as an act of aggression. In the case of Somalia, a fight between UN peacekeepers and domestic political parties broke out. Second, UN peacekeepers could avoid intervening in conflicts between warring political factions and thus fail to prevent humanitarian crisis situations from occurring, as demonstrated in the case of Rwanda where, despite warning signals of genocide, the international community and the United Nations did not forestall or stop the genocide from taking place. Third, the unclear division of roles between peacekeeping forces and other international agencies and the lack of coordination among them, as well as the delayed reaction and inadequacy of peace operations as witnessed in the Liberian civil war, led to a failure to respond effectively to human rights violations and secure enabling environments for humanitarian aid. Fourth, peacekeepers could violate the human rights of local citizens. Sexual abuse or torture by members of an international contingent of UN peacekeepers have been problematic, as revealed in the cases of Bosnia-Herzegovina, Sierra Leone, Kosovo, Somalia and the DRC.[21]

Case I: Somalia

General Muhammad Siyad Barre of the Marehan clan assumed dictatorial control of Somalia after a successful coup d'état in 1969. There were various armed anti-governmental uprisings from the early 1980s, and in January 1991 Barre was deposed in an anti-government campaign led by the United Somali Congress (USC). After the collapse of Barre's regime, civil war erupted as several clan-based military factions competed for power. Fighting broke out between the two rival factions of the USC, respectively led by interim President Ali Mahdi Mohammed and General Mohammed Farah Aidid (formerly in charge of military operations in the USC). In 1993, after two years of civil war, Aidid's Somali National Alliance (SNA) emerged as the dominant force in Mogadishu, the capital city.[22]

The crisis in Somalia attracted international attention when a severe drought, coupled with the devastation of civil war, struck the country in 1991–1992; an estimated one-third of the entire Somali population was at risk of dying from starvation. The United Nations authorized the deployment of the United Nations Operation in Somalia (UNOSOM I) with an initial force of 4,500 troops in April 1992 and successfully prevented further starvation. In addition to UN peacekeeping forces in the country, the US-led multinational Unified Tasked Force was deployed in December 1992 in order to facilitate the safe and effective delivery of humanitarian assistance to people in need. In January 1993, under the mediation of the United Nations, the 15 warring factions, including the forces of interim President Mohammed and General Aidid's SNA, gathered in Addis Ababa to sign a cease-fire agreement. However, Aidid opposed the establishment of the UN-administered Transitional National Council and did not submit to disarmament agreements.[23]

In May 1993, UNOSOM I was replaced by a stronger and larger UNOSOM II, which had a force composition of 30,800 troops. However, clashes between UNOSOM and the SNA escalated, resulting in the deaths of 24 Pakistani soldiers in June. Consequently, UNOSOM II launched retaliatory attacks on the SNA and attempts to disarm the SNA and capture Aidid lasted through October, provoking hostile reactions in Mogadishu. In the same month, an operation by a force of US Army Rangers and Delta Force operators to capture Aidid's militia members in Mogadishu resulted in the deaths of 18 American soldiers and some 350 Somalis. This incident completely reversed the course of events and hastened a US withdrawal from Somalia by March 1994. The United Nations also concluded that there was nothing more to do and declared all UN operations in Somalia a failure. UN peacekeeping contingents started to withdraw in December 1993 and completed all UN operations by March 1995. Aidid then launched a campaign to drive all opposing factions out of Mogadishu and declared himself president of a new Somali government that failed to receive international recognition.

The original mandate of UNOSOM I was to support the effective delivery of humanitarian aid to starving Somali people. However, during the course of the mission, the mandate was first changed to the mediation of political reconciliation among all the warring factions and the establishment of a "secure environment" in the country, then to the removal of Aidid, and eventually to seek a compromise with him. By choosing to expand the mandate of the mission beyond its original focus (i.e. providing a secure environment for humanitarian assistance to reach the intended beneficiaries, which was a success), the UN mission (directly and by association with the US Rangers) lost its impartiality and became a party to the conflict and, in so doing, lost the ability to achieve its core mandate of supporting humanitarian assistance. This, in turn, led to local misunderstanding of UN intervention as an act of aggression, drawing UN peacekeepers into the fighting. Although UNOSOM I and II were successful in alleviating the suffering of famine victims in the country and repatriating thousands of refugees, they were forced to withdraw without achieving their ultimate goal of resolving the civil war, thus leaving the Somali crisis unresolved. Aidid died in August 1996 in a fight with competing factions, raising the prospect of peace in Somalia. However, it is questionable if there will ever be any future efforts by the United Nations and the international community to bring about peace in the country, because numerous warlords and factions are still fighting in several parts of the country, making the country a harsh environment for any reconciliation, mediation or even peace enforcement efforts.

Case 2: Rwanda

The Rwanda civil war was the outcome of violent conflict between the majority Hutu and minority Tutsi ethnic groups, which was aggravated by Belgian colonial authorities who gave the Tutsis a monopoly of political and administrative power.[24] Independence in July 1962 resulted in the empowerment of the Hutu majority and ended the dominance of the Tutsi minority. In the wake of bloody inter-ethnic conflicts between 1963 and 1967, many Tutsis were killed and tens of thousands of Tutsis fled to neighbouring countries, though most of them fled to Uganda. In 1988, Tutsi refugees and dissident Hutus in Uganda formed the Rwandan Patriotic Front (RPF), which invaded the northern part of Rwanda in October 1990. In August 1993, the government of Rwanda and the RPF signed a peace accord in Arusha, Tanzania. In October 1993, the United Nations Assistance Mission for Rwanda (UNAMIR) was established with the mandate to monitor the observance of the cease-fire agreement, repatriate Rwandan refugees and coordinate humanitarian assistance efforts. However, the security situation in the country continued to deteriorate in the early months of 1994. On 11 January 1994, Romeo Dallaire, UNAMIR's Force Commander, informed UN Headquarters of plans for ethnic attacks on the Tutsis, as well as of the existence of accumulating arms caches, which UN Headquarters did not take seriously.

The genocide in Rwanda was unleashed on 6 April 1994, immediately after the death of President Habyarimana in a plane crash. On the following day, the prime minister, a moderate Hutu, was killed by Rwandan militia, together with 10 Belgian soldiers. As a result, the Belgian contingent (the most well-equipped in UNAMIR) withdrew and killings of Tutsi civilians escalated. In the midst of all these events, discussion at the UN Security Council on Rwanda in April 1994 had little to do with the possibility of a civilian massacre, but rather was focused on the cease-fire agreement between the government and the RPF. Furthermore, on 21 April, the Security Council unanimously decided to reduce the size of UNAMIR to 270 from 2,539 troops. On 17 May 1994, the Security Council adopted a resolution to expand UNAMIR to a maximum of 5,500 forces. However, this resolution was too late in stopping the killings that took place during the five weeks between early April and mid-May in 1994. The genocide lasted a total of 13 weeks until the Tutsi-dominated RPF defeated the Hutu-led government on 18 July. At least 800,000 (with claims as high as 1 million) Rwandans were killed, mostly by *interahamwe* militia – or gangs of Hutu youths.

UNAMIR was intended to be an impartial third-party mediation operation, but because of Belgian participation it was not seen as one by the Hutus. In addition, the 2,500 troops that were deployed were under-equipped and lacked both coordination and discipline. There was also confusion within the mission over the rules of engagement, not to mention the fact that there was insufficient planning for any possible humanitarian crisis situations that could arise. Still, it is unfortunate to note that the genocide in Rwanda took place in a country where UN peacekeepers were deployed and expected to maintain peace. The overriding causes of the failure were, on the one hand, a lack of resources on the ground and, on the other hand, the limited political will and commitment of UN member states to act. Moreover, the mandate of UNAMIR appears to have been based on an over-optimistic assessment of the peace process at the time, and thus was inadequate to meet the needs of the real situation in the country.

There were also problems of command and control owing to a lack of communication between UN Headquarters and UNAMIR. In his cable of 11 January 1994, Dallaire announced his intention to take action to disarm the militia. However, his action plan was rejected by UN Headquarters because it was outside UNAMIR's mandate. Furthermore, UNAMIR was often called an "orphan operation", because it was created in the aftermath of Somalia. UN member states, fearing for the lives of their soldiers, were also reluctant to send their forces to Rwanda, leaving UNAMIR unable to assemble the quantity and quality of troops it required to effectively manage the situation in the country.

The delay in identifying events in Rwanda as genocide was also moti-vated by a lack of political will among the UN member states to act. This is because states that were parties to the 1948 Genocide Convention would have been obliged to intervene if the killings that were taking place in Rwanda had been identified as acts of genocide. Another critical issue related to the Rwandan case was that the UNAMIR mandate did not keep pace with the developments that were rapidly taking place and was, therefore, neither precise nor relevant to the prevailing situation. In light of the above, UNAMIR was unable to function as a cohesive oper-ation once the killing started in early April.

The Rwandan tragedy indicates that the UN Security Council failed to give the peace operation (UNAMIR) the authority and means to prevent or stop the genocide. The mission made several attempts to seek author-ity to take preventive steps, but each time the Headquarters ordered the mission to stop its intended actions and reminded it of its limited man-date. Indeed, there can be no neutrality in the face of the threat of geno-cide or massive violations of human rights. As a result most new missions are deployed under a Chapter VII mandate so that they would be able to react to similar developments without having to first seek additional au-thorization from the Security Council.

It is also crucial to recognize that the mere presence of a UNPKO, whether or not its mandate includes the protection of civilians, will create a certain expectation, if not "false illusion", that it will protect people from violence and create an enabling environment for humanitarian as-sistance. Failure to do so will cause serious harm to the UN reputation, as observed in Rwanda and the Srebrenica massacre, where more than 8,000 Bosnian Muslim men and boys were killed by Bosnian Serbs in July 1995, while the town of Srebrenica was designated a "safe area", guarded by the United Nations Protection Force (UNPROFOR) during the 1992–1995 war in Bosnia.[25] UN peace operations should thus, as a minimum, include sufficient authorization to protect civilians in imminent threat of violence and guarantee a hospitable environment for humani-tarian action.

Case 3: Liberia

Liberia, which was founded in 1847 by freed American slaves, was a US forward base for anti-communist operations during the Cold War. The Reagan administration offered substantial financial assistance to Liberia during the first half of the 1980s.[26] In particular, Samuel Doe, who estab-lished a military regime through a military coup in 1980, diverted much of US aid of tens of millions of dollars from development and investment spending to the military budget. Consequently, Liberia's highly developed military later became the main tool for Doe's long-term dictatorship as it was used for removing political opposition forces in the process of consolidating the regime.[27]

This oppressive regime came to an end when the National Patriotic Front of Liberia (NPFL), led by Charles Taylor, waged an insurrection in December 1989 and captured Monrovia, the capital city, in July 1990. However, in the course of the fighting, the NPFL was divided into two factions, one led by Taylor and the other by Prince Johnson, thus leading the country into a civil war. The civil war (1989–1996), which left 200,000 people dead and displaced at least 850,000 people from their homes, came to an end through an enforced cease-fire in 1995 with the intervention of the United States, the United Nations, the Organization of African Unity (now the African Union) and the Economic Community of West African States (ECOWAS).[28]

Although elections were held under UN supervision and Taylor was elected as president in July 1997, many of the Liberian people questioned the legitimacy of Taylor's government. As a result, political opposition and fighting between various political factions continued, eventually leading to a second civil war (1999). There were two main opposition groups: (1) Liberians United for Reconciliation and Democracy (LURD), which was based in the northern part of the country and had been fighting Taylor's forces since 1999, and (2) Movement for Democracy in Liberia (MODEL), which began incursions into Liberia from Côte d'Ivoire in April 2003, uprooting an estimated 700,000 Liberians.[29] Several aborted attempts were made to enforce a cease-fire agreement between LURD, MODEL and the government in June and early July of 2003, increasing international pressure for US military intervention. On the other hand, President George W. Bush kept calling on Taylor to step down from power. In August 2003, Taylor fled to Nigeria and power passed to an interim government.[30]

As in the first civil war, ECOWAS intervened during the initial stage of the second civil war. Security Council Resolution 1509 also authorized the United Nations Mission in Liberia (UNMIL) to provide support for implementing the cease-fire agreement and the peace process, provide protection to UN staff and civilians, support humanitarian assistance efforts and provide support in forming a new and restructured military.[31] However, there are several issues that remain, which indicate that the UN mission is far from complete.

The primary problem was the delay in troop deployment on the ground. Although the United Nations approved the deployment of 15,000 peacekeepers in September 2003, the mission reached only half its total authorized strength by the end of 2003. Troop numbers hovered at 14,665 in September 2004 and 15,775 in January 2005.[32] The delay of UN troops has slowed the post-conflict reconstruction operations of UN administrative officials and humanitarian relief workers. Also, the UN failure to deploy a sufficient number of peacekeeping forces prevented peacekeepers from effectively responding to cases of severe human rights violations such as robbery, abduction, torture and rape.

Although the primary task of UNMIL was to disarm rebel forces by collecting small arms in return for economic compensation, this process of what is called "DDRR" (disarmament, demobilization, reintegration and repatriation)[33] was not properly implemented owing to the lack of thorough preparation and, accordingly, it generated negative effects. For one, there were not enough troops to carry out the task, not to mention the lack in financial resources to provide the promised support. In addition, poor border control allowed the flow of small arms into the country to continue, driving more arms into the black market along the border with Sierra Leone. This in turn provided Sierra Leone with another threat factor at the stage of the peacemaking process in 2003. Moreover, the two rival groups, MODEL and LURD, whose cooperation was essential to the peace process, continued to demand more influence than the other group in establishing the new government. Yet, UNMIL launched several public campaigns in order to disconnect the rebel leaderships from the rest of their respective groups. As a result, there still exists potential conflict between UNMIL and the two rebel groups.[34]

UNMIL has also failed to develop effective and sustained cooperation with other UN agencies such as the World Food Programme, the UN High Commissioner for Refugees (UNHCR), the United Nations Development Programme and the United Nations Children's Fund, as well as other non-governmental organizations. According to a high official serving in UNMIL, UNMIL's coordination, partnership and control structure was paralysed to the point that rebel groups easily looted humanitarian relief supplies for refugees. Furthermore, refugee camps have become a main target for rebel soldiers, turning the camps into a hotbed of systematic rape and pillage.[35]

It can be argued that the aforementioned problems of the Liberian case, such as slow deployment of peacekeeping troops and their poor coordination with humanitarian agencies, resulted from unfulfilled or poorly executed intended actions rather than from unintended ones. Yet, this case clearly shows that, owing to the delay and inadequacy of peace operations, the UN mission lost its capability to effectively stop severe human rights violations. Also, unclear role distinctions between UN peacekeepers and other international agencies, and the lack of coordination among them, caused critical damage to the authority and reputation of the UN mission in conflict-ridden Liberia, thus making humanitarian assistance difficult. These problems should be seriously considered in the context of unintended consequences of peace operations for humanitarian purposes.

Conclusion

In the aftermath of the chain of unintended consequences, a full review of peace operations was initiated through the Independent Panel on UNPKO (and the Brahimi Report). The panel's work, which took place after two UN independent inquiry reports (on the UN failures to prevent the genocide in Rwanda in 1994 and to protect the civilians of Srebrenica in Bosnia and Herzegovina in 1995) were released in 1999, acknowledged that civilians have increasingly become the target of assault and killings as warring parties have sought to forcibly displace, annihilate or intimidate groups or individuals that do not share ethnicity with, or are perceived as hostile to, one of the conflict parties. This casualty pattern suggests that it is crucial to identify a more comprehensive approach to peacekeeping, as well as identify the conditions for successful intra-state peacekeeping missions.[36]

In addition, the Security Council and the General Assembly examined the structure, deployment and mission operation procedures of peacekeeping operations in order to better counter the changing nature of recent conflicts. Among the topics that were examined, the following were included: the need to clearly identify the definition and principles of humanitarian activities; the reinforcement of the Code of Conduct among individual peacekeepers; the enhancement of the observation and human resource capacities of missions; and improved cooperation with other UN agencies and NGOs. In anticipation of future cases of UN intervention, further studies on successful cases, along with an evaluation and analysis of cases of failure, are needed. Further research on the unintended consequences of UN peacekeeping is also needed in order to increase the international community's control over peace operations.[37] It is important too to improve the UN response to the challenge of increasing "grey zones" that require UN action, which will be neither in the form of traditional peacekeeping activities nor in the form of full-blown enforcement action.[38]

For all these, a paradigm shift in the politics of the United Nations, and the Security Council in particular, is required. UN member states have no legal and political responsibility, and at most a moral responsibility, to respond to the humanitarian crisis situations, with the exception of genocide.[39] The Security Council has often been criticized for its uneven "case-by-case" decisions to rescue victims of war and violence.[40] Unless the humanitarian imperative is not overshadowed by the strategic interests of the member states, particularly power politics, the role of UN peace operations as a whole would be at risk of being discredited, as demonstrated in the failed peacekeeping missions in Somalia, Bosnia-Herzegovina and Rwanda.

Moreover, the understanding of various examples of unintended consequences of UN peacekeeping should be incorporated into the present PKO system as part of the short-term reform plans concerning UN peacekeeping. Of course, its long-term reforms, which would be in line with the long-term reform plans of the organization as a whole, would be pursued at the same time. As seen through the cases of Somalia and Rwanda, the United Nations would have to develop a credible way to assess a particular conflict situation before and after it deploys a mission, and thus adapt a method to define its mandate and strategy according to developments on the ground. Also, sufficient explanation of the purpose of the mission and its mandate should be made in advance to the local parties in order to increase their trust of UN forces. On the other hand, UN forces should be sufficiently equipped so that they would be able to respond effectively to emergency situations that might erupt. In addition, a clearly defined command system would need to be established within the mission, not to mention the fact that peacekeepers should be sufficiently informed of the social dynamics in the area of conflict before they begin their activities.

Still, it would be difficult to prevent or minimize the unintended negative consequences of peacekeeping through the reform of UNPKOs, given the limited resources and the lack of political will of member states due to differences in their national interests and positions. Also, assistance at the official and governmental level would not be the only means to avoid a large-scale crisis. It would be possible to stop or decrease the possibility of humanitarian crisis situations from occurring through the network of international NGOs and coordination between field workers. The thorough review of lessons learned from both successful and failed cases of UN peacekeeping missions should be continued in order to improve the United Nations' capacity to deal with such unintended consequences. It is also important to seek ways of adapting the cases that have produced positive consequences (e.g. the United Nations Operation in Mozambique and the United Nations Observer Mission in El Salvador) to other crises through the process of classifying them.

In conclusion, despite the malfunctions and negative consequences of UN peace operations, it would be wrong to denounce peacekeeping altogether because of its past failures. It would be imprudent and invalid to decide that the absence of peace operations would do less harm than the harm that peacekeeping has done. Just as we should continue to provide international aid to people in conflict zones, despite the possibility that assistance efforts could be distorted by local politics and misappropriated by warriors to aggravate conflict, peacekeeping missions should proceed.[41] In fact, a decision to suspend or postpone peace operations in conflict zones would very likely result in greater negative humanitarian consequences and thus threaten the future of UN peacekeeping itself.

Notes

1. O. A. Otunnu, "The Peace and Security Agenda of the United Nations: From a Crossroads into the Next Century", in *Envisioning the United Nations in the Twenty-first Century, Proceedings of the Inaugural Symposium on the United Nations System in the Twenty-first Century*, Tokyo, Japan: UNU Headquarters, 21–22 November, 1995.
2. S. Lee, "International Conflict and the United Nations: The Role of Peacekeeping Operations" (in Korean), *New Asia*, 11(4), 2004, pp. 61–83.
3. United Nations Peacekeeping Operations, "Background Note: 30 September 2006", available at ⟨http://www.un.org/Depts/dpko/dpko/bnote.htm⟩ (accessed 29 November 2006).
4. K. A. Mingst and M. P. Karns, *The United Nations in the Post-Cold War Era*, 2nd edn, Boulder, CO: Westview Press, 2000.
5. United Nations, *United Nations Peacekeeping: Meeting New Challenges*, available at ⟨http://www.un.org/Depts/dpko/dpko/faq/q6.htm⟩ (accessed 29 November 2006).
6. R. Dwan and C. Holmqvist, "Major Armed Conflict", in Stockholm International Peace Research Institute (SIPRI), *SIPRI Yearbook 2005*, New York: Oxford University Press, 2005, p. 121.
7. J.-M. Guehenno, "United Nations Peacekeeping Today", address presented at United Nations Under-Secretary-General for Peacekeeping Operations, Workshop on UN Peacekeeping Operations, Mexico City, 28 November 2002.
8. S. Lee and B. Heldt, "UN Peacekeeping in Civil War and Genocide: Rwanda and Beyond", in *Peace and Stability on the Korean Peninsula*, Seoul: Korean Association of International Studies, 2001, pp. 229–261.
9. OCHA, *Humanitarian Issues*, available at ⟨http://ochaonline.un.org/print_page.asp?Page=64&Lang=⟩ (accessed 29 November 2006).
10. The Christian Science Monitor, "Aid Workers Increasingly a Target in Conflict Zones", 5 November 2004, available at ⟨http://www.csmonitor.com/2004/1105/p07s02-wosc.html⟩ (accessed 29 November 2006). "On 11 June 2004, nine days after five MSF [Médecins Sans Frontières] staff members were killed in Afghanistan, a Taliban spokesperson offered the following justification for their murder: 'Organisations like Médecins Sans Frontières work for American interests and are therefore targets for us'". Fabrice Weissman, Research Director, MSF-Foundation, Paris, "Military Humanitarianism: A Deadly Confusion", 16 December 2004, available at ⟨http://www.msf.org/msfinternational/invoke.cfm?component=article&objectid=762E8B7B-2F5F-448A-8EC26F2039794E54&method=full_html⟩ (accessed 29 November 2006).
11. US Department of State, *Indonesia: Country Reports on Human Rights Practices – 2003*, released by the Bureau of Democracy, Human Rights, and Labor, 25 February 2004, available at ⟨http://www.state.gov/g/drl/rls/hrrpt/2003/27771.htm⟩ (accessed 29 November 2006).

12. United Nations, *Report of the Panel on United Nations Peace Operations*, General Assembly (A/55/305) and Security Council (S/2000/809), New York, 21 August 2000, available at ⟨http://www.un.org/peace/reports/peace_operations/⟩ (accessed 29 November 2006).

13. M. B. Anderson, *Do No Harm: How Aid Can Support Peace or War*, Boulder, CO: Lynne Rienner Publishers, 1999, p. 145.

14. Ibid.

15. *The Comprehensive Report on Lessons Learned from United Nations Operation in Somalia (UNOSOM), April 1992–March 1995*, available at ⟨http://www.un.org/Depts/dpko/dpko/lessons/somalia.htm⟩ (accessed 29 November 2006).

16. S. Chesterman, "The Use of Force in UN Peace Operations", UN Department of Peacekeeping Operations, Peacekeeping Best Practices External Study, 31 August 2004, available at ⟨http://pbpu.unlb.org/pbpu/library/Chesterman%20External%20Paper%20(31-08-2004).pdf⟩ (accessed 29 November 2006).

17. United Nations, *Report of the Special Committee on Peacekeeping Operations and Its Working Group at the 2004 Substantive Session*, UN General Assembly UN Doc. A/58/19, New York, 29 March–16 April 2004.

18. "Faced with a protection crisis at the Blace border post, and the need to prepare sites for a massive influx of refugees, UNHCR made an official request to NATO on 3rd April for assistance with the humanitarian aid operation. This agreement with a warring party was without precedent and seriously undermined the impartiality of the assistance programme." Toby Porter, "The Partiality of Humanitarian Assistance – Kosovo in Comparative Perspective", *Journal of Humanitarian Assistance*, 22 June 2000, available at ⟨http://www.jha.ac/articles/a057.htm⟩ (accessed 29 November 2006). Porter also quotes A. Suhrke, M. Barutciski, P. Sandison and R. Garlock, "The Kosovo Refugee Crisis: An Evaluation of UNHCR's Emergency Preparedness and Response", January 2000, p. 109: "UNHCR's decision to work with NATO during the air strikes therefore meant a deviation from the traditional norm that humanitarians be impartial and neutral."

19. Weissman, "Military Humanitarianism: A Deadly Confusion".

20. W. J. Durch, V. K. Holt, C. R. Earle and M. K. Shanahan, *The Brahimi Report and the Future of UN Peace Operations*, The Henry L. Stimson Center, 2003, available at ⟨http://www.stimson.org/fopo/pdf/BR-CompleteVersion-Dec03.pdf⟩ (accessed 29 November 2006).

21. The topic of sexual abuse or torture by members of an international contingent of UN peacekeepers is addressed by other chapters in this book.

22. GlobalSecurity.org, "Somalia Civil War – Southern Somalia", available at ⟨http://www.globalsecurity.org/military/world/war/somalia-south.htm⟩ (accessed 29 November 2006).

23. O. Ramsbotham and T. Woodhouse, *Encyclopedia of International Peacekeeping Operations*, Santa Barbara: ABC-Clio, 1999.

24. This section has been prepared based on the *Report of the United Nations Independent Enquiry into the Actions of the United Nations during the 1994 Genocide in Rwanda*, 16 December 1999, Security Council, UN Doc. S/1999/1257, for which I served as a special adviser.

25. UN General Assembly, *Report of the Secretary-General Pursuant to General Assembly Resolution 53/35, The Fall of Srebrenica*, UN Doc. A/54/549, 15 November 1999, available at ⟨http://www.un.org/peace/srebrenica.pdf⟩ (accessed 29 November 2006).

26. David S. Hauck, "Why Liberia Turns to Its American 'Big Brother'", 1 August 2003, available at ⟨http://www.csmonitor.com/2003/0801/p07s01-woaf.html⟩ (accessed 29 November 2006).

27. Public Broadcasting Service, Global Connections, "Liberia and the United States: A Complex Relationship", available at ⟨http://www.pbs.org/wgbh/globalconnections/liberia/essays/uspolicy/⟩ (accessed 29 November 2006).
28. "The Liberian Crisis: 1980–1996", available at ⟨http://pages.prodigy.net/jkess3/Civilwar.html⟩ (accessed 29 November 2006). Amnesty International, *Liberia: Time to Take Human Rights Seriously – Placing Human Rights on the National Agenda*, 1 October 1997, available at ⟨http://web.amnesty.org/library/Index/engAFR340051997⟩ (accessed 29 November 2006).
29. J. Drumtra, "West Africa's Refugee Crisis Spills across Many Borders", *Migration Information Source*, Migration Policy Institute, 1 August 2003, available at ⟨http://www.migrationinformation.org/Feature/display.cfm?id=148⟩ (accessed 29 November 2006).
30. CBC News Online, "Indepth: Liberia – Land of the Free", 29 March 2006, available at ⟨http://www.cbc.ca/news/background/liberia/⟩ (accessed 29 November 2006).
31. Department of Peacekeeping Operations, "United Nations Mission in Liberia", available at ⟨http://www.un.org/Depts/dpko/missions/unmil/⟩ (accessed 29 November 2006).
32. Africa Action, "Liberia: UN Peacekeeping", *Africa Policy E-Journal*, 28 September 2003, available at ⟨http://www.africaaction.org/docs03/lib0309.htm⟩ (accessed 29 November 2006).
33. United Nations, "The United Nations Mission in Liberia (UNMIL): Tubmanburg", January 2004, available at ⟨http://www.un.org/av/photo/subjects/tubmanburg.htm⟩ (accessed 29 November 2006).
34. International Crisis Group, *Rebuilding Liberia: Prospects and Perils*, London: ICG, 30 January 2004.
35. W. G. O'Neil, *A New Challenge for Peacekeepers: The Internally Displaced*, The Brookings Institution-Johns Hopkins SAIS Project on Internal Displacement, 2004, p. 31.
36. Lee and Heldt, "UN Peacekeeping in Civil War and Genocide".
37. United Nations Department of Public Information, Peace and Security Section, "Past, Present & Future Challenges in Peacekeeping", 2002, available at ⟨http://www.un.org/Depts/dpko/dpko/dpkoseminar/⟩ (accessed 29 November 2006).
38. Otunnu, "The Peace and Security Agenda of the United Nations".
39. Still, it is not easy to define whether a situation is genocide. For instance, the delay in identifying the events in Rwanda as genocide was motivated by a lack of political will to act. Although Boutros Boutros-Ghali, the Secretary-General at the time, was labelling the situation as genocide, the UN Security Council was much more circumspect with its words and actions. Just as the United Nations as a body was reluctant to use the word "genocide" to describe Rwanda, so too were individual member states.
40. T. J. Farer, D. Archibugi, C. Brown, N. C. Crawford, T. G. Weiss and N. J. Wheeler, "Roundtable: Humanitarian Intervention After 9/11", *International Relations*, 19(2), 2005, pp. 211–250.
41. This argument is a modified version of Mary B. Anderson's argument in her book *Do No Harm: How Aid Can Support Peace or War*, p. 2.

6

Unintended consequences of civil–military cooperation in peace operations

Stuart Gordon

The end of the Cold War witnessed increasing occurrences of external military and peacekeeping forces being deployed alongside civilian political and humanitarian agencies in pursuit of "coherent" responses. These presupposed both a shared objective, a sustainable peace, and the possibility of synergies between the various elements of the intervention. Simultaneously, there has been a wider debate on what constitutes an appropriate relationship between politico-military and humanitarian action and whether the latter could, and should, simultaneously and impartially relieve suffering while also contributing to building a peace. The core of this discourse has been a recognition that differing aspects of an international intervention may both hinder and mutually reinforce one another.

From the military perspective, the concept of "civil–military cooperation", or CIMIC, is frequently portrayed as the mechanism that can unlock synergies between the politico-military and humanitarian aspects of an intervention. Although this is often the underlying assumption, this chapter suggests that CIMIC may often result in a set of, frequently negative, unintended consequences.

The growth of policy "coherence"?

Debates over the viability and desirability of CIMIC take place in the context of the broader debate over the relationship between political and humanitarian activity. There is a strong sense within the humanitar-

Unintended consequences of peacekeeping operations, Aoi, de Coning and Thakur (eds), United Nations University Press, 2007, ISBN 978-92-808-1142-1

ian community that "integrating" diplomatic, military and humanitarian responses to conflict has led not necessarily to synergies, but to encroachments upon humanitarian space. In effect, humanitarianism is perceived to be under siege from both the military and the political strands of the international response. This reflects broader changes within international interventions in conflict. Slim argues that international intervention is increasingly conceived of as an "impartial humanitarian pursuit through the UN rather than an aggressive and side-taking military strategy carried out on a bilateral basis" but is conducted in the context of live wars. Consequently, such interventions have increasingly engaged in building peace within conflict environments.[1] The Brahimi Panel paralleled Slim's analysis, concluding that, in circumstances where neither belligerent had achieved a decisive military victory and not all parties had fully committed themselves to a peaceful resolution, the United Nations' role should be transformed from underpinning a peace agreement into creating the conditions in which one could be achieved. Peacekeeping and peacebuilding have, therefore, been transformed from largely "sequential" activities into parallel, simultaneous and interdependent ones. Arguably this has resulted in the co-option of humanitarian action by the "the dominant neo-liberal political agenda" using "humanitarian assistance as part of a wider policy of state-repair which aims to produce liberal democracies from war-torn societies".[2] In effect, Brahimi conceives of humanitarian action as a tool in the diplomatic armoury of state repair.

Such changes are part of a much broader trend involving the general politicization of aid policy. In an apparent return to the Cold War era, states, once more, have demonstrated a tendency to pursue both domestic and foreign policy objectives through essentially humanitarian means. The global war on terror has accentuated this process, causing a more considered and deliberate link between the failed state, development and traditional state security agendas in an increasingly "integrated" approach to interventions. The belligerent status of major donors, the prevalence of donor power and donors' obvious strategic agenda have also caught the humanitarian community almost unawares, throwing the relationship between political and humanitarian action into disarray and complicating humanitarian agencies' operational responses.

The blurring of distinctions between political and humanitarian action has not simply been imposed upon the humanitarian community. In part it also results from the greater convergence of (or at least a much stronger recognition of the link between) humanitarian and human rights norms. The institutional topography of relief has also changed with the expansion of the role of non-governmental organizations (NGOs) in peace support operations (PSOs). This has resulted, at least in part, from claims that appropriately configured assistance may contribute to peacebuilding strategies.[3] Furthermore, commentators such as Abiew argue that:

> [this has also occurred in the context of a greater degree of reliance upon NGOs by western governments] in relief operations and the delivery of development programs. The NGO community itself has argued that it and other civil society actors are more effective than governments in delivering assistance to people in need. Thus, much of the proliferation of NGO activity has come at the expense of states and international organizations.[4]

This has enhanced both the role of NGOs in the process of delivery and the perceived links between the various aspects of an international response to a crisis. It has also raised the prominence of a number of "operational challenges" for the humanitarian community. Slim describes these as "the art of mid-war operations; the need to protect civilian populations (who are now within reach) from violence; the management of military-humanitarian combinations in UN operations; and the focus on peace programming as a means of ending war".[5] These challenges have raised the importance of understanding the interaction of international political, military and humanitarian responses to conflict. Few would disagree with the idea that international interventions are likely to be at their most effective when all of the instruments of influence are deployed in a manner that retains the integrity of each, yet secures synergies in a "complementary" fashion. Yet diplomacy, sanctions, humanitarian action, military, economic, development, judicial/rule of law, social and human rights instruments have a unique capacity to interfere with one another if their interaction is not effectively regulated. Such encroachments are most likely to be visible in terms of the specific interaction of international military and humanitarian responses. However, CIMIC is frequently portrayed as the mechanism that prevents unintended and negative consequences.

CIMIC definitions: Besieging humanitarian space?

The reality is often different, in that negative and unintended consequences are not always prevented. NATO defines CIMIC in terms of:

> [t]he co-ordination and co-operation, in support of the mission, between the NATO commander and civil actors, including national population and local authorities, as well as international, national and non-governmental organisations and agencies.[6]

NATO's approach stresses a presumption not of maintaining humanitarian space but of synergies with the commander's mission entailing rather obvious implications for humanitarian principles. In particular, "commanders must take into account the presence of large numbers of IOs [international organizations] and NGOs with their own aims, methods and perspectives, all of which may have to be reconciled with those of NATO".[7] The purpose of CIMIC for NATO commanders is to "establish and maintain the full co-operation of the NATO commander and the civilian authorities, organisations, agencies and population within a commander's area of operations in order to allow him to fulfil his mission".[8]

NATO's definition makes clear that, in any clash between the humanitarian imperative and mission primacy, the latter will dominate. This approach is largely echoed within national doctrines and approaches. Even French military doctrine, often quite independent by NATO standards, reflects the mission primacy and strategic framework inherent in the broader NATO definition.[9] The US military tend to employ an even more *active* term, namely "civil affairs" (CA), to describe operations that can involve the assumption of executive and administrative authority by soldiers, defining this in terms of:

> those interrelated military activities that embrace the relationship between military forces and civil authorities and populations. CA missions include civil-military operations and civil administration. CA encompasses the activities that military commanders take to establish and maintain relations between their forces and the civil authorities and general population, resources and institutions in friendly, neutral or hostile areas where their forces are employed. Commanders plan and conduct CA activities to facilitate military operations and help achieve politico-military objectives derived from US national security interests.[10]

In effect, it appears that, notwithstanding protestations as to the sanctity of humanitarian space, CIMIC doctrines are generally converging upon the idea that CIMIC action is defined solely by the strategic framework of the intervention as a whole. The promotion of humanitarian space may, or may not, be a feature of this framework; potentially leading one to the conclusion that the promotion of humanitarian space and civilian dominance within this framework may in fact be an unintended consequence of CIMIC.

The particular need to regulate this relationship is encapsulated in the virtual abandonment by the Office for the Coordination of Humanitarian Affairs (OCHA) of the term CIMIC, adopting in its place "humanitarian civil military coordination" or CMCoord, defining this as:

The essential dialogue and interaction between civilian and military actors in humanitarian emergencies that is necessary to protect and promote humanitarian principles, avoid competition, minimize inconsistency, and when appropriate pursue common goals. Basic strategies range from coexistence to cooperation. Coordination is a shared responsibility facilitated by liaison and common training.[11]

However, even within the UN system itself, concepts of civil–military cooperation differ in terms of the importance assigned to the maintenance of humanitarian space. The headline definition adopted by the UN Department of Peacekeeping Operations (DPKO) contrasts with that of OCHA in its rather bland downplaying of the possibility of military encroachment upon humanitarian space, defining CIMIC in terms of a "system of interaction, involving exchange of information, negotiation, de-confliction, mutual support, and planning at all levels between military elements and humanitarian organizations, development organizations, or the local civilian population, to achieve respective objectives".[12]

Whereas OCHA's CMCoord concept makes a positive feature of its attempt to limit the degree to which humanitarian imperatives are subordinated within civil–military coordinating structures, it contrasts strongly with the almost imperialistic overtones of definitions used by several international and national military establishments. The general failure to provide definitions of CIMIC that seek unambiguously to guarantee humanitarian space is problematic in a number of ways, particularly because it does not firmly close the door to behaviour that protects humanitarian principles. Increasingly, national armies are developing CA capabilities to manage CIMIC. In part, these reflect the genuine demands of contemporary multidimensional military operations, but they also reflect a type of institutional mimicry explored later in this chapter. These new civil affairs organizations have developed reinforcing bureaucratic and personal interests, leading them to demand a strong profile, role and status within operations that are often readily accepted by their parent armies as being fully in accordance with a predetermined "cognitive script". (The phrase "cognitive script" is employed to describe themes, thoughts and conclusions that are employed or arrived at habitually and influence our decisions and actions. They are not usually used consciously.) These aspirations are leveraged by other factors (the military monopoly of information on security, control of road routes, sea and airport control and access to needs assessment information in particularly dangerous and volatile areas) to provide them with the means for "encroachment" through controlling access and information flows. These largely bureaucratic pressures for military "growth" are reinforced by other factors, in particular the concept of "integrated mission" structures.

Peacekeeping and the "integration" debate

Although the concept of integrating politico-military and humanitarian responses within peacekeeping missions is the dominant *concept* within the United Nations, particularly within the DPKO, there is actually no dominant *organizational* model. The key organizational principle is the placement of the humanitarian, military and political responses under the Special Representative of the Secretary-General, generally reporting back through the DPKO. The intention is to create a structure that can harness UN efforts in support of the consolidation of peace, and support the creation of stable and viable institutions of governance. This is often mooted as offering three principal advantages. It:

1. facilitates a common strategic vision, harnessing collective, system-wide action;
2. ensures the capacity to rationalize resources and systems (e.g. procurement, services);
3. allows for overall direct management of UN system resources.[13]

Broadly speaking there are two principal versions of integration. In the maximalist guise, there is no separate identity for OCHA and the United Nations' humanitarian leadership is integrated fully within the overall mission structure. In the minimalist version, OCHA tends to have a separate identity, even though a separate Deputy Special Representative of the Secretary-General (DSRSG) is appointed with responsibilities in this area. It is also fair to say that in most cases the DSRSG is generally at least double "hatted", with both development and humanitarian responsibilities, as well as serving as a focal point for integrating the work of mission field offices.

The "integrated" model (maximalist) is championed largely by the DPKO, and is viewed with far less enthusiasm elsewhere, particularly within the specialized humanitarian agencies, which fear the compromises that it potentially engenders in humanitarian and human rights agendas as well as operational and institutional autonomy. "Organizational" (minimalist) integration threatens to ensure that political agendas drive, rather than inform, decisions on humanitarian assistance. Furthermore, the blurring of distinctions between military and humanitarian responses potentially compromises humanitarian space (and therefore the security of agencies) and the perceived independence and impartiality of responses.

The UN missions in Liberia and Côte d'Ivoire highlight the latter issue. In Liberia, peacekeeping troops have engaged in "hearts and minds" activities (including small-scale food distributions[14] and budgeted for approximately US$1 million annually). However, previously, troops of the cease-fire monitoring group of the Economic Community of West African States (ECOMOG) used humanitarian assets such as transport and communications systems in order to facilitate routine military missions while supporting humanitarian programmes generally only in order to facilitate mission legitimacy. Furthermore, several NGOs have routinely used military (logistical and medical) assets to pursue essentially humanitarian objectives. The United Nations Mission in Liberia (UNMIL) has also directly, albeit inadvertently, linked the *security* and *humanitarian* agendas through engagement in Security Sector Reform, particularly the disarmament, demobilization and reintegration processes.[15] This involved food distributions linked to the withdrawal of weapons. There are also occasions when UNMIL contingents, engaging in hearts and minds activities, have failed to coordinate sufficiently. Raj Rana records one occasion on which the International Committee of the Red Cross (ICRC) chose to withdraw its assistance to a hospital once an UNMIL battalion began, unilaterally, to support it.[16]

The blurring of roles and institutional responses may ultimately have negative consequences. There was a possibility that the Liberian elections, which took place in 2005, would be opposed, raising the possibility that the United Nations would employ force or other enforcement measures. Equally, the breakdown in relationships between French and UN peacekeeping troops and the Ivorian Army in late 2004 raised similar difficulties in Côte d'Ivoire. In such circumstances, as well as in the context of an integrated mission structure, drawing distinctions between the responsibilities, mandate and actions of humanitarian actors and the UN politico-military strategy obviously becomes increasingly difficult – with obvious implications for humanitarian space and independence.

Such difficulties are amplified by the increased probability that force will be used in peace support operations as (particularly) western states have moved away from the application of consent-based doctrinal frameworks in volatile environments. Largely as a consequence of the fragility of the concept of consent, and the controversies its failure creates, states such as the United Kingdom have sought to apply a concept of "peace enforcement" (PE) between traditional consent-based peacekeeping and war-fighting operations. Peace enforcement emphasizes the application of "impartiality" rather than consent, endeavouring to create conditions in which "legitimate" force can be employed by the "Peace Support Force". Philip Wilkinson, one of the authors of this approach, concluded that:

A new doctrine of impartial PE has been designed around an international consensus to ensure that military forces do not become party to a conflict but use a combination of coercion and inducement to create the conditions in which other diplomatic and humanitarian agencies can build peace.[17]

Amongst many others, this "compellence" approach[18] has been echoed in the US Army's Field Manual 100-23, *Peace Operations*,[19] and in French, Swedish and NATO peace support doctrines.[20] It also influenced the Brahimi Panel's report on the reform of UN peacekeeping.[21] Brahimi's Panel stressed that "consent", "impartiality" and the use of force only in self-defence "should remain the bedrock principles of peacekeeping". It also identified that the result of consent-maintaining techniques, maintaining "equidistance" between the parties where one party to the peace agreements is incontrovertibly "violating its terms", can "in the best case result in ineffectiveness and in the worst may amount to complicity with evil". Brahimi's conclusion was a call for the Security Council to show a greater willingness to distinguish "victim from aggressor" and to call upon the Security Council to provide UN troops with the wherewithal to defend themselves. The report specifically called for missions that are larger and more powerful, with credible forces operating with "robust rules of engagement" and mandates that "specify an operation's authority to use force".[22]

The convergence of peacekeeping doctrines on more robust approaches, combined with the increasing prevalence of integrated missions, is likely to have profound and unintended consequences in terms of the maintenance of humanitarian space generally.

Afghanistan and CIMIC

By far the greatest perceived challenge to humanitarian space has arisen from the integration of military, political, reconstruction and humanitarian responses in Afghanistan. These have been integrated both at the level of the United Nations' original Integrated Mission Task Force in New York and at the field level in the UN Assistance Mission in Afghanistan (UNAMA). Also, both the NATO-led International Security Assistance Force (ISAF) and the US Operation Enduring Freedom (OEF) combat forces have employed "integrated" civil–military Provincial Reconstruction Teams (PRTs). Arguably, and notwithstanding the enormous controversy that they have generated, these latter structures represent the epitome of CIMIC and "integrated" structures, combining security, reconstruction, humanitarian and diplomatic responses within one overarching, tactical-level and operational (as opposed to planning and management) structure.

Criticisms of PRTs tend to revolve around three broad themes. "[F]irst, that the military does development work poorly; second, that the military's focus on minor reconstruction projects through PRTs is an inefficient use of resources; and third, that PRTs contribute to the blurring of the lines between military and humanitarian actors, thereby potentially increasing the risk to NGO staff in the field."[23] Barbara Stapleton's excellent analyses provide useful summaries of NGO objections, suggesting that the PRTs' essentially "politically" driven approach to both humanitarian assistance and reconstruction programmes is fundamentally at odds with the principles upon which humanitarian assistance should be provided: namely that it should be provided in a neutral and impartial manner and on the sole basis of need. She also highlights a range of practical oppositions – that they duplicate NGOs' services, compete for funding, are less cost effective and, as a consequence of the militaries' lack of training and expertise, increase the probability of harmful side-effects and damage to the relationship between NGOs and local communities. Furthermore, many NGOs have argued that PRT encroachment upon humanitarian space has dangerous consequences in terms of humanitarian space and NGO security.[24]

The impact of Provincial Reconstruction Teams on NGO insecurity

NGO security has definitely declined since the fall of the Taliban. In August 2003, Mullah Omar famously described the United Nations and "western aid groups" as the enemy. Added to this, the number of aid workers targeted by insurgents has steadily grown. However, establishing a direct *causal* link between the existence of PRTs and the erosion of humanitarian space is enormously difficult. The fact of NGO insecurity is not disputed, but its causality most certainly is. Senior ISAF and coalition commanders tend to portray it as an inevitable product of the logic of the insurgency, focusing on the insurgents' decisions to hit softer, civilian targets associated with the political end-state pursued by the Karzai government, rather than any supposed effect induced by the existence of PRTs.

Nevertheless, the blurring of politico-military and humanitarian responses by PRTs has been profound. OEF and ISAF PRTs have combined "hearts and minds" and humanitarian operations. US and coalition Special Forces have engaged in simultaneous combat and "hearts and minds" operations and OEF PRT activity has frequently preceded and continued alongside combat operations.[25] The scale of this activity has also been significant. By February 2004 the coalition claimed to have been involved in the reconstruction of some 125 schools, 82 wells and 50 health facilities across seven provinces. They have also participated in and even driven the overall needs assessment process, sending representatives to the range of meetings between the Afghan government officials and the NGO community and collating information for the Afghanistan Information Management Services project managed by the United

Nations Development Fund. As a consequence, PRTs are widely viewed as exerting an undue influence on information flows as well as being seen as deeply enmeshed in the setting and communication of priorities. Equally, the direct provision of humanitarian assistance by (particularly US) PRTs clearly breaches the "spirit" of a range of existing "military-humanitarian" guidelines, all of which stress the *in extremis* and civilianized control of the provision of assistance.[26]

The direct links among combat, reconstruction and humanitarian action have been particularly controversial. The *New York Times* covered the activities of a US combat patrol (from Ghazni) using humanitarian assistance as leverage to extract information on al-Qaeda and the Taliban, quoting US Lieutenant Reid Finn as stating that "the more they help us find the bad guys, the more good stuff they get".[27] Equally, there have been inadvertent links between PRT action and humanitarian or reconstruction work. Christian Aid, for example, records how, within two days of the completion of a 12 kilometre rebuild of a road to Ghazni, PRT members rented a house at the end of the road, giving the impression of a direct link between them and organizations involved in construction.[28]

The blurring of politico-military and humanitarian responses has also been brought on by other factors, particularly the reliance by the US military and UNAMA on commercial logistics, reconstruction and private security companies. This results in the blurring of distinctions between civilian non-combatants and the combatant community. Equally, there have been pressures blurring such distinctions from the civilian side. Also, NGOs, taking advantage of reconstruction money, have proliferated. Before 11 September 2001, there were some 220 national and 80 international NGOs (INGOs) operating. These figures have expanded to over 1,500 national NGOs and 500 INGOs. National NGOs have subcontracted reconstruction work from PRTs, INGOs and "for profit" organizations such as the Louis Berger Group – eroding distinctions between profit-based, politically motivated and exclusively humanitarian responses. This makes it very difficult to identify and separate the international political, military, cultural, commercial and humanitarian responses to a crisis and creates a sense of a multidimensional "western" engagement.

Equally, many humanitarian organizations have found it difficult to separate their own humanitarian and essentially politicized responses. There is a clear dividing line between those agencies that view the ISAF/UNAMA/Afghan authorities as a belligerent party to the conflict (e.g. Médecins Sans Frontières and ICRC) and those that view them as enjoying a legitimate status derived from their own sovereignty or the United Nations' legitimacy. The latter position leads them to advocate policies that strengthen the status of the Afghan central state structures and

UNAMA's capacities to support this – such as calls for the extension of ISAF beyond Kabul[29] and vocal criticisms of the failure to contain the growth of poppy production.

Nevertheless, many of the international NGOs have consistently sought to avoid blurring wherever possible. In particular, agencies of the UK Steering Committee for Humanitarian Response and the Agency Co-ordinating Body for Afghan Relief limit their interaction with ISAF and OEF military forces, avoid using military assets, share only information that relates to security and are critical of military involvement in humanitarian assistance that falls outside of established guidelines. However, the creation of an "organizational" continuum from US combat-related "hearts and minds" activities through to ISAF PRTs' reconstruction work and NGO-managed humanitarian assistance projects increases the possibility that humanitarian and political objectives would be viewed as inextricably bound together – potentially making more likely the type of response espoused by Mullah Omar.

PRTs' impact on NGO acceptance strategies

Humanitarian agencies have also encountered difficulties in gaining or maintaining acceptance by Afghan communities, with some agency staff ascribing this to the militarization of reconstruction and assistance strategies. Although it is difficult to prove such a *direct* causal link, it is clear that many agencies lack the degree of active support of community leaders that they find in other regions. Although elements of this are attributable to the overall weakness of Afghan civil society, it also results from a negative image of NGOs generally. Minear implies that this may have arisen from the behaviour of some elements of the humanitarian community itself during the Taliban period:

> There have also been serious lapses of professionalism in the form of offensive individual and collective behavior which has undermined not only effectiveness but also credibility. The widely observed consumption of alcohol (albeit on private premises) by international staff, insensitivity to the lack of separation of the sexes in agency living quarters, the high profile of female officials, and the derision often expressed in public of Taliban edicts give international assistance providers – and the assistance provided – an unnecessarily provocative profile.[30]

More recently, the NGO community has been publicly undermined by elements within the Kabul authorities who, seeking to establish themselves as a credible provider of services, have portrayed NGOs as operating on a much larger scale than they really did and as taking financial advantage of the system.

The quality of military development work

A further difficulty with the PRT concept stems from the perceived and general ineffectiveness of military-led reconstruction and humanitarian work. Clearly, the 1990s witnessed an increasing military involvement in the direct delivery and provision of humanitarian assistance. Nevertheless, there is a clear consensus within the humanitarian community that humanitarian assistance has not been dealt with effectively by the military. Pugh argues that:

> military personnel are not ideally suited to humanitarian work; they lack training, expertise and appropriate policy configurations for building local capacities and accountability to local populations; above all, military acts are inherently political and usually connote partisanship – in contrast to traditional "humanitarianism", which is idealized as morally autonomous and not politically conditioned or imposed.[31]

On the other hand, he continues: "it is [not] feasible simply to rule out military involvement in relief". At times this may be indispensable. For example in 1999, when the combination of Yugoslav ethnic cleansing and NATO bombing led to large-scale civilian displacement, NATO's role in the construction of refugee camps was of critical importance. Furthermore, the military *can* play a vital role in circumstances where the humanitarian community cannot gain access (for security reasons) or where the scale of the crisis or the speed of onset overwhelms the humanitarian community. Peacekeeping troops' involvement in immediate post-conflict recovery of infrastructure may also be useful in the absence of civilian capabilities. Furthermore, they might also have legal obligations to become directly involved (e.g. in Iraq in 2003 prior to the resumption of governmental and INGO services). The dangers, at least those felt in terms of encroachments upon humanitarian space, tend to arise in circumstances where these military forces are, or may become, potential belligerents and rely upon "militarized humanitarianism" as a force protection strategy.

However, "militarized humanitarian assistance" may be extremely inefficient and, at times, even counterproductive. In the aftermath of the Kosovo refugee crisis, donor states literally threw bilateral development and reconstruction funding at the region, often channelling this through their own national military contingents and frequently with damaging consequences. Over the course of a decade, Kosovar Albanians had constructed a parallel civil society, providing healthcare, media and educational services largely through their own efforts. European and North American bilateral and CIMIC interventions in this context were frequently non-participatory, often superficial, unsustainable and poorly managed. These projects were done "for" rather than "with" local communities and ran the risk of "dispossessing" domestic coping mechanisms and creating fragile dependency cultures.[32] In effect, the western pursuit of political legitimization may have undermined the pursuit of a sustainable peace. This may also be an unintended consequence of PRT activity in Afghanistan. Despite evidence suggesting that some PRTs have made positive contributions to building Afghan state capacity,[33] some commentators warn that donor efforts to coordinate reconstruction efforts more effectively through highlighting the PRT role may ultimately have a detrimental effect on the development of the core Afghan subnational administrative and governance structures. PRTs may create alternative, better-funded and more effective processes that fall outside the Afghan constitutional and state-building processes.

There is also evidence that military assistance is routinely more expensive than that provided by either NGOs or commercial organizations. Military engineers and medical staff routinely apply gold-plated technical standards of assistance despite their formal, but often only declaratory, adoption of the standards of the Sphere Project and the United Nations High Commissioner for Refugees (UNHCR). This has generated well-documented difficulties in handing over programmes such as refugee camp management to the humanitarian community.[34]

The militarization of relief efforts may also have unintended consequences felt in other ways. During NATO's 1999 Kosovo intervention, NATO–humanitarian relationships were generally cordial and NATO troops constructed refugee camps with a view to handing them over to the humanitarian community as soon as possible. This positive relationship was based on a set of implicit assumptions about the justice and legitimacy of the intervention. However, highly visible cooperation with western forces may generate dangerous associations in the minds of belligerents engaged in conflicts elsewhere. For them this raises the possibility that "humanitarian space" and the principles upon which it is based are not a fixed and universally applicable reference point, but rather a confidence trick disguising hidden agendas. These suspicions may be raised by other factors, such as some NGOs' dependence on western donors and the largely western face of humanitarian action. Together they may bring the impartiality and independence of humanitarian action into question.

Further unintended consequences may be felt in terms of the failure to create sustainable projects. NGOs have a "hard won appreciation for the importance of sustainable reconstruction interventions", says CARE's Paul Barker. He continues:

It is not enough to build a school or clinic or well or irrigation system if there is not at the same time equal attention given to creating and empowering the structures at the community level which will ensure the maintenance, operation and equitable use of whatever is being built. NGOs work to ensure real community ownership of a project through joint planning, training and requiring limited cash and/or in-kind contributions. PRTs do not have the time or training to engage communities in a complete and well-thought-out development process. The quick impact-output oriented approach used by PRTs often results in buildings used for purposes other than those intended, wells going idle when pump pieces inevitably break, irrigation projects being designed to serve the fields of an already rich farmer, etc. The fact that military QIPs [quick impact projects] require no community contribution and only superficially engage communities in a development process means that the communities will have little sense of ownership over things built.[35]

Furthermore, there is little training of CIMIC/civil affairs specialists in the promotion of minority groups or women or of approaches that promote equity of access to development resources. CIMIC and civil affairs specialists (both regular and reservist) rarely have appropriate training or backgrounds in development or a genuine understanding of local customs and norms – raising the risk that they will misread local power relations and reinforce forces that are best undermined.

It is with CIMIC projects that require significant community engagement that criticisms tend to emerge most strongly. The Danish Committee for Aid to Afghan Refugees (DACAAR), one of the largest of the NGOs operating in Afghanistan and a specialist in water projects, has identified a range of problems. In particular, PRTs have been unaware of the need to encourage community participation in the design and management of the programmes at all stages or contributions to the construction of these programmes. Wells are frequently sited in order to serve the often wealthier and self-appointed community elders, and there is no creation of a water committee and therefore the wells are not maintained. Similarly, the NGO Ibn Sina records an incident in which a CIMIC team in Paktika province took over a clinic that it had been running for a week. The PRT dispensed free medicines, unaware of the requirement for cost recovery under the Ministry of Health protocols (under which Ibn Sina had been working), thereby compromising Ibn Sina's relationship with many of its erstwhile beneficiaries.

Compared with CIMIC and PRT teams, NGOs tend to take longer to complete projects and require greater commitment from the community (in terms of meetings, labour and even cash). PRTs and CIMIC teams often simply deliver projects (largely out of unsubstantiated claims that it fosters force protection) and rarely engage communities. The absence of cost recovery mechanisms may make them popular and speed implementation, but a price may also be paid by the NGO community in terms of their own programmes and relationships. Raz Mohammed Dalili, executive director of a Christian Aid partner organization in Afghanistan, argues that PRTs "do not engage in good local needs assessment, but set up projects on an ad-hoc, 'pick and choose' basis with no coherence. When other NGOs come, people get tired of the lengthy selection process for projects, and the two approaches become confused."[36] He argues that Afghans have become politically "intelligent" and, as a consequence of living through both the Taliban period and the Soviet occupation, have become "suspicious of external invaders who come claiming to be friends. The Americans think that if they get involved in local communities it is good for propaganda, but in fact the opposite is true. Everyone knows that it is an American idea and not for the benefit of Afghans."[37]

Unregulated military activity may also crowd out humanitarian agencies. The Swedish Committee for Afghanistan (SCA), for example, relates the story of a school in Laghman where it had already laid the foundations and had generated sufficient resources to complete the building. The local PRT commander, apparently under pressure to spend his budget within the financial year, insisted on building another school, forcing the SCA to give up on its project after more than a decade of involvement with this community.

Nevertheless, PRT reconstruction is not without its success stories. Numerous pieces of government infrastructure (Bamiyan University, several governors' offices, police stations and road infrastructure development) would not have been built without PRT efforts and, consequently, many NGOs recognize this as a valuable contribution. However, these are largely "technical" projects that do not require community participation and would not necessarily attract NGO engagement.

The "integrated approach" as organized hypocrisy?

States' pursuit of "policy coherence" through integrating diplomatic, military and humanitarian responses has increasingly been reflected in most western military doctrines – despite the range of potential and actual difficulties. Lipson implicitly provides an insight into why militaries have assiduously pursued such approaches in the face of sustained criticisms and problems. In his study of the application of organizational theory to the evolution of peacekeeping structures, he suggests that these structures are subject to what he describes as "mimetic isomorphism, or modeling under uncertainty". In cases where it is difficult to identify and evaluate output criteria for the measurement of success, success becomes defined in terms of the mimetic evolution of structures and doctrines (isomorphism). In such cases, success is measured in terms of organizational mimicry rather than calculating the specific costs and benefits of particular courses of action. Lipson concludes that the practical consequences of following such cognitive scripts may be the "standardization of suboptimal practices that acquire the status of 'best practices' for reasons of legitimacy rather than performance".[38] In part, this may explain the apparent convergence of CIMIC doctrines and the strong support of "integrated" approaches (as currently framed) despite evidence suggesting that they may often be suboptimal approaches.

PRTs and integrated mission structures are not the only mechanism for reconciling the civil (humanitarian) and politico-military agendas. From a (largely western) military perspective, Civil–Military Operations Centres (CMOCs) are increasingly recognized as the industry standard for institutionalizing civil–military cooperation in all types of military operation (from war-fighting to PSO). CMOCs are one of a range of related coordination structures – Humanitarian Assistance Coordination Centres (HACCs), Humanitarian Operations Centres (HOCs)/Assistance Centres (ACs), Civil–Military Cooperation Centres (CIMIC Centres) – that represent an almost infinite variability in terms of approach, services offered and structures employed. Nevertheless, they all share the idea that they are essentially vehicles for NGO, IO and military interaction and information exchange with varying degrees of provision for host nation and civil community involvement and interaction. Lipson quotes Michael Williams:

> A Civil-Military Operations Centre (CMOC) was established [in Bosnia] in 1993 to share information and make coordination with other agencies, including NGOs, easier. The Centre was to prove a major innovation, and was copied in subsequent peace operations, among them the UN Operation in Somalia (UNOSOM II).[39]

CMOCs and their numerous variants represent essentially optional structures for commanders, to be adopted or adapted according to the prevailing circumstances. Lipson draws from this the idea that this optional status and ad hoc approach represent a failure to institutionalize the idea of civil–military coordination. Many military commanders would be uncomfortable with the *logic* underlying this conclusion. Most modern armies "task organize" military formations and units and the idea of a one-size-fits-all type of institutional arrangement would be anathema. Nevertheless, even doctrine writers such as Philip Wilkinson appear to agree with Lipson's conclusion. Lipson quotes Wilkinson's observation that:

"[w]hile the new doctrinal consensus reflects the broader political, diplomatic, and humanitarian context of PSO, much that is stated on civil–military coordination remains an aspiration, not yet reflected in current practice."[40]

The question then becomes, if this is true, why? There is some evidence that, in both the UK and US experience during the 2003 invasion of Iraq, the civil dimension of military operations was not effectively managed and that the various CMOC structures often did not work particularly effectively. They suffered from a paucity of resources, an ineffective plan and organizational fragmentation. In part, this reflects the issues raised by the belligerent status of the United States and the United Kingdom, but there may also have been other causal factors. Nils Brunsson offers some interesting insights into what these may have been. His research into organizational behaviour leads him to conclude that organizations subjected to strongly conflicting pressures, values, etc. may create declaratory or symbolic organizational charts and underwrite them with alternative, action-centred structures that are often unrelated. For Brunsson, this is a normal (and possibly even healthy) response on the part of organizations to divergent or strongly conflicting norms and demands.[41]

The declaratory structures represent a formal, symbolic and/or ritualized commitment to particular norms or aspirations whereas actual organizational structures reflect the deeper substructure of the relationship and the real demands for outputs that may, or may not, have an action component. Brunsson argues that there is, at times, a pressure to decouple organizational responses and structures and that this pressure is greatest when there are apparently irreconcilable or strongly divergent norms at play. He raises the possibility that structures designed to manage the humanitarian interface (such as CMOCs) may have a function apart from simply seeking purely optimal outcomes. They may also be the product of a cognitive script, a formal commitment to "norms such as inclusiveness and humanitarianism without actually giving NGOs a greater voice, or providing aid more efficiently".[42] In effect, structures of civil–military cooperation may be a part of the symbolism and superstructure of military peacekeeping structures, driven by a normative commitment (or cognitive script dedicated) to the concept of cooperation between militaries and humanitarian organizations, but subject to other pressures, such as combat mission primacy, that actually define the militaries' responses.

Perhaps the key point arising from this discussion is that the increasingly widespread use of CMOC- and CIMIC-type structures does not *necessarily* imply that the humanitarian–military interface is being managed more effectively or that the terms of the relationship between humanitarian and military action have become easier as a consequence.

Conclusion

It is clear that the consequences of civil–military cooperation are still not fully understood or easily managed. In particular, there is a clear requirement to protect humanitarian space and principles more adequately. When the humanitarian imperative meets the dogma of mission supremacy, the former does not simply need to roll over and die.

Although clear limitations need to be in place in order to prevent military encroachment on humanitarian space, Afghanistan has demonstrated that western militaries often lack sufficient knowledge of where the already agreed boundaries lie. More effective mechanisms need to be in place within the militaries to encourage institutional recognition of the *in extremis* involvement of the military in the direct provision of humanitarian assistance and, wherever possible, external military forces should limit their role to the provision of framework security. In circumstances in which the humanitarian community is unable to respond (for security reasons or absence of sufficient capacity), the military may play a useful role in the direct provision of assistance or the immediate restoration of critical infrastructure, but largely as a last resort. In circumstances where the external military may be drawn into belligerent action, however defined, it is incumbent upon *both* the humanitarian and the military communities to defend the separation between them. Equally, the militaries' blind acceptance that their participation in reconstruction and humanitarian projects automatically equates to force protection needs to be explored on a case-by-case basis, rather than simply representing the default setting.

Soldiers will also need to be more aware that coordination structures such as CMOCs are not always an appropriate response and that they must be aware of institutional mimicry. Lipson provides a warning, arguing that "according to organizational field theory: 'Early adopters of organizational innovations are commonly driven by a desire to increase performance ... [But as] an innovation spreads, a threshold is reached beyond which adoption provides legitimacy rather than improves performance'."[43]

All of the problems do not fall on the military side. There is a clear sense of humanitarianism overextending the objectives of humanitarian action. In particular, some NGOs have realigned their operational responses around robust interpretations of impartiality in order to provide legitimization of their advocacy positions. Although this approach may be understandable, NGOs might benefit from Oliver Ramsbotham's suggestion that international humanitarian law generally, and humanitarian action in particular, are predicated upon the assumption that it is largely possible to separate out political and humanitarian issues.[44]

The humanitarian community also needs to more actively develop structures to counterbalance the "power" of the military and political agendas in integrated structures. Committees serving to guard humanitarian principles and lobby on their behalf are already in existence. In Sierra Leone, several humanitarian organizations have established a committee (comprising various national and international NGOs, donors, UN humanitarian agencies and the ICRC) in order to develop, implement and monitor operational procedures and principles, with the object of opening up humanitarian space. It may be that such committees are simply symptomatic of a problem, but they may also be a major part of the solution. Integration is a process rather than an event, and committees such as these may contribute to keeping the unintended consequences in check. It is also important to maintain the vitality of "fixed" policy reference points such as the "MCDA" and "Oslo" guidelines.[45] Both enshrine principles that can leverage the maintenance of humanitarian space.

Nevertheless, there are dangerous developments. The blurring of commercial, humanitarian, military and political agendas has been reinforced and distorted by the global war on terror's dangerous fusion of the security, failed state and humanitarian strategies. Undoubtedly this has and will continue to complicate CIMIC.

Notes

1. H. Slim, "International Humanitarianism's Engagement with Civil War in the 1990s: A Glance at Evolving Practice and Theory", A Briefing Paper for ActionAid UK, *Journal of Humanitarian Assistance*, 19 December 1997, available at ⟨http://www.jha.ac/Ref/ r021.htm⟩ (accessed 6 November 2006).
2. Ibid.
3. J. Macrae, *Lost in Translation: The Coherence Agenda from Rwanda to Iraq*, March 2003, available at ⟨http://www.odi.org.uk/hpg/meetings/coherence.pdf⟩ (accessed 6 November 2006).
4. F. Abiew, "From Civil Strife to Civic Society: NGO–Military Cooperation in Peace Operations", Occasional Paper No. 39, Norman Paterson School of International Affairs, Ottawa, 2003, pp. 5–6.
5. Slim, "International Humanitarianism's Engagement with Civil War in the 1990s".
6. NATO, Military Committee Document (MC) 411/1 (Final), NATO Military Policy for CIMIC, 17 July 2001, cited in *NATO Civil-Military Co-operation Doctrine*, Allied Joint Publication (AJP), 9 June 2003, p. 1-1, available at ⟨http://www.nato.int/ims/docu/AJP-9. pdf⟩ (accessed 6 November 2006).
7. *NATO Civil-Military Co-operation Doctrine*, p. 1-2.
8. *NATO Civil-Military Co-operation Doctrine*, pp. 1-2–1-3.
9. *NATO Civil-Military Co-operation Doctrine*.
10. US Department of Defense, *Dictionary of Military and Associated Terms*, Joint Publication 1-02, 12 April 2001, as amended August 2002.

11. OCHA, Civil Military Coordination Section, *Guidelines on the Use of Military and Civil Defence Assets [MCDA] to Support United Nations Humanitarian Activities in Complex Emergencies*, March 2003, p. 5, available at ⟨http://www2.apan-info.net/mpat/documents/MCDA%20Guidelines.pdf⟩ (accessed 6 November 2006).

12. DPKO, 10th Standard Generic Training Module (SGTM), "Civil-Military Coordination", 30 June 2003.

13. UN Executive Committee on Humanitarian Affairs, Expanded ECHA Core Group Joint Study, "The Peacekeeping-Humanitarian/Development Interface", 2004, author's copy.

14. United Nations Office for the Coordination of Humanitarian Affairs, Integrated Regional Information Networks (IRIN), "Liberia: Key Northern Liberian Town Faces Relief Crisis", 19 May 2004, available at ⟨http://www.reliefweb.int/w/rwb.nsf/0/89a7aa1f5fc3d78085256e9900705551?OpenDocument⟩ (accessed 6 November 2006).

15. S. Gordon, "The Changing Role of the Military in Assistance Strategies", unpublished mimeograph, Overseas Development Institute, London, 2005.

16. R. Rana, "Contemporary Challenges in the Civil-Military Relationship: Complementarity or Incompatibility?", *International Review of the Red Cross*, 86(855), September 2004, pp. 565–591.

17. Colonel (ret.) Philip R. Wilkinson, "Sharpening the Weapons of Peace: The Development of a Common Military Doctrine for Peace Support Operations", ISIS Briefing Paper No. 18, April 1998, cited in Michael Lipson, "Interorganizational Networks in Peacekeeping and Humanitarian Relief: An Institutional Theory Perspective", paper prepared for presentation at the 2003 annual meeting of the American Political Science Association, Philadelphia, PA, 28–31 August 2003, p. 12, available at ⟨http://alcor.concordia.ca/~mlipson/apsa_proceeding_1687.pdf⟩.

18. T. Schelling, *Arms and Influence*, New Haven, CT: Yale University Press, 1966, p. 2.

19. US Army, *Field Manual 100-23: Peace Operations*, Headquarters, Department of the Army, Washington, DC, December 1994.

20. See, for example, NATO, *Peace Support Operations*, Allied Joint Publication 3.4.1, July 2001.

21. *Report of the Panel on United Nations Peace Operations* (Brahimi Report), UN Doc. A/55/305–S/2000/809, 20 August 2000, available at ⟨http://www.un.org/peace/reports/peace_operations/⟩ (accessed 6 November 2006).

22. Ibid.

23. Personal correspondence with Michael Kleinman, Advocacy Co-ordinator, CARE, Afghanistan, 2005.

24. B. Stapleton, "The Provincial Reconstruction Team Plan in Afghanistan: A New Direction?", Bonn, May 2003, available at ⟨http://www.ag-afghanistan.de/arg/arp/stapleton.pdf⟩ (accessed 6 November 2006); see also B. Stapleton, "Security Developments in Afghanistan", background paper for the Liechtenstein Institute on Self Determination at Princeton University, presented in Vienna, Austria, December 2003.

25. J. Bishop, "War in Afghanistan and Iraq: Aberration, or the Shape of Things to Come", *The Liaison*, 3(2), 2004, available at ⟨http://coe-dmha.org/Liaison/Vol_3No_2/Feat08.htm⟩ (accessed 6 November 2006).

26. See, for example, *Guidelines on the Use of Military and Civil Defence Assets to Support United Nations Humanitarian Activities in Complex Emergencies*.

27. David Rohde, "New U.S. Tactic in Afghanistan Has Old Ring", *New York Times*, 31 March 2004.

28. Christian Aid, "Afghanistan: Caught in the Crossfire", in *The Politics of Poverty: Aid in the New Cold War*, 2004, available at ⟨http://www.christianaid.org.uk/indepth/404caweek/chapter4.pdf⟩ (accessed 6 November 2006).

29. Agency Co-ordinating Body for Afghan Relief, "Afghanistan: A Call for Security", Kabul, 17 June 2003.
30. L. Minear, *Report to the Headquarters Colloquium on the InterAgency Strategic Framework Mission to Afghanistan*, 2003, available at ⟨http://hwproject.tufts.edu/publications/electronic/e_rtth.pdf⟩ (accessed 6 November 2006), p. 6.
31. M. Pugh, "Civil-Military Relations in the Kosovo Crisis: An Emerging Hegemony?", *Security Dialogue*, 31(2), June 2000, p. 236.
32. A. Suhrke, M. Barutciski, P. Sandison, R. Garlock, *An Independent Evaluation of UNHCR's Emergency Preparedness and Response*, Geneva: UNHCR, February 2000.
33. S. Lister, "Caught in Confusion: Local Governance Structures in Afghanistan", AREU Briefing Paper, Kabul: Afghanistan Research and Evaluation Unit, 2005, available at ⟨http://www.reliefweb.int/library/documents/2005/areu-afg-2mar.pdf⟩ (accessed 6 November 2006).
34. Suhrke et al., *An Independent Evaluation of UNHCR's Emergency Preparedness and Response*.
35. Paul Barker, "Why PRTs Aren't the Answer", Institute for War & Peace Reporting, London, 3 November 2004, available at ⟨http://www.globalpolicy.org/ngos/aid/2004/1103prts.htm⟩ (accessed 26 November 2006).
36. Dalili, quoted in Christian Aid, "Afghanistan: Caught in the Crossfire", pp. 49–50.
37. Christian Aid, "Afghanistan: Caught in the Crossfire", p. 50.
38. Lipson, "Interorganizational Networks in Peacekeeping and Humanitarian Relief", p. 12.
39. M. Williams, "Civil-Military Relations and Peacekeeping", Adelphi Paper 321, London: International Institute for Strategic Studies, 1998, p. 37, cited in Lipson, "Interorganizational Networks in Peacekeeping and Humanitarian Relief", p. 13.
40. Wilkinson, "Sharpening the Weapons of Peace", cited in Lipson, "Interorganizational Networks in Peacekeeping and Humanitarian Relief", p. 13.
41. N. Brunsson, *The Organization of Hypocrisy: Talk, Decisions, and Actions in Organizations*, New York: Routledge, 1993.
42. Lipson, "Interorganizational Networks in Peacekeeping and Humanitarian Relief", p. 22.
43. Lipson, "Interorganizational Networks in Peacekeeping and Humanitarian Relief", p. 14, citing Paul J. DiMaggio and Walter W. Powell, "The Iron Cage Revisited: Institutional Isomorphism and Collective Rationality", in Walter W. Powell and Paul J. DiMaggio, eds, *The New Institutionalism in Organizational Analysis*, Chicago, IL: University of Chicago Press, 1991, p. 65.
44. O. Ramsbotham, *Humanitarian Intervention in Contemporary Conflict; A Reconceptualisation*, London: Polity Press, 1996.
45. See OCHA, Civil Military Coordination Section, at ⟨http://ochaonline.un.org/webpage.asp?Page=774⟩ (accessed 6 November 2006).

Part IV

Troop-contributing countries

7

Unintended consequences of peace operations for troop-contributing countries from West Africa: The case of Ghana

Kwesi Aning

There is an underlying liberal assumption that peace operations and the interventions they undertake are necessarily beneficial and helpful to those communities in which they serve. By extension and definition, peacekeepers are perceived as being "do-gooders". Although this is generally true, this perception of peace operations and peacekeepers as "do-gooders" has recently been questioned, and in certain instances challenged, as stories of diverse and sometimes disturbingly excessive atrocities committed by peacekeepers have started to emerge.[1]

The emerging public discourse about the roles, activities and actions of peacekeepers in theatres of peace operations has two facets. First is the gradual exposure of such excesses by individuals within the organizations sending these forces who, through this exposure, hope to generate debates that might result in improved and better oversight of the performance of peacekeepers. Second are the vehement denials and endeavours by affected states to explain these occurrences and, in most instances, to debunk such claims as orchestrated attempts at tarnishing the image of particular states. However, several countries that have engaged in peace operations are now beginning to interrogate and discuss the actions of their troops in different theatres of peace operations both far and near.

One of the countries with a respected and enviable tradition for peace operations internationally is Ghana.[2] As of July 2004, the 10 largest troop contributors to UN peace operations were from developing nations, with Ghana ranking fourth.[3] There is now a generally accepted

Unintended consequences of peacekeeping operations, Aoi, de Coning and Thakur (eds), United Nations University Press, 2007, ISBN 978-92-808-1142-1

perception in Ghana that "if peacekeeping was an exportable commodity, Ghana would have been a rich country by amassing a huge amount of money from it".[4] Since Ghana's first involvement in peace operations activity in Congo-Kinshasa – now Democratic Republic of Congo (DRC) – in the early 1960s, "Ghana has subsequently participated in more than twenty-nine United Nations peace operations around the world". Such peace operations have spanned over 40 years of activities and contributed a total of over 80,000 men and women to this cardinal role.[5]

Under the aegis of UN peace operations alone, 98 Ghanaians have made the ultimate sacrifice of giving their lives in the service of peace.[6] Participation in UN peace operations has included different activities, such as undertaking military patrols, providing civilian police officers, electoral observers, de-miners, cease-fire monitors, and humanitarian aid workers, fighting rebel forces and collaborating with private military contractors. According to Margaret Novicki, a former director of the UN Information Centre in Ghana, "few [states] can boast of Ghana's consistent and steadfast willingness to answer this call".[7] Ghana's participation in international peace operations is a political decision, perceived as furthering the national interest and contributing to the attainment of global peace. However, there is no doubt that such participation also impacts unintentionally on troop-contributing countries. In the case of Ghana, it reduces economic hardship among troops and helps keep them "on track" and away from potential domestic mutinies. But is this all that there is to Ghana's peace operations activities?

In this chapter, I argue that such international exposure through subregional (Economic Community of West African States – ECOWAS), regional (African Union) and global (United Nations) peace operations duties has had an immense impact on the Ghana Armed Forces (GAF) and, since 1995, on the Ghana Police Service (GPS). Public discourse about Ghana's participation in such UN peacekeeping operations, and since August 1990 in the ECOWAS intervention schemes in Liberia and Sierra Leone, has normally focused on the intended or expected spin-offs from such participation. As a result, the overarching aims of Ghana's outside engagement have usually been phrased in typically identical terms: either "to [contribute] to lay[ing] the foundation for lasting peace"[8] or to "restore peace and order".[9] There is hardly any discussion (or, if there is, certainly not in the public domain) about the "unintended consequences" of Ghana's international peace operations activities arising from such involvement. In this chapter, the emphasis will be on the two key components of these activities that deal with the impact of such international exposure on: (a) the GAF as an institution; and (b) the rank and file of individuals who participate in these activities.

I shall undertake a comparative evaluation and analysis of the peace operations missions of Ghana, Nigeria and Senegal as a means of understanding and appreciating the unintended consequences and spin-offs arising from such peace operation activities. Although the main focus is on Ghana, the cases of Nigeria and Senegal will as much as possible be applied as controls to contrast and compare with the information gathered on Ghana to examine the extent to which Ghana's experiences are either similar to or dissimilar from those of these other countries. I will not undertake a strict account of such consequences in terms of the individual peace operations in which these countries have participated; rather I will apply a thematic approach. This approach analyses the multiple ways in which Ghana, a state that since the mid-1970s has been characterized by severe resource stringency, has managed to utilize peace operations to attain specific as well as unspecified results. To this end, some of the themes I will be examining are the multiple and differentiated methods through which Ghana's participation in peace operations has become both a resource-generating endeavour for the state and, for the individuals involved, a scheme to supplement or generate an income. Especially for individuals, such outcomes have critical and distinguishing impacts on domestic economies (both national and individual) in multiple ways.

Although these mutually reinforcing processes are still in operation, the resource-generating aspect of peace operations for Ghana has moved into a higher gear with the acquisition of critical weapons that revert to the GAF after particular operations under the Wet Lease system.[10] Although this system enables the replenishment of military stocks and, in some cases, legitimizes military expenditure in Ghana in terms of particular military acquisitions, it also opens new vistas for potential misunderstandings relating to military acquisitions during such peace operations.[11]

Two consequences of peace operations, which are almost unwritten and unspoken about, deal with what in popular parlance have become known as ECOMOG (ECOWAS cease-fire monitoring group) babies – the products of relationships between locals and internationals in theatres of peace operations – and the impact of HIV/AIDS on these troops. Especially in the case of the latter, two dynamics apply: there is the distinct possibility of troops infecting recipient communities with the virus; and, inversely, there is the potential for troops serving in high-prevalence countries to get infected.

This is not a comparative chapter, but it may be useful to discuss briefly the impact of Ghana's international experience on its ECOMOG activities and how such interactions impart knowledge to other ECOMOG troop-contributing countries such as Nigeria and Senegal. Although these concerns are widespread, one cannot say that, officially, Ghana has engaged in or undertaken any official evaluations of how its wider international peace operation activities have affected the GAF specifically and the wider country as a whole.[12]

Peace operations and resource stringency: The Ghana case

It has been argued that, for the GAF, the utility of peace operations comes in different forms and shades. Although countries such as Ghana are more than willing to contribute troops for UN peace operations, it must be recognized that, for Ghana and the GAF, international peacekeeping operations have started to raise particular hurdles and difficulties. Some of the difficulties arise from the increasing regionalization of peace operations, which, according to Hutchful, poses particular challenges and complications. He posits that:

> This shift in the nature of peacekeeping is imposing unaccustomed strain on regional and domestic resources, as poor countries are forced to *divert scarce resources* into peacekeeping with little hope of compensation by the UN or the international community.[13]

There are several critical points here. First, there is the argument that there has been a definite shift in emphasizing and giving key roles to regional and subregional players in international peace operation interventions.[14] Secondly, there is the implicit assertion that scarce domestic resources are diverted into peace operation endeavours.[15] Finally, there is the contention about the relative uncertainty of Ghana's chances of recouping what it "invests" materially and financially from the UN system. Although aspects of the argument may be tenable, the point about recovery of invested assets from the United Nations is at best tenuous. This inability to use the UN system implies two separate but complementary developments: first, the initial Ghanaian involvement in the Liberian intervention, which reflects Hutchful's points above; and, second, the inability or unwillingness of the Ghanaian authorities to use the available options within the UN system to claim for compensation.[16] The following point has been succinctly made:

> Ghana is currently involved in five peacekeeping missions in Lebanon, Liberia, Sierra Leone, Cote d'Ivoire and the Democratic Republic of Congo (DRC). All these missions have stringent logistic requirements, but Ghana has been able to partially meet these demands. The Wet Lease System only reimburses the equipment meeting the specifications and in working condition. *Ghana loses significant sums of money for her failure to meet these requirements ... The Wet Lease System has, therefore, become a recurring theme on Ghana's military agenda.*[17]

This has, however, changed since 1995. Through the Wet Lease system, Ghana now pre-finances it troops' material needs, to be refunded and compensated for by the United Nations at a later time. A recent typical example of this change of procedure for material acquisition as a contribution to Ghana's peace operations activities was the 2003 acquisition of four helicopters to help with its engagement in peace operations in the DRC. This shift in procedure and the possible controversies that such processes can create domestically are discussed in full below.

In previous years, however, Ghana's peace engagements in the subregion have been used as an excuse to seek external funding to support the structural development of its armed forces in terms of the acquisition of military hardware and the improvement of buildings. A classic example of such disbursement is the Chinese government's provision of "10 million yuan to assist the Ghana Armed Forces (GAF) to acquire military hardware". This support was extended because of the "GAF['s] role in peacekeeping operations, particularly around the West Africa sub-region".[18] The exploitation of Ghana's peace operation history to attract external support and funding demonstrates the deeper structural and financial constraints faced by the GAF and opens the country to potential political manipulation by its financial and material benefactors. This is because Ghana perceives peace operations as purely political and humanitarian ventures and hardly exploits the Wet Lease system and the self-sustaining options for the business opportunities that it provides. According to a February 2005 newspaper report, China's rationale for donating equipment worth US$2 million was "Ghana's consistent adherence to China's policies and common concern in international affairs".[19]

For the GAF, funds accruing from peace operations are vital for the upkeep of the armed forces in different ways, including paying for basic acquisitions such as land. Budgetary constraints have made it impossible for the Ministry of Defence (MoD) to pay land compensations, which have accrued since the First Republic (1957–1966). As a result, the cumulative debt resulting from non-payment for land in 2004 totalled 75 billion cedis.[20] A typical case in point is the GAF's acquisition of 271 acres of land for the establishment of the 60th Artillery Regiment at Ho in the Volta Region, which is still not paid for.[21]

Ghana has also made peacekeeping into a veritable resource-generating phenomenon. Although the financial resources accruing to Ghana are earmarked for the GAF, they eventually get to the Government of Ghana (GoG). In 2003, the US government provided an additional sum of US$4 million in support of Ghana's peace initiatives in the West African sub-region. This was in response to an earlier request to the United States and European states for assistance for the ECOWAS monitoring mission in Côte d'Ivoire.[22] Furthermore, under the African Contingency Operations Training Assistance (ACOTA) programme, the United States has supplied over US$3.4 million worth of training equipment to the GAF. The training capabilities and equipment provided through ACOTA have helped the GAF in training peace operations contingents to support UN operations in the DRC, Liberia, Lebanon, Sierra Leone and Côte d'Ivoire.[23] Although not explicitly stated, there is no doubt that, for a military with the historical burden of intrusion into Ghana's body politic, peace operations are increasingly serving as a diversionary strategy to keep the military from domestic mutinies.[24]

The process for helicopter acquisition

The acquisition of military assets, either for peace operations or primarily for utilization by the GAF, is not usually subject to public debate. Nonetheless, since the Fourth Republic of 1992, there has been an improvement in terms of transparency, public debate and access to information. This does not, however, pertain to all acquisitions. An example of this is the acquisition of helicopter assets for Ghana's peace operation activities in the DRC.

Because of the nature of the process through which these helicopter assets were procured, there was no public bidding process or competition among different arms manufacturers.[25] However, with the deepening of the democratic ethos in Ghana, and the improvement in the conditions for investigative journalism and a more active parliament, other procurement processes since the reintroduction of democracy in 1992 have resulted in more open "competitive" tendering processes.

In this particular case, in January 2003 Ghana's parliament approved a US$55 million budget for the Ministry of Defence to "acquire equipment including helicopters to facilitate Ghana's participation in UN peacekeeping operations" in the DRC.[26] These included four Mi-17-V5 transport helicopters, of which two were to be used for the UN operations and two kept for the GAF. The original estimated cost for these helicopters was US$14.64 million, with "contract provision made for the training of ... personnel as well as spares and tools [for] US$5 055 600 million. The total contract sum therefore amounted to US$19 695 600".[27]

The main issue here was that, on 20 August 2002, the MoD signed an agreement with Wellfind Ltd, a UK company, for the supply of four Mi-17-V5 helicopters, spares and flight training. Wellfind subsequently signed an agreement with Kazan helicopters, a Russian manufacturing company, for the supply of these helicopters, spares, tools and flight training on 24

September 2002. However, before deliveries could be made, the MoD realized that the contract process "had developed some problems". The MoD therefore decided to suspend the contract "due to some unanticipated financial circumstances beyond its control".[28] According to the MoD, "it became imperative ... to take steps to ensure that the national interest was not compromised as a result of the disagreements between the two companies".[29] As a result of this suspension, the minority in parliament criticized the "suspen[sion of] a contract ... without due process of law"[30] and raised the spectre of possible corruption in the procurement process. Parliamentarians and several newspaper editors raised concerns about what was widely perceived as an unexplained increase in cost outlays and the general necessity for these acquisitions.[31]

For example, the minority party in parliament, the National Democratic Congress (NDC), made allegations of corruption in the procurement process.[32] The leader of the NDC opposition, John Attah Mills, also described the circumstances in which these purchases were being made as "bizarre" and justified his personal and his party's concern and criticism about the need to "raise serious concerns for public attention and discussion [since] this transaction is [not] in the public interest".[33] However, the leader of the opposition party has so far not indicated what this expenditure could have been used for. Kwame Addo-Kufuor, the sector minister, in responding to the NDC's criticism of the wholly untoward cancellation of the Wellfind/Kazan contract, argued that the suspension had come about "due to some unanticipated financial circumstances beyond its [MoD's] control". The MoD promised that it "would in future ... revisit the contract when our finances improve".[34] In spite of the media and political criticism, the MoD argued that the procurement process, prior to its abrupt abrogation, had been "guided by the policy of transparency and adherence to the laid down procedures in the procurement of military hardware in all its transactions [and] that the [MoD] had sought to protect state resources so that there will be no financial loss to the state".[35]

However, public knowledge about the suspension of this helicopter deal can hardly be related to the sector minister's penchant for openness. On the contrary, he is known for his strong opposition to being open to the general Ghanaian public with respect to military expenditure, and is on record as asserting that, "though the military is subjected to civilian authority, there is a limit to which military spending should be exposed to the public".[36] Therefore, public knowledge about this helicopter deal is a consequence of great assiduity by parliament and the media, certainly not the MoD's desire to be forthcoming with information. The MoD has, since the exposure of these dealings, revised plans for the purchase of these helicopters by insisting that it will deal only with Rosoboron Export, yet another Russian company.

Although the process through which these four helicopters were acquired and delivered to the GAF has generated controversy, it is possible not only that their presence has contributed to helping Ghana perform its peace operations in the DRC creditably, but that they have certainly enhanced Ghana's chances of fully satisfying the UN criteria for provision of equipment under the Wet Lease system.

Impact on individual resource mobilization

Over the past three decades, Ghana has participated in 29 peace operations all over the world. As a result, the GAF is internationally recognized as a capable force for peace operations. One impact of such peace operations activities on the GAF has been the perception among the troops that participating in peace operations is an irrefutable way of improving one's financial situation. Thus, being selected to participate in such a force has become a major *raison d'être* for members of the GAF to stay in the forces and implicitly serves as both a restraint and an incentive to individuals in the armed forces. Although, as is discussed later, the selection process is fraught with its own problems, for the military top brass such involvement and the rotation of large numbers keep the armed forces in check.

However, what is probably seen to be more important is the extra income that accrues to those who are selected. While these officers and men are on mission, all their pay and allowances due to them in Ghana are paid in full by the MoD. During their stay in the theatre of operation, they are given a daily allowance of US$20 out of the US$32 paid by the United Nations. Finally, upon the completion of the mission, all goods and services that are freighted or shipped into Ghana are brought in duty free. It is fairly common knowledge that the convertible currency earned is normally used to purchase trade goods, which are sold in Ghana for a good profit. Those who have managed to invest their peacekeeping funds profitably have subsequently purchased plots of land, built houses, purchased household goods and generally sent their children to better schools and improved their standard of living. Being chosen to participate in peace operations has become synonymous with an improvement in one's standard of living. This leaves no doubt that the process of getting selected is competitive.

If military personnel perceive participation in peace operations as a major input into the private economies of participating soldiers and the state with the salaries paid, then it is not surprising that the officers of the Ghana Police Service (GPS) who serve under the United Nations equate their service and its remuneration as a "goldmine".[37] Under such peace operations, officers earn mission service allowances of US$100–135 per day depending on the volatility of the conflict area. But such opportunities for improved earning power also open the potential for corruption in the selection of officers for such UN peace operations. Allegations of favouritism, nepotism and lack of transparency in the selection processes have already started to emerge.[38]

According to one report, the "officers that were tasked to supervise the selection process of the officers for the AU [African Union] mission have allegedly turned the process into a lucrative business for generating quick money for their selfish interest".[39] The selection process is so fraught with falsifications that "after [applicants went] through the selection process blameless, it came as a surprise to a number of [them] when the final list was released most of [them] had [their] names missing while officers who never showed up in the selection process had been short-listed for the mission".[40] In the newspaper story it was reported that this anomaly was corrected when, "after persistent demands, *they were made to do something* [and] their names have re-emerged on the final list".[41] Although this development may seem surprising, the GPS has a history of internal falsification with respect to examinations and promotions. Such incidents have become so problematic that the GoG had to establish what was called an "Enquiry into Promotions within the Police Service" in August 1986. Upon submission of its report (known as the "Tibiru Report"), the GoG subsequently issued a White Paper.

Selection procedures for participation in UN peace operations in Ghana have created opportunities for a reversal of the previous practices where fraudulent appointments were almost the norm. Now, in the aftermath of complaints about the selection process, the officers implicated in this case were redeployed and the GPS has streamlined its selection process to reflect more transparent selection and rotational processes based on merit.

"ECOMOG babies" and HIV/AIDS

The phenomenon of ECOMOG babies arose as a result of the introduction of the Economic Community of West African States (ECOWAS) cease-fire monitoring group (ECOMOG) troops in different theatres of peace operations in the West African sub-region. These forces were first inserted in Liberia and subsequently in Sierra Leone and Guinea Bissau and since January 2003 in Côte d'Ivoire. There are widespread anecdotal stories about the liaisons that were formed between these ECOMOG

Table 7.1 Nexus between HIV prevalence and length of peacekeepers' duty tour

Length of duty tour (years)	Prevalence rate (%)
1	7
2	10
3	15

Source: Based on graph in A. Adefolalu, "HIV Prevalence among Nigerian Troops", paper presented at the Third All African Congress of Armed Forces and Police Medical Services, Pretoria, 1999.

troops, especially Ghanaian and Nigerian troops, with local women in the countries where they served.[42] The departure of these troops and their inability to bring their babies or their liaisons with them have created occasional friction between host states and troop-contributing states.

If ECOMOG babies are problematic, then the impact of HIV/AIDS on troop-contributing countries can be potentially devastating. The degree to which conflicts contribute to the spread of HIV/AIDS is uncertain. Added to this is the fact that the conditions that increase the risk of HIV infection in war zones also make it difficult to gather dependable information. The limited data available nevertheless make for very disturbing reading. One of the few studies on the Nigerian military has argued that HIV prevalence among Nigerian troops is directly related to the numbers of years spent away from home on duty as peacekeepers (see Table 7.1).

This study seems to confirm the results of an earlier study of Nigerian troops returning from peacekeeping activities in West Africa. The study found that infection rates were more than double that of the average for Nigeria overall. More interestingly, the study also found that a soldier's risk of infection doubled for each year spent on deployment in conflict regions, suggesting a direct link between duty in a war zone and HIV transmission.[43] Part of the explanatory dynamic here is the combination of conflict, young men and commercial sex workers, where military culture tends to exaggerate male behaviour. It can therefore be argued that there is a context within peacekeeping activities, and in particular in conflict zones, that contributes to the spread of infectious diseases, including sexually transmitted diseases. Thus, although the apparent infection rates are worrying in all three countries (Ghana, Nigeria and Senegal), there is a high probability that HIV infections may begin to erode and degrade combat readiness.

In Ghana's case for example, it is estimated that the prevalence rate among troops returning from peacekeeping is almost 2 per cent. This is lower than the rate among the general population, which is 3.6 per cent.[44] But the relationship between Ghanaian peacekeepers, HIV infection and national politics goes back to the early 1970s when testing of potential peacekeepers for communicable diseases became mandatory. However, in June 1979 the Armed Forces Revolutionary Council took power in a coup d'état. Medical officers who were perceived to have "failed" potential peacekeepers by finding that they had communicable diseases were chased out of the 37 military hospitals in Accra, in retaliation for having denied soldiers the opportunity to serve and earn extra income. For a period after 1979, all rank-and-file soldiers who went for testing prior to a peacekeeping activity were passed and "therefore people went with diseases and came [back] with more".[45] A similar incident occurred after the coup d'état of 31 December 1981. Since 1994, however, the GAF has made it compulsory for all troops participating in UN operations to be tested for HIV before deployment, and has actually developed and printed a policy document that is given to all soldiers. Because of the new dangers posed to these armies, plans of action have been adopted that seek to:

- reduce the rate of new infection among soldiers by 5 per cent annually through educational and preventive measures,
- ensure that new recruits are HIV negative,
- undertake voluntary, anonymous and confidential testing of military personnel,
- counsel and provide generic medications to sick soldiers,
- provide social and economic assistance to the families and survivors of sick soldiers.

In the general discourse about states that have generally managed to reduce the prevalence of HIV/AIDS among troops, Uganda is perceived to have achieved phenomenal successes by reducing HIV prevalence from 18 per cent in 1992 to 6 per cent in 2003. The statistics coming out of Senegal seem to imply that this West African country has chalked up equally impressive achievements in its fight against this pandemic. According to the head of the Senegalese Armed Forces SIDA-Armee Program, Lieutenant Colonel Mbaye Khary Dieng, "since 2002 we have tested 2000 troops serving abroad and found the prevalence rate in the military to actually be a bit lower than the national figure".[46] The army estimates "our national prevalence to be between 1.4 and 1.7%, while in the army the rate is between 0.94% and 1.09%".[47] This development seems to go against the generally accepted perception, supported by the Joint United Nations Programme on HIV/AIDS (UNAIDS), that, "even in peacetime, sexually transmitted diseases ... among military forces tend to be two or five times higher than the general population, and surge even higher during times of conflict".[48]

The issue of potential corruption

There are several types of possible corrupt practices associated with Ghana's participation in international peacekeeping activities. This section will concern itself with two key issues, namely financial corruption and avenues for corruption in the selection process of officers and men undertaking peacekeeping operations.

Corruption in the management of peacekeeping finances seems to be a major problem in Ghana, Nigeria and Senegal.[49] In terms of the GAF, different types of "protocol" facilities are extended by junior officers to their senior officers, either to get their duty tours extended or to be selected to participate in a peacekeeping operation as a whole. This seems to be a fairly widespread practice in the GAF. Two cases of alleged corruption and financial irregularity in relation to peacekeeping duties will be cited. The first case deals with the dismissal of 20 senior officers in the GAF who had participated in UN peace operations duties in Lebanon in the early 1990s,[50] and the second case deals with a more recent incident involving the GPS in 2003 and 2004.

Probably, the most well-known and well-documented case of corruption away from the anecdotal stories of such incidents involved a Nigerian contingent in Sierra Leone. An internal UN audit report of alleged cases of corruption exposed the huge gap between the rhetoric of peace operation ideals expressed by the United Nations and the reality on the ground in a conflict zone such as Sierra Leone. According to the UN report, the issue revolved around the obstruction of peace moves in Sierra Leone because Nigerian officers and men were enriching themselves through illegal trading in diamonds. Diverse reports alleged that "the Nigerian army was heavily involved in diamonds, false passports, drug-smuggling and other illegal activities".[51] At the very top of this corruption cabal was the leader of the Nigerian forces in Sierra Leone, Brigadier-General Maxwell Khobe, nicknamed "Ten Million man" for allegedly accepting large sums of money from the Revolutionary United Front of Sierra Leone (RUF/SL) to allow them to operate. In spite of this damning report, there was also acceptance that "[a]gainst the corruption has to be balanced the fact that the Nigerians [i.e. the army] are one of the most effective fighting forces in Sierra Leone, with the most success in taking on the rebels".[52] Subsequent to the release of this report, written by the Indian commander, General Vijay Jetley, the simmering misunderstandings between Nigerian and Indian forces broke out into the open, leading to the eventual withdrawal of Indian troops.

Potential financial misappropriations: The case of the Ghana Police Service

With respect to the case involving the GPS in early January 2004, several articles appeared on a Ghanaian website alleging that several senior public officials, including the Inspector General of Police, the minister of the interior and other unnamed top government officials, were extorting money "by proxy" from the Ghanaian police contingent on the UN peacekeeping mission in Kosovo.[53] The whole story started when 54 personnel of the Ghanaian police contingent in Kosovo were given a three-month extension after their original duty tour ended. There is some element of controversy and misunderstanding about the "agreement" and the terms of this unusual extension. However, when these 54 officers were given their first post-extension salary, they realized that €500 had been deducted from their salaries. Upon enquiry, the explanation subsequently provided was that these "unauthorized" deductions were to "top government officials back home".[54] After intense pressure exerted on these men by their contingent leaders, it was discovered that Assistant Superintendent of Police (ASP) Garibah and ASP Kontomah had collected a total sum of €27,000.

When these allegations were made public, they sought to attack the integrity of the Inspector General of Police, the minister of the interior, senior police officers, the GPS and the GoG as a whole. Subsequently, the police administration denied any complicity of its senior officers in this corruption scandal. To limit the expanding crisis, the Police Council, which is the constitutionally mandated oversight body of the GPS, attempted to institute an internal inquiry to determine the truth of this damaging allegation.[55] The Police Council, which has 10 members, is the constitutional body responsible for advising the President on matters of policy relating to internal security, including the role and functioning of the Police Service.[56] The Council may, with the approval of the President, make regulations for the performance of its functions and for the effective and efficient administration of the Police Service.[57]

As a damage control measure, the Chair of the Police Council, J. B. da Rocha, issued a statement on 8 January 2003 that, "even though the police administration had responded with a full statement, which denied the allegation, the matter called for a thorough investigation, both locally and on the spot in Kosovo, to ascertain the real source of the story and whether it was true or false".[58] Although promises were made by the

Police Council to publicize the results of its own investigations, almost 18 months after these promises were made nothing had been published. In response to persistent requests for information, different authorities have been involved in shifting the blame for the release of the report between the Police Council secretariat, the Police secretariat and the United Nations. The officers involved in this case are convinced that the reluctance on the part of the Police Council and the Police secretariat to publish their findings is a cover-up and an unwillingness "to clear widespread rumours that those alleged to have collected the monies on behalf of the [senior public] officials had been promoted by the police administration".[59]

There is a further interesting twist to this saga of potential extortion. Two different emphases have been placed on the crux of the matter by the protagonists in the case. First, the police administration is more concerned about finding out how the story about an internal corrupt praxis was placed on the Internet;[60] secondly, the officers who feel robbed are interested in the outcome of the investigation against those who were alleged to have taken their money illegally. In the course of this research, several junior police officers who also served on the mission confirmed that different sums of money were taken under the guise of contributing to a "welfare" or development fund. However, very few returns seem to have been provided from this fund to those who contributed to it. Apparently it was widely known that these sums went to senior officers.[61] The discontent about this "development or welfare fund" centres on the amount of peacekeeping funds it has accrued, who actually controls the "fund" and how it is audited, if at all.

Finally, it is important to deal with the critical role that peace operations play in generating and supplementing incomes for ranking officers. Officers' annual savings on such a mission could easily be more than US$20,000, which is equivalent to a lifetime of savings by Ghanaian standards. It is a generally held opinion that "while we keep the peace, we improve our quality of life", thus indicating the general satisfaction with undertaking such activities.

The case of the Ghana Armed Forces

The following empirically proven examples concerning the GAF straddle two aspects: the processes through which personnel are selected to participate in peace operations, and financial misconduct.

From all indications, some level of corruption frequently occurs in the selection process of officers and men to participate in international peace operations. The procedure for selection is that, if a unit is instructed to provide, say, 734 men, 500 will be selected through the normal procedures and the remaining 234 will be given out as a "Protocol List". Initially, this widely accepted praxis in the selection of officers and men was meant to permit commanders to reward hard-working individuals in their units. Added to this, commanders could also give these officers and men turns to travel. More recently, however, this system has been systematically and widely abused. Although several retired and junior officers confirmed that potentially less qualified personnel were selected to serve on UN peace operations, serving officers were reluctant to accept that this occurred.[62]

What explains the prevalence of this widely accepted practice? According to a retired senior officer, it is almost impossible for a commander to avoid using such patrimonial practices within a unit because, as a commander, you end up creating serious animosity among the rank and file, as well as other institutional difficulties. The Ghana Navy, for example, has 17 such protocol places on any one mission but the number of protocol places available varies for different battalions, normally ranging between 17 and 25 places. For senior commanders, such patronage gives them immense power and access because, if one commands a unit that has not gone out for several years, then the desire to be selected is immense. In one case, a naval officer drove from the naval base in Sekondi to Navy Headquarters to enquire about the chances of being sent out. A civilian staffer got the chance to participate in a peacekeeping operation but gave the allotted place to a naval officer with a tacit agreement to share the proceeds accruing from the salary paid.

The second aspect concerns the manner in which financial gains accruing from peace operations and activities are controlled by senior officers. In this particular case, the estimated financial sum accruing to a particular battalion was calculated and subsequently a percentage of this amount was released to the Commanding Officer (CO), who utilized these sums in two ways. First, a CO and his senior staff would invest the principal sums privately, earning substantial interest that was pocketed by the senior officers, and they delayed releasing the principal to those who deserved it. As a result, instead of paying the monthly disbursements of assessed pay to the rank and file, these sums were kept until the end of a duty tour, which usually lasted between four and six months. When this became known in the late 1980s among the army hierarchy, Lieutenant-General Arnold Quainoo, who was then Army Commander, had all the officers involved in this scam dismissed in one day.

Another area for potential corruption arises from the money due to particular battalions. These calculations are based on assessed but approximate budgets. As a result, whatever surplus may accrue is not returned but used in purchasing goods for senior officers from unit funds. From all indications, the "willingness" of a unit to contribute to the purchase of expensive presents to "sweeten" the officer corps is to ensure and improve the unit's chances of being sent out quickly.

Purchase of the Gulfstream Jet

There is widespread public support for peace operations among Ghanaians, convinced that their men and women deployed around the world are contributing to the attainment of international peace and a reduction in human suffering. However, there is one incident that has brought the profitability of international peacekeeping and the potential for state exploitation of the financial resources accruing to its peacekeepers into question. This is what, in the public mind, is known as the "Gulfstream Jet G-III Scandal" and the conditions surrounding the operation of the Special Reserve Account for peace operation funds.

The Special Reserve Account came about because the United Nations pays Ghana a daily sum in relation to the actual number of men on the ground. The Government of Ghana (GoG) pays every soldier a basic sum of US$20 and the difference in relation to what the United Nations pays Ghana, which essentially becomes a profit for Ghana, is paid into this Special Reserve Account.[63] The initial reason for the establishment of this account was the fact that Ghana needed to pre-finance its involvement in peace operations prior to being reimbursed by the United Nations later. So, the "profits" that were kept in this account were to ease the financial burden on the GoG in pre-financing its troops. Apart from pre-financing troop participation, this special account was also used for the purchase of special equipment for the GAF as and when necessary.

The crux of the story is that, on the day that Ghanaian soldiers were deployed, the money that should have been partly paid to them was used for other purposes. The former finance minister under the erstwhile National Democratic Congress government, Kwame Peprah, instructed Ghana's Controller and Accountant-General to instruct the treasury officer attached to Ghana's UN embassy in New York to transfer two separate sums of money – US$14.5 million and US$1.5 million, respectively, a total of US$16 million. This money was then transferred from the Ghana Mission Peacekeeping account into the account of Gallen Limited, a single-purpose offshore company in the Cayman Islands.[64] This sum of money was supposed to be taken from an escrow account specially set up in New York for the purchase of a presidential jet.[65] According to aviation experts, whereas the actual price of the jet was US$13.5 million, the Ghana government pledged to pay US$17 million.

After the jet was purchased, there was a public outcry and scandal concerning (a) the procedures under which peacekeeping money had been diverted for what was perceived to be frivolous expenditure; and (b) the shady nature of the financial transaction which made Ghana pay considerably more for an ageing jet than its true commercial value. The unfolding scandal had two impacts. First, there were rumblings within the GAF that the rank and file were being cheated out of money that should legitimately be paid to them. Secondly, this led to heated parliamentary debates as the leading opposition party in 1999 and 2000, the New Patriotic Party (NPP), criticized the government and urged it to divulge what appeared to be a dubious financial transaction. As an opposition party, the NPP promised not to use this jet if it came into power. Since winning the December 2000 elections, the NPP has kept its campaign promise: the jet sits on the tarmac and Ghana still meets its financial repayment obligations with peacekeeping funds.

Peacekeeping and private contractors

Probably one of the less glamorous aspects of Ghana's peace operation activities is the collaboration between its peacekeepers and private military contractors or mercenaries. Although this may not necessarily be Ghana's fault, and rather represents new international dynamics relating to the wider discussion of privatization and outsourcing, it certainly does raise questions of morality and ethics in peace operations and the potential impact on national armies. With the emergence of a global trade in hired military services, better known as the privatized military industry, it has been argued that,

> [it] is one of the most interesting developments in warfare over the last decade.... [M]eeting humanitarian needs with private military solutions is not necessarily a terrible or impossible thing. But, it clearly carries both advantages and disadvantages that must be constantly weighed and mitigated through effective policy and smart business sense.... [W]e must be doubly sure of our dealings with private industry. We should not let our frustrations lead us down the dangerous path of privatization without due consideration.[66]

Both Nigeria and Ghana have had extensive dealings with such companies, which has had a far-reaching impact on the military in both countries. Probably the best known of such collaborations was between the Ghanaian and Nigerian armies on the one hand and Executive Outcomes in Sierra Leone.[67] Two obvious effects have been noticed in both countries since this "unholy alliance" occurred in Sierra Leone: first, the increase in the privatization of security in both countries; and, secondly, the exponential growth in the number of companies established by officers who have returned to their respective countries from these encounters, a development that has been characterized as a "growing industry".[68] The privatization of security in Ghana and Nigeria, for now, is associated with high walls, massive gates, *concertino* fencing and uniformed security men who patrol wealthy neighbourhoods, large companies and corporations. In the Nigerian case, it has been argued that

> [t]he private security industry is creating a separate and unequal system under which the rich protect their privileges and guard their wealth from perceived *barbarians* at the gate. Many of the affluent live in enclaves, gated communities, where private security forces control entrances, screen visitors and hired help, and patrol grounds. These guards are accountable not to the public but to the well-manicured hand that feeds them.[69]

The disparate rationales for what these private security forces represent shift from representations of a *nouveau riche* culture to a failure of the state and its inability, along with that of the Police Service, to respond in an adequate and qualified manner to societal needs and security concerns. But the trend towards privatization is increasingly evident and the argument that supports this move is as follows:

> Engaging the private sector to provide public security efficiently, effectively, and relatively cheaply is a logical outgrowth of a neo-conservative theology that preaches that the private sector will do a more competent job ... profiting from what used to be "public works" in many countries.[70]

As to whether the emerging collaboration between peacekeepers and private military contractors will continue and what the potential impact on armies might be, this issue will need more empirical work to establish a clear answer. But, at present, neither Ghana's nor Nigeria's armed forces seem to have benefited in any measurable way from this cooperation.

Assessing other potential dimensions of peace operations on troop-contributing states

In spite of these potentially damaging revelations, on balance the participation of officers from the GPS in peace operation activities has had a positive reverse impact on the service. For example, the core duties performed by GPS officers include monitoring, checking on arms collection to reconcile collected numbers, guiding and guarding bomb squads and contributing to the research and planning of field activities. More importantly, the collaborative processes involved in peace operations ensure that officers from a resource-constrained country such as Ghana are exposed to the use of new equipment and contemporary methods of twenty-first-century policing.[71]

Furthermore, several senior officers were enthusiastic about the institutional cultural change experienced during peace operations. While in Ghana, officers are normally in offices. During peace operations, however, they are actively on patrols and thus acquire a better understanding of the challenges of front-line peace operations. This increased exposure to other cultures and political issues leads to soldiers and policemen learning about human rights, thus bringing this to bear on their work in Ghana.

Conclusion

This chapter has attempted to go beyond the norm of showering praise on peacekeepers and on states contributing to peace operations, by examining the unintended consequences of the processes and mechanisms of their engagement. The picture that emerges, tentative as it is, demonstrates the institutional and political complexities that underlie decisions to participate in such peace operations. I argue for the need for a closer examination of the unintended consequences of such international engagements on troop-contributing states' finances, their armies and the lives of individual officers and men in the recipient states. Although Ghana's continuous peacekeeping is mainly used and perceived as an opportunity for gaining wider front-line training experience and the acquisition of new armaments that would otherwise be difficult to obtain, such engagements also improve the purchasing power of participating officers and men. However laudable these positive aspects are, the possibilities for corruption, intimidation and institutional decay are also present. Although these negative tendencies and developments have not yet reached crisis proportions, the examination of these issues is worthwhile so that they can be confronted before they undermine and tarnish the image of proud and effective UN peacekeeping troop-contributing states.

Notes

1. K. Holt and S. Hughes, "Sex and Death in the Heart of Africa", *Independent Review*, 25 May 2004, pp. 2–4.
2. For the Ghana case, see "Ghanaian Troops Win Praises in Sierra Leone", *Ghanaian Times*, 29 January 2005, p. 1; Emmanuel Kwesi Aning, "The United States and Africa's New Security Order", *Critical Perspectives*, 7, 2001; see also A. Abdoulaye, "Liberia in the Hands of Nigeria and Ghana, Once Again", *The Perspective*, 21 May 2003.
3. Pakistan, Bangladesh and Nigeria are the top three leading contributing states to UN peacekeeping operations. India, Ethiopia, South Africa, Uruguay, Jordan and Kenya follow Ghana, in that order. See T. Deen, "UN Rejects Private Peacekeepers", *Dawn*,

30 August 2004, available at ⟨http://www.dawn.com/2004/08/30/int14.htm⟩ (accessed 6 November 2006).

4. M. Afele, "Peacekeepers are Ghana's Treasured Export", PanAfrican News Agency, 2000, available at ⟨http://www.library.yale.edu/~fboateng/peace.htm⟩ (accessed 6 November 2006).

5. Ibid.

6. Interview with Ghana Armed Forces Information Department, Accra, 14 October 2004.

7. Interview with Margaret Novicki, Accra, 27 August 2004.

8. *Journal of ECOWAS*, 21, 1992, p. 7.

9. OAU, *OAU Conflict Management Review*, Addis Ababa, 1996, p. 4.

10. Wet Lease is the process through which UN member states under agreement provide particular resources and equipment during a particular operation at an agreed price. "Wet" refers to the agreement that the troop-contributing country makes to provide all the necessary equipment and its associated direct support (maintenance, replacement). See *UN Contingent Owned Equipment Manual*, New York, 2002. See also UN General Assembly Resolution 55/274 of 22 June 2001, which adopted the recommendation of the Post-Phase V Working Group. Some of the areas considered under the Wet Lease system include troop costs, major equipment and the ability to sustain the troops.

11. E. Kwesi Aning, "Military Imports and Sustainable Development: The Case of Ghana", paper presented at an OXFAM and Ploughshares Canada seminar, Oxford, UK, 3–5 March 2004, see especially pp. 12–15.

12. The only known work that analyses such impacts on Ghana from a logistical point of view is Julian Nii Adjetey Otinkorang, "The United Nations Wet Lease Logistics System and Challenges for Ghana's Participation in Peace Support Operations", MA (International Affairs) Dissertation, University of Ghana, 2005.

13. Eboe Hutchful, "The Ghana Armed Forces in Liberia", in Greg Mills and Jakkie Cilliers, eds, *From Peacekeeping to Complex Emergencies? Peace Support Missions in Africa*, Johannesburg: SAIIA/ISS Press, 1999, p. 98 (my emphasis).

14. For a succinct discussion of such an issue and the way in which it potentially generates controversy, see Ewen MacAskill, "UN Gets Warning Shot on Peacekeeping – Special Report: Sierra Leone", 9 September 2000, available at ⟨http://www.guardian.co.uk/international/story/0,,366269,00.html⟩ (accessed 7 November 2006).

15. It is impossible to gauge the actual amounts disbursed by Ghana on peacekeeping activities. A close study of the military expenditure estimates presented by the Ministry of Defence (MoD) to parliament does not disaggregate how much of these sums is utilized on peacekeeping activities. For a tentative estimate of the cost to Ghana of the first Liberian war, see Emmanuel Kwesi Aning, "Ghana, Liberia and ECOWAS: An Analysis of Ghana's Policies in Liberia", *Liberian Studies Journal*, 21(2), December 1996.

16. Interview with a retired senior military officer, Accra, 5 June 2004.

17. Otinkorang, "The United Nations Wet Lease Logistics System and Challenges for Ghana's Participation in Peace Support Operations", p. 2 (my emphasis). Because of this inability to meet the specification of the Wet Lease system, "[a] 2001 estimate put Ghana's loss for a two year operation in UNAMSIL at US$2 382 768 due to [Ghana's] inability to meet the self-sustainment criteria stipulated by the UN. This loss could have been redeemed with a business approach to peace support operations and the injection of capital into PSO in order to fully satisfy the UN criteria under the Wet Lease system".

18. Michael Donkor, "China Supports GAF", *Daily Graphic*, March 2004, p. 1.

19. "Vehicles from China for Defence Ministry", *Accra Daily Mail*, 8 February 2005, p. 5.

20. F. Muzzu, "Military Cannot Pay for Parcels of Land", *Daily Guide*, 2 July 2004, p. 4.
21. The regiment was formerly known as the Medium Mortar Regiment. This land acquisition was covered by Executive Instrument 72 of 1964. The GAF's inability to pay for land requisitioned in the 1960s for barracks is increasingly becoming public knowledge. For example, see I. Essel, "Military, Civilians in 40-Year Land Litigation", *Accra Daily Mail*, 10 February 2005, pp. 1 and 3.
22. See "Ghana: USA Provides Additional US$4 million for Sub-Regional Peacekeeping Effort", Ghana Broadcasting Corporation Radio 1, 3 June 2003.
23. "US Ambassador Hands over Equipment to Ghana Armed Forces", *Crusading Guide*, 3–9 February 2005.
24. Interview with senior military official, Accra, 1 March 2005.
25. It is important to understand that the fact that there was no public bidding was not related to Ghana's democratic status. The lack of public bidding reflected the lack of funds to purchase vessels. The British had offered an AMAZON class frigate for £2 million and the Canadians had also offered a vessel for C$1.8 million through a British firm. It is important to note that military procurement is always by selective bidding.
26. Ministry of Defence, "Update on the Supply of Helicopters to the Ghana Armed Forces by Wellfind Ltd.", confidential memo, January 2003, p. 1.
27. Ibid., p. 2.
28. Ibid., p. 4.
29. Ibid., p. 3.
30. See *The Insight*, 3–4 September 2003, p. 8.
31. The *Insight* newspaper was particularly vocal in questioning (a) the need for such a purchase, and (b) the cost outlays for these procurements. Almost all its publications in September 2003 had an article or two about this transaction. See, for example, "Minority on Supply of Four Helicopters", *The Insight*, 3–4 September 2003, p. 8.
32. "Minority Responds to Defence Minister", *The Insight*, 10–11 September 2003, p. 8.
33. "Mills Wades into Helicopter Deal", Myjoyonline.com, 19 September 2003, available at ⟨http://www.myjoyonline.com/ghananews.asp?p=3&a=6516⟩ (accessed 7 November 2006).
34. Part of the minority's concern was that this letter alleging the suspension of a legally binding contract owing to financial constraints was not copied either to the Ministry of Finance or to the Parliamentary Select Committee on Defence and Interior, although the approval had been granted by parliament and the money transferred to the MoD. See "Minority Responds to Defence Minister", *The Insight*, 10–11 September 2003, p. 8.
35. This is a politically loaded statement because the phrase "causing financial loss to the state" has, since April 2003, been in vogue in Ghana and refers to the procedures whereby public officers who are found to have been remiss in their duty and thus caused avoidable financial loss to the state can be imprisoned. See "The Republic of Ghana vs. Kwame Peprah and three others", *Daily Graphic*, 26 September 2003, pp. 20–21.
36. A. K. Salia, "Military Spending Can't Be Exposed", *Daily Graphic*, 28 February 2001, pp. 16–17.
37. T. Fosu, "Scandal Rocks Police Heads", *Daily Guide*, 4 March 2005, p. 1.
38. Ibid.
39. "Police Boil over Recruitment Exercise ... for AU Peace Mission in Sudan", *Ghanaian Chronicle*, 4 March 2005.
40. Ibid.
41. Ibid.
42. F. Olonisakin and E. Kwesi Aning, "Humanitarian Intervention and Human Rights: The Contradictions in ECOMOG", *International Journal of Human Rights*, 3(1), 1999.

43. This study was undertaken by the Civil-Military Alliance to Combat HIV/AIDS, cited in Michael Fleshman, "AIDS Prevention in the Ranks", *Africa Recovery*, 15(1–2), 2001, p. 16.
44. Interview with retired senior commander, Accra, 25 June 2004.
45. Ibid.
46. See N. Crockett-Ntonga, "Senegalese Army Shows Success with HIV/AIDS Program", *The Bulletin*, 3(1), February 2005, p. 1.
47. Ibid., p. 4.
48. Ibid., p. 1.
49. These are not the only states to have experienced some level of corruption in the management of peacekeeping finances. In Sierra Leone, a crisis within peacekeeping forces resulted in the overthrow of the Joseph Momoh regime by Captain Valentine Strasser. Similarly in The Gambia, Yaya Jammeh overthrew Dauda Jawara in a coup d'état. In October 2004, a mutiny occurred among 600 Guinea-Bissau troops who had returned home from nine months of UN peacekeeping operations in Liberia; this resulted in "the killing of General Verissimo Seabra, the chief of the armed forces, and Colonel Domingos de Barros, its head of human resources". The mutineers complained that "they were still owed special payments associated with the mission, which ended in July, along with other pay arrears. They also aired grievances about poor living conditions in military barracks and rampant corruption in the upper echelons of the armed forces." See "Yet Another Soldiers' Mutiny", at ⟨http://www.irin.org⟩ (accessed 9 October 2004).
50. Interview with Lieutenant General Arnold Quainoo, former Commander, GAF, 11 August 2004.
51. MacAskill, "UN Gets Warning Shot on Peacekeeping".
52. Ibid.
53. O. Garblah, "Blackmail & Extortion in Kosovo", *Ghanaian Chronicle*, 5 July 2004, p. 1; also available at ⟨http://www.ghanaweb.com⟩ (accessed 7 November 2006). One of the individuals accused in this story subsequently accused Ghanaweb of "wrong[fully] ... us[ing] the name 'Ghana' because it creates the impression that the website is the official national website". This idea was immediately rebutted by an MP: "Hackman [Owusu Agyeman] probably knows next to nothing about the internet and how it operates". See "Hackman: Ghanaweb is Misleading", *The Statesman*, 31 July 2005.
54. Ibid., p. 8.
55. Some of the internal regulatory mechanisms are Police Service (Administration) Regulations, 1974, L.I. 880; Police Force (Disciplinary Proceedings) Regulations, 1974, L.I. 993; Police Force Disciplinary Proceedings (Amendment) Regulations, 1977, L.I. 1104, L.I. 1335 (Amendment).
56. Article 203 (1), 1992 Constitution.
57. Article 203 (2) and (3), 1992 Constitution. Matters that should be covered under such regulations include the control and administration of the service, conditions of service, and powers and discipline of members of the service.
58. Garblah, "Blackmail & Extortion in Kosovo", p. 8.
59. Ibid., p. 1.
60. An internal inquiry by the UN Mission in Kosovo (UNMIK) internal investigation section dated 26 February 2003 by UN investigator Eyas Mahaden absolved two of the four Ghanaian officers accused of having posted the articles.
61. Interviews with several officers who had served in Bosnia and Kosovo.
62. The selection of less qualified personnel to engage in peacekeeping activities does not seem to be a problem just for Ghana and is more widely practised than hitherto known. See review of *Emergency Sex and Other Desperate Measures* by Kenneth Cain, Heidi

Postlewait and Andrew Thomson, Miramax Books, 2004, by Mark Hammersley, available at http://forum.aidworkers.net/cgi-bin/discuss/board-profile.pl? (accessed 27 May 2004). In this article it is asserted that "Bulgarian peacekeepers in Cambodia were not actually trained soldiers … [T]he Bulgarian government, strapped for hard currency, offered a deal to inmates, pledging them pardons if they accepted a six-month assignment in Cambodia. For sending troops the UN would give Bulgaria financial compensation."

63. I must emphasize here that increases in the amount that soldiers are paid are purely institutional and political decisions. Usually, increments are given when there is a perception of potential unrest among the troops.

64. B. Ansabah, "Presidential Jet Scandal: Who Faces the Music?", *Daily Guide*, 6 January 2004, p. 1 and 8.

65. Interview with Baby Ansabah, Accra, 7 July 2004. According to Baby Ansabah, an escrow account is one in which a creditor pledges to put money for payment into an account but the creditor does not have access to that account.

66. Deen, "UN Rejects Private Peacekeepers", citing Peter W. Singer of the Brookings Institution.

67. For a detailed analysis of this relationship, see Emmanuel Kwesi Aning, "Africa's Security in the New Millennium: State or Mercenary Induced Stability?", *Global Society: Journal of Interdisciplinary International Relations*, 15(2), May 2001; also see Doug Bandow, "The End of U.N. Peacekeeping", *The Freeman*, 50(10), October 2000, available at ⟨http://www.fee.org/publications/the-freeman/article.asp?aid=2442⟩ (accessed 7 November 2006).

68. "Private Security Firms to Blame – Rejoinder", *Daily Graphic*, 13 June 2001, p. 9.

69. I. Chukwuma, "Privatisation of Security in Nigeria", *Law Enforcement Review*, March 2001, pp. 14–18; and interview, Lagos, Nigeria, 18 October 2004.

70. K. R. Nossal, "Roland Goes Corporate: Mercenaries and Transnational Security Corporations in the Post-Cold War Era", *Civil Wars*, 1(1), 1998, p. 31.

71. In one interview, an officer informed me that some of these were the use of flak jackets and walkie-talkies, arms usage, learning how to use coded messages and learning about cultural sensitivity. Interview at Police Headquarters, Accra, 25 February 2005.

8

Unintended consequences of peace operations for troop-contributing countries from South Asia

C. S. R. Murthy

South Asia and peace operations have a special and mutually supportive relationship, and three countries in particular on the subcontinent – India, Pakistan and Bangladesh – merit attention here. Since 1949, India and Pakistan have hosted the second-oldest UN peace operation, known as the United Nations Military Observer Group in India and Pakistan (UNMOGIP) in Jammu and Kashmir. India remains among the most experienced contributing countries to peace operations since it first contributed its troop contingents to the United Nations Emergency Force (UNEF) in 1956.[1] In the 50 years since then, India has taken part in 39 out of the 61 operations launched to date, with an average contribution of nearly 70,000 troops. Indian troops, along with civilians and police personnel, have participated in many major multinational peace operations deployed under UN auspices in Cambodia, the Democratic Republic of Congo (DRC), Egypt, El Salvador, Mozambique, Namibia, Sierra Leone, Somalia and the former Yugoslavia. Eight Indians have been made force commanders of 13 such operations.[2] According to UN official statistics, the Indian fatality figure (120 have died while on UN peace operations duty, mainly in the Congo in the 1960s, during the Suez crisis and in Somalia) is the highest among 150 troop-contributing countries, which have lost, in total, 2,298 soldiers.[3]

Though not contributing for as long as India, Pakistan and Bangladesh also have much to be proud of as troop-contributing countries (TCCs). Although Pakistan's troop contribution to UN peace operations started in 1962 (with the West New Guinea operation), the active phase of its

Unintended consequences of peacekeeping operations, Aoi, de Coning and Thakur (eds), United Nations University Press, 2007, ISBN 978-92-808-1142-1

participation started much later when it took part in the UN mission deployed to help Namibia attain independence in 1990.[4] Relative to India or Pakistan, Bangladesh is a late entrant as a TCC; it registered its presence for the first time as part of the peace operation the United Nations sent to supervise cease-fire and troop withdrawals between Iran and Iraq in 1988. However, it soon emerged as an ardent supporter of UN peace operations, with the gross participation of nearly 40,000 troops in the short span of 15 years.[5] Having taken part in 36 and 34 UN operations, respectively, so far, Pakistan and Bangladesh have suffered high fatalities, including the loss, respectively, of 40 and 25 lives in the Somalia and Sierra Leone operations.

According to official information available in early 2005, the South Asian trio – India, Pakistan and Bangladesh – are among the top five TCCs. Indeed, as a pioneer, India can be said to have laid the firm foundations to turn the subcontinent into the favourite troop contributor for international peace operations. The share of these three countries of South Asia constituted 25 per cent of the aggregate strength of military personnel during the early 1990s when the size of the UN peace operations reached its peak.[6] Paradoxical as it might seem, India and Pakistan have worked together as co-contributing countries in numerous peace operations, while much of the world is worried about the political friction between the countries as a consequence of a military flare-up concerned with nuclear issues.

Before turning my attention to aspects of unintended consequences, it is appropriate to explore the question of what motivates the South Asian countries to send troops to peace operations abroad.

Motivating factors

The approach of South Asian countries to UN peacekeeping is an integral part of these countries' outlook towards this world organization. In the pursuit of world peace and development as interlinked missions, India for instance has favoured a multilateral approach in preference to unilateral actions. India believes, as many non-aligned countries do, that the UN mechanism should be strengthened to serve the cause of world peace effectively. In India's world view, the organization's potential lies not in perfecting strategies of coercion and force, but in sustaining peaceful means such as mediation, moderation and negotiation.[7] Furthermore, although recognizing the importance of the major powers, which enjoy certain privileges in UN decision-making, India has been interested in the evolution of the United Nations as a democratic and inclusive institution that cares about the problems and aspirations of small and weak countries and aims to act in their best interest.

To India and the other two South Asian neighbours, participation in all facets of UN activities affords a valuable opportunity to gain a variety of experiences and to evolve as an enlightened member of the community of nations. These South Asian countries compensate for inadequacies in terms of hard power and project their soft power potential by working for, in and with the United Nations. It is this aspiration to seek active and independent influence that pushed them to contribute actively to the evolution of peace operations under the UN umbrella. Participation in UN peace operations and the contribution of troops provide concrete experience in testing on the ground, beyond negotiation chambers, some of the South Asian countries' potential – particularly in the case of India – for leadership in the immediate neighbourhood and beyond.[8] Through peacekeeping, India has had the opportunity of relating with the problems of the people of Asia, Africa and South America and promoting future economic, commercial and cultural ties with them.

Moreover, over the years, the military capabilities of both India and Pakistan have grown in terms of manpower, training and the inventory of advanced equipment. Despite the combat experience gained in wars with external enemy forces and also in controlling armed insurgencies within the country, the armed forces view participation in peace operations as an opportunity to enhance professional exposure in combat and non-combat situations while learning how to use new equipment. However, India and Pakistan are not keen to take part in any and all peacekeeping operations. Understandably they make their assessment of costs and benefits when responding to requests for troop contributions. India looks for the assurance that the countries hosting the troops actually want the presence of its troops, in addition to keeping in view the considerations of solidarity and empathy with the affected country.[9] The urge to be regarded as a "good international citizen" seems to govern decisions by Pakistan and Bangladesh to involve themselves in peace operations. For example, Pakistan's top political leadership asserted in the 1990s that it was ready to commit its "prestige, energy, resources and above all the lives" of its troops as a mark of its "unwavering support for an active role by the UN for the preservation of international peace and security".[10] There was also presumably the need for Pakistan to repair its negative image as a country affected adversely by the political instability marked by military coups and a troubled economy.[11] An extension of this motive is the desire of the political leadership to keep the army purposefully busy in peace operations abroad, so that the fledgling constitutional and democratic order is allowed its legitimate space. In addition,

Pakistan has been guided by considerations of Islamic solidarity when deciding to send troops to certain operations, such as the ones in Bosnia-Herzegovina and Somalia. Further, in line with the India-centric thrust in its foreign policy, Pakistan does see its national interest in demonstrating that its capabilities as a troop contributor are as professional and praiseworthy as those of India. The motive of earning foreign exchange may not be decisive in the case of India and Pakistan, but it does appear to be a factor in the case of Bangladesh. And, like Pakistan, Bangladesh uses peacekeeping operations as a way of keeping its army away from meddling in the political sphere of the country.

Although recognition is an intended outcome for the South Asian troop contributors, what can be stated about the unintended consequences? What significance do they have both for TCCs and for the international community? Would it be possible to group the unintended consequences into either positive or negative columns as far as South Asian TCCs are concerned? These aspects will be addressed in the next section.

Medley of unintended consequences

South Asian troop-contributing countries have much in common in their approach to peace operations, but an interesting nuance may be noted with regard to their contrasting attitudes as hosts to peace operations. India's non-cooperation with UNMOGIP stands quite in contrast to the maturity it shows as a TCC. This otherwise cost-effective operation in Kashmir has been caught up in a kind of "one-upmanship politics" between India and Pakistan since the mid-1960s. Given a chance, India would have liked to see UNMOGIP pulled out from Kashmir way back in 1971. Since that remains unachieved, India has reduced its contact with UNMOGIP to the barest minimum and does not take up with UNMOGIP its complaints about Pakistani violations of the line of control.[12] Pakistan, in contrast, does not miss an opportunity to present itself as a model of an enthusiastic and cooperative host of the UN observer mission. Notably again, India's attempt in some of its bilateral engagements during the 1980s to reaffirm its track record as an impartial and non-fighting troop contributor to UN operations abroad ended in a major embarrassment. The reference here is to the bitter experience of the troops sent to Sri Lanka under the name of the Indian Peace Keeping Force between 1987 and 1990. Having paid a heavy price for misappropriating the label of "peacekeeping" in Sri Lanka in the late 1980s, India seems to have learnt its lesson quickly and has renewed its interest in UN peace operations.[13] India now lets others know that it would not want to send troops abroad outside of UN auspices – a position it repeated when rejecting the United States' request for Indian troops to be sent to Iraq to restore order in US-occupied Iraq after the 2003 war.

No doubt, there are a number of specific unintended consequences linked to India and other South Asian TCCs. These consequences can be broadly grouped as political, diplomatic, financial, social and military. Let us take a close look at each of them to see if the consequences can be seen as positive or negative.

Mixed political and diplomatic consequences

The pre-eminent unintended political consequence is the vigour and self-confident tone in India's advocacy of its case for a permanent seat in the enlarged UN Security Council. In particular, India's recommendation for adding new permanent members on the basis of their contribution to peace operations reflects the hope that its track record as a troop contributor would speak for itself. It may not, however, be true or fair to say that India has taken part in peace operations with the motive of boosting its case for the much sought after seat. Nor can anyone argue that India's participation by itself will get it a permanent seat. It is true that the issue of the expansion of the Security Council is among the trickiest reform issues before the international community, and it would be simplistic to expect an early outcome. And India faces the gigantic task of dealing with potentially damaging its relationship with China, the United States, Pakistan and other countries.[14]

Another positive consequence peculiar to Bangladesh with regard to troop contributions to UN peace operations is the unwillingness of the army to overthrow the civilian government and seize power by exploiting the perennial bickering between the two major political parties in the country. According to media analysts, the Bangladesh army, "earning dollars and plaudits" while doing peacekeeping jobs around the world, "is in no mood to return to politics".[15]

In certain cases, peacekeeping has emerged as a cementing force in India's bilateral relationships with other countries, especially the United States. India's participation in the DRC and Somalia operations provided positive resonance in bilateral relationships during the 1960s and in the 1990s. Cooperation on peacekeeping matters appeared prominently in the talks between the Indian and US leaders between 1993 and 2000. The two countries established a Joint Working Group on UN Peacekeeping Operations, which meets twice a year to review the problems of peacekeeping and to draw appropriate lessons for joint action.[16] The Joint Working Group is aimed at developing institutional linkages between the two countries to facilitate training in peacekeeping and the exchange of observers, students and guest faculty. Other countries such as the United Kingdom followed suit by setting up similar joint working groups with India.

It may be noted that Pakistan also found an opportunity to repair and strengthen its relations with the United States and to return to serving as a troop contributor in Somalia. For instance, since 1990 the US administration could not certify, as required under the 1984 Pressler amendment, that American military aid would prevent Pakistan from acquiring nuclear explosive devices. As a result, congressional sanction for aid had to be stopped until the Pressler amendment was repealed in 1998.[17]

There have been several occasions when the Indian and Pakistani units have worked together as TCCs in the UN mission areas (Cambodia, the DRC, Mozambique and Somalia are pertinent examples). Whatever political strains have marked relations between the two countries, Indian and Pakistani troops have worked in camaraderie when they have put on "blue helmets" in a third country. An element of positive competition has also been noticed between India and Pakistan. Pakistan seemed to have picked up positive signals from the revival of Indian participation in the post–Cold War peace operations of the United Nations and so it too actively resumed troop contributions in the 1990s.[18] Likewise, Pakistan withdrew its contingents from Sierra Leone, citing risks as a compelling reason after India's withdrawal. India's decision to pull troops out of Sierra Leone in 2000 represents an unfortunate aberration in the "staying power" it painstakingly showcased during numerous difficult operations, such as in Suez or Somalia.[19] Although not as dangerous as Mogadishu, where many peacekeepers from Pakistan and the United States lost their lives, Indian troops did not panic when, within a few months of deployment in April 1993, the Indian contingent suffered 14 casualties among its troops. But in Sierra Leone a completely different view has emerged in favour of withdrawal. The decision to withdraw from Sierra Leone was prompted by Indian unhappiness with Secretary-General Kofi Annan's decision to replace General Jetley as the Force Commander after the working relationship between the Force Commander, his deputy (a Nigerian officer) and the Special Representative (Oluyemi Adeniji) rapidly deteriorated.[20] India refused to heed the UN Headquarters' plea to continue its troop presence. The timing of the withdrawal of its contingent was synchronized with General Jetley's replacement, which was aimed to save the Indian army's face.

Again, the Sierra Leone withdrawal decision was linked to the strong disquiet expressed by Indian political parties and parliamentarians over the hostage crisis involving 500 personnel belonging to contingents from India and other TCCs, and the negative publicity about the role of the

Force Commander, Major General Vijay Jetley.[21] In fact, unlike in the past, decisions about participation in peace operations came under close scrutiny in parliament and outside during the 1990s. Questions were raised about the need to send soldiers to dangerous areas of Somalia or Sierra Leone where their lives were put at risk, or even the wisdom of contributing troops to peace operations in far-away lands (such as Haiti) where India's national interests are not at stake.[22] In this context, the remarks of a former senior army officer assume significance: "It's good for Indian troops to get a multilateral experience and earn UN salaries, but if the situation degenerates into war, they will be embroiled in a regional conflict that is of no concern to them."[23]

Tough questions have been raised in Pakistan too. In the context of the loss of soldiers' lives in Somalia in 1993, members of Pakistan's senate criticized the government for allowing the troops to abandon their humanitarian role and adopt the American line.[24]

Long delays in the reimbursement of costs to TCCs by the UN Secretariat (owing to deliberate withholding of payments by the United States – the largest assessed financial contributor for the peace operations) presented a rather peculiar and unintended consequence. The gap between the growth of peacekeeping activities and the level of assured financial resources resulted in huge arrears to the troop-contributing countries of South Asia and other regions of the world. The outstanding payments from the United Nations to India and Pakistan amounted to US$60 million and US$50 million, respectively, during the years 1996 and 2000. According to estimates, the United Nations owed Pakistan, Bangladesh and India nearly US$549 million at the end of 2003.[25] This also appeared to strain the capacity of these countries readily to spare troops even when troops were urgently needed (as in the DRC since 2000). India has reason to call for the formulation of "rules of disengagement" that run parallel to "rules of engagement", in order to ensure the settlement of all financial claims and the reimbursement of costs before the liquidation of a peace operation.[26]

Moderate economic and financial gains

The economic and financial gain for individuals deputed by the army in all three South Asian countries under study could be described as substantial as well as attractive. The subsistence and other allowances (approximately US$1,000 a month) that an officer or a person below the rank of officer may get are much higher than his/her salary would be in the country of origin. (In certain cases, such as Cambodia, the daily allowance exceeds the per capita annual income in the host country.)[27] In other words, to an individual soldier or officer, assignment to a peace operation may mean a financial "jackpot", in that they are able to save, within a year, something equal to the amount they might get as a lump sum retirement benefit after 20 or 30 years of service! It does make a qualitative improvement in the financial status of the individuals concerned.

What the individuals have done with the earnings brought back home is hard to quantify. Some may have invested in real estate, and others may have invested in the stock market. Incidentally, the early 1990s witnessed a surge in the number of small investors, but many – like those who invested in the Unit Trust of India – suffered losses owing to share market crashes and scandals. A similar situation seems to have prevailed in Bangladesh too.[28] In any event, it is not possible to establish clearly whether the earnings made any noticeable difference to the economic situation of the local community after the return of soldiers.

With regard to the financial earnings for the army on account of troop contributions, the situation does not appear to be as clear as it is in the case of individuals. In Bangladesh, where nearly half of the national army has taken part in UN peacekeeping at one time or another, the economic returns could be described as substantial: its earnings on account of troop contributions are US$766 million in a span of 15 years.[29] On the other hand, it is very doubtful if troop contributions in UN peace operations brought substantial financial benefits to the Indian or even the Pakistani army establishment. The gains that accrued as a result of contributions are described as a "drop in the ocean". The highest number of Indian troops deployed at any one time was 6,000, which was in the mid-1990s.[30] Presently, the annual turnover of officers is around 250. According to knowledgeable quarters, one needs to get the percentages right to realize that, in a huge army of more than 1 million soldiers, a few extra thousand dollars would not make a marked difference. In the past 50 years only around 60 units in the Indian army have had UN peace operation assignments so far. And, going by the current rate of deployment, it will take 250 years for all 360 units to get this opportunity at least once! In comparison, in a small country with a small army (as in the case of Bangladesh), virtually every infantry unit will spend some time in UN peace operations (at least once), sooner or later.[31]

It is also possible to perceive reimbursement of equipment-related costs as a positive unintended economic incentive. However, informed sources insert a note of caution on this score. On the one hand, it is true that the rate of reimbursement is quite high by Indian standards and, if the equipment is maintained properly, it could be in service long after the entire costs have been neutralized by UN reimbursements. However, this does not hold true in the case of special equipment, whose import costs are too high to be met out of reimbursement earnings alone.[32]

Manageable social consequences

It is true that public opinion and the media consider participation by Indian troops and police in UN peace operations as an expression of national pride. Ironically, however, coverage by the print or visual media of the activities or achievements of Indian personnel is at best sporadic, with knee-jerk reactions to the news of death, injury or kidnapping. The reception that returning or departing contingents get at railway stations or airports is nowhere comparable to the welcome given to soldiers returning from a war front (as after the Kargil war in 1999). The government does not seem to feel the need to offer compensation in the form of the allotment of land or petrol pumps to the victims' families.[33]

With regard to growing concern about the incidence of prostitution and HIV/AIDS as unintended consequences of UN peacekeeping activity,[34] many TCCs are known to take offence at any hint that the spread of the killer disease is to be linked to the presence of their contingents. Responding to US criticism of the United Nations for unsatisfactory work in combating the spread of HIV/AIDS, India once told the Security Council the following:[35]

> We find objectionable the imputation that peacekeepers are either necessarily at risk or carriers of the disease.... Not one Indian peacekeeper has either arrived in the theatre in Africa with HIV/AIDS or left with it. Our soldiers have died in Africa and elsewhere of diseases – most recently in Sierra Leone from a particularly virulent form of cerebral malaria – but no one has died of AIDS.

Verifiable information on the nature, scale and follow-up of cases of sexually transmitted diseases is not available. Nonetheless, according to estimates of officers at the Centre for United Nations Peacekeeping (CUNPK) in New Delhi, nearly 100 cases might have been detected among the troops and civilian staff who returned from Cambodia in 1993, and 25 per cent of them are thought to have tested HIV positive.[36] Indian diplomats have vigorously rejected reports of the occurrence or spread of HIV/AIDS among the troops that came back from Sierra Leone. No figures are available for Pakistan, but in Bangladesh 188 army men were reportedly affected.[37]

In any event, India appears to have been progressively sensitized to the threat and has initiated some corrective steps in the wake of experiences during the Cambodian operation in the early 1990s.[38] Preventive measures have been launched by strictly enforcing a code of conduct for the personnel deputed for peace operations abroad and including awareness modules in the pre-deployment training programmes. Alarmed over the deadly consequences of AIDS, new procedures are in place requiring every single individual proceeding to UN missions or being repatriated to be tested for HIV. However, even if the Cambodia and Sierra Leone statistics are correct, these figures account for less than 1 per cent of the actual HIV prevalence in the Indian armed forces.

Complaints about the sexual misconduct of troops in various peace operations are growing. According to media reports, in the Bunia province of the DRC alone, UN investigators documented 68 cases of rape, prostitution and paedophilia involving Pakistani personnel, along with contingents from Nepal, South Africa, Uruguay and others in 2004. Furthermore, some of them reportedly tried to bribe witnesses to retract or dilute the damaging charges originally made regarding the alleged sexual abuse. Officials in Pakistan's permanent mission in New York expressed a willingness to take the "strictest" disciplinary action against those who were found guilty in a proper investigation. At the same time, Pakistan saw a plot in these allegations to "defame" the country's troops.[39] Only 1 out of nearly 250 complaints concerned the behaviour of the Indian troops. The action on that seems to be firm: in 2005 the Indian army dismissed a soldier from service on charges of misconduct in the DRC.[40]

No information is made public about the number of disciplinary proceedings against those charged with major (rape, murder) or minor (traffic accidents) crimes during the period of a peace operation or about the outcomes of such proceedings. It may still be pertinent to note the relevant procedures in place. The standard practice under the terms of the Status-of-Forces Agreement is that neither the United Nations nor the host country has the authority to prosecute the offenders; this responsibility rests with the authorities of the contributing government. When complaints are lodged, a Court of Inquiry or Summary of Evidence is conducted by the concerned contingent's authorities in the mission area on their own initiative or on the advice of the mission headquarters. On completion of the inquiry, the accused is repatriated to face proceedings for disciplinary action, if necessary.[41] Notably, however, the disciplinary proceedings are carried out in camera with a view to avoiding adverse publicity. The less than transparent nature of proceedings often gives rise to doubts in the host countries about the credibility of the contributing country.

Miscellaneous professional effects

Working shoulder to shoulder with soldiers from a multitude of developed and developing countries may have been professionally rewarding to the Indian and other contingents from South Asia in many ways. According to one peacekeeper, "the opportunities in terms of international training exposure, interoperability with multi-national forces and cross-cultural exchanges make definite improvement in the professional outlook of the peacekeepers".[42] The professional conduct of Indian officers has received praise except on rare occasions. To cite examples of exceptions, complaints were publicly aired against the Sierra Leone Force Commander, Major General Vijay Jetley. It was said that he was "high-handed and aloof, often acting without consultation with close colleagues" and he "surrounded himself with an inner circle of Indian officers".[43] On a different point, according to a report brought out by the US-based Henry L. Stimson Center, India has a rather "low" overall level of specialized training for peace operation purposes, despite conducting pre-deployment orientation and unit training.[44] The lessons drawn and the best practices identified from the experiences in peace operations surely are contributing to the strengthening of the Standard Operating Procedures and work culture of the forces.

One of the most notable effects of increased participation in peace operations is said to be the steady rise in the levels of aspiration of the army officers. With the likelihood of assignment for nearly 300 officers each year, every upcoming officer remains optimistic about such career prospects. On the other hand, in view of the limited opportunities and the possibility of many being left out of the intensely competitive process, soldiers may perceive favouritism or feel professional jealousy. It may be noted here that Pakistan reportedly developed a policy of not allowing any of its soldiers more than one assignment in peace operations abroad. This approach is not above criticism, for it can be argued that, if soldiers or officers are given the opportunity to serve in a peace operation only once, this might hinder them from building on their experience and doing better another time, unless institutional memory is ensured through appropriate mechanisms for imparting pre-deployment and post-deployment training.[44]

The extensive experience of Indians in UN peace operations has equipped them to develop and conduct training programmes for military personnel, both Indian and foreign. With encouragement from the UN Department of Peacekeeping Operations, the Indian army set up a Centre for United Nations Peacekeeping (CUNPK) in Delhi in 2000 on the premises of the well-known military academy, the United Services Institution of India (USI), to develop and conduct regular training programmes.[45] The United Nations and the CUNPK collaborated in organizing a training course for Military Observers and police officers in October 2003. Since then, bilateral joint working group seminars have been held in cooperation with the United States, Norway and the United

Kingdom separately. These and other exercises attracted participation from 45 countries. Besides these, countries such as Japan, China, South Korea and Iran (which are relatively less experienced in peace operations) are showing interest in formalizing arrangements for training and other professional exchanges. Other South Asian contributing countries have taken similar initiatives: Bangladesh has set up a training institute, the Bangladesh Institute of Peace Support Operation Training.

Finally, whether UN peace operations experience has improved the work culture of the army in handling intra-state tasks such as containing insurgencies or alleviating human suffering in natural disasters is a moot question. In any event, the effect is likely to be negligible because only 1 or 2 units out of about 360 infantry units of the army are engaged in such jobs within the country every year, even though a cumulative effect cannot be ruled out over a long time frame.

Conclusion

As can be discerned from the foregoing analysis, the ongoing troop contributions by India, Pakistan and Bangladesh have been instrumental in the success of a good number of UN peace operations – a service for which these countries have received wide appreciation. Both common and particular factors have motivated the South Asian countries actively to contribute troops. Although they are happy about their vital role in furthering the common cause of world peace and security, participation in peace operations has served as a vehicle for countries such as India to advance ambitions for regional or global leadership. The three South Asian countries' strong and sustained association as troop contributors points to a variety of important and interesting shades of unintended consequences ranging from the political and diplomatic, to the economic, social and professional realms. Nevertheless, these unintended consequences for the South Asian region cannot be characterized in either exclusively positive or negative terms. In other words, the positive and negative aspects coexist, in nuanced forms, in each of these segments. For example, the financial gains may have brought riches to the individual peacekeepers, but not necessarily to the local community or to the army. Likewise, peacekeeping activism may have boosted India's case for a permanent seat in the expanded Security Council, but India may not be able to obliterate major obstacles to the achievement of its aspiration. Again, as has been shown in the discussion, some aspects of the unintended consequences are peculiar to each of the South Asian trio, whereas other aspects are common to India, Pakistan and Bangladesh as leading TCCs to peace operations.

Notes

1. For historical aspects, see F. Parakatil, *India and United Nations Peace-Keeping Operations*, New Delhi: S. Chand, 1975; and Indar Jit Rikhye, "United Nations Peace-keeping Operations and India", *India Quarterly*, 41(3–4), 1985, pp. 303–319.
2. This information is drawn essentially from a write-up on "UN Peace Keeping" available at ⟨http//www.indianarmy.nic.in/arunpk1.htm⟩ (accessed 7 November 2006).
3. Website of the Department of Peacekeeping Operations, available at ⟨http://www.un.org/Depts/dpko/fatalities/StatsByNationalityMission.htm⟩ (accessed 7 November 2006).
4. See K. Hasan, "Kasuri Highlights Pakistan's Peacekeeping Record in UNSC", *Daily Times*, 12 October 2004.
5. Z. Haque, "Bangladesh Armed Forces Contribution in United Nations Peacekeeping Operation", *The New Nation*, 16 September 2004.
6. K. Krishnasamy, "'Recognition' for Third World Peacekeepers: India and Pakistan", *International Peacekeeping*, 8(4), 2001, p. 58.
7. These aspects are elaborated in, for example, *India and the United Nations, Report of the Study Group of the Indian Council of World Affairs*, New York: Manhattan, 1957; Ross N. Berkes and Mohinder S. Bedi, *The Diplomacy of India: Indian Foreign Policy in the United Nations*, Stanford, CA: Stanford University Press, 1958; and S. Mehta, "India, the United Nations, and World Peace", in M. S. Rajan, ed., *India's Foreign Relations during the Nehru Era*, Bombay: Asia Publishing House, 1976.
8. K. Krishnasamy, "The Paradox of India's Peacekeeping", *Contemporary South Asia*, 12(2), 2003, p. 264.
9. Foreign Minister Inder Gujral's statement in the General Assembly, UN Doc. A/51/PV.22, 4 October 1996, p. 15. It may be stated parenthetically here that India agreed to send the second-largest contingent as part of UNEF-I because Egypt strongly wanted an Indian presence and India wanted to demonstrate its solidarity with Egypt at the time of crisis in a concrete way. Conversely, India's reluctance to send troops to former Yugoslavia or to East Timor can be traced to its feelings of discomfort with regard to the implications of separatism under way and its continuing friendly sentiments towards the governments in trouble in both theatres.
10. Remarks by Prime Minister Benazir Bhutto and her defence minister at that time quoted in K. Krishnasamy, "Pakistan's Peacekeeping Experiences", *International Peacekeeping*, 9(3), 2002, p. 105.
11. Ibid., pp. 111–114.
12. C. S. R. Murthy, "India and UN Peacekeeping Operations: Issues in Policy and Participation", *Man and Development*, 8(2), 1998, pp. 172–183; and also A. James, *Peacekeeping in International Politics*, London: Macmillan for International Institute for Strategic Studies, 1990, pp. 161–163.
13. A. Bullion, "India and United Nations Peacekeeping Operations", *International Peacekeeping*, 4(1), 1997, pp. 98–114, discusses the influence of the Sri Lanka experience on India's peacekeeping activities in Somalia and Sierra Leone.
14. For details, see C. S. R. Murthy, "Reforming the UN Security Council: An Asian View", *South Asian Survey*, 5(1), 1998, pp. 113–124.
15. S. Varadarajan, "Limited Room for Mullahs, Military but Not Mastans", *The Hindu*, 14 September 2004.
16. "Statement by the US-India Joint Working Group on UN Peacekeeping Operations", Washington DC, 29 June 2001.
17. Krishnasamy, "Pakistan's Peacekeeping Experiences", p. 113. Also see Robert M. Hathaway, "Confrontation and Retreat: The U.S. Congress and the South Asian

Nuclear Tests", *Arms Control Today*, January–February 2000, available at ⟨http://www.armscontrol.org/act/2000_01-02/rhjf00.asp⟩ (accessed 7 November 2006).

18. Krishnasamy, " 'Recognition' for Third World Peacekeepers: India and Pakistan", pp. 56–76.
19. Krishnasamy, "The Paradox of India's Peacekeeping", pp. 269–270.
20. Ibid., p. 272.
21. A. Bullion, "India in Sierra Leone: A Case of Muscular Peacekeeping", *International Peacekeeping*, 8(4), 2001, pp. 77–91.
22. See, for example, "Opposition Seeks Forces' Withdrawal", *Times of India*, 24 August 1994.
23. Lt. Gen. (Retd.) A. K. Sharma's critical comments quoted in Alan Bullion, "India and Its Rationale for Participation in United Nations Peacekeeping Operations" (forthcoming publication made available by courtesy), p. 27.
24. Remarks of a Jamaat-i-Islami party senator quoted in K. Krishnasamy, "Pakistan's Peacekeeping Experiences", pp. 109 and 119.
25. See Thalif Deen, "UN: Bullies and Beggars", Inter Press Service, 28 May 2004, available at ⟨http://www.antiwar.com/ips/deen.php?articleid=2680⟩ (accessed 7 November 2006).
26. See the statement by Ambassador Vijay K. Nambiar in the UN General Assembly Special Committee on Peacekeeping Operations, 4 March 2003, Press Release, UN Doc. GA/PK/178, available at ⟨http://www.un.org/News/Press/docs/2003/gapk178.doc.htm⟩ (accessed 20 November 2006). These concerns are common to other South Asian TCCs; see, for example, the statement by Pakistan's permanent representative, Ambassador Munir Akram, in the same Committee, 30 March 2004, available at ⟨http://www.un.int/pakistan/00home110104⟩ (accessed 20 November 2006).
27. M. R. Berdal, "Whither UN Peacekeeping?", Adelphi Paper No. 281, London: International Institute of Strategic Studies, 1993, p. 46.
28. The experience of bad investments has been noted in T. A. Zearat Ali, "Bangladesh in United Nations Peacekeeping Operations", BIISS Paper No. 16, Dhaka, July 1998, p. 53.
29. I. Rahman, "Dhaka Facing Problems in Peacekeeping", *Arab News*, 29 September 2004.
30. I wish to thank officials, especially Col. P. Purushottaman of the Centre for United Nations Peacekeeping (CUNPK) and the United Services Institution of India in New Delhi, for their input in this section.
31. In Bangladesh, one-third of the nearly 100,000 strong army has served in 28 peacekeeping operations located in 23 countries in a relatively short space of time, namely since 1988. See Haque, "Bangladesh Armed Forces Contribution in United Nations Peacekeeping Operation"; and also K. Krishnasamy, "Bangladesh and UN Peacekeeping: The Participation of a 'Small' State", *Commonwealth and Comparative Politics*, 41(1), 2003, pp. 24–47.
32. On the other hand, according to CUNPK, the Indian armed forces incur high expenditures for creating administrative facilities for the UN-bound or returning personnel. The army is making a big effort to create a world-class infrastructure for training the peacekeepers. There are several sources of hidden costs which, when added up, equal or even surpass the financial and material advantages accruing from UN reimbursements. The contingents are equipped according to international standards, which entails the purchase of equipment and stores that would otherwise not be included in the unit inventory or equipment requirements. These are, however, passed down to the relieving units. If the Indian troops deployed in the current missions remain in service for some years, these items may more or less complete their "life cycle".

33. This is a common practice to benefit the families of soldiers killed or injured during combat operations against insurgent groups within the country or against enemy troops from outside.

34. According to Assistant Secretary-General for Human Resources Management, Rosemary McCreery, a system-wide investigation was triggered by reports that 6 out of 48 UN agencies operating in the field had received reports of new cases of sexual exploitation or abuse, mostly by blue-helmeted UN peacekeepers in Kosovo and the Bunia region of the DRC during 2003. Cited in Deen, "UN: Bullies and Beggars".

35. Statement by India's Permanent Representative, Kamalesh Sharma. In the same meeting, the Under-Secretary-General for Peacekeeping Operations, Jean-Marie Guehenno, questioned the possible damage caused by 50,000 military and civilian personnel deployed worldwide, when actually tens of millions were affected by the disease already. See Thalif Deen, "Politics: Outgoing US Envoy Blasts UN Peacekeeping Department", Inter Press Service, 19 January 2001, available at ⟨http://www.aegis.org/news/ips/2001/IP010105.html⟩ (accessed 7 November 2006).

36. Personal communication from Col. P. Purushottaman, 30 September 2004.

37. W. Rahman, "Aids Warning for Bangladesh Army", BBC News Online, 6 December 2001, available at ⟨http://news.bbc.co.uk/1/hi/world/south_asia/1696063.stm⟩ (accessed 7 November 2006).

38. According to some estimates, 45 Indian peacekeepers in Cambodia were infected with HIV/AIDS (Stefan Elbe, "Strategic Implications of HIV/AIDS", Adelphi Paper 357, London: International Institute of Strategic Studies, 2003, p. 41).

39. For details, see the story filed by Colum Lynch, "UN Sexual Abuse Alleged in Congo", Washington Post, 16 December 2004, p. 26.

40. Josy Joseph, "Indian Contribution to UN Peacekeeping Highest Ever", DNA India, 1 April 2006, available at ⟨http://www.dnaindia.com/report.asp?NewsID=1021385&CatID=2⟩ (accessed 10 November 2006).

41. Communication with Col. R. K. Rajput of CUNPK, New Delhi, 2 March 2005.

42. Views and opinions of Col. P. Purushottaman of CUNPK, New Delhi, in a personal note, 30 September 2004.

43. Bullion, "India in Sierra Leone: A Case of Muscular Peacekeeping?", pp. 78 and 81.

44. Report discussed in S. Rangarajan, "The Perils of Peacekeeping: Training United Nations Forces", Frontline, 30 June 1995, p. 55; cited in Bullion, "India in Sierra Leone", p. 83.

45. This point was made by one of the participants in the discussion on the preliminary draft of the chapter during the authors' workshop in Cape Town in November 2004.

46. CUNPK, Training for Peace, New Delhi: United Service Institution, 2003.

9

Unintended consequences of peace operations for troop-contributing countries in South America: The cases of Argentina and Uruguay

Arturo C. Sotomayor

Participation in United Nations peace operations is thought to have important and positive effects on civilian control of the military among troop-contributing and democratizing states. In fact, a large body of literature concludes that participation in peace operations is universally beneficial for military institutions and for civilian control. Authors such as Charles C. Moskos argue that peace operations change military organizations, as civilians become intimately involved in peace operations. As he argues, "the armed forces themselves have been increasingly democratised, liberalised, and civilianised".[1] Likewise, Michael C. Desch and Gabriel Marcella find that, in order to ensure military subordination to civilian rule in peacetime, civilian politicians have to encourage their armed forces to adopt externally focused missions, such as peace operations.[2] As Desch argues, "The Argentine government, in an effort to keep the country's once internally-oriented military externally focused, has recently been having the military participate in international peacekeeping missions. This is a realistic and beneficial post-Cold War military mission."[3] Similarly, Deborah L. Norden considers that transitions from authoritarian rule to democracy pose serious challenges for military institutions and identities. For this reason, she believes participation in international peace operations can have significant domestic consequences: "by engaging the armed forces in a worthwhile, professional endeavour, international peacekeeping can help ease these tensions".[4]

In this chapter I will examine the relationship between engagement in UN peace missions and civilian control of the armed forces in the

Unintended consequences of peacekeeping operations, Aoi, de Coning and Thakur (eds), United Nations University Press, 2007, ISBN 978-92-808-1142-1

Southern Cone of South America. I identify a policy-relevant and theoretically important intellectual puzzle: whereas conventional wisdom and case-study evidence suggest that engaging the military in UN peace operations is universally positive for reducing the military's political influence in recently democratizing states, the body of cross-national research that I conduct finds that participation in peace operations can have many and varying consequences, which are not always conducive to increasing democratic civilian control. Participation in peace operations has positive effects in some places, but not in others. Moreover, the effects are different in some places than in others.

In order to explore the relationship between engagement in UN peace operations and civilian control of the armed forces, I assess the varying effects of peace involvement on four separate indicators of civilian control – the defence sector, bureaucratic control of international security policies, military professionalism and the civilianization of the soldier. I use the comparative method of case studies to explain the different effects of peace operations' involvement on civilian control of the military. I argue that domestic factors (such as different types of military prerogatives and divergent forms of bureaucratic decision-making processes) and external variables (such as dissimilar forms of social interaction in peace operations) can influence the potential effects of participation in peace operations on civilian control of the military. The influence of these domestic and external factors can sometimes have unintended consequences; that is, effects or outcomes that are not always perceived or intended by policy-makers when forces are deployed to a peace mission.[5] The project engages in a two-step analysis. It first aims to identify the domestic conditions under which participation of the armed forces in UN peace missions is likely to strengthen democratic civilian control. Second, it explores the mechanisms through which international participation in peace operations exerts its influence on the military and on civilians.

For this purpose, I have selected two cases in the Southern Cone of South America: Argentina and Uruguay. Both countries have substantial UN peace experience and have deployed infantry battalions to the United Nations. The comparison would seem to be a natural one for two nations that are members of the same sub-region and experienced authoritarian regimes in the 1970s and early 1980s and transitions to democracy in the mid-1980s. They are both highly urbanized countries and have professional militaries. But the similarities are not as intriguing as are the differences. Divergent bureaucratic politics and policies can be traced to evaluate the impact of participation in peace operations on civilian control. In order to develop the main argument this chapter will proceed with a brief discussion of Argentina's and Uruguay's peacekeeping experience. I shall then discuss how involvement in peace operations had consequences for the defence sector, bureaucracies, military professionalism and the civilianization of the soldier.

From praetorianism to peace operations: Argentine and Uruguayan peacekeeping contributions

In August 1991, two Argentine frigates with 450 naval officers were deployed from the port of Belgrano, Argentina, to the Persian Gulf to aid the United States in the blockade against Iraq. The blockade was sanctioned by several resolutions of the UN Security Council (Resolutions 661, 665, 669 and 670). After the Gulf war experience, Argentina made a commitment to the United Nations and pledged to send a 900-man battalion to Croatia. Since then, the country has undertaken three other significant troop commitments in Cyprus, Iraq/Kuwait and Haiti. In fact, Argentina increased its UN contribution from 30 peacekeepers in 1989 to almost 3,000 in 1995. This is a 100-fold increase in less than six years. The Argentine troop contribution eventually stabilized at about 500 military personnel per year. Since 1992, Argentina has sent more than 14,000 volunteers to more than 13 peace operations worldwide.[6] In total, about 40 per cent of the army's commissioned officers have had some kind of peace operation exposure since 1991. Progressively, Argentine military officers became ubiquitous peacekeepers in Central America, Africa and Europe. As a result of this experience, Argentina became the most active Latin American troop supplier and one of the top five troop-contributing countries in the period 1992–1996.[7]

The Argentine engagement with UN peace operations may be seen as an uneventful fact, since the country was merely assuming its responsibility as a founding member of the United Nations. Article II of the UN Charter clearly specifies that all members shall give the United Nations every assistance in any action it takes and shall refrain from giving assistance to any state against which the United Nations is taking preventive or enforcement action. However, what is interesting about the Argentine case is that the deployment of the two Navy ships to the Persian Gulf took place only months after the 1990 coup attempt against the democratically elected government of President Carlos Saúl Menem. Paradoxically, officers and soldiers who had revolted at least three times against the re-emerging Argentine democracy were now being sent to missions abroad, miles away from the capital city of Buenos Aires. In fact, Argentina's engagement with the United Nations – including peace operations and other missions, such as involvement in the UN-sanctioned Persian

Gulf war – coincided with the government's effort to restructure the armed forces and impose firm civilian control on the military. The re-democratization process of Argentina left the military without a role and in a moribund state, as civilians drastically cut budgets and closed military industries. In such a context, military leaders were susceptible to different forms of engagement, such as peace operations. Therefore, participation in UN peace missions offered a low-cost opportunity to receive additional payments and perform a positive military role abroad. The policy also converged nicely with President Menem's foreign policy, which focused on realigning Argentina with the United States.

Similarly, since the 1950s, Uruguay has sent Military Observers to missions in the Sinai and the India–Pakistan border.[8] However, in 1992, Uruguay sent its first peacekeeping battalion to Asia as part of the United Nations Transitional Authority in Cambodia. In total, 1,330 soldiers (about 5.5 per cent of the country's armed forces) were deployed across Cambodia's provinces. This was significant for two main reasons. First, it was the first large-scale deployment abroad, involving troops and contingents from different services. Second, it symbolized a radical departure in military politics, because it shifted the role of the armed forces from domestic politics towards internationalism. The deployment took place only 6 years after the return to democracy and following 13 years of bureaucratic authoritarian rule. The military dictatorship that ruled Uruguay from 1973 to 1985 was not as brutal as Pinochet's regime or the Argentine military junta, but guerrilla and labour repression and the percentage of people detained for questioning by the military were higher than in any other country of the Southern Cone.[9] Hence, it was somewhat paradoxical that thousands of Uruguayan military officers, who were once responsible for state repression, were now being sent abroad to help UN conflict resolution processes.

Within a decade of the 1992 deployment, Uruguay became the world's largest per capita contributor to UN peace operations. The number of Uruguayan blue helmets sent to UN missions increased from roughly 100 officers in 1982 to 2,486 in 2004, an increase of over 1,000 per cent. In 1982, Uruguay participated in only two peace missions (the India–Pakistan mission and the Multinational Force Operation in the Sinai); by 2003 it was involved in more than 18 UN peace operations. As of today, more than 10,370 soldiers have been involved in at least one peace mission. To date, more than 50 per cent of army officers and 34 per cent of all non-commissioned officers have had some kind of peace mission experience. Similarly, in 2005, more than 10 per cent of Uruguay's total armed forces were deployed in more than six UN missions, ranging from Kashmir in Asia to the Democratic Republic of Congo (DRC) in Africa and Georgia in Central Europe.[10] Given the increasing involvement in peace operations and the rate of participation, how did such engagement affect civilian control in both Argentina and Uruguay? I shall analyse this question in the following sections.

Peacekeeping and civilian control of military missions

First, I wish to assess the effect of participation in peace operations on military missions. Do large UN troop contributions have varying effects on politicians' abilities to monitor military missions, deployment, education and budgets? In Argentina, civilians pressured the military to undertake major changes after the Falklands/Malvinas war and severely disciplined the armed forces with reduced budgets and trials, thus undermining military prerogatives. Ultimately, some of the policies undertaken by civilians backfired, because the military rebelled and demanded a reversal of trials, a change of command and even a new foreign policy. Between 1987 and 1991, Argentina experienced three military revolts and one failed coup attempt. It is safe to assert that in Argentina the military was caught in a severe crisis after the transition to democracy. The absence of purpose, low salaries and decreasing budgetary allocations led to a downward spiral of morale among the armed forces and resentment against the civilian authorities for failing to provide an alternative mission. In this context, policy-makers in Argentina then reasoned that participation in peace operations would compel the military to implement reforms and perhaps become less focused on domestic politics at a time when political changes were being introduced. In other words, the expectation was that, in providing an externally oriented mission to the armed forces, they would become less politicized, hence enabling civilians to focus on domestic politics without military contestation.[11]

Participation in peace operations had important consequences for civil–military relations. First, peace operations logistics were fully coordinated by the Ministry of Defence and its Joint Chief of Staff, which in turn undermined the traditional political importance of the service commanders (Army, Air Force, and Navy). Slowly but surely, colonels and majors who had once revolted against the government began to accept the leadership of the President and the Joint Chief of Staff in the Ministry of Defence. Second, peace operations provided a new externally oriented mission that modified the structure and organization of the military. Procurement, purchase and recruitment policies were transformed as a result of Argentina's engagement in UN affairs. The military went from being a praetorian institution, focused on national security doctrines, to a relatively modern force inspired by UN doctrines. Third, peace operations served as a tool for civilians to divide and conquer.

The recruitment process benefited the cadre of officers (young, junior army officers and non-commissioned officers) who in the past had been associated with revolts against the government and the military leadership. Participation in UN peace operations was thus part of a civilian strategy to purge insubordinate staff by sending large numbers of soldiers abroad and keeping them busy in an activity that was radically different from their previous mission. That is, in the Argentine case, it worked as a diversionary strategy that effectively defused the military as a domestic factor by changing the role and focus of a particular group of uniformed personnel from domestic issues and towards external functions.

Nevertheless, it was in the economic realm where the unintended outcomes were more evident. Peace operation contributions provided individual sources of income to a politically dissatisfied military. On average, the UN payment for a member of a peace unit is US$1,000 per month. This money was paid from the United Nations directly to the government, which in turn provided extra supplements for its soldiers. In some cases, officers sent on a peace mission received an additional 25 per cent pay increase as part of the supplement. For instance, the standard payment for a peacekeeper at the rank of army sergeant was US$1,400 per month, including the UN salary and the supplement. When one considers that a sergeant in Argentina was paid US$760 dollars per month (before the 2001 devaluation), the peace operation pay supplement was of considerable consequence. Military Observers (who are sent as individuals and not as part of a unit) were paid on a different scale and system, receiving a daily allowance directly from the United Nations ranging from US$85 to US$120, depending on the mission. The devaluation of the Argentine peso in December 2001 drastically affected salary incentives for participation in peace operations. By 2002, 63 per cent of all armed forces personnel were making less than 716 Argentine pesos a month (about US$250). Conversely, on a peace mission, non-commissioned officers were being paid US$1,000 a month. Not surprisingly, when the government announced a possible deployment to Afghanistan, the army received almost three times as many applicants as positions available for a unit consisting of 600 infantry men.[12]

Therefore, UN peace operations were accepted by the military as a partial solution to its institutional and financial crisis. In due course, the extra salaries placated complaints about decreasing military budgets and facilitated relations between civilian politicians and soldiers, as the government provided monetary incentives for military subordination. In other words, participation in UN peace missions was a carrot in exchange for institutional military obedience. Peace wages were not incompatible with civilian control, since the sources of money were known, discussed by several ministries and eventually approved by civilians. Argentina's defence policy consisted of reducing the number of soldiers and dividing the forces to eradicate the sources of future military revolts.[13] In this sense, participation in peace operations did fulfil the expected outcomes that Argentine decision-makers envisioned from the very beginning.

Participation in peace operations also had a positive unintended effect on military procurement, which began to change as a result of Argentina's increased engagement in UN missions. In 1982 the United Kingdom imposed a military embargo against Argentina that banned all military exports from NATO members to Buenos Aires. But, because of Argentina's commitment to UN peace missions, the Clinton administration granted the country the status of major non-NATO ally in 1997, in effect reversing the embargo by the United Kingdom. This measure made it possible for Argentina to buy outmoded equipment from NATO states, participate in interoperability exercises and obtain credit to buy military gear.[14]

Some Argentine officials, however, expected more assistance from the United States, and members of the Menem administration even harboured the illusion of being accepted as a full NATO ally. Notwithstanding this disillusionment, the extra-ally partnership did change Argentina's foreign suppliers. In the past, Argentina had relied on Soviet, European and local military technology. But the involvement in UN missions made the United States Argentina's main supplier of military procurement. It obtained equipment from Washington through either donation or direct purchase. For example, Deborah Norden found that, in order to fulfil UN commitments, the Navy acquired 2 ships and 20 Mohawk reconnaissance planes, and the Air Force bought 36 Skyhawk fighter planes from the United States.[15]

However, involvement in peace operations was also a very expensive endeavour into which the Argentine state had to pour a lot of resources to maintain contented troops abroad. Eventually, those resources generated corruption among top civilian decision-makers, as money was transferred from the UN Headquarters in New York to Buenos Aires. For instance, in 1992 the United Nations paid US$3 million to compensate for injuries and deaths caused during service in Croatia. The money, however, never reached the actual victims. Sergeant Sergio Balia lost both his legs in a landmine accident and for this tragedy the United Nations paid US$230,000, but he received only US$1,800; civilian authorities in the Ministry of Economics kept the rest.[16] Paradoxically, military budgets were becoming more transparent in Argentina because the sources of money were known. There was, indeed, more civilian control over military budgets, but no one made civilians accountable for their decision-making on UN peace operations.

Another unintended consequence generated by Argentina's involvement in UN peace operations was that a far more profound internal reform within the military, regarding the modernization of the fleet and its rapid deployment in the country, was halted, because the best and brightest were being detailed to the United Nations for peace operations.

Analogous to neighbouring Argentina, the Uruguayan military lacked public recognition and was in desperate need of a mission. The Uruguayan transition to democracy in 1985 left the armed forces in a defensive position, where they had to continuously justify their existence to citizens who were traditionally critical of their role. Faced with domestic criticism and economic shortages, military advisers in the Uruguayan Ministry of Defence reasoned that participation in peace operations would help alleviate budgetary ills by providing both additional salaries and operational incentives. The expectation was that the United Nations would pay the salaries of all participating peacekeepers plus equipment depreciation. UN peace missions promised an alternative mission to address the identity crisis and guaranteed resources for salaries and for future defence procurement. In other words, the military engaged in peace missions merely for institutional survival reasons. In so doing, it went from being an inward-oriented service to an outward-oriented institution that dedicates most of its energies to UN peace operations.

UN peace operations have transformed procurements, budgets and even the internal structure and organization of the Uruguayan military. Indeed, the military has strong monetary incentives to join UN efforts. Salaries can be more than tripled during peace service. For example, a lieutenant colonel is paid roughly US$700 a month. While on a UN mission, the same officer can make up to US$6,000 a month; this is more than quadruple his or her normal salary because of all the extra incentives the state provides, such as a 50 per cent pay increase. Likewise, a non-commissioned naval officer earns US$100 a month; while on a UN mission, the same soldier can make up to US$1,000 a month.[17] Certainly, some of the expectations about the automatic economic benefits of UN peace participation were unrealistic. The government did not realize that UN payments were slow and could take up to two years for full reimbursement. But, overall, the armed forces had more to win than to lose from UN engagement.

Nevertheless, in contrast to Argentina, participation in peace operations did not substantially increase civilian control in Uruguay. Today, civilians do not have sufficient information about Uruguayan peacekeepers, nor do they know about the levels of expenditure for training and equipping peacekeeping personnel. For instance, Uruguayan soldiers are participating on a large scale in UN missions in Africa, where the levels of HIV infection are high, yet no civilian authority has information about cases of HIV contracted during these peace missions. The military believes that, unless that information is explicitly requested, it has no obligation to share it or make it public. Some of the variation in effects on civilian control between the two *río platense*[18] countries can be best explained in terms of military prerogatives. In Uruguay, there is still a high level of military prerogatives. In particular, the coordination of the defence sector, which in effect manages policies regarding peace operations, is still in the hands of active and retired officers, with very few civil servants or civilian appointees, except for the minister of defence and her very close personnel. Ultimately, civilians exercise very weak comprehensive planning of Uruguay's UN peace contributions, which in turn prevents higher levels of effective civilian control.

Nowhere are the differences between Argentina and Uruguay more evident than in the educational component of UN peace operations. Both Argentina and Uruguay have established peace operation training centres to prepare their corps of peacekeepers. In both cases, a certain degree of adjustment has occurred since the engagement in UN peace operations took place in the early 1990s. The armed forces have adjusted their training programmes to UN demands, providing English courses for their troops, offering specialized instruction on military observer and monitoring missions, and recruiting former peacekeepers as instructors. However, such policies have had varying effects on civilian control.

In Argentina's Joint Peace Operations Training Centre (CAECOPAZ), civilians actively participate, either as instructors or as students. Diplomats, politicians and psychologists give courses on several issues, including international law, humanitarian intervention and psychological adjustment to pre- and post-deployment stages. Instructors at CAECOPAZ invite scholars and international participants to train and provide information to Argentina's peacekeepers. An intensive course for journalists is also given every year at Campo de Mayo's CAECOPAZ, in Buenos Aires.

The Uruguayan Peacekeeping Operations School, in contrast, is informal in its approach and institutionally underdeveloped. The curriculum is not stated in manuals, there is no debriefing and there are virtually no civilian components. Despite the fact that the training provided at the centre is joint and inter-service, the instruction is strictly military with little or no civilian intervention. Military officers provide courses on international and humanitarian law and rarely invite outsiders or expert scholars to their lectures.[19]

In sum, the evidence from the case studies suggests that participation in peace operations strengthens civilian control in some cases, but it is epiphenomenal in others. Different levels of military prerogatives have varying consequences when they interact with variables such as participation in peace operations. The more prerogatives a country has at the initial stage of UN engagement, the more likely that civilian control will remain unchanged. Involvement in peace operations is likely to improve civilian control in democratizing countries that have low levels of military prerogatives. In these circumstances, the institutional and legal frameworks provide less constraining conditions for civilians and thus allow for increasing levels of civilian intervention when the armed forces are engaged in UN peace operations. Conversely, participation in UN peace missions may be inconsequential and even decrease military subordination to civilian authorities in institutional settings where military prerogatives are high. In these latter cases, best exemplified by Uruguay, military autonomy and reserved domains insulate the armed forces from civilian intervention,[20] even if they are engaged in externally oriented missions.

Peacekeeping participation and intervention by foreign policy bureaucrats

Active participation and engagement in official international organizations are believed to help civilian political leaderships increase their control over the military security sector. This is because, in peace operations, civilian officials in governments and international organizations lead the missions. The evidence, however, suggests that there is a high degree of variation in terms of civilian intervention by Foreign Ministry bureaucrats.

Argentina is a case where civilian intervention by Foreign Ministry bureaucrats had the largest positive effects on civilian control. In fact, most experts agree that Argentina used two-level strategies to deal with UN peace operations. That is, the government's policies were influenced by domestic and international considerations. Domestically, extensive UN engagement was a political strategy to deal with the *cuestión militar* (the military issue). Internationally, Argentina's active involvement in UN politics stemmed from President Carlos Menem's desire to satisfy the United States.[21] As Carlos Escudé, a former foreign policy adviser, explains, "We reached our bottom line in 1982 with the Malvinas fiasco.... We were *de facto* a pariah state in the international arena. It was clear that in order for us to enter the club of modern nations, we had to unequivocally declare that Argentina was a Western, reliable and predictable nation."[22] Therefore, troop deployments to missions in the Persian Gulf, the former Yugoslavia and Haiti, which were highly esteemed and valued by US government officials at the time, were a way of expressing international commitment.

The domestic consequence of this policy is that, by making participation in peace operations a foreign policy issue, Menem in effect transferred powers and decision-making authority to the Foreign Ministry. Indeed, the Foreign Ministry went beyond its legal mandate, trespassing on ground that would normally have been reserved for the Ministry of Defence. Argentine diplomats in New York and Buenos Aires set the criteria for participation in peace operations, determining who the peace-keepers would be and when and where they would be sent abroad. This is a rather unusual procedure, since, as David Pion-Berlin reminds us, nothing in the constitution or the Law of Ministries specifically allows the Foreign Ministry to represent the nation's interests in security or defence affairs abroad, although it may do so in a host of other areas.[23] Hence, slowly but surely, decision-making powers were delegated to ambassadors at the expense of military organizations. This shifting of power and resources improved military screening, because Argentine peace-keepers were forced to report information to the Foreign Ministry and to follow diplomatic instructions. Politicians appointed ambassadors to key positions in the Ministry of Defence and used diplomatic missions to monitor deployments, thus strengthening civilian control.

Likewise, involvement in peace operations generated a national debate about Argentina's foreign policy. Scholars and practitioners with knowledge on international relations began publicly to debate defence and peace operation matters as part of Argentina's external affairs. In so doing, a qualitative expansion of the defence policy community took place, thus increasing civilian expertise and contributing to improve the quality of civilian control.

The most solid evidence that participation in peace operations generated a wide debate on security issues among civilian experts is the amount of literature on peace missions published during this period. At least 34 books, articles and working papers on peace operations were written by civilians in Argentina between 1993 and 2001. From a cursory view, the amount of literature seems rather small compared with the large number of articles that are available in military journals, such as *Revista Militar*.[24] However, if one considers that security studies in Argentina was a field once dominated exclusively by the military, then the appearance of civilian-led publications on military affairs is a radical and welcome change. In fact, Argentina has the largest academic production on matters regarding peace operations in the Southern Cone of Latin America. Equally surprising is the fact that some Argentine civilian experts have written articles in military journals. This suggests that there has been a certain degree of acceptance of civilian views on defence and military matters.

Argentina fits Samuel Huntington's model of subjective civilian control, in which civilians violate the military's professional autonomy and compell the armed forces to defer to civilians in the military realm. For Huntington, this model introduces serious pathologies, since subjective control impairs military effectiveness and leads to failure in the battle-field.[25] For most Argentines, however, subjective control (the unintended effect) is better than no control at all. Nevertheless, congressional oversight was not improved and diplomats were not fully accountable for their decisions and actions; hence, civilians had more control over the armed forces but democratic institutions were somewhat eroded.

Uruguay offers a contrasting case, where weak diplomatic organizations have facilitated military interference in foreign policy issue areas. In contemporary Uruguay, there has not been an explicit attempt to incorporate the armed forces into foreign policy objectives. In fact, unlike India, Canada, Sweden, Argentina or Brazil, countries that actively participate in the UN system, Uruguay has never been part of the UN Security Council and there are no plans to join the body as a non-permanent member. The unintended consequence of this policy is that the Ministry of Foreign Affairs does not participate in the decision-making process regarding peace operations. The system effectively increases the policy leverage of the Ministry of Defence because it has more information on peace operations than any other civilian agency in Uruguay. Furthermore, the information is not always shared, debriefed or diffused among other civilian-led bureaucracies. In other words, there are no political or civilian institutions monitoring or controlling Uruguay's UN peace contributions.

Consequently, policies on peace operations in Uruguay are perceived exclusively in security terms and not as a complex response to post-conflict peacebuilding, where the military component is but one element of a multidimensional system that combines security, political, socio-economic and reconciliation dimensions under one complex peace operation mandate. Part of the problem is that civilian defence policy communities in Uruguay are small and not very influential. Civilians rarely discuss or debate matters such as peace operations. This is a surprising finding for a country that has almost 1 peacekeeper for every 280 citizens. In theory, almost every Uruguayan inhabitant knows or has been in contact with at least one peace soldier. In practice, however, there is little knowledge about peace operations.

Another unintended effect of Uruguay's engagement in peace operations is that the quality of civilian defence expertise has been somewhat eroded. For instance, there are at least 117 articles on peace operations in Uruguayan military journals. Conversely, only two articles were found in academic civilian journals and not a single book or major volume has been produced by a commercial or academic publisher.[26] Engagement in peace operations has not encouraged military officers to share information about peace missions with civilians nor has it increased civilian interest in military affairs. This leads to problems of information asymmetry, accountability and lack of civilian control. For example, the most recent

Uruguayan involvement in the UN mission in the DRC (MONUC), where more than 2,000 peacekeepers were deployed from Montevideo, created a foreign policy controversy because this peace enforcement operation (under Chapter VII of the UN Charter) is opposed by most politicians because of the implicit political/military risks. The military argues that such a mission provides resources for survival, whereas civilians consider foreign policy consistency to be far more important than economic benefits. At the time of writing of this chapter, military preferences seemed to have prevailed, since peacekeepers have not been withdrawn from the DRC. This fact questions not only foreign policy decisions but also civilian control. If civilians are against participation in UN peace enforcement operations but the military succeeds, then who is in charge of defence and peace policies? Uruguay's involvement in UN peace operations suggests that the armed forces either ignore civilian preferences or have sufficient power to influence politicians; in either case, civilian control is weakened. This poses a serious challenge to civil–military relations because, if the military prevails most of the time, then what should we expect if more serious divergences between soldiers and civilians emerge in the future?

Furthermore, another important unintended effect of the current Uruguayan decision-making process is that the military has become less risk averse, especially with regard to peace enforcement operations. This seems to be the result of the lucrative nature of participation in these missions – individual officers are now more willing than in the past to engage in dangerous operations in exchange for higher salaries. I have not argued that military views are necessarily incompatible with civilian perspectives but, as Georges Clemenceau's old adage reminds us, "war is too important to be left to the generals". If this adage is valid for war issues, it is even more compelling for peace matters, which, under normal conditions, are dealt with by politicians and diplomats, not generals or commanders. The findings of this study, however, suggest that some countries are entrusting their armed forces with the implementation of key decisions, but at the expense of civilian control. Consequently, it may be hypothesized that participation in peace operations can have unintended and even negative consequences for civilian control, unless Foreign Ministry and civilian bureaucrats assume a very active role in the decision-making process regarding peace deployments.

Peacekeeping and its civilizing and professional effects on soldiers

Engagement in peace operations can also have an effect on individual military officers as people. Peacekeepers can be involved three types of

184 ARTURO C. SOTOMAYOR

activities when they are deployed abroad: traditional observer missions, multidimensional missions and peace enforcement missions. By performing several types of military and civilian tasks and interacting with foreign armies and civilian personnel, participation in peace operations can affect the military personnel as individuals. Social interaction in the mission can dilute military organizational interests and may have consequences for civilian control if officers become more civilianized or more professional.

I define civilianization as the inclusion of functions that are not inherently military but create greater flexibility and civil–military penetrability. Civilianization effects take place when soldiers perform civilian tasks in peace operations or when, over a protracted period, they become heavily dependent on civilian infrastructures, as they train for and perform their civilian duties rather than strict military activities. Peace officers so trained are likely to bring to their jobs a wider world view, certainly more civilian in perspective than that of their purely military peers. By contrast, I define professionalism as the development of military expertise, involving skills, training, knowledge and operation for war-making and the management of violence. Professionalism occurs when peace soldiers establish contacts with foreign armies and execute highly specialized military duties in peace operations, such as imposing sanctions or monitoring armies.[27]

The task of testing hypotheses about social interaction involves analysing how different types and mandates of peace operations exercise divergent effects on the levels of civilianization and professionalism. First, there is ambiguous evidence about the effects on the levels of civilianization. Civilianization effects were strong in some multidimensional peace operations where peacekeepers assist civilians in national reconstruction processes. In UN operations in Central America, East Timor and Mozambique, South American peacekeepers had the opportunity to rebuild armies, train police forces and provide security for UN personnel and non-governmental organizations (NGOs), build refugee camps and help monitor electoral processes. The degree of cooperation between civilians and soldiers in these missions was high and smooth. Logistics were well coordinated, civilians cooperated and peacekeepers were subordinated to civilian international and local authorities.

Nevertheless, Argentine officers were not particularly exposed to these operations, since less than 0.22 per cent of all Argentine peacekeepers participated in multidimensional missions under Chapter VI. Furthermore, a substantial number of Uruguayan peacekeepers (54.4 per cent) participated in multidimensional missions where cease-fire agreements were violated, as in Angola, Cambodia, the DRC, Rwanda and Sierra Leone. In these cases, the peacekeepers were involved in policing and internal security functions, sometimes suppressing civilian unrest rather than assisting civilian reconstruction. In other cases, as in Angola, Cambodia and the DRC, blue helmets were responsible for deterring or halting active combatants; this work in part resembled their previous domestic mission, focused on counter-insurgency and deterrence of guerrillas. Therefore, it is unclear whether these missions increased the civilianization of the soldiers or simply reinforced old doctrines. It seems that, for some soldiers, participating in peace operations involves fulfilling the types of function for which they have been traditionally trained and from which civilian reformers want to wean them.

Similarly, this study could not find substantial evidence suggesting that observational missions increase civilianization effects. Argentina has the most experience in these types of operation, with a participation rate of 35.6 per cent, followed by Uruguay (19.5 per cent). Interviews with South American blue helmets engaged in UN observational missions in Cyprus, India/Pakistan, Iran/Iraq and the Middle East (Israel/Syria) did not indicate high levels of civilian inter-penetrability. In these cases, Military Observers were in charge of monitoring troop movements and interacted mostly with foreign armies, not with civilians. The only civilian interaction took place outside the mission, when observers were off duty.

Of all the operations examined in this project, peace enforcement operations exercise the fewest civilianization effects. Uruguay is currently engaged in its first peace enforcement operation in the DRC and Haiti. About 62 per cent of all Argentine peacekeepers have participated in peace enforcement operations in Europe, Latin America and the Middle East (including Haiti, Yugoslavia and Iraq/Kuwait). In personal interviews with 13 commanders, Argentine officers emphasized the military benefits of participation in peace enforcement operations. The tasks they performed included eliminating landmines, deterring Serbian forces, controlling garrisons and coordinating logistical support with NATO-participating countries. Civilian components were coordinated by UN staff and NGOs, but with little civil–military inter-penetrability. These blue helmets did interact with civilians, but for them the most important aspect of the mission was the military component. This does not imply that peacekeepers were not involved in the delivery of humanitarian relief and the protection of NGOs. However, the main functions performed in these operations are strictly military in nature. Officers engaged in these missions put into practice skills that they learned as professional soldiers, using military force if necessary rather than negotiation and persuasion (the so-called soft power elements). Consequently, the argument about the civilianization of the soldier in peace enforcement missions is somewhat questionable.

Secondly, I found substantial variation between participation in peace operations and military professionalism. Argentine peacekeepers continuously socialized and interacted with NATO forces in several UN missions in Cyprus, Croatia, Haiti, Iraq/Kuwait and the former Yugoslavia (Kosovo, Prevlaka and Slovenia.) Personal accounts and debriefings of Argentine peacekeepers suggest that they increased certain professional military skills in peace enforcement operations.[28] In Cyprus, Argentine peacekeepers interacted mostly with British soldiers. Ironically, 10 years after the Falklands/Malvinas war, the two former foes would meet once again on an island far from the South Atlantic.

The mingling of Argentine and British troops had interesting cultural and professional consequences. I was told of numerous accounts of passionate and intense soccer and rugby matches between the two former rivals, but there were other far more revealing exchanges. For instance, a Malvinas veteran from the Argentine Navy who cooperated with the British Royal Navy in Cyprus described his personal experience as follows: "I will never concede the Malvinas to the British, but I recognize their professionalism. Now I understand why we lost the war."[29] This comment implies that peacekeepers were learning more than just war-making techniques. They also developed a sense of corporateness, as soldiers identified themselves with other foreigners of the same profession. Argentine peacekeepers were re-educating themselves using role models as they interacted with armies that were already under firm civilian control. They observed the institutional behaviour and personal conduct of professional officers who were experts in their field, shared a sense of organic unity and performed their missions with responsibility. They saw how US and European troops carried out their missions professionally and responsibly, even if they disagreed with their civilian commanders. Ultimately, Argentines internalized the procedures of NATO officers, in the expectation that in so doing they would be acclaimed too. As a result, when the Argentine officer asserted that he knew why they had lost the war in 1982, he implied that the involvement of the military in Argentina's domestic politics had been a major mistake and an abandonment of the distinguished characters of the military profession.

Analogous experiences were not replicated in Uruguay, where blue helmets have interacted and socialized mostly with armies from developing countries in Africa and the Caribbean. Uruguay has sent its largest UN troop contributions to missions in Angola, the DRC, Mozambique and now Haiti. In these cases, Uruguayan peacekeepers have mingled with forces from Ghana, India, Nepal, Nigeria, Malaysia and Pakistan. Compared with the South American armed forces, the militaries of these countries have fewer resources and deploy non-commissioned soldiers rather than commissioned officers. So, it is unlikely that Uruguayan blue helmets in UN missions in Africa are acquiring or developing new professional or technical skills. Again, in most cases, peacekeepers are developing police and national guard duties rather than conventional military skills.

Prospects for the future and contributions to theory and policy

Some of the empirical results in this project are still largely inconclusive. Statistical and survey studies are required to test more rigorously the effects of participation in peace operations. Governments, the United Nations, military institutions, think tanks and foundations have to be convinced that surveys and polls are needed to evaluate the (intended and unintended) consequences of internationalism on soldiers. Unfortunately, there is still a huge informational gap in Latin America on military affairs since data are not always disclosed or are simply not available because no one has bothered to generate them. I hope that this contribution will create new avenues of research and will encourage future scholars to engage in peace studies in South America in a more systematic way.

This study provides a number of empirical and policy contributions. A large body of literature concludes that participation in peace operations has positive effects on civil–military relations, particularly in reinforcing civilian control of the armed forces. I have exposed a serious flaw in this research. There are many different types of peace participation that have divergent effects on civilian control. When militaries have prerogatives, face few constraints from diplomats and parliamentarians, and interact with less developed armies, involvement in peace operations has perverse effects on civilian control. My research suggests that, instead of focusing exclusively on successful cases, we should try to explain the variations in order to understand better why engagement in UN peace operations can lead to unintended consequences that ultimately undermine civilian control. Explaining variation also facilitates the identification of clear causal mechanisms and underlying conditions.

My research on South American peace contributions is an initial attempt to theorize and elucidate how the UN policies of transitional and democratizing regimes differ and vary in their effects from the UN peace contributions of consolidated democracies. A growing trend in the United Nations is to recruit peacekeepers from third world countries, some of which are experiencing transitions from dictatorial rule. My research goes beyond so-called area studies because the findings in this study provide insights for other states that are currently using peace policies as a strategy to reform their armies. My arguments give some theoretical clues to what we should expect when countries such as Nigeria,

Serbia or Mexico (my native country) decide to deploy peacekeepers to UN operations.

One of the most significant barriers to strong democratic and civilian control of the military in Latin America is the lack of civilian policy-makers with expertise in military matters. Perhaps the most important policy prescription derived from this project is that, although participation in UN peace operations remains important for socializing militaries, it will have little success if it is not supplemented with programmes reaching out to civilians, who also need to develop defence expertise. Peacekeepers cannot be effective in consolidating civilian control when diplomats and politicians leave peace and war matters in the hands of soldiers. Embracing peacekeeping when the country is not diplomatically prepared challenges civilian control, because it provides opportunities for the military establishment to perform as it deems necessary without much political monitoring. Therefore, programmes and policies need to be designed to empower and strengthen diplomatic organizations and civilian institutions in democratizing states. This involves training more career diplomats and members of civil society in security affairs and engaging civilians in the decision-making process.

Acknowledgements

For comments on earlier drafts I thank Chiyuki Aoi, Richard K. Betts, Douglas Chalmers, Cedric de Coning, Rut Diamint, Michael Doyle, Page V. Fortna, Matthew Kocher, Farid Kahhat, Kimberly Marten, Covadonga Meseguer, Susan Minushkin, Antonio Ortiz Mena, Katia Papagianni, Lorena Ruano, Juan Rial, Alfred Stepan, and participants at the UNU/TfP/ACCORD Unintended Consequences of Peacekeeping Book Project Author's Workshop. I am also grateful to the Columbia University Center for International Conflict Resolution, the Institute for the Study of World Politics and the Academic Council for the United Nations System, which provided generous funding to conduct field research in Argentina and Uruguay in 2002 and 2003 respectively.

Notes

1. C. C. Moskos, J. A. Williams and D. R. Segal, "Armed Forces after the Cold War", in Charles C. Moskos, John Allen Williams and David R. Segal, eds, *The Postmodern Military: Armed Forces after the Cold War*, New York: Oxford University Press, 2000, pp. 1–13.
2. M. Desch, *Civilian Control of the Military: The Changing Security Environment*, Baltimore, MD: Johns Hopkins University Press, 1999, p. 122; G. Marcella, "Warriors in

Peacetime: Future Missions of the Latin American Armed Forces", in Gabriel Marcella, ed., *Warriors in Peacetime: The Military and Democracy in Latin America*, Portland, OR: Frank Cass, 1994, pp. 1–21.

3. Desch, *Civilian Control of the Military*, p. 122.

4. D. L. Norden, "Keeping the Peace, Outside and In: Argentina's UN Missions", *International Peacekeeping*, 2(3), Autumn 1995, pp. 346–347.

5. Robert Jervis has used the term "unintended effects" for actions that have unexpected consequences "on the actor, others, and the system as a whole, which means that one cannot infer results from desires and expectations and vice versa". See Robert Jervis, "Realism, Neoliberalism, and Co-operation: Understanding the Debate", *International Security*, 24(1), Summer 1999, p. 62. See also Robert Jervis, *Systems Effects: Complexity in Political and Social Life*, Princeton, NJ: Princeton University Press, 1997.

6. Ejército Argentino, *Soldados Argentinos por la paz*, Buenos Aires: Servicio Histórico del Ejército Argentino, 1997.

7. Col. Ricardo José Etchegaray, "Operaciones militares de paz", Permanent Mission of Argentina to the United Nations in New York, mimeo, 1999.

8. Ejército de la República Oriental del Uruguay, *El ejército Uruguayo en misiones de paz*, Montevideo, Uruguay: Ejército de la República del Uruguay, 1999, pp. 20–38.

9. See A. Stepan, *Rethinking Military Politics: Brazil and the Southern Cone*, Princeton, NJ: Princeton University Press, 1985, p. 325; C. G. Gillespie, *Negotiating Democracy*, Cambridge, MA: Cambridge University Press, 1991, pp. 50–76; C. Perelli, "The Legacies of Transitions to Democracy in Argentina and Uruguay", in Louis W. Goodman, Johanna S. R. Mendelson and Juan Rial, eds, *The Military and Democracy: The Future of Civil–Military Relations in Latin America*, Lexington, MA: Lexington Books, 1991, pp. 39–54; A. Barahona de Brito, *Human Rights and Democratization in Latin America: Uruguay and Chile*, New York: Oxford University Press, 1997, pp. 38–66.

10. Personal interview with General Héctor R. Islas, Director General of the School of the Arms and Services, and Lt Col. Pablo Pintos, Director of the School of Peacekeeping Operations at the School of the Arms and Services, Uruguayan Army, Montevideo, Uruguay, 8 August 2003.

11. The literature on Argentina's peacekeeping operations is vast. See, for instance, Deborah L. Norden and Antonio L. Palá, "Peacekeeping and Its Effects on Civil–Military Relations", in Jorge I. Domínguez, ed., *International Security and Democracy: Latin America and the Caribbean in the Post-Cold War Era*, Pittsburgh, PA: University of Pittsburgh Press, 1998, pp. 130–150; Antonio L. Palá, "The Increased Role of Latin American Armed Forces in UN Peacekeeping: Opportunities and Challenges", *Airpower Journal*, Special Edition, 1998, pp. 1–10; Andrés Fontana, "Seguridad internacional y transición democrática: La experiencia Argentina, 1983–1999", working paper, Facultad de Estudios para Graduados de la Universidad de Belgrano, Buenos Aires, Argentina, 2001; Marcelo Fabián Saín, "Seguridad regional, defensa nacional y relaciones cívico-militares en Argentina", in Francisco Rojas Aravena, ed., *Argentina, Brasil y Chile: Integración y seguridad*, Santiago, Chile: FLACSO, 1999, pp. 125–162; Ricardo E. Lagorio, "Institutionalization, Cooperative Security, and Peacekeeping Operations: The Argentine Experience", in Jorge I. Domínguez, ed., *International Security and Democracy: Latin America and the Caribbean in the Post-Cold War Era*, Pittsburgh, PA: University of Pittsburgh Press, 1998, pp. 121–129.

12. D. Gallo, "El 63% de los uniformados del Ejército cobra menos de $716", *La Nación*, 28 October 2002, available at ⟨http://www.lanacion.com.ar⟩.

13. Arturo Sotomayor, "The Peace Soldier from the South: From Praetorianism to Peacekeeping", unpublished PhD dissertation, Department of Political Science, Columbia University, United States, 2004.

14. See "Lauding its Peacekeeping, Clinton Offers Special Ally Status to Argentina", *International Herald Tribune*, 17 October 1997, p. 12. See also Carlos Escudé and Andrés Fontana, "Argentina's Security Policies: Their Rationale and Regional Context", in Jorge I. Domínguez, ed., *International Security and Democracy: Latin America and the Caribbean in the Post-Cold War Era*, Pittsburgh, PA: University of Pittsburgh, 1998, pp. 51–79; Rafael Grossi, "Los límites del intervencionismo humanitario", Instituto del Servicio Exterior de la Nación-Nuevohacer-Grupo Editorial Latinoamericano, Buenos Aires, Argentina, 2000; and Saín, "Seguridad regional, defensa nacional y relaciones cívico-militares en Argentina".
15. Norden, "Keeping the Peace, Outside and In", p. 345.
16. See "Indemnización a heridos y víctimas fatales: Controversia por fondos para cascos azules argentinos, la mayor parte no llegó a los destinatarios", *La Nación,* 12 January 2003, Sección política, p. 9.
17. Personal interviews with Ricardo J. Schunk, Director of Peacekeeping Operations, Uruguay's Navy, Montevideo, 20 August 2003, and Col. Picabea, Director of Peacekeeping Operations, Army General Staff's Office, Uruguayan Army, Montevideo, 5 August 2003.
18. The term *río platense* refers to the Plata River area, which is shared by Argentina and Uruguay.
19. Arturo Sotomayor, "The Peace Soldier from the South", pp. 92–149.
20. Reserved domains are areas of policy that elected government officials would like to control in order to assert governmental authority or carry out their programmes but are prevented from controlling by veiled or explicit threats of a return to authoritarian rule. They are imposed by the military, which often has crucial access to state power to make credible threats against recently elected governments. J. S. Valenzuela, "Democratic Consolidation in Post-Transitional Settings: Notion, Process, and Facilitating Conditions", in Scott Mainwaring, Guillermo O'Donnell and J. Samuel Valenzuela, eds, *Issues in Democratic Consolidation: The New South American Democracies in Comparative Perspective*, Notre Dame, IN: University of Notre Dame, Press, 1992, pp. 66–67.
21. See Deborah L. Norden, "The Transformation of Argentine Security", in Richard L. Millet and Michael Gold-Biss, eds, *Beyond Praetorianism: The Latin American Military in Transition*, Miami: North-South Center Press, 1996, pp. 241–260; Norden, "Keeping the Peace, Outside and In", pp. 330–349; Joseph S. Tulchin, "Continuity and Change in Argentine Foreign Policy", in Joseph S. Tulchin and Allison M. Garland, eds, *Argentina: The Challenges of Modernization*, Wilmington, DE: Scholarly Resources, 1998, pp. 163–197; Jorge Bolívar, "La cuestión de la identidad en la nueva política exterior argentina", in Andrés Cisneros, ed., *Política exterior Argentina, 1989–1999: Historia de un éxito*, Buenos Aires, Argentina: Nuevohacer-Grupo Editorial Latinoamericano, 1998, pp. 213–236; Escudé and Fontana, "Argentina's Security Policies".
22. Personal interview with Carlos Escudé, scholar and former foreign policy adviser to Minister Guido de Tella, Buenos Aires, Argentina, 29 January 2002.
23. David Pion-Berlin, *Through Corridors of Power: Institutions and Civil–Military Relations in Argentina*, Pennsylvania: Pennsylvania State University Press, 1997, p. 152.
24. Arturo Sotomayor, "The Peace Soldier from the South", pp. 112–130.
25. Samuel Huntington, *The Soldier and the State: The Theory and Politics of Civil-Military Relations*, Cambridge, MA: Harvard University Press, 1957, pp. 80–94.
26. The two articles published by Uruguayan scholars are: Selva López Chirico, "Forças Armadas e democracia: Um olhar para o passado recente a partir do final do século", in Maria Celina D'Araujo and Celso Castro, eds, *Democracia e forças armadas no Cono Sul*, Rio de Janeiro, Brazil: Editora FGV, 2000, pp. 179–213; and Julián González, "Fuerzas armadas en tiempos de escasez: El riesgo de la desnaturalización funcional",

Observatorio Político, 3, Spring 2003, pp. 101–103. For a complete list of publications on peacekeeping available in Uruguay, see Arturo Sotomayor, "The Peace Soldier from the South", pp. 175–206.

27. Samuel Huntington's classic work, *The Soldier and the State*, contributed to my understanding of military professionalism and its impact on civilian control. One of Huntington's main arguments is that, in order to instil organizational loyalty and obedience, military organizations have to develop their own area of expertise, distinguished by an emphasis on war skills, hierarchy, tradition, rituals and a sense of "corporateness". For Huntington, the key to objective civilian control is professionalism, which maximizes military fighting power and minimizes civilian interference. Civilian control is achieved when, in exchange for professional autonomy, the armed forces voluntarily subordinate to civilian authority and refrain from intervening in domestic politics. Morris Janowitz disagreed with Huntington and took a more sociological approach to military professionalism. In his landmark book *The Professional Soldier*, he showed that the military will be a reflection, although not a copy, of the society it serves. For Janowitz, the self-conception of the military can be somewhat apart from society, but not fully separated. In his view, the professional soldier has to reflect the dominant values of the society he or she serves, for which the civilianization of the military is required. In this context the importance of a broad liberal education on the part of military leaders becomes relevant for achieving civilian control. For example, educating officers in liberal arts colleges as a complement to the official military academies constitutes an important form of civilian control. For Janowitz, officers so trained are likely to bring to their jobs a wider world view, certainly more civilian in perspective than that of their purely military peers. See Huntington, *The Soldier and the State*, and Morris Janowitz, *The Professional Soldier: A Social and Political Portrait*, Glencoe, IL: Free Press, 1960.

28. See Ejército Argentino, *Soldados Argentinos por la paz*.

29. Personal interview with Lt Col. Francisco Alejandro Ramirez, Chief of the Department of Peacekeeping Operations in Development, Argentine Joint Chief of Staff, Ministry of Defence, Buenos Aires, Argentina, 23 February 2002.

Part V
Accountability

10

The accountability of personnel associated with peacekeeping operations

Françoise J. Hampson and Ai Kihara-Hunt

The underlying purpose of a peacekeeping operation is undermined when personnel actually or apparently associated with it break the rules. That is exacerbated when no action is or appears to be taken against the suspected perpetrator. In other words, effective accountability not only is to be desired in itself but is essential if the goals of the operation are not to be subverted.

Scope of the study

The operations

The operations include all operations created by or endorsed by the United Nations, other than enforcement actions or Security Council endorsed exercises of the collective right to self-defence.[1] Operations *created* by the United Nations include those with a mandate under Chapter VI or Chapter VII of the UN Charter. They include operations to be carried out by UN forces ("blue berets") and those carried out by military forces not under UN command. They include traditional peacekeeping and so-called peace enforcement operations. They include operations that do not have a military component. Operations *endorsed* by the United Nations include operations authorized, lawfully or otherwise, by some other organization and subsequently endorsed by the United Nations, such as the Economic Community of West African States'

Unintended consequences of peacekeeping operations, Aoi, de Coning and Thakur (eds), United Nations University Press, 2007, ISBN 978-92-808-1142-1

cease-fire monitoring group (ECOMOG) operation in Liberia and the Kosovo Force (KFOR) in Kosovo, provided that the operation endorsed by the United Nations was of a peace support operation (PSO) type.[2]

The personnel

The range of personnel included in the study is wide. They include members of armed forces, "civilians accompanying the armed forces",[3] foreign civilians working for companies under contract to a military contingent, Military Observers (MOs), Civilian Police (CIVPOL), international civil servants, including UN Headquarters employees, UN employees in the field, UN Volunteers, the staff of intergovernmental organizations (IGOs), including specialized agencies, Headquarters' employees in the field, the foreign staff of international non-governmental organizations (NGOs) and civilians (whether national or foreign) performing services for any of these categories of personnel.

Accountability

The principal focus of this chapter is not the possible vicarious liability of the United Nations as an employer or the general civil liability of the international organizations.[4] This will, however, be addressed in passing. The focus is rather on examining who has the responsibility to address criminal conduct or breaches of applicable disciplinary codes on the part of the employees described above.

Misconduct

Allegations of misconduct can be divided into three categories: acts that are within the ostensible mandate of the mission; individual criminal acts; and acts that are disciplinary offences. Individual criminal acts are either (i) acts that are criminalized in the majority of states (e.g. rape, murder), or (ii) acts that amount to international crimes. In some circumstances, that may give rise to a problem where behaviour in many states is regarded as criminal but is not regarded that way in the host state and is not an international crime (e.g. spouse rape).

In the case of acts within the ostensible mandate of the mission, there are two issues. First, it may be clear that the mandate gives the authority, in certain circumstances, to take the action in question. The issue will be whether those circumstances existed at the relevant time (e.g. killing resulting from the use of potentially lethal force during the course of a confrontation with members of a PSO mission). Secondly, there may be doubt whether the mission has the mandate to take that action at all and, if it can, there may be doubts with regard to the manner in which it is done (e.g. the authority to detain[5]). Where acts are within the ostensible mandate of the mission, questions may arise regarding the liability under human rights law of the sending state in relation to military contingents. In relation to other personnel, it is not clear who might have responsibility under human rights law (see further below).

Where individuals engage in conduct in breach of a disciplinary or contractual code binding on them, they may be liable to punishment of a disciplinary or contractual nature. Although such conduct can include behaviour not of a criminal nature, it may overlap with criminal conduct (e.g. harassment). Where individuals engage in conduct of a criminal character, they ought to be subject to criminal proceedings. It is treated as self-evident that, where misconduct is criminal in character, it is not sufficient for the United Nations to offer compensation. It is also necessary to attempt to identify the suspected perpetrator and then to bring criminal proceedings against him or her.

In virtually all PSOs there have been allegations of misconduct, but to varying degrees. This study seeks to:
- determine whether it is possible to evaluate the scale and seriousness of the problem accurately,
- identify what is supposed to happen,
- determine whether what is supposed to happen actually happens in practice.

Methodology

In order to evaluate the scale and seriousness of the problem and to determine what actually happens in practice, research was conducted into allegations of misconduct in PSOs since 1990. Information was gathered from official reports by the United Nations, from reports by sending governments and from NGO reports and the media. The trigger was an allegation of a violation of the rules. In each case, there was an attempt to identify whether administrative or criminal proceedings had ensued and whether there was any information available about the ultimate outcome. General accusations could not usually be followed up. The database that was created was therefore confined to specific allegations, even if the suspected perpetrator was not identified.[6]

There is no reason to believe that each UN mission has been evenly reported. Furthermore, since a significant number of reports come from sending states, alleged wrongdoings that result in action are more likely to be reported than an allegation where no action was taken. Since the responsibility of the sending state is most obviously engaged in the case of military personnel, it is likely that allegations against such personnel are better reported by sending states. There are also more reports about some kinds of individual criminal act than others, such as offences of a sexual nature (101 cases out of 230 allegations, excluding allegations of widespread misconduct). This makes it impossible to draw conclusions with regard to the scale and seriousness of misconduct. The evidence may, nevertheless, reveal possible patterns, such as the relative number of allegations made against members of armed forces or CIVPOL. It should, however, be remembered that there are significantly different numbers of different types of personnel in different missions.

Category of personnel and immunity

It is essential to analyse the different categories of personnel because that is likely to determine whether they are subject to a disciplinary or a contractual code and whether they may benefit from some form of immunity. Different categories of personnel have different chains of command.

Members of national contingents

The first, and often the biggest, component of PSOs is the members of national military contingents. They are employed not as individuals but as part of contingents. This means that the command chain remains within the contingent. They are subject to the exclusive criminal and disciplin-

Table 10.1 Immunity and jurisdiction

Types of personnel	Immunity from host state jurisdiction	Disciplinary authority	Criminal jurisdiction
1. Members of national contingent	AI	SS	SS/(TS)
2. Military Observers	FI	UN/SS	HS/SS/(TS)
3. CIVPOL	FI	UN/SS	HS/SS/(TS)
4. Very senior UN official	AI	UN	x(TS?)
5. UN official	FI	UN	HS/(SS)/(TS)
6. Non-UN official mission staff	FI	UN	HS/(SS)/(TS)
7. International IGO staff	FI/x	IGO	HS/(SS)/(TS)
8. Other foreign personnel	x	employer	HS/(SS)/(TS)
9. Local person working for categories 1–7	FI/x	UN/employer	HS/(TS)
10. Local person working for category 8	x	employer	HS/(TS)

Notes: AI = absolute immunity; FI = functional immunity; x = no immunity; SS = sending state; HS = host state; TS = third state.

ary jurisdiction of the sending state. They are protected by absolute immunity from host state jurisdiction, normally by a Status-of-Forces Agreement (SOFA – either a bilateral SOFA or application of the Model SOFA[7]). Even without any SOFA, they are protected by sovereign immunity.[8] Which categories of "civilians accompanying armed forces" are included (in the exclusive jurisdiction of the sending state) will depend on the law of the sending state. This makes the follow-up even more difficult, especially if there is a lack of will on the part of the sending state to take action. Where they are UN forces, they should come under the ultimate command of the Force Commander. In international law, there is no legal obligation to obey the orders of the Force Commander. It is absolutely clear that in practice the majority of contingents reserve the right to consult their own capital, particularly in difficult operations, such as those in Somalia and Rwanda.[9]

Military Observers

Military Observers (MOs) are recruited as individuals, and they have to be full-time serving members of armed forces.[10] They are recruited through the government of the sending state. Under the sending state's legislation, its authorities should have criminal and disciplinary jurisdiction over them. Their status is that of Experts on Mission, based on the SOFA. This means that they enjoy immunity from the host state jurisdiction with regard to official acts.[11] They come under the command of the United Nations while on mission.[12]

CIVPOL

CIVPOL officers are recruited as individuals, and they have to be serving or retired members of a national police force.[13] They are recruited through their sending state governments. Whether they are subject to the disciplinary jurisdiction of the sending state may depend on whether they are still serving officers and on whether the police/gendarmerie code of discipline applies outside the national territory.[14] Their status is that of Experts on Mission, based on the SOFA, and thus they are also protected by functional immunity from the host state jurisdiction.[15] They should come under the command of the CIVPOL commander, who will in turn be under the command of the Special Representative of the Secretary-General (SRSG).

International civil servants

UN international civil servants have different levels. Very senior officials of this category enjoy absolute immunity.[16] It is not clear whether this protects them from the exercise of criminal jurisdiction by third states, including their home state.

UN civil servants who are holders of the UN laissez-passer are "officials" and are protected by functional immunity.[17] It is not clear if the home state can bring proceedings against them, because their functional immunity appears to be universal, including from their home state jurisdiction.[18]

UN civilian staff members without the status of "officials" are also protected by functional immunity.[19] They are regarded as Experts on Mission mainly based on a SOFA, and such functional immunity is only from the host state jurisdiction.[20] Recent missions have tended to treat more civilian staff as "officials" for this purpose. For example, UN Volunteers are treated as "officials" in recent SOFAs.[21] All UN international civil servants are normally either directly or indirectly subject to the UN Staff Rules.

In PSOs, other intergovernmental organizations (IGOs) are normally present. Some of the foreign employees of intergovernmental organizations are "officials" of the United Nations, if the organization they work for is within the "UN family". The status and immunities of other foreign members of intergovernmental organizations depend on the Memorandum of Understanding (MOU) that is normally agreed between the organization and the host state. They are normally subject to a separate agency-specific code of conduct. Such codes and disciplinary proceedings are to some extent coordinated (Common System).[22]

Other foreign staff

Foreign staff working for NGOs normally enjoy no special status. This means that they are subject to the host state jurisdiction. Whether or not the home state law applies to them depends on the home state law with regard to criminal jurisdiction, but, as a matter of practice, it is difficult for the home state to exercise jurisdiction over them. They may be subject to the disciplinary code of the NGO they work for, or in some cases it may be written in their contract that they are also subject to other codes. In the case of the NGO they work for being an implementing partner of one of the UN components or agencies, there may be some agreement to subject them to UN codes.

There are also foreigners employed by any of the people already mentioned, usually contractors such as lorry drivers and security guards. They are usually employed under a contract between their employer and the other agency. In some cases, they may be discharging functions previously carried out by armed forces.[23] The disciplinary code to which they are subject depends on their contract. Whether or not the home state law applies to them depends on the home state legislation, but, as a matter of practice, it is difficult for the home state to exercise jurisdiction over them.

Local staff

All the above categories normally have national staff working for them (i.e. nationals of the host state). Those working for the United Nations or intergovernmental organizations enjoy limited functional immunity, based on the SOFA, apart from staff paid by the hour. Except for the above, they are subject to the host state jurisdiction.[24] They are normally subject to the disciplinary codes of the organization they work for.

Types of immunity

Some measure of immunity serves an important purpose. It is designed to enable a person or organization to discharge its responsibilities independently.

Host state immunity

Different categories of personnel have different types of immunity from the jurisdiction of the host state under the General Convention, bilateral SOFA, Model SOFA or MOU.

Full immunity

Very senior UN international civil servants are entitled to full diplomatic immunity.[25] Members of a national military contingent are protected by absolute immunity from the host state jurisdiction, usually as provided in a SOFA.[26]

Functional immunity

Functional immunity or provisional immunity is an immunity from legal process in respect of words spoken or written and all acts performed by them in their official capacity, or in the course of the performance of their mission in the case of the Experts on Mission.[27]

MOs, CIVPOL, the majority of UN international civil servants and some local personnel working for one of the above are protected by functional immunity, either by the General Convention or by the SOFA. Foreign personnel working for intergovernmental organizations are protected by functional immunity, depending on the agreements between the relevant organization and the host state. Other foreign persons are normally not covered by immunity.

There remain uncertainties in the area of functional immunity. The meaning to be given to "during the course of their duty" is determined by the SRSG. This has caused some confusion in the field. For example, in a case of rape in the United Nations Transitional Administration in East Timor (UNTAET), the alleged perpetrator's immunity was declared inapplicable owing to the alleged act being outside of official functions.[28] On the other hand, in a case of murder in the United Nations Interim Administration Mission in Kosovo (UNMIK), the suspect's immunity was waived.[29] In the latter case, one would have expected the act to be outside the scope of the immunity.

Where immunity is not applicable, foreigners working under contract for one of the components above or foreign staff working for international NGOs are subject to the host state jurisdiction.

In many situations in which PSOs are deployed, there is no national authority with which to negotiate a SOFA (e.g. Somalia) or no agreement. There have been PSOs where the international component has gone into the territory before negotiating the SOFA with the host state.[30]

Even where the exercise of host state jurisdiction is a theoretical possibility, it should be remembered that, in many of the types of situation in which a PSO is deployed, there *is* no functioning legal system. Impunity in practice is not solely attributable to the existence and exercise of immunity; it may be the product of the lack of a local legal system.

Waiver of immunity

The absolute immunity of members of a national contingent is not normally subject to waiver.[31] Apart from that, other immunities can, in theory, be waived.

Immunities granted for MOs, CIVPOL, UN international civil servants and local personnel can be waived by the SRSG (in the name of the Secretary-General), where he or she considers the immunity would impede the course of justice, and where it can be waived without prejudice to the interests of the United Nations.[32] In the case of SRSG, the Secretary-General has a right and duty to waive.[33] In the case of personnel of intergovernmental organizations, waiver of immunity is normally determined at the Headquarters.

The function of immunity is not to give impunity. Particular difficulties arise where the United Nations is not simply present in a territory but is, in effect, acting as its government.[34] Governments do not have immunity. On the contrary, human rights law requires that governments should be capable of being called to account. Any proposals designed to avoid the risk of immunity giving rise to impunity should distinguish between situations where the United Nations is, in effect, the government and those in which it is present alongside some form of national government.

Sending states and immunity

Members of national contingents are subject to the exclusive criminal and disciplinary jurisdiction of the sending state. In some states, criminal proceedings against members of armed forces are conducted by court martial. In others, all nationals, including members of the armed forces, are subject to normal (i.e. civil) criminal jurisdiction, even for acts committed abroad. Where that is not the case, special legislation may provide for the possibility of normal criminal proceedings for acts committed abroad specifically in the case of members of armed forces.

For MOs and CIVPOL, there is no legal basis for immunity from the sending state's criminal jurisdiction. MOs are serving officers of a national defence force and should be subject to the criminal and disciplinary jurisdiction of the sending state. For CIVPOL, too, there is the possibility of prosecution by the sending state, but that depends on whether the state has laws in place that permit the prosecution of all nationals for acts committed abroad or that permit the prosecution of police officers for acts committed abroad.[35] Generally, civil law countries are able to exercise criminal jurisdiction over nationals for acts committed abroad, whereas common law countries can do so only where there is express legislative provision to that effect. MOs and CIVPOL, as Experts on Mission, are not entitled to immunity from their sending state criminal jurisdiction.[36] Wherever functional immunity is based on a SOFA, the sending state immunity question does not arise.[37]

There being no legal barrier for the exercise of criminal jurisdiction by the sending state does not, however, mean that such proceedings are likely. There may be a need for express legal provision and, above all, for the necessary practical arrangements to be put in place. There are also likely to be practical difficulties in having access to the victim, witnesses and other evidence.

UN international civil servants, who are entitled to functional immunity under Article V of the General Convention, seem to be protected by immunity against the exercise of their home state jurisdiction as well.[38] By contrast, some categories of UN civilian staff, such as UN Volunteers or consultants, do not enjoy functional immunity in their home state, because their immunity is provided on the basis of the SOFA.[39]

Some foreign personnel of intergovernmental organizations appear to have functional immunity from the courts of their national jurisdiction. For those appointed for a short term, immunity derives from an MOU, and immunity in the state of nationality will depend on its provisions. Other foreigners, such as foreign staff of NGOs and foreign contractors, do not enjoy immunity. Depending on national legislation on extraterritorial jurisdiction and practical barriers, there is the possibility of their being prosecuted in their home state. The right and duty to waive immunity in relation to a staff member's home state rest with the Secretary-General.

Immunity and third states

In the exceptional case of the alleged misconduct taking the form of an international crime, any state is permitted to exercise jurisdiction in relation to a person located within that state's territory, based on universal jurisdiction, provided that the suspect is not protected by immunity. There is no known example of a third state claiming jurisdiction over a member of a PSO.

In addition to the usual questions regarding the applicability of immunity outside the host state, there may be questions of diplomatic immunity.[40] The same practical problems may be expected to arise as in the case of prosecution by the sending state.

Jurisdiction of international criminal courts

Where an international or hybrid court is created under international law to address violations in a particular region or conflict, the scope of its jurisdiction will be determined by the statute of the court. Such courts may have jurisdiction over persons who would otherwise be protected by immunity (e.g. the trial of Milosevic before the International Criminal Tribunal for the former Yugoslavia). The International Criminal Tribunal for the former Yugoslavia, for example, examined the possibility of war crimes proceedings arising out of NATO operations in Kosovo.[41] The position is the same in relation to the International Criminal Court (ICC). It would appear that national courts are required to give effect to the personal immunity of senior officials.[42]

Practical problems are likely to arise in relation to the collection of evidence and access to the victims and witnesses. Political opposition to the ICC and limited resources may also act as deterrents.

The civil liability of the United Nations

As indicated at the outset, this will be touched on only briefly. Whether or not compensation is provided, there is still a need to identify and to bring criminal proceedings against suspected perpetrators of misconduct that is criminal in character. The issue of the United Nations' civil liability as an employer may arise when civil wrongs are committed by its staff. The United Nations, as such, is immune from legal proceedings in local courts.[43] The United Nations generally provides compensation for civil wrongs through a Civil Claims Unit.[44] One case is unusual in that a complaint alleging wrongful arrest and unlawful detention was brought against the SRSG personally, and not against the United Nations. A Japanese national made the claim against the SRSG, the minister of justice of East Timor, the Prosecutor-General and a judge. The District Court in East Timor failed to rule that the matter was covered by diplomatic immunity, at least in the case of the SRSG. The District Court awarded compensation and the matter was then appealed. The Court of Appeal overturned the decision by the District Court, based on an argument that such a complaint should be made against the United Nations instead of individuals working for the United Nations. The complainant was awarded compensation outside the Court.[45]

In addition to claims against the United Nations, national contingents may establish mechanisms to deal with civil claims. For example, many of the national contingents serving in Somalia had some form of civil complaint system open for the local population.[46] Where such a system is put in place, the United Nations needs to know of the existence of such complaints, what information has been gathered regarding the complaint and what the contingent has done regarding the complaint. The United Nations should ensure that complainants are kept informed. There may be the possibility of civil claims being brought against the sending state in its own courts.[47] The operation of civil claims seems to be less than transparent.[48] Where a PSO has a Civil Claims Unit, transparency depends on whether the procedures are translated into the local language and whether the public knows about them.

How allegations of misconduct are handled

It is necessary to emphasize that there is no way of knowing what proportion of actual misconduct results in some form of official complaint and what proportion of complaints appear in official documents. In the types of situation in which a PSO is deployed, there may be difficulties of communication, making it difficult to ensure that the population knows how to complain. There could be difficulties in travelling, making it difficult to reach the place where complaints should be lodged, and, above all, a lack of confidence in any form of complaints procedure. This may be because the population never had the experience of effective accountability for governmental acts or its experience of the PSO may lead it to assume that effective accountability will not be delivered in practice, whatever the rhetoric. In addition, there may be a cultural reluctance to report certain types of crimes, particularly those of a sexual nature.[49] The only way of obtaining a more accurate picture would be if all missions included human rights monitors whose responsibilities included the seeking out of information of alleged misconduct by any PSO personnel. It should also be remembered that the victim of misconduct may be not a member of the local population but another member of the PSO.

Alleged criminal conduct

Internal proceedings

The following account describes what is supposed to happen. When there are allegations of criminal acts by members of military contingents, MOs, CIVPOL officers or UN civilian personnel, such allegations are normally reported to one of the components of the mission. All the personnel in the mission are supposed to report allegations of serious misconduct by members of national contingents, MOs and CIVPOL to the SRSG, who should conduct a preliminary investigation.[50] It is assumed that the same thing should occur in the case of allegations against civilian personnel, although there is no express provision in the Staff Rules. Based on the result of the investigation, the SRSG may call a Board of Inquiry (BOI), which is composed of at least three senior staff. Where the alleged perpetrator is a member of a national contingent, the BOI normally invites a representative from the contingent to sit on the board. The same applies for allegations against MOs and CIVPOL. The Board will recommend appropriate action against the perpetrator if the allegation is substantiated. The SRSG will make recommendations on subsequent measures based on the BOI recommendations in the case of members of national contingents, MOs and CIVPOL.[51] Some uncertainty remains as to the power of the SRSG at this stage (e.g. can the SRSG ignore a BOI recommendation? Can he or she waive immunity before BOI proceedings?[52] What happens if the allegation is against the SRSG?). For members of armed forces, the SRSG can make recommendations, but it is up to the national contingent to subject the alleged perpetrator to criminal/ disciplinary proceedings.[53] For MOs, CIVPOL and UN civilian personnel, the United Nations can take disciplinary measures, but it lacks criminal jurisdiction over anyone. There are two main possibilities for criminal proceedings: proceedings in the host state and in the home state.

Where the victim is a member of staff of the United Nations, he or she may invoke the internal grievance procedure. That process is not the subject of the current study but it should be noted that it has been said to give rise to a variety of difficulties. They include allegedly defective processes for investigating the facts, notably concerns over the independence of those responsible for the investigation and a lack of oral hearings. During these oral hearings, each party may call witnesses and cross-examine witnesses. There should be an appeal mechanism that accepts the facts as found by the other body and which again does not hold oral hearings. A concern is also expressed at the significant number of cases in which a person who invokes the grievance procedure then finds that his or her contract is not renewed. This issue raises squarely the extent to which the United Nations itself should be bound by the requirements of due process in human rights law.

Other intergovernmental organizations normally have their own system, which is similar to the one for PSO personnel. For "UN family" agencies (e.g. the United Nations High Commissioner for Refugees, the United Nations Children's Fund), the "Common System" has been developed, and proceedings are centralized in New York.[54] Other categories of personnel are normally treated in the same way as other foreigners present in the state. They may be subject to some form of disciplinary proceedings by virtue of a term in their contract.

External proceedings – host state

When allegedly criminal acts may be within the official function of the alleged perpetrator and where the host state is contemplating bringing proceedings, issues of functional immunity may arise (see above). Thus, it may be necessary for the SRSG either to declare immunity not to be applicable or to waive the immunity. The borderline between the two (declaration of non-applicability of immunity and waiver of immunity) is not clear, and the decision is left to individual SRSGs. In a case involving an alleged rape by a Jordanian member of CIVPOL, the SRSG initially waived immunity and later said that immunity was not applicable.[55]

Even in cases where a host state is in a position to request permission from the SRSG to exercise criminal jurisdiction, it may choose not to do so for a variety of reasons. The host government may feel too intimidated to ask for jurisdiction over the staff of agencies and organizations that are providing assistance.[56] In particular, it may feel incapable of asking for jurisdiction over nationals of powerful countries.[57] It may be misled by the SOFA and think that that confers absolute immunity or it may lack the capacity to deal with cases involving difficult issues (immunity and waiver) before the already overstretched courts.

The problem is further exacerbated by the frequent rotation of personnel. Even if action against an alleged perpetrator starts, that person's contract may be over before the action is completed.[58] For example, many of the CIVPOL officers serving for PSOs have one-year contracts, but some, such as Australian CIVPOL officers in UNTAET, had contracts for three months only.[59] The host state may become even more reluctant to request criminal proceedings against a CIVPOL officer if its perception of the UN accountability mechanisms is that nothing ever happens to personnel found guilty of criminal misconduct. There are provisions in the Directives that prohibit alleged perpetrators from leaving the host state's jurisdiction before all the proceedings are complete. The number of cases where alleged perpetrators leave the jurisdiction in mysterious circumstances before or during the proceedings against them is striking. We have a report of at least five cases where suspects fled during the proceedings against them.[60] In one case, the alleged perpetrator was detained by the host authorities and had surrendered his passport at the time of his flight.[61]

The problems caused by rotation affect not only suspected perpetrators. Senior officials complain that staff involved in investigations, supervisors, members of BOIs and witnesses rotate during the proceedings, which makes the process slow and difficult.

There may be additional issues in the host state exercising criminal jurisdiction. There may be no functioning court system in the host state. The host state jurisdiction may not be compatible with human rights law, either because the criminal code itself is not compatible with it or because the way in which the criminal code is enforced is not compatible with it. Where the United Nations is acting in effect as the government, there may previously have been special difficulties in calling state agents to account in the host state. In such cases, waiving the immunity of the alleged perpetrator either may not be an acceptable option for the United Nations or may not result in prosecution.

External proceedings – home state

For members of national contingents, these are the only criminal proceedings they may face for acts that do not constitute international crimes. For MOs, CIVPOL and all UN civilian personnel who are under the disciplinary control of the United Nations, the maximum action the United Nations can directly take is repatriation. After repatriation, criminal proceedings may be brought in the home state (see earlier for possible problems with the rules on jurisdiction of the home state and practical difficulties in bringing proceedings).

There are four possible difficulties in securing the effective exercise of the criminal jurisdiction of the sending state:
• allegations may not be investigated thoroughly,
• the investigation may not have been effective,
• proceedings may not always be brought where they should be,
• the charge may not adequately reflect the seriousness of what is alleged to have taken place.

Even where a person is convicted, the sentence or penalty may not adequately reflect the seriousness of what has been proved to have occurred. For members of national contingents, MOs and CIVPOL, the BOI files may be made available to the sending state for following up.[62]

The sending state may be in breach of human rights norms in relation to these issues.

The follow-up mechanism on the part of the SRSG is not sufficiently institutionalized and depends too much on the individual discharging the role. The United Nations is supposed to make enquiries as to what actions the sending state has taken for repatriated members of national contingents, MOs and CIVPOL.[63] In practice, there is evidence of a lack of follow-up. Apparently at least 90 per cent of repatriated CIVPOL officers' cases are not followed up by the United Nations.[64]

Part of the problem is that there is no obligation on the sending state to supply information with regard to disciplinary/criminal proceedings against repatriated officers. Another possible difficulty is the administrative burden that might be imposed by effective follow-up. It should be recalled, however, that any apparent lack of accountability is not only bad in itself but seriously weakens the authority and credibility of the mission as a whole and undermines the possibility of securing accountability in the future within the host state. It gives the appearance that the United Nations is requiring states to accept practices to which it itself is not willing to conform. For these reasons, it needs to be made mandatory for any allegation, even one made directly to the national contingent itself, to be referred to the SRSG and he or she needs to be required to follow up any allegation with regard to a member of a national contingent. In other words, the SRSG should be required to obtain information regarding the result of the investigation, whether charges have been brought and, if so, for what offence and the result of any such proceedings. To that end, it would be useful if national contingents were required to provide that information to the SRSG.

For UN civil servants and staff of intergovernmental organizations, there are no "sending states" and this makes it even more difficult to follow up on the cases where the alleged perpetrators are dismissed. There are also practical barriers, such as evidence collection and access to witnesses/victims. Considering that one of the principal rationales for prosecution is to deter the commission of crime, the impact of any proceedings in the sending state may be less than if the suspect was prosecuted in the host state. That effect could be reduced if it was required that the SRSG be informed of such proceedings. The SRSG would then be able to publicize them in the host state. The sending state may not see very much interest in prosecuting its national after the suspect returns home, because the victim is far away from the place of prosecution.

Where a BOI finds that an accused person is responsible for criminal conduct, the United Nations ought to be able to ensure that that person is never employed in a PSO again, whatever the recommendations of the BOI.

Disciplinary codes and proceedings

Acts of misconduct may include acts that are against disciplinary codes but are not criminal in character. There are different disciplinary codes for different categories of personnel. Most of the organizations, from the United Nations, intergovernmental organizations and NGOs, to companies working under contract, have disciplinary codes. UN staff members are subject to the Staff Rules. Other UN civilian personnel, with fixed or short-term contracts, are normally also indirectly subject to the UN Staff Rules. Either their contracts provide such provisions or the Code of Discipline to which they are subject refers back to the Staff Rules. Staff of NGOs contracted as implementing partners for UN agencies may be subject to the disciplinary code of the UN agency, depending on their contract. Foreigners working for companies may be subject to some form of disciplinary code by virtue of the terms of their contract. Other foreigners may not be subject to any form of disciplinary proceedings.

For the United Nations, BOIs are the main disciplinary proceedings to which PSO mission personnel are subject. All allegations of serious misconduct against all the PSO personnel must be dealt with by BOIs.[65] BOI procedures are the same as those for criminal acts, as the BOI includes criminal acts in the "serious misconduct" category.[66] If claims against members of national contingents are substantiated, the only and maximum disciplinary measure BOIs can recommend is repatriation.[67] For MOs and CIVPOL, there are a range of actions that BOIs can recommend, including recovery of the mission subsistence allowance, redeployment and repatriation.[68] In relation to UN staff members, the penalties available are those set out in the Staff Rules.[69] Other UN civilian personnel are normally indirectly subject to the Staff Rules, and thus the penalties are the same as for staff members.

Allegations of minor misconduct against members of national contingents, MOs or CIVPOL are dealt with by the national contingent and senior officers of MOs/CIVPOL. Whether a particular act constitutes serious misconduct or minor misconduct may not be obvious in some cases. In the case of the military and CIVPOL, that determination is made by the superiors who receive the allegation.[70]

The Directives impose an obligation on all the people working for PSO missions to refer all allegations of serious misconduct to the SRSG. However, there is little evidence that this obligation is known to personnel in the field, especially to local personnel.[71] An additional problem is that there may be no obligation on, for example, personnel working for intergovernmental organizations to refer allegations of serious misconduct to anyone.

Transparent accountability for disciplinary offences is important. If it is perceived that the alleged authors of misconduct are left unpunished, that may undermine the credibility of the mission itself. It is particularly important where the misconduct has an impact on the host population and where it regards the misconduct in question as criminal in character. In places with no functioning judicial system, disciplinary proceedings may well be the only proceedings to deal with every kind of misconduct.

There are, however, certain concerns regarding disciplinary codes and proceedings. First, each intergovernmental organization has its own disciplinary rules and mechanisms. This may contribute to the confusion in the host population as to what to expect. It may be unclear for some categories of personnel, such as UN Volunteers or personnel employed by an NGO but working for the United Nations, what code applies. In addition, foreigners who are not subject to disciplinary codes may be perceived as enjoying impunity by the host population.

Disciplinary jurisdiction by the perpetrator's home state usually exists over its armed forces, MOs, members of CIVPOL and seconded civil servants. For members of national contingents, their sending state's disciplinary jurisdiction is the primary one. It is easier for them to ensure disciplinary accountability, at least in theory, because contingents function within the national chain of command. Even in cases where the United Nations recommends disciplinary action against a member of a national contingent, its enforcement will be left to the contingent.[72] There is, again in theory, little problem in enforcing national disciplinary codes for MOs, because they are serving members of their national armed forces. Disciplinary proceedings for retired CIVPOL officers is dependent upon the applicability of the disciplinary code in such circumstances (see above).

It has been said, with regard to national disciplinary proceedings, that some CIVPOL officers and military personnel have been repatriated without any proper proceedings. This was apparently so in at least some cases in the International Police Task Force (IPTF) in Bosnia.[73] In practice, in many cases, as soon as an allegation is made of serious misconduct, the member of CIVPOL concerned is repatriated by his or her national authorities or encouraged to return home voluntarily, without any form of proceedings taking place.[74] Some evidence is available regarding the practice of some contractors persuading the alleged perpetrator of misconduct to resign voluntarily.[75]

Disciplinary charges may be brought where the conduct alleged ought to give rise to criminal proceedings. Conversely, in certain cases a disciplinary charge may in fact amount to a criminal charge, if the nature of the offence and of the potential penalties is of the requisite gravity. Where disciplinary proceedings in effect determine a criminal charge, the due process guarantees of human rights law are likely to be applicable.

Ombudspersons

The United Nations has set up other mechanisms that also deal with misconduct. An ombudsperson's office was set up in UNTAET and UNMIK, and the ombudsperson was authorized to receive complaints against all the people employed by the United Nations, as well as against personnel working for local authorities.[76] A local ombudsperson's office was also set up in other PSO missions, including in the United Nations Mission of Support in East Timor (UNMISET).[77] Ombudspersons have the authority to receive complaints, investigate and make recommendations to the relevant authority, but lack the authority to enforce the recommendations.

Ad hoc mechanisms

In addition, in response to increasingly visible allegations of misconduct appearing in the media, there have been some ad hoc mechanisms in recent PSO missions. These include the Personnel Conduct Committee in the United Nations Mission in Sierra Leone (UNAMSIL)[78] and the Code of Conduct Committee in the United Nations Operation in Burundi (ONUB).[79]

Such mechanisms normally have the authority to receive and look into complaints and make recommendations to the relevant authority, but they lack the authority to enforce the recommendations. An additional problem with such quasi-judicial mechanisms is that they are often very ad hoc and are set up in response to particular claims. They are consequently often not well known to the public. Many such mechanisms use people in high positions working part time for the mechanism.[80]

Office of Internal Oversight Services

There is also the Office of Internal Oversight Services (OIOS), established in 1994 to increase the strength of internal oversight within the United Nations. Part of its mandate is internal investigation. Reports of possible violations of rules or regulations, mismanagement, misconduct, waste of resources or abuse of authority can be followed up by the OIOS Investigation Division. Such reports can be made by any individual, and the OIOS can also initiate its own investigation for serious cases.[81]

The OIOS has taken up investigations into serious misconduct by PSO personnel, such as sexual exploitation in the Democratic Republic of Congo, and brought the reports to the attention of the General Assembly. It called for coercive action against the perpetrators of 20 substantiated cases, which was accepted by the Department of Peacekeeping Operations (DPKO) and the United Nations Organization Mission in the Democratic Republic of Congo (MONUC).[82]

The OIOS does not have criminal jurisdiction over any of the personnel, but it can recommend various disciplinary and administrative actions against perpetrators of substantiated misconduct.

General conclusions with regard to the operation of the various systems in practice

Significant changes have been made in the past few years to attempt to deal with criminal and disciplinary matters outside the mandate. The United Nations, however, does not appear to accept accountability for acts committed *within* the mandate. This poses particular difficulties in the case of PSOs where the United Nations is, in effect, the government of the territory or in the case of personnel other than military personnel.[83]

The problems in practice appear to include the following.

- *Prevention*: although the codes of conduct are in place, the institutional infrastructure to guarantee that all misconduct is reported and then acted upon is not yet in place. This issue is within the mandate of the Best Practices Unit of the Department of Peacekeeping Operations (PBPU).[84] The DPKO has been making considerable efforts to clarify what is expected of personnel, such as the 2003 Directives, and it provides training on related issues, such as gender awareness and HIV. However, gaps remain, such as the position of foreign civilian contractors providing services previously provided by military contingents or CIVPOL.[85] More needs to be done to specify precisely what powers are given by the mandate. Sending states should be required to guarantee that members of military contingents and CIVPOL have been adequately trained. Spot checks should be carried out to ensure that this in fact occurs. The training should include mission-specific information, such as the local age of consent and the local age of criminal responsibility. The focus should not be exclusively on misconduct of a sexual character.[86]
- *Operationalization of the system*: there is no guarantee that the SRSG is informed of all allegations. There are two elements to this. Public information campaigns need to be part of each PSO to ensure that the population knows how to complain and can do so easily. This needs to take account of realities on the ground.[87] Second, every member of a PSO should be required to ensure that any complaint is referred to the SRSG, even if it is dealt with elsewhere (e.g. within a national contingent).

The procedures to be followed need to be institutionalized.[88] A member of staff of the SRSG should be required to follow up every allegation against a member of a military contingent, to discover the outcome of any investigation, whether proceedings have been brought and the result of such proceedings. Sending states should be responsible for bringing criminal proceedings against "civilians accompanying the armed forces" and civilians employed under a contract with a national contingent.

It should be the responsibility of a state providing members of CIV-POL to bring criminal proceedings against individuals found responsible by a BOI for what amounts to criminal conduct, where that is not done by the host state. The SRSG should be required to follow up such cases. Where other personnel are found responsible for serious misconduct by a BOI, which recommends dismissal, that person should not be employed in the future in any other PSO. Where the misconduct constitutes a criminal offence and criminal proceedings do not take place in the host state, the person should be repatriated and proceedings should be brought in his or her home state.

It is recognized that these proposals would require some states to modify their rules on the exercise of criminal jurisdiction. The alternative would be for the United Nations to run its own criminal courts within the host state. That would be likely to give rise to very real difficulties in practice.

The obligations towards the complainant need to be clarified. There should be a requirement that the complainant be informed of the results of the investigation and proceedings.[89] The only reference in the Directives is "the SRSG may if necessary use the BOI report to appropriately inform the victim/individuals concerned of the action taken".[90] With regard to an investigation or proceedings within CIVPOL, the CIVPOL Commissioner also does not have an express responsibility to notify the complainant of the process or the result of the investigation/proceedings, although it is apparently done usually as a matter of course.[91] In practice, in at least one mission, that does not seem to have occurred.[92] This undermines the victim's trust in the proceedings themselves. It is crucial to instil the notion of accountability and of the rule of law in a post-conflict society.

There is a need to address the problem of reluctant witnesses, especially civil servants who are requested to testify against their superior(s). For various reasons, including the fear of suffering adverse consequences in the workplace, they may not be willing to give evidence to the investigating authority. UN officials believe that it is compulsory for all civilian staff to give testimonies when called upon to do so by a BOI.[93] However, there is evidence that, even while confirming orally that they know the allegation to be true, they are not willing to give evidence to a BOI.[94]

This suggests that UN personnel have little faith in the United Nations' capacity to deal with allegations.[95] This may be related to a perceived lack of independence of the accountability mechanisms.[96]

The operation of the mechanisms in practice at present is not transparent and does not ensure effective accountability. In addition to being wrong, in and of itself, this also severely undermines the credibility and integrity of the mission. Creating or restoring the rule of law is usually an important part of the function of a mission. Such efforts are badly damaged when the United Nations is not seen to practise what it preaches.

There are conflicting signals regarding the seriousness with which the United Nations views these issues. On the one hand, there have been the 2003 Directives and the Secretary-General's Bulletin,[97] which speaks of zero tolerance. On the other hand, the Special Committee on Peacekeeping Operations in 2004 noted that the meeting called for in the previous session, to discuss ways and means of meeting the challenges to minimize misconduct,[98] had not been held. The United Nations has shown some willingness to address some issues. It remains to be seen whether there is the willingness in the United Nations and amongst member states to examine all the issues thoroughly, to institute all reforms found to be necessary and to ensure that they are all implemented in practice.

Notes

1. This excludes only the operation to liberate Kuwait following the Iraqi invasion of 1990.
2. Initially, the NATO operation in Kosovo involved an international armed conflict. By the time KFOR was endorsed by the United Nations, the nature of the military operation had changed and it had become a PSO not carried out by UN forces.
3. For example civilian aircrew; this is a technical term in the law of armed conflict.
4. The responsibility of international organizations is currently being examined by the International Law Commission (Mr Giorgio Gaja, Special Rapporteur).
5. The authority to arrest, detain, search and seize may be given to both armed forces and CIVPOL. The mandate may be far from clear. KFOR, for example, appears to base its authority to detain on the "all necessary means" formula in the mandate (UN Doc. SC/Res/1244, adopted 10 June 1999). It is not clear whether this provides sufficient legal basis for detention, particularly for states bound by the European Convention on Human Rights, Article 5 of which lists exhaustively the only legitimate grounds of detention. No state participating in KFOR has submitted notice of derogation. The issue is currently before the European Court of Human Rights.
6. Ai Kihara-Hunt, PSO Accountability Database, at the University of Essex, UK, ⟨http://www2.essex.ac.uk/human_rights_centre/⟩ (accessed 8 November 2006). The database is not currently accessible, but funding is being sought to put it on-line.
7. United Nations, *Model Status-of-Forces Agreement for Peace-keeping Operations, Report of the Secretary-General*, UN Doc. A/45/594, 9 October 1990.
8. In certain states, notably common law jurisdictions, the exercise of criminal law jurisdiction is essentially territorial. This makes it essential that special arrangements are made

to ensure that criminal proceedings can be brought against members of armed forces for acts committed outside national territory.

9. It is difficult to see how, being realistic, this problem can be solved. It is equally clear that this gives rise to very real difficulties in practice for Force Commanders; see Roméo Dallaire, *Shake Hands with the Devil*, London: Arrow Books, 2004.

10. This excludes retired officers. *Selection Standards and Training Guidelines for United Nations Military Observers (UNMILOBS)*, First Draft, United Nations Department of Peacekeeping Operations, 2002, p. 15.

11. *Model Status-of-Forces Agreement*, para. 2.

12. It is not clear to what extent, in practice, they take orders from national capitals.

13. United Nations Department of Peacekeeping Operations, *Selection Standards and Training Guidelines for United Nations Civilian Police (UNCIVPOL)*, First Draft, May 1997, available at ⟨http://www.un.org/Depts/dpko/training/tes_publications/books/ civilian_police/selstand_civpol/selstand_civpol.pdf⟩ (accessed 8 November 2006), pp. 6–8.

14. In the normal course of events, states have to ensure that they can exercise jurisdiction over their armed forces for extraterritorial acts on account of the possibility of the commission of criminal acts during an international armed conflict. If they fail to make adequate provision, states will be in breach of their obligations under the Geneva Conventions. There may, however, be no expectation of their police forces or gendarmes serving outside national territory. The necessary provisions may therefore not exist.

15. *Model Status-of-Forces Agreement*, para. 26; *Convention on the Privileges and Immunities of the United Nations*, adopted 13 February 1946 by the General Assembly of the United Nations, entry into force 17 September 1946 [hereinafter *General Convention*], Article VI, available at ⟨http://www.unog.ch/80256EDD006B8954/(httpAssets)/ C8297DB1DE8566F2C1256F2600348A73/$file/Convention%20P%20&%20I%20(1946) %20-%20E.pdf⟩ (accessed 20 November 2006).

16. *Model Status-of-Forces Agreement*, para. 24; *General Convention*, Article V, Section 19.

17. *General Convention*, Article V, Section 18.

18. *Applicability of Article VI, Section 22, of the Convention on the Privileges and Immunities of the United Nations, Advisory Opinion of 15 December 1989, I.C.J. Reports 1989*, p. 194, available at ⟨http://www.icj-cij.org/icjwww/idecisions.htm⟩ (accessed 9 November 2006); *Difference Relating to Immunity from Legal Process of a Special Rapporteur of the Commission on Human Rights, Advisory Opinion of 29 April 1999, I.C.J. Reports 1999*, available at ⟨http://www.icj-cij.org/icjwww/idecisions.htm⟩ (accessed 9 November 2006).

19. *General Convention*, Article VI, Section 22.

20. *Model Status-of-Forces Agreement*, para. 2.

21. Zeid Ra'ad Zeid Al-Hussein, "A Comprehensive Strategy to Eliminate Future Sexual Exploitation and Abuse in United Nations Peacekeeping Operations", attached to UN Doc. A/59/710, 24 March 2005, Annex.

22. Bruno Simma, *The Charter of the United Nations – A Commentary*, Oxford: Oxford University Press, 1995, pp. 1091–1094.

23. For example, conducting interrogation or running detention facilities in Iraq; Ariana Eunjung Cha and Renae Merle, "Line Increasingly Blurred between Soldiers and Civilian Contractors", *Washington Post*, 13 May 2004, p. A01.

24. *Model Status-of-Forces Agreement*, para. 25; General Assembly Resolution 76 (I) of 7 December 1946, "Privileges and Immunities of the Staff of the Secretariat of the United Nations", UN Doc. GA/Res/76(i), 7 December 1946.

25. *General Convention*, Article V, Section 19.

26. Independently of the existence of a SOFA, a question may arise regarding armed forces, whether they are entitled to sovereign immunity.

27. *General Convention*, Article VI.

28. Kihara-Hunt, PSO Accountability Database, Cases aet001 and aet002.

29. Kihara-Hunt, PSO Accountability Database, Case mik009.

30. To avoid this problem, recent UN deployments have taken place only once the state into which forces have been deployed agrees to accept the provisions of the UN *Model Status-of-Forces Agreement*. Dieter Fleck, *The Handbook of the Law of Visiting Forces*, New York: Oxford University Press, 2001, p. 535.

31. Where foreign forces are stationed on a long-term basis in another state, the SOFA may well provide for waiver. It is unlikely that waiver will be used in PSOs. There may be real concerns regarding the fairness of any possible proceedings, particularly if the deployment does not have the consent of the host state.

32. *General Convention*, Sections 20, 23; *Model Status-of-Forces Agreement*, para. 47.

33. *General Convention*, Article V, Section 20.

34. It should be noted that the Ombudsperson in Kosovo objected to the scope of the immunity that the SRSG had given to his mission under his law-making capacity. Kosovo Ombudsperson Institution in Kosovo, "Special Report No. 1 on the Compatibility with Recognized International Standards of UNMIK Regulation 2000/47 on the Status, Privileges and Immunities of KFOR and UNMIK and Their Personnel in Kosovo (18 August 2000) and on the Implementation of the Above Regulation", April 2001.

35. Some states' penal codes specifically mention that the state holds jurisdiction with regard to its police officers for their criminal acts committed abroad, e.g. the Swedish Penal Code; see, generally, note 8 above.

36. Whether that is in fact the case depends on considerations previously discussed.

37. *Model Status-of-Forces Agreement*, para. 2.

38. See above pp. 197–198.

39. *Model Status-of-Forces Agreement*, para. 2.

40. *Case Concerning the Arrest Warrant of 11 April 2000 (Democratic Republic of the Congo v. Belgium)*, *I.C.J. Reports 2002*, p. 121, available at ⟨http://www.icj-cij.org/icjwww/idecisions.htm⟩ (accessed 9 November 2006).

41. *Final Report to the Prosecutor by the Committee Established to Review the NATO Bombing Campaign against the Federal Republic of Yugoslavia*, available at ⟨http://www.un.org/icty/pressreal/nato061300.htm⟩ (accessed 8 November 2006).

42. *Case Concerning the Arrest Warrant of 11 April 2000 (DRC v. Belgium)*. This calls into question the decision of the tribunal in Sierra Leone confirming the arrest warrant for Charles Taylor. The lawfulness of the arrest warrant may depend on whether the Special Court for Sierra Leone was sitting as an international or a national tribunal. The International Court of Justice is to examine this issue again in *DRC v. France*.

43. *General Convention*, Article II, Section 2; *Model Status-of-Forces Agreement*, para. 15.

44. The standing claims commission, as provided in para. 51 of the *Model Status-of-Forces Agreement*, has never been established. United Nations General Assembly, *Report of the Secretary-General, Administrative and Budgetary Aspects of the Financing of United Nations Peacekeeping Operations*, 37 ILM 700 (1998).

45. Amnesty International, "East Timor: Justice Past, Present and Future", London: 2001, AI Index: ASA 57/001/2001; Asia Press Club, "Houjin Dansei ni UNTAET ga Shazai, wakai seiritsu, hutou taiho meguru teiso juken", 1 February 2002, available at ⟨http://apc.cup.com/?no=93.0.0.33.0.0.0.0.0⟩.

46. Some were open only one morning a week, and others were open more frequently. Many of these mechanisms were not systematic and most of them insisted that they were dealing with *ex gratia* payments; African Rights, "Somalia, Human Rights Abuses by United Nations Forces", London, July 1993.

47. For example, *Bici and Bici* v. *Ministry of Defence*, [2004] EWHC 786, para. 84, in which two Kosovars sought compensation from the UK Ministry of Defence for the wrongful act of a soldier.
48. The matter of civil claims is not the same as *ex gratia* payments. The latter, by definition, do not deal with formal liability.
49. John Van Kesteren, Pat Maythew and Paul Nieuwbeert, *Criminal Victimisation in Seventeen Industrialised Countries: Key Findings from the 2000 International Crime Survey*, The Hague: Scientific Research and Development Centre, 2000.
50. DPKO, *Directives for Disciplinary Matters Involving Civilian Police Officers and Military Observers*, 2003, DPKO/CPD/DDCPO/2003/001 [hereinafter *CIVPOL Directives*], para. 9; DPKO, *Directives for Disciplinary Matters Involving Military Members of National Contingents*, 2003, DPKO/MD/03/00993 [hereinafter *Military Directives*], para. 9. If the alleged perpetrator is a member of a national contingent, the UN-led preliminary investigation and subsequent proceedings do not prevent any investigation or proceedings against the alleged perpetrator by the contingent.
51. *Military Directives*, paras 20–21; *CIVPOL Directives*, paras 19–20.
52. According to a senior official who worked for several BOIs in different missions, the authority of the SRSG to waive immunities before BOI recommendations is taken for granted.
53. *Military Directives*, paras 8, 28.
54. See Simma, *The Charter of the United Nations – A Commentary*.
55. PSO Accountability Database, Cases aet001 and aet002.
56. Pam Spees, "Gender Justice and Accountability in Peace Support Operations: Closing the Gaps", A Policy Briefing Paper by International Alert, London: International Alert Gender and Peacebuilding Programme, 2004, p. 23.
57. For example, it was claimed that the new local authorities found it very difficult to ask for jurisdiction over a case caused by a UN civil servant. "Ribeiro's Widow: There Is No Justice", *Timor Post*, 5 May 2004.
58. Colette Rausch, "The Assumption of Authority in Kosovo and East Timor: Legal and Practical Implications", in Renata Dawn, ed., *Executive Policing, Enforcing the Law in Peace Operations*, SIPRI Research Report No. 16, Oxford: Oxford University Press, 2002, p. 30.
59. Personal communication with Australian CIVPOL officers.
60. PSO Accountability Database, Cases aet001, aet008, mik005, mik010, and msi007. It is difficult to avoid the suspicion of collusion on the part of a variety of institutions in these cases.
61. PSO Accountability Database, Case aet008.
62. *Military Directives*; *CIVPOL Directives*.
63. *Military Directives*, para. 28; *CIVPOL Directives*, para. 31.
64. E-mail communication with a Human Rights Advisor to the CIVPOL Commissioner, UNTAET.
65. *Military Directives*, para. 14; *CIVPOL Directives*, para. 14.
66. *Military Directives*, para. 4; *CIVPOL Directives*, para. 4.
67. *Military Directives*, paras 24–25.
68. *CIVPOL Directives*, para. 23.
69. United Nations Staff Rules, *Staff Regulations of the United Nations and Staff Rules*, UN Doc. ST/SGB/2002/1, 1 January 2002, Rule 110.3.
70. Both the *Military Directives* and the *CIVPOL Directives* provide examples of major and minor misconduct, but the details are open to interpretation.
71. In at least some cases, staff members were not given a copy of directives on this matter. Local personnel may not even get verbal instructions. The report by the Office of Inter-

nal Oversight Services on allegations of sexual exploitation and abuse acknowledges this: "Few military or civilian staff seemed aware of the directives, policies, rules and regulations governing sexual contact that they were obligated to follow". *Investigation by the Office of Internal Oversight Services into Allegations of Sexual Exploitation and Abuse in the United Nations Organization Mission in the Democratic Republic of the Congo*, UN Doc. A/59/661, 5 January 2005, p. 11.

72. *Military Directives*, para. 28.

73. "Hopes Betrayed: Trafficking of Women and Girls to Post-Conflict Bosnia and Herzegovina for Forced Prostitution", *Human Rights Watch*, 14(9), 2002.

74. Duncan Chappell and John Evans, *The Role, Preparation and Performance of Civilian Police in United Nations Peacekeeping Operations*, Vancouver: International Centre for Criminal Law Reform and Criminal Justice Policy, 1997, available at ⟨http://www.icclr.law.ubc.ca/Publications/Reports/Peacekeeping.pdf⟩ (accessed 9 November 2006), p. 154. Commissioner O'Rielly in the United Nations Protection Force had cases investigated. If there was evidence of serious wrongdoing, he gave the alleged perpetrators a choice. They could choose to return home or he would institute proceedings, which would result in the person being repatriated, with the offence (fraud) on their record.

75. PSO Accountability Database, Cases ibh008 and ibh011.

76. UNTAET Daily Briefing, "Twenty Cases Examined by Ombudsperson", 1 June 2001, available at ⟨http://www.reliefweb.int/rw/rwb.nsf/AllDocsByUNID/a0e90ae0fac3f82785256a62005b5929⟩ (accessed 9 November 2006); Ombudsperson Institution in Kosovo Report, "Ex Officio Registration No. 10/01", available at ⟨http://www.ombudspersonkosovo.org/doc/reps/elion%20kuci_summary.htm⟩ (accessed 9 November 2006).

77. UNMISET, "UNMISET to Support Timor-Leste's Office of the Provedor for Human Rights and Justice", 20 April 2005, available at ⟨http://www.unmiset.org/UNMISETWebSite.nsf/0/a927b68a145c3c3f49256fee00271e64?OpenDocument⟩ (accessed 9 November 2006).

78. UNAMSIL Press Release, "Special Representative of the Secretary-General Launches UNAMSIL Personnel Conduct Committee", 26 August 2002, available at ⟨http://www.un.org/Depts/dpko/unamsil/DB/260802⟩ (accessed 9 November 2006).

79. PeaceWomen, "Burundi: UN Mission Sets up Units to Check Sexual Abuse", 15 November 2004, available at ⟨http://www.peacewomen.org/un/pkwatch/News/04/ONUBConductUnit.html⟩ (accessed 9 November 2006).

80. E-mail communication and phone interviews with a senior official who worked for several missions on disciplinary issues. This is true for BOI members as well. *Military Directives*, para. 17; *CIVPOL Directives*, para. 17.

81. United Nations Office of Internal Oversight Services website, ⟨http://www.un.org/Depts/oios/investigation.htm⟩ (accessed 9 November 2006).

82. *Investigation by the Office of Internal Oversight Services*.

83. There may be some measure of sending state responsibility for the acts of military personnel under human rights law; see Human Rights Committee, *General Comment No. 31 on Article 2 of the Covenant*, CCPR/C/74/CRP.4/Rev.6, 21/04/2004, Geneva: Office of the United Nations High Commissioner for Human Rights.

84. The PBPU is involved in compiling the knowledge and experiences, analysing and advising on policies, training and public information regarding applicable laws and rules and proceedings against alleged authors of misconduct; PBPU website, ⟨http://www.un.org/Depts/dpko/lessons/⟩ (accessed 9 November 2006).

85. DPKO, "Guidance and Directives of Disciplinary Issues for All Categories of Personnel Serving in UN Peacekeeping and Other Field Missions", CD-ROM, 19 March 2004,

details available on PeaceWomen website at ⟨http://www.peacewomen.org/un/pkwatch/ discipline/DPKODirectivescompilation.html⟩ (accessed 9 November 2006).

86. About half of the cases registered in the database are related to other kinds of misconduct; 129 cases out of 230 cases registered (excluding general allegations) were not of a sexual nature. The majority of misconduct appears to relate to motoring offences (e-mail communication and phone interviews with a senior official who worked for several missions on disciplinary issues).

87. UNAMSIL has set up a hotline through which the local population can report sexual abuse or exploitation, but the line is criticized for not adequately taking account of the realities on the ground; Paul Higate, "Peacekeeping and Gender Relations in Sierra Leone", Chapter 2 in *Gender and Peacekeeping. Case Studies: The DRC and Sierra Leone*, ISS Monograph No. 91, March 2004, available at ⟨http://www.iss.org.za/pubs/ Monographs/No91/Chap2.pdf⟩ (accessed 9 November 2006), p. 49.

88. A wide variety of issues appears to be left to the discretion of those involved, e.g. the determination of whether an act is major or minor misconduct, the lack of the sending state's reporting obligation on the action taken against repatriated personnel, notification of the progress of proceedings to the victim.

89. The requirement to involve the complainant in the process of investigation and to inform him or her of the result is part of the right to an effective remedy under human rights law.

90. *Military Directives*, para. 26; *CIVPOL Directives*, para. 29.

91. E-mail communication with a senior official who worked for several missions on disciplinary issues.

92. We know of a complainant of sexual assault who was not notified of the result of proceedings following her complaint.

93. E-mail communication with a senior official who worked in the office of an SRSG on disciplinary issues.

94. Interviews with various personnel involved in peacekeeping operations.

95. UN Wire, "Survey Finds U.N. Staff Fear Retribution for Reporting Misconduct", available at ⟨http://www.unwire.org/UNWire/20040610/449_24749.asp⟩ (accessed 2004).

96. The only issue being addressed here is the problem of proceedings arising out of a PSO. There is known to be a more general, and related, problem within international organizations generally; see above.

97. *Secretary-General's Bulletin on Special Measures for Protection from Sexual Exploitation and Sexual Abuse*, UN Doc. ST/SGB/2003/13, 9 October 2003.

98. *Report of the Special Committee on Peacekeeping Operations and Its Working Group at the 2004 Substantive Session*, UN Doc. A/58/19, 26 April 2004.

11

A beacon of light in the dark? The United Nations' experience with peace operations ombudspersons as illustrated by the Ombudsperson Institution in Kosovo

Florian F. Hoffmann

Citizen's advocate: The theory and practice of ombudspersonship

The idea of ombudspersonship originally evolved in the context of the relationship between national administrations and the citizens they are responsible for. Its pioneer was Sweden, which established the first ombudsperson's office (the *Justitieombudsman*) in its 1809 constitution.[1] It was to be entirely independent from the executive agencies it was to supervise, empowered to receive complaints directly from aggrieved citizens and endowed with far-reaching powers of prosecution, investigation and publication. The Swedish model has provided the central tenets of ombudspersonship up to the present day, with now over 90 countries having some kind of public sector ombudsperson. Although in many of these the ombudsperson has originally and essentially been seen as an instrument of national administrative law and practice, a broader association with the general protection of human rights has developed over the years, culminating in a "third wave" of the spread of ombudspersonship in the context of the various post-1990 transitions to democracy.

The United Nations and its agencies are no strangers to the ombudsperson idea. In fact, under the catch-all heading of "national institutions for the promotion and protection of human rights", the United Nations has considered (national) ombudspersons as a priority element of its "implementation and monitoring" methods as set out in the Vienna Declaration and Programme of Action (adopted by the World Conference on

Unintended consequences of peacekeeping operations, Aoi, de Coning and Thakur (eds), United Nations University Press, 2007, ISBN 978-92-808-1142-1

Human Rights in Vienna on 25 June 1993).[2] Through the United Nations Development Programme (UNDP) or the United Nations High Commissioner for Refugees (UNHCR), the United Nations has supported many nascent national ombudsperson institutions.[3] It has also increasingly used ombudsperson-type institutions in post-conflict theatres, where they are seen to serve as "a viable forum for the investigation and resolution of human rights complaints ... [in situations] where the judicial system is weak, politicized, slow or otherwise incapacitated".[4] Hence, UN-promoted ombudspersons in post-conflict situations such as in Bosnia-Herzegovina, Haiti or Kosovo have been accorded a double role as alternative, quasi-judicial mechanisms for the investigation and remedy of human rights abuses, and as general promoters of the rule of law and democratic governance.

Although the United Nations' objective with regard to ombudspersons has primarily been to support reconstructed or nascent *national* structures, it has slowly but steadily come to understand that the accountability provided by ombudspersons may, in principle, also apply to itself where it exercises functions of government, and that this may, in fact, be a desirable thing. As early as 1995, for example, the Department of Peacekeeping Operations (DKPO) suggested the creation of an ombudsperson for each peace operation,[5] a suggestion that was then taken up officially by the Secretary-General,[6] several UN organs[7] and the Security Council in 2000.[8] However, it has not yet been acted upon and seems destined to further bureaucratic meandering.[9] Furthermore, it has been suggested that a unit be set up within the UN Department of Humanitarian Affairs that could "serve as ombudsman to which any party can express a concern related to provision of assistance or security".[10] In a similar vein, there has for some time been some loose discussion on the idea of special-issue ombudspersons for vulnerable groups.[11]

However, leaving aside these ongoing, if so far inconclusive, discussions on UN-internal ombudspersonship,[12] none of the UN-promoted national ombudsperson institutions has ever had a mandate covering the United Nations itself. This is true even in places such as Bosnia-Herzegovina, where the United Nations maintained a significant civil and military presence, and, in effect, came to exercise many governmental functions. The reason for this was, evidently, that, no matter how deeply involved, the United Nations saw itself still as essentially a sophisticated aid agency rendering assistance within existing state structures and in collaboration with often weak but nonetheless existing governments. From this perspective, the United Nations could not possibly be directly responsible for maladministration or human rights mishaps, and it could, therefore, not be subject to the very accountability mechanisms it helps states to set up in their domestic spheres.

This perspective has, however, been fundamentally challenged through those last-generation "peace operations" where the United Nations exercises state-like functions or, as with fully international administrations, is actually the main sovereign in a particular territory, such as until the end of 2002 in East Timor and until now in Kosovo. In these cases, the United Nations cannot "externalize" responsibility to any domestic government but would, at least in theory, be expected to assume all the functions and obligations of government. As such, it would also be subject to any accountability mechanism set up for the territory in question. In particular, it would face the same level of scrutiny of its human rights record as any ordinary domestic government. The international administrations of Kosovo and East Timor would, therefore, seem to be ideal test cases of whether and how the United Nations has been living up to the accountability standards it promotes vis-à-vis states. Yet, in actual fact, only the Kosovo mission represents a testing ground for UN accountability, because the East Timor ombudsperson, despite having been endorsed by the United Nations early on, became operational only in May of 2001. This was barely a year before independence, so that its oversight of the United Nations never became a significant issue. This fact can by itself be seen as a symptom of the United Nations' continuing reticence to subject itself to independent accountability mechanisms, since the delay in implementing an ombudsperson scheme in East Timor was, arguably, due to a lack of attention and funding for the institution by the United Nations Transitional Administration in East Timor (UNTAET).[13]

This chapter aims to assess the performance of the ombudsperson institution as an institutional remedy for some unwanted and unintended consequences of peace operations through the illustrative case study of the Ombudsperson Institution in Kosovo (OIK).

The Kosovo experience: David versus Goliath

Literally within hours of the end of NATO's bombing campaign on 10 June 1999, the UN Security Council passed Resolution 1244 by which it simultaneously established the civil United Nations Interim Administration Mission in Kosovo (UNMIK) and the NATO-led Kosovo Force (KFOR). Not only was UNMIK's mandate, as phrased in the resolution, entirely removed from the realities that the civil war and the NATO bombing had left on the ground, but it also combined mutually incompatible objectives so as to essentially leave everything open to everybody.[14] Hence, in a gesture to the Kosovars, and then at least to most western states, the resolution speaks of the establishment of "an interim administration for Kosovo under which the people of Kosovo can enjoy substantial autonomy", adding, however, the crucial "within the Federal Republic of Yugoslavia", to express compliance with its own promise in the peace accord and as a gesture to Russia. The key to any permanent solution in Kosovo, notably its future status as either an independent state or a semi-independent province of Yugoslavia, is therefore left undefined, to the immediate and ongoing disappointment of the Albanian side. The resolution then goes on to specify that UNMIK will "provide transitional administration" that will, however, simultaneously establish and oversee "the development of provisional democratic self-governing institutions".

Ironically, it thereby creates the structural fault-line that haunts UNMIK to this day, namely the impossible combination of the top-down, military-style imposition of peace and the centrally planned building of state institutions under conditions of ongoing ethnic tension, with a simultaneous commitment to democratic decision-making, the rule of law and human rights for the local population. Lastly, the resolution has UNMIK "ensure conditions for a peaceful and normal life for all inhabitants of Kosovo", a promise that sounds not merely hollow, but is indeed farcical.[15]

UNMIK's problems stem from both exogenous and endogenous factors. Although its "impossible" mandate may, from the beginning, have prejudiced its attempts to reconcile the various ethnic communities in Kosovo, it is nonetheless also true that the challenge was always a rather stiff one no matter how well the mission performed. The confident assertion of an early American enthusiast that "[Kosovo] is the ideal foundation upon which to help them [presumably all Kosovans] build what they already want"[16] has turned out to be almost exactly the reverse, with Kosovo being, as Julie Mertus puts it, a house of cards that will collapse at the slightest false move.[17] Indeed, it is no wonder that the long prehistory of mutual distrust and occasional violence between ethnic groups, combined with the vicious circle of repression and rebellion since 1989, has poisoned inter-ethnic relations almost beyond repair. As "battle-hardened" Bernard Kouchner, the first Special Representative of the Secretary-General (SRSG) in Kosovo, observed, "here I discovered hatred deeper than anywhere in the world, more than in Cambodia, or Vietnam or Bosnia".[18]

This highly volatile situation on the ground has haunted UNMIK from the beginning. As soon as Serb forces had left, there were outbreaks of spontaneous "revenge attacks" against Serb Kosovars and alleged collaborators, most notably the various Roma communities who have traditionally lived in Kosovo. These attacks soon emerged into increasingly well-planned campaigns against the non-Albanian population, which essentially amounted to an attempt of "reverse ethnic cleansing".

Parallel to this, Serbs in northern Mitrovica and in the Serb-dominated areas in the northern part of Kosovo did the same with regard to Albanians, with extremist elements in both communities doing all they could to create irreversible facts on the ground. While these small-scale yet sustained attacks have exacerbated a climate of fear and distrust, there have also been periodic outbreaks of larger-scale violence, most recently in March 2004, when, following inaccurate reports on the drowning of three young Albanian children, violence erupted for two days in more than 30 places across Kosovo, involving more than 50,000 people and resulting in 19 deaths and over 900 injured. The challenge that these almost "civil war-like" occurrences pose for international peace operations is daunting.

In addition to the precarious security situation in Kosovo itself, the continuing political haggling over the status and, thus, the future of the province has been bound to undercut many of UNMIK's good-faith efforts to bridge the seemingly unbridgeable divides. For as long as Serbia – and hence Yugoslavia – was still dominated by Milosevic, no admissions of guilt or other reconciliatory gestures towards Albanian Kosovars were to be expected, nor any relaxation of Belgrade's insistence on its territorial integrity, which, of course, includes Kosovo. Once the Yugoslav regime changed, however, and in response to international pressure became somewhat more open-minded about Kosovo, it was the Kosovar side that hardened its attitude, fearing that the goal of full Kosovo independence would be prejudiced by a Yugoslavia that was reintegrated into the international community. It is, therefore, fair to say that in all probability *any* international mission would have found its state-building efforts marred by the geopolitical uncertainty that continues to surround Kosovo.

However, these exogenous factors cannot solely account for the precarious state that Kosovo continues to be in today. Nor is it merely the usual Security Council impasse that is responsible for the fact that Kosovo, after several years as an international protectorate, is not much nearer to being a functioning multi-ethnic democracy ready for substantive autonomy than it was when UNMIK first arrived. It is arguably the very structure and running of UNMIK and its related missions that have frequently exacerbated the problems that seem to impede its success. The reasons for this are manifold, but are all essentially related to two overall factors, namely the mission's scope and objectives and its institutional structure.

As for the former, the breadth of the mission's scope and the depth of its powers, as well as its dual objective of peacebuilding and territorial administration, were at the time of UNMIK's establishment nearly unprecedented challenges for the United Nations.[19] They led, to some extent, to contradictory mission objectives and a partial inability to deal with the (exogenous) challenges on the ground, which, taken together, have from the outset beset UNMIK with a degree of institutional schizophrenia. An example is the apparent confusion on the part of different UNMIK actors in the early phase of the mission about how the much-needed provision of security could be squared with its more general governmental functions, most notably the upholding of international human rights standards. Here, some argued that, given the precarious security situation and the measures required to quell the violence, UNMIK should formally derogate a number of the rights protected in the covenants – most notably in the International Covenant on Civil and Political Rights. This would allow it to gain some manoeuvring space for robust peacemaking, while not appearing hypocritical in relation to its human rights obligations.[20]

Yet, somewhat typically, UNMIK ended up doing neither: it did not dare openly to prioritize peacemaking for a limited initial period, nor did it formally derogate from any human rights standards. Instead, it officially upheld the parity of its mission objectives and, thus, the full validity of international human rights standards. However, in practice, it continuously subverted the latter with its ad hoc and purely reactive approach to security.[21] This has led, for example, to such plainly paradoxical stances as the commitment to train an independent and human rights conscious judiciary, as well as fully to cooperate with the International Criminal Tribunal for the former Yugoslavia. It also includes the simultaneous practice of regularly extending the detention of suspected trouble-makers by executive order, even when, on some occasions, detainees had been set free by the UNMIK-created domestic court system.

As for institutional structure, although UNMIK was very much set up from a lessons learned perspective that tried to avoid, in particular, the hydra-headed mission structure in Bosnia,[22] it has nonetheless suffered from a multiplicity of partially complementary, partially competing components that have prejudiced its overall coherence. Although formally under UN leadership in the form of the SRSG, UNMIK's original four so-called pillars were respectively administered by UNHCR (refugees), the United Nations proper (civil administration), the Organization for Security and Co-operation in Europe (OSCE) (institution-building and human rights) and the European Union (economic reconstruction). Given the very different institutional logics and field experience of these organizations, problems of communication and coordination were bound to arise. Whereas UNHCR and, arguably, also the OSCE showed themselves well prepared and experienced for their respective tasks, the European Union has tended to be slow, bureaucratic and ill equipped to respond to an emergency situation. The United Nations' civil administration component, for its part, has suffered from its initial lack of expertise and experience in "running a government", including such tasks as social service provision or the administration of justice.

This lack of governmental experience cannot, as such, be held against the UN administration, but the way it has dealt with this challenge has not always maximized the mission's effectiveness. Hence, for example, rather than make extensive use of the long-time Kosovo experience of the Secretariat's Department of Political Affairs, the first and subsequent SRSGs have tended to centralize expertise and decision-making, which led to the recruitment of large numbers of committed but inexperienced field staff. This slowed down local deployment, which may, in turn, have contributed to Ushtria Çlirimtare e Kosovës (UÇK – Kosovo Liberation Army) filling in the authority gaps with its own parallel structures, which have caused so many subsequent problems and have proved to be very difficult to dismantle.[23]

In addition to these UNMIK-internal problems, the mission's relations with other peace operation components have not always been either straightforward or easy. The main parallel actor has, of course, been NATO's KFOR, which, like the Implementation Force and the Stabilisation Force in Bosnia beforehand, has from the very beginning insisted on a parallel but not subordinate relation with UNMIK. This has meant that the inner logic of KFOR has often been able to prevail over the more general objectives set by the civilian mission, such as close cooperation with the Civilian Police (CIVPOL), especially in emergency situations. Other general objectives set by the civilian mission include the disinterested prevention of inter-ethnic violence, or, indeed, the protection of minorities and other vulnerable groups. Instead of following general objectives, different KFOR contingents have frequently implemented their own security policy within their respective sectors, without sufficient collaboration with the civilian peace operation components and, as a result, with occasionally far-reaching (negative) consequences.[24]

Indeed, part of KFOR's problem appears to be the fact that its "real" functioning significantly diverges from its official mission structure. It should operate as a clear hierarchical structure, with the Commander of KFOR heading the four multinational brigades, but each of the brigades practises, in fact, a significant degree of autonomy and is more directly linked with its respective national command structure than with that of NATO. As a result, important decisions are often taken not by the central command structure in close cooperation with UNMIK and CIVPOL, but rather by regional commanders who consult with national capitals.[25]

To be sure, part of these problems also stem from the significant decrease in KFOR troop strength, from 50,000 in 1999 to just over 18,000 in early 2004, which reflects more the changed priorities of the international community than any significant improvement in the security situation in Kosovo.

Another actor that is meant to complement UNMIK's work is, of course, CIVPOL, the civil policing component of the mission and the largest force like this in all UN missions.[26] Its effectiveness has, however, suffered from initial deployment problems, over-cautiousness and difficulties in establishing a relation of trust and cooperation with the local population.[27] Collaboration with KFOR, even if that collaboration has been far from smooth, has often been vital in policing an environment that ranges from common, and frequently organized, crime, to mortar attacks and the like.[28] Despite some successes, there are a good number of cases where KFOR conducted military-style raids on places that had been under covert investigation by CIVPOL, thereby prejudicing the latter's efforts.

Along with CIVPOL, the OSCE-trained Kosovo Police Service is part of UNMIK's Provisional Institutions of Self-Government (PISGs) and is meant to replace the international police component eventually. Although strong efforts have been made on the part of UNMIK to make it a multi-ethnic and modern police force, it has partly functioned as a receptacle for ex-UÇK fighters. It is severely under-funded, and it is generally not trusted by KFOR (and, to a lesser degree, CIVPOL), resulting in its systematic under-appreciation, especially in crisis moments such as the March 2004 violence.[29] Lastly, there is the notorious Kosovo Protection Corps (KPC), which, upon strong pressure from NATO, was created by UNMIK as a demilitarized, humanitarian successor of the UÇK. During the bombing campaign, NATO had enjoyed relatively cordial relations with the UÇK leadership and had come to regard it, in effect, as a surrogate ground force.

As a consequence, KFOR, and to some extent UNMIK, have been less than stringent in their supervision of KPC activities, and both have, on occasion, shown reticence in pursuing misconduct by high-ranking KPC operatives.[30] To the former UÇK leadership, the KPC has always been the army-in-the-making of an independent Kosovo, and it has pushed hard to transfer its personnel and its structures *ad integro* into the KPC. Thus, KPC conduct has tended to converge on that displayed by the UÇK before the international presence, including the exercise of (illegal) "policing" functions, as well as involvement in premeditated violence against minorities, as well as organized crime. This partial spinning out of control has led one senior UN official to state that "I think we have created a monster".[31] The KPC's "parallel" regime has since been curtailed as the result of a policy shift by its most important international ally, the United States, following reports of KPC involvement in the destabilization of neighbouring Macedonia. Finally, the presence of more than 250 non-governmental organizations (NGOs) adds to the colourful institutional cocktail that characterizes government and governance in Kosovo.

One for all – one against all: The Ombudsperson Institution in Kosovo

The Ombudsperson Institution in Kosovo (OIK) was created in the midst of this complex institutional matrix in a highly volatile environment. In fact, its particular configuration is less a representation of the textbook ombudsperson than a product of political and administrative haggling during the early days of the international administration. While, as stated above, the United Nations has generally endorsed the idea of peace operations, ombudspersons and member states (the United States, in particular) exerted strong pressure to create such an institution for the Kosovo mission.[32] Its powers and institutional standing were far from uncontroversial. As a result, it took the civil administration, the OSCE (which, as pillar III, was formally responsible for the institution's creation) and KFOR a good year to haggle out the ombudsperson's institutional formula, eventually promulgated as UNMIK Regulation 2000/38, and to secure the required funds. The latter represents a much watered-down version of the model of a completely independent institution with strong investigatory and sanctioning powers over all aspects of the international administration.

The reasons for this, to be examined in greater detail below, are linked to the mentioned duality of UNMIK's objectives, notably to more or less forcibly pacify the province while, at the same time, establishing the rule of law, human rights and democratic institutions. Although the SRSG, the OSCE and KFOR all share a basic commitment to human rights, at least the SRSG and KFOR have also, and perhaps primarily, been concerned with the humanitarian and the security situation, and have been unwilling to let their efforts on that front be hampered by independent bodies holding them to the letter and spirit of international human rights instruments. This attitude clearly transpires in the institutional set-up of the Ombudsperson. His mandate as stipulated in Regulation 2000/38 is broad:

1.1 The Ombudsperson shall promote and protect the rights and freedoms of individuals and legal entities and ensure that all persons in Kosovo are able to exercise effectively the human rights and fundamental freedoms safeguarded by international human rights standards, in particular the European Convention on Human Rights and its Protocols and the International Covenant on Civil and Political Rights.

> 1.2 The Ombudsperson shall provide accessible and timely mechanisms for the review and redress of actions constituting an abuse of authority by the interim civil administration or any emerging central or local institution.[33]

In addition, the OIK is entrenched in Chapter 10 of the Constitutional Framework for Provisional Self-Government of May 2001.[34] Yet, although the OIK is mandated to attend to "all persons in Kosovo", its jurisdiction is formally curtailed *ratione temporae, materiae* and *personae*. The mandate excludes issues that took place before 30 June 2000, issues outside Kosovo, disputes between UNMIK and its staff and, most importantly, KFOR *in toto*, even though the OIK's founding regulation allows for a "special agreement" with the Commander of KFOR regarding its jurisdiction, which has, up to this day, not happened.[35] The Ombudsperson's functions are wide-ranging, including "receiving complaints, monitoring, investigating, offering good offices, taking preventive steps, making recommendations and advising on matters relating to his or her functions",[36] as well as promoting inter-ethnic reconciliation and providing advice to the civil administration on the compatibility of its acts with international human rights instruments. To fulfil these functions, the OIK has extensive investigatory powers, both in response to complaints received and *ex officio*, and UNMIK authorities are obliged to cooperate fully with any OIK investigation, which includes the duty of a prompt response to any enquiry on the part of the OIK. Crucially, however, the SRSG has the authority to deny the release of documents to the OIK, though he or she has to inform the latter in writing of any such decision.

One power that brings the OIK close to the model of the French *Médiateur* is the ability to recommend the case-by-case suspension of the application of administrative decisions where this causes, in the OIK's view, "irreparable damage". Finally, its sanctioning power is limited to making recommendations to the relevant authorities, which may include the suggestion that that authority – not the OIK itself – institute civil or criminal proceedings against a person. In a case of non-compliance, the only further formal sanction the OIK has is the dubious right to draw the matter to the attention of the SRSG. However, the fact that, unless otherwise determined by the OIK itself, both recommendations and SRSG petitioning are public, adds the important informal instrument of "shaming" to the ombudsperson's arsenal. What severely compromises the OIK's independence is the ultimate grip that the SRSG, the head of the very structure that OIK is meant to control, has over it. The SRSG appoints and, in cases of misconduct, dismisses the Ombudsperson and his/her deputies. The OIK reports to none other than the SRSG. The issue of misconduct includes the rather catch-all "failure in the execution of his or her functions",[37] which is very obviously problematic. In addition, Regulation

2000/38 only specified financial backing for the year 2000, and left follow-up financing to an unspecified mix between international donors and the Kosovo Consolidated Budget (KCB).

Next to the KCB, which is also controlled by the SRSG, the OIK's funds were provided by the Permanent Council of the OSCE, as well as a number of committed donor states, most notably the United States, Switzerland, Poland, Denmark, Sweden, Norway, France, Turkey and Liechtenstein. In addition, a number of international organizations supported individual aspects or projects of the OIK, namely the Council of Europe and the European Court of Human Rights, the OSCE's Office of Democratic Institutions and Human Rights, UNICEF and the United Nations Development Fund for Women. Some private foundations, such as the Kosovo Open Society Foundation, as well as a number of national ombudsperson offices, have also assisted the OIK. Yet, the OIK's budget is not consolidated enough for the Ombudsperson not to have to lobby actively to donor states for complementary funding, nor is its financial dependence on UNMIK purely nominal. This is illustrated by the considerable problems caused in 2003 when the OSCE significantly reduced local staff salaries, thereby prompting the imminent threat of a mass exodus of senior professional OIK staff, which would have crippled the institution and wasted three years of intensive (and costly) professional training. At the time, this worst-case scenario was averted after internal negotiations, but it exposed the financial precariousness of the OIK.[38]

In practice, the OIK has so far fared better than these institutional deficiencies might suggest, though this is arguably largely the work of the actual office-holder, Marek Nowicki. A Polish human rights lawyer and pro-democracy activist, he has risen to the difficult task of building confidence in the OIK across ethnic lines. He has acted as assertively and independently, vis-à-vis UNMIK and KFOR, as his institutional framework allows him. He has also consistently promoted the reconceptualization of the international presence as a "surrogate state" that exercises all the functions of national government in the territory and that should, therefore, be accountable in the same way as is expected of states proper. This was and is by no means how the United Nations has tended to view this kind of situation.[39] Moreover, he has won the confidence of many ordinary Kosovars across the ethnic spectrum, so much so that the OIK is occasionally the only institution they trust enough to place any confidence in. He has also overseen the institutional consolidation of the OIK, with three developments in particular being noteworthy. First, the initial and serious problems of providing adequate access to the OIK for all population groups across the province were gradually overcome. There are now three field offices in Gnijlane, Pec and Prizren Mitrovica – including an outpost in the Serbian-dominated northern part of that city – as well as periodic Open Days in these and other municipalities during which the Ombudsperson can be met in person. Secondly, the OIK created two special "teams", the Children's Rights Team (CRT) and the Non-Discrimination Team (NDT), which aim to improve the OIK's effectiveness on these especially problematic thematic fronts. Thirdly, the OIK has worked towards the gradual "kosovanization" (*sic*) of the OIK, in line with general UNMIK policy. Between 2003 and 2004, the numbers of international staff were radically reduced so that, at present, only the Ombudsperson himself is an international, although there is still a network of *in-* and *ex-loco* international consultants. While Nowicki has publicly endorsed the eventual indigenization of the OIK, he has also made it clear that he thought UNMIK's approach to the issue was hasty and premature, as the institution's sustainability could be severely prejudiced by an imposed lack of international training and advice. UNMIK's stance on "kosovanization" showed, once again, its under-appreciation of the fact that the OIK was "the only independent entity with a mandate to engage on human rights and rule of law issues both with the international administration, which will remain in place and in power beyond [the time-frame for full kosovanization of the OIK], and with emerging local institutions, which have yet to develop fully".[40] Therefore, he favoured, for the time being, the maintenance of a hybrid international–national institution.[41]

Lastly, the OIK has also fostered relationships with a number of national ombudspersons, as well as with relevant forums on democratic institution-building, such as the Council of Europe's Round Table on National Human Rights Institutions. In this context, it is interesting to note that virtually all of these important inter-institutional exchanges have been facilitated by the OSCE and the Council of Europe, with the United Nations, despite its nominal commitment to the promotion of "national human rights institutions" (see above), being conspicuously absent. It would appear that the potential for synergies with the various other peace operations ombudspersons, such as those in and around Bosnia, has been largely unexplored.

The importance of the OIK within the UNMIK structure is underlined by its overall use patterns. Since its inception, the number of Kosovars using the institution has increased four-fold (from roughly 1,000 up to mid-2001 to 4,000 between mid-2003 and mid-2004[42]), with the increase in registered cases rising steadily, if less exponentially (from 344 in mid-2001 to 420 in mid-2004). This is surely due to the much improved access possibilities, as well as to the fact that the OIK is increasingly seen by the local population as a trustworthy accountability mechanism at their disposal. The much lower number of Final Reports is a reflection both of the semi-judicial and hence somewhat time-consuming process of the

OIK (see below), as well as of the persistent difficulties it has had in obtaining prompt and adequate reactions from respondents, most notably of UNMIK and PISG bodies. This is particularly grave because UNMIK is, as would be expected, the principal respondent. KFOR ranked as the number two respondent up to mid-2002, but it has since dropped to fourth place, both because the absolute number of registered complaints is down by roughly two-thirds, and because complaints related to PISGs and UNMIK's Housing and Property Directorate have taken second and third place, respectively. In all, the OIK has issued nine Special Reports, five in its first few months of operation in 2001, one in 2002, and (up to the time of writing) three in 2004.

In general, the OIK would seem to have used its special reporting competence[43] to address controversial issues that underlie larger complaint patterns but are not amenable to resolution on a case-by-case basis and, instead, require high-level decisions of principle. The issues dealt with by the Special Reports include most of the bigger "structural" problems of UNMIK administration, notably UNMIK and KFOR immunities,[44] "executive" detention,[45] the sale of property,[46] judicial due process issues,[47] the display of religious symbols[48] and the applicable law.[49] Analysis in the reports is with reference to international human rights instruments, and the European Convention of Human Rights in particular, and, where applicable, to relevant UNMIK regulations. In terms of applying these standards to the general facts in question, the OIK has been employing strict legal reasoning, underlining the para-judicial nature of the institution. In its conclusions, however, it has been able to go beyond a purely judicial logic, and it has frequently proposed new UNMIK legislation as a remedy. Moreover, it has generally set a deadline for the fulfilment of its proposals, and has requested to be informed of any measures taken.

Given the considerable odds which have stood against it over the past four years, the OIK could be seen as a success simply for having managed to consolidate and expand its role, for having earned the trust of the local population and for having had the audacity to ignore and rise up against UNMIK's consistent under-appreciation. However, to evaluate how effective the OIK has been as an accountability mechanism in a peace operations context, its performance in relation to its two main challenges have to be examined, namely the difficulties of accountability promotion under conditions of ethnic tension, and difficulties arising from the mixed-up priorities of the mission for the benefit of which the OIK was created.

One of the structural fault-lines built into the OIK from the very beginning is its dual role as a UN-promoted national human rights institution in the sense of the Paris Principles[50] and, at the same time, as a peace operations ombudsperson in the sense of the UN Secretary-General's Report to the Security Council on the Protection of Civilians in Armed

Conflict.[51] Both roles are bound to converge in a situation where the United Nations is in effect a surrogate government, though this still leaves the various institutional paradoxes of such a dual role unresolved.

"Between all chairs": The OIK and accountability promotion under conditions of ethnic tension

As was hinted at earlier, the environment within which the OIK has to promote human rights, the rule of law and democratic accountability is probably one of the most challenging possible. There are clear indications that, even after five years, without the international presence in Kosovo a vicious civil war-like situation would rapidly re-emerge, with attempted ethnic cleansing, imposed social "apartheid" and a collapse of whatever democratic institutions have been painstakingly built up by the mission. Radicals on either side of the ethnic divide continue to foster a climate of mutual distrust and fear, and the international presence seems to have made little headway in significantly curtailing their activities. This is amply illustrated in the issues and complaints attended to by the OIK, which range from administrative problems resulting from the undefined status of the province via ethnically discriminatory practices and behaviour, to the most rampant human rights violations. The OIK is, of course, not the only institution attempting to remedy these grievances, and, indeed, they are at the heart of UNMIK's, KFOR's and CIVPOL's activities. This, however, frequently complicates the OIK's position, because it has simultaneously to work on the causes and consequences of interethnic tension and to supervise UNMIK's, KFOR's and CIVPOL's responses to these. Hence, the provision of general human rights accountability is almost inevitably entangled with UNMIK's administrative review, leaving the OIK with the heavy burden of fighting on two fronts at the same time.

An example is the issue of impunity or lack of criminal investigation or prosecution, which has accounted for between 10 per cent and 15 per cent of registered complaints. The underlying issue is almost invariably ethnically motivated murder or grave bodily harm which, as one CIVPOL source put it, is "planned and directed – possibly by terrorist groups, extremist and violent groups and no-one takes credit for them".[52] However, such incidents become administrative issues once their investigation by CIVPOL and/or KFOR is, as is frequent with inter-ethnic incidents, ineffectual or negligent.[53] It is usually only once the other "surrogate" authorities have acted inadequately that the OIK is seized, or seizes the issue itself through its *ex officio* reporting powers.

A case in point for the severity of the crimes involved is the February 2000 killing of six Albanians – including one child – during rioting in northern Mitrovica, which in turn followed a rocket attack on a Serbian bus. The investigation concerning two of the Albanian victims was delayed for more than a year and remained inconclusive. The OIK opened an investigation into the possible violation of the victims' right to life as protected by Article 2 of the European Convention on Human Rights.[54] There are a number of similar cases on which the OIK has taken analogous action. An equally severe case arose from the remote-controlled bombing of the lead bus of the Nis express convoy, which was carrying Serbs from Serbia proper to Kosovo. It left 11 Serbs dead and over 40 injured. Shortly thereafter, four Albanian men were detained by CIV-POL in connection with the bombing, three of whom were, however, subsequently released and one ordered to one month of "executive" detention on a dubious legal basis. The three released men were then re-arrested for violation of the court order, and, together with the fourth, transferred to the US detention facility at Camp Bondsteel. There, the fourth detainee, serving his executive detention, managed to escape, allegedly with the help of a wire-cutter hidden in a pie, although rumours also circulated of connivance of US forces. The three remaining detainees were released six months later, after a court review found the charges against them unsubstantiated. No one has since been charged with any crime in connection with the bombing. The OIK has followed the investigations, and enquired with UNMIK police about their progress, only to be told that that force was committed to bringing justice to those responsible for the crime, but that it could not reveal any details of its investigation on account of its covert nature.[55]

Other types of incident include the destruction of minority cultural heritage and the severely restricted freedom of movement that most minority Kosovars experience in practice. This has resulted in grave economic hardship and various other impediments, such as the day-to-day dependence on KFOR and UNMIK police protection and escort, which, in turn, has hampered various access rights, such as those enjoyed by school children to education facilities or by all Kosovars, regardless of ethnicity, to a competent court. The OIK has monitored all these issues and raised them with UNMIK, UNMIK police and KFOR, though its annual reports all too frequently state that "there has been no response to this letter". There have also been many less severe types of incidents that can nonetheless be attributed to the trials and tribulations of an internationally administered province of a (nominally) sovereign nation-state that is socially fragmented along ethnic lines. These include such seemingly trivial issues as the lack of arrangements for pension payments from Serbia proper or the international recognition or non-recognition of travel and other documents. The licensing of vehicles or the non-compliance with the requirement to make official documents available in Serbian, one of Kosovo's three official languages, is also an issue. In the latter case, the OIK wrote directly to the prime minister of Kosovo urging him to ensure the full implementation of the linguistic specifications of the Constitutional Framework. Ironically, it received a response in Albanian, stating that the relevant PISG institutions were doing all they could to respect the Constitutional Framework.[56]

Two other issues that have continuously occupied the OIK concern the treatment of displaced persons in and outside of Kosovo, as well as property disputes. As to the former, there continues to be an outflux of minorities from Kosovo to Serbia proper, Montenegro and the former Yugoslav Republic of Macedonia (FRYROM), with an already high number of de facto refugees present in these territories finding themselves in precarious situations. An additional problem factor is that neither Serbia nor Montenegro officially recognizes them as refugees, because Kosovo is, evidently, considered by them to be a part of the former Yugoslav Republic. In the FRYROM, the situation of Roma refugees from Kosovo is highly precarious, whereas some West European states that accepted some of these refugees expressed their intention to return them to Kosovo as soon as possible. In all these cases, the OIK, interpreting its territorial mandate broadly, has written to the relevant authorities and governments to relieve what has become a regional refugee crisis that is the direct result of the continuously unstable security situation for minorities in Kosovo.[57]

The other significant issue concerns the enforcement of respect for property rights, which involves both property issues stemming from the period of Yugoslav rule before 1999, as well as the question of the return of minority-owned property illegally taken during and after the conflict. Large numbers of houses and agricultural lands were taken from their rightful owners, who were often displaced persons unable to resist the seizure of their land. In response to this, UNMIK established the Housing and Property Directorate (HPD) early on in order to process claims by dispossessed land owners, but, hampered by mismanagement, infighting and chronic lack of funds, it had a very slow start. Up to the present day it lags far behind in its processing of claims. To make matters worse, occupants formally evicted by the HPD have occasionally either refused to leave or subsequently returned and threatened the previous owners who have taken back possession of their land. Again, in a climate and culture of lawlessness, it is all too often only by means of "robust enforcement" through an already overburdened UNMIK police that settled property claims can be realized. Here, the OIK has played a crucial role in bringing together the pieces and presenting it as a problem to UNMIK. Given the inadequacy of HPD procedures, the OIK has, in effect, become the principal recipient of complaints concerning property claims, a fact confirmed by the high numbers of registered complaints concerning property issues.[58]

Finally, an event that has overshadowed the "routine" violation of human rights in the province was the March 2004 outbreak of violence across the whole of Kosovo.[59] The grave failings of especially KFOR that are connected to this will be discussed below. What is relevant here is the rapidity, scale and unexpectedness with which the violence broke out, and which seemingly took the entire international presence in Kosovo by complete surprise. It thereby exposed the fragility of the bits and pieces of "normality" that UNMIK has been trying to construct, and brutally brought to the fore what many had come to suspect, namely that, at least for as long as the final status of Kosovo and the issues related to it remained uncertain, there could be no pull-out of the international presence. Immediately after the violence had subsided, the Ombudsperson publicly called for calm, pleaded for people to put a stop to the violence and set out on a travelling marathon to Serbian and Roma communities throughout Kosovo. He also appealed to international and local humanitarian organizations to address the urgent needs of the many persons displaced by the violence. Subsequently, he petitioned the Kosovan prime minister to make good on his promise to rebuild non-Albanian properties destroyed in the violence, and he initiated an *ex officio* investigation into the human rights issues relating to the international and PISG response to the crisis, which is still pending at the time of writing.[60] He has sought to use the public trust in the OIK and in his person to quell further violence and to promote a return to "the road ahead", though he must himself have been aware of the razor's edge he was treading. The OIK's reaction to the March 2004 violence shows how difficult it is to construct a culture of human rights, rule of law and democratic governance in an apparently unwilling environment.

"A peril unto itself": The OIK and UNMIK's mixed-up priorities

If the OIK's exogenous challenges are daunting, its endogenous ones are perhaps even more so. Indeed, the two are related insofar as the OIK's ability to do what it was set up for, namely to resolve the day-to-day problems of UNMIK-governed Kosovars, is severely hampered by the very organizational structure that created it. UNMIK appears to be profoundly perplexed about its impossible mandate and its multiple roles, with the result that it has not pursued a consistent course since its establishment. Most of all, UNMIK – and with it KFOR and the related components – seems never to have taken on board the idea that it truly is a "surrogate state" in Kosovo, and that it must therefore not behave like a mere humanitarian complement to a weak but existing government. It must assume all the responsibilities of such a government. Insofar as the kind of national governance promoted by the United Nations is democratic, rule of law based and oriented to the fulfilment of human rights, it must, by implication, represent these principles where it acts itself as the government. It must, in other words, be accountable to the people it governs according to the principles it stands for. This, however, has been insufficient in the case of UNMIK, and its core failure is one of governance. It has blundered in two areas, namely the separation of powers and the establishment of a functioning legal system, both of which are essential for accountability.

With regard to the separation of powers, UNMIK is, as the Ombudsperson has observed, not just a democratic institution;[61] but it also concentrates nearly absolute power in the SRSG. The SRSG is both the executive with supreme personnel appointment powers and the final legislator, empowered by Resolution 1244 "to change, repeal or suspend existing laws to the extent necessary for the carrying out of his functions, or where existing laws are incompatible with the mandate, aims and purposes of the interim civil administration".[62] All PISG institutions with their state-like positions are ultimately subordinate to the SRSG. Finally, the SRSG also exercises ultimate appointment powers over the new Kosovo judiciary, which severely compromises the latter's independence. Showing complete awareness of this "plenitude of powers" for which many heads of regular state governments would envy him/her, the first SRSG, Bernard Kouchner, remarked that his "authority comes directly from the Security Council resolution 1244, which gives ultimate legislative and executive authority in Kosovo to UNMIK, of which the SRSG is the legally appointed head".[63]

From the United Nations' perspective, this despotism is, of course, meant to be benevolent,[64] as well as necessary given the humanitarian and security situation it first encountered in the province. Yet, instead of using it transparently in the initial "emergency" phase by declaring a clearly bounded martial law as some think (retrospectively) would have been best,[65] successive SRSGs responded in an ad hoc and reactive way to the situation, which has, from the OIK's perspective, created rather than solved problems.

One issue in particular continues to be a recurrent source of complaints filed with the OIK. This concerns the questionable practice of the SRSG and the KFOR Commander being able to shorten or extend the detention period of individuals by executive order without any adequate court proceedings and beyond periods considered compatible with international human rights standards. The argument UNMIK and KFOR have brought to support this practice is the allegedly continuing emergency situation during which certain derogations from human rights standards were permissible. As the *UNMIK News* conveniently put it, "international human rights standards accept the need for special measures that, in the wider interests of security, and under prescribed legal conditions, allow authorities to respond to the findings of intelligence that are not able to be presented to the court system".[66] This argument and the practice it is meant to support generated a wave of protests, as well as a Special Report by the OIK,[67] whereupon UNMIK half-heartedly established a Sentencing Review Commission.[68] However, this commission largely confirmed and agreed with the detentions ordered, and did not have its mandate renewed after a three-month period.[69]

In general, the delay and lack of preparedness with which UNMIK has gone about establishing the legal system have resulted in what the OIK has called "legal chaos", which persists until the present day. One of the first but most consequential blunders was the seemingly blind application of a UN general policy directive (which was also applied by UNTAET) that mandated the immediate reinstatement of the law applicable in Kosovo up to the beginning of the bombing campaign in March 1999, subject to it being compatible with international human rights standards and the mission's objective.[70] The rationale behind this was to avoid a legal vacuum and to minimize the need to re-train local lawyers. However, in Kosovo, the measure proved untenable, because the Albanian legal profession, which, in truth, consists to a considerable degree of "recycled" (Albanian) lawyers from the old FRY times, had already rejected the measure as a reimposition of Serbian law. When UNMIK initially insisted on its validity, the newly appointed, largely Albanian, judiciary resorted to civil disobedience, which eventually forced UNMIK to reverse its stance and issue Regulation 24/1999, which established the Kosovo codes valid before the imposition of Serbian direct rule in 1989. However, because the new Kosovan judiciary has freely borrowed from Yugoslav codes when the Kosovo ones did not clearly regulate a matter, general confusion, not only among the judiciary but also among law enforcement agencies, not to mention the general population, has prevailed. This is aggravated further by UNMIK's parallel efforts to elaborate new codes, which it then, however, fails to promulgate across the province.[71]

Lastly, any borrowed Yugoslav law is, by Regulation 24/1999, subject to a non-discrimination test, for which there is no uniform judicial procedure, let alone the equivalent of constitutional judicial review. A further problem has been UNMIK's difficulty with promulgating, as well as enforcing, its own legislation. As to the former problem, the issue of *vacatio legis* has continuously occupied the OIK, because the period between the promulgation and the entry into force of UNMIK regulations frequently provides insufficient time for the legal profession and the wider population to gain knowledge of the new law. This creates an awkward legal uncertainty that the OIK has found clearly violates international human rights standards.[72] Lastly, even several years after the first steps for the establishment of a new legal order in Kosovo were undertaken, the new judiciary is still not functioning satisfactorily. Lack of legislation on the administration of justice, insufficient training and low remuneration have marred its efficiency.

In addition, the appointment process for judges, controlled ultimately by the SRSG, is still not transparent, nor is the judiciary independent in the strict sense of the term. Minority representation has been difficult to obtain, not least because minority judges frequently face grave security risks and are often in need of police protection. In northern Kosovo, parallel Serbian–Yugoslav court structures continue to operate illegally. Ethnic bias and unfairness in proceedings have by no means been rooted out, nor has occasional pressure on the judiciary from different quarters. Most pressing from the OIK's perspective is, however, the slowness of the system, which has resulted in a huge backlog in civil and also in criminal cases. The OIK is bound to find European Convention of Human Rights violations for excessive length of proceedings almost as routinely as the European Court of Human Rights does vis-à-vis certain Convention states.[73] In all, the OIK has felt bound to state that "the situation as it stands today is a serious impediment to the proper administration of the rule of law in Kosovo".[74]

Given the precarious state of the governance and legal systems, the OIK should be one, if not the, principal accountability mechanism in the province. Although still a comparatively small and potentially underfunded institution, it has clearly shown itself well prepared and unrelenting in its monitoring of democracy, the rule of law and human rights. Yet, in actual fact it has very little real power to take on UNMIK and KFOR. Formally, the reason for this can be attributed to the immunity enjoyed by all senior UNMIK officials, and the general restriction of the OIK's mandate over KFOR. The notorious UNMIK Regulation 2000/47 grants both its staff and KFOR's immunity,[75] a state of affairs that the OIK, in its very first Special Report, found to be not consistent with international conventions for human rights and to be failing to protect individuals in Kosovo from arbitrary behaviour by UNMIK and KFOR, or by their personnel.[76] Just before UNMIK's deadline to repeal the legislation expired, the SRSG answered with a letter announcing "further consultations with UNHQ and others".[77] No further response has thus far been received by the OIK.

However, in practice, UNMIK and KFOR immunity is not the main reason for the OIK's relative weakness. Rather, it is the continuing unwillingness on the part of those two mission components to cooperate fully and in good faith with the OIK. OIK has repeatedly complained of a lack of cooperation with its investigations, with both UNMIK and PISG representatives who either do not respond or respond insufficiently to its requests. UNMIK police have been frequently unwilling to share important documentation. In such cases, the OIK has no follow-up powers apart from repeating its appeals for cooperation, and it may not initiate or become a party to judicial proceedings, which severely limits its reach. If UNMIK, PISG and KFOR were to freely share information with the OIK, it would then be able to make its case against particular officials, and could, as a second step, ask the SRSG to lift that official's civil or criminal immunity. In a hypothetical context of good faith, cooperation between the SRSG and the OIK would then render the formal immunities enjoyed by UNMIK and KFOR officials no longer an impediment to their being held responsible for any crimes or misdemeanours.

Yet, it is precisely the lack of such cooperation in good faith that severely curtails the potential of the OIK as both an accountability and human rights promotion mechanism. And there can be no doubt that this lack is, to a large extent, not accidental but due to a deliberate unwillingness on the part of UNMIK to let the OIK monitor its conduct. Indeed, there have been subtle and continuous attempts to weaken the OIK's position further, be it by creating potentially competing institutions, such as the currently discussed idea of a separate Gender Ombudsperson, or by the already mentioned drive to fully indigenize the institution, which would, in all likelihood, imbue it with the same problems as those faced by the judiciary. UNMIK's stance towards the OIK betrays a worrying lack of interest in independent and competent human rights protection mechanisms in Kosovo. This is a situation that the OIK has found to "[create] a paradox, whereby those entities that are in Kosovo to help preserve human rights and the rule of law are themselves not answerable to the very persons they are obliged to protect".[78] Given the fact that UNMIK is the largest and most sophisticated UN peace operation to date, it is somewhat tragic that the Ombudsperson has felt quite powerless to close what he has strikingly described as a "human rights black hole in Europe".[79]

Conclusion: Lessons to be learned and the road ahead

How can that black hole be closed? And is an ombudsperson institution such as the OIK the right means to do it? It is, for reasons of space, not possible to appraise all the many general lessons that ought to be learned from the United Nations' Kosovo experience so far. It must suffice merely to point again to the main structural fault-lines that continue to affect UNMIK. Perhaps the most crucial one is also the one for which the mission is least directly responsible, notably the future status of the province, which has yet to be determined. It is clear that many of the more radical political actors in Kosovo thrive precisely on that indeterminacy, and it is largely their persistent sabotage of UNMIK's attempts to pacify and to "normalize" Kosovo life that has kept the mission on the defensive. This position is doubly problematic, because it has also provided the excuse for UNMIK to govern in an inconsistent and unprincipled way.

The continuing need for peace and its apparent corollary, namely executive, order-type government, has in UNMIK's case meant that close attention to the rule of law and human rights standards is seen as an impediment rather than a complement. The mission has not sufficiently understood that it cannot externalize its good governance, rule of law and human rights efforts and apply them only to the nascent PISGs without applying them to itself. This "do-as-I-say-not-as-I-do"[80] attitude is profoundly counterproductive, not only with regard to nation-building but also with regard to peacebuilding. The United Nations does not appear to realize that, in a theatre such as Kosovo, the traditional idea that it is, by definition, "there to help" is not enough. With real and exclusive power over people and territory, the only way to ensure that the United Nations attains the role it has traditionally desired to fulfil, namely to make a positive and tangible difference where state actors have failed, is to lead by example. That lesson, however, does not seem to have penetrated yet.

Given UNMIK's unfortunate stance and its resulting unwillingness to see in the OIK an equal partner that helps it to govern by example, OIK's impact is by necessity limited. OIK's judicial enforcement authority is weak, and even its potential for political pressure is restricted by its very independence. Since it has refused to side with either UNMIK or local political interests, it constantly finds itself in between all chairs, and is able to make any headway only by appealing to select and varying audiences. In addition, the OIK's formal association with the OSCE has, arguably, also contributed to its relative weakness vis-à-vis UNMIK, because relations between UNMIK and OSCE have not always been harmonious, which may have further hampered the OIK's effectiveness. That said, the Ombudsperson has successfully managed to earn the trust of ordinary Kosovars across ethnic lines, and it is perhaps the only institution to have gone as far down the nation-building road. Indeed, it is the only UN institution in the territory that does not pathologically mistrust the population it is responsible for. As Marek Nowicki put it succinctly, "the people in Kosovo need the Ombudsperson Institution because, as one of my first interlocutors stressed as early as 2000, thanks to our existence and actions they feel less abandoned and left to their own devices".[81]

What lessons are to be learned from the OIK experience? And would these be applicable only to the territorial administration contexts in which the United Nations finds itself, or would they also be valid for the many other less intensive peace operations? In the particular context of territorial administration, the OIK experience shows that even a small and financially restricted institution with committed and professional staff can step into the accountability gap and provide fast and "easy-to-use" remedies. Even though these remedies consist largely of the comparatively "soft" intermediation between the governed and the government, the OIK has proved to be an indispensable device in adverse conditions such as Kosovo. Hence, despite and because of its difficulties vis-à-vis UNMIK, the OIK is a positive example that ombudspersons are well suited to the United Nations' accountability needs and that they provide a much-needed channel for civil society to voice specific complaints.

Yet, the OIK experience also shows that much needs to be improved for ombudspersons to utilize their full accountability potential in peace operation contexts. One evident step is to strengthen any future ombudsperson's formal mandate vis-à-vis both the civil and the military components of a mission. The ombudsperson's work must not be hampered by ill-conceived immunities for the very actors who need to be rendered accountable. The institution's jurisdiction must extend to all those capable of affecting the lives of the people inhabiting the territory in question, be they international or domestic actors. Moreover, the independence of a prototype peace operation ombudsperson would need to be significantly more entrenched than is currently the case with the OIK. The OIK has, to its great credit, effectively acted entirely independently and is, as an institution, politically and financially dependent on the civil administration, the very body it is meant to scrutinize.

A future ombudsperson should, therefore, be established entirely outside the framework of the particular mission, and receive its mandate and its funding from sources not controlled by the people it is aiming to regulate. Both mandate and funding must be guaranteed over at least a medium period of time, so that the institution does not need to haggle periodically for influence and funds, as may be the case with other mission components. Finally, any model ombudsperson will also need to have wider-ranging powers of investigation and prosecution. By no means must it be dependent on the mere goodwill of the civil or military administration to provide it with information. Rather, it must be endowed with statutory powers of investigation, which must include the power to request any piece of information and to question any official, whether international or domestic. In addition, it should be competent enough to become a party to domestic legal proceedings in the territory in question, so as to provide it with a more robust means to pursue wrongdoers where necessary.

The question these proposals raise is, of course, the legal and institutional basis on which such a fortified ombudsperson institution could be established. As regards the legal basis, the preferable option would be a direct Security Council mandate, rather than an indirect foundation on a Secretary-General's report, as is the case with the OIK. Similarly, to guarantee its institutional autonomy, either peace operation ombudspersons could be established as auxiliary bodies of the Security Council, in a similar vein to, for example, the United Nations Monitoring, Verification and Inspection Commission, or their institutional cradle could be situated in mission-independent UN bodies, such as the Department of Political Affairs or the Office of the UN High Commissioner for Human Rights. In general, an overall policy of peace operation ombudspersonship would need to be established that would allow the designated "mother" institution to develop an accountability expertise that would be independent of mission-political contexts, yet easily adaptable to the specific challenges of each theatre.

However, the political obstacles to such proposals remain high, even if one excludes the fundamental question of the attainability of international, and specifically Security Council, consensus on general peace operation ombudspersonship. The main challenge may lie in the fact that an ombudsperson's central feature, namely his or her independence, is incompatible with the kind of political bargaining between different mission components and levels that characterizes current UN governance. This is one of the lessons to be learned from the OIK experience, notably that the de facto independence displayed by the OIK's office-holder has led to its being sidelined from the mission-internal political processes that determine the mission's day-to-day policy and its general direction. In the absence of a tighter legal framework compelling all mission components to be responsive to ombudsperson-type accountability mechanisms, this state of affairs is unlikely to change. Unless the United Nations comes fully to accept its role as a surrogate state, and the state-like responsibilities this implies, it will not be able to overcome the accountability gap.

Lastly, the response to the question of whether ombudsperson-type accountability is applicable only to fully fledged international (UN) administrations, or whether all peace operations can and ought to have them is clear: all forms of UN governance, whether it acts as the formal government of a territory or just as one of the power-holders of a failed or destroyed state, are amenable to the kind of accountability provided by an ombudsperson. Indeed, the institution is ideally suited correctly to appreciate the extent of UN responsibility in a particular situation, and clearly to separate the ombudsperson from other state or non-state actors. Hence, in non-territorial administration scenarios, it is only an independent ombudsperson with jurisdiction over all the actors involved who is able to ensure that the United Nations is held accountable for what it is truly responsible for. That said, the most effective solution to the United

Nations' accountability gap is probably not the establishment of ad hoc ombudspersons for each mission, but the creation of one, system-wide UN Ombudsperson. Only such a unified and independent institution could muster the authority and formal standing to push accountability to the centre of the United Nations' concerns.[82]

Acknowledgements

This chapter has greatly benefited from a thorough reading by Elizabeth Griffin, formerly of Amnesty International and currently of the Law Department of Essex University; additional thanks are due to Frédéric Mégret (University of Toronto), Maarten Keune (European Trade Union Institute) and Nizar Messari (Instituto das Relações Internacionais, PUC-Rio).

Notes

1. See, generally, D. C. Rowat, ed., *The Ombudsman: Citizen's Defender*, London: Allen & Unwin, 1968.
2. UN General Assembly, *National Institutions for the Promotion and Protection of Human Rights*, UN Doc. A/RES/48/134, 4 March 1994.
3. UNDP, for one, currently supports post-conflict ombudspersons in 21 countries, in many cases jointly with the Office of the UN High Commissioner for Human Rights – see Bureau for Development Policy – Management Development and Governance Division, *Survey of UNDP Activities in Human Rights*, New York: UNDP, 1999.
4. Linda C. Reif, "Building Democratic Institutions: The Role of National Human Rights Institutions in Good Governance and Human Rights Protection", *Harvard Human Rights Journal*, 13, Spring 2000, pp. 1–70.
5. See DPKO Lessons Learned Unit, *A Comprehensive Report on Lessons Learned from United Nations Operation in Somalia (UNOSOM), April 1992–March 1995*, available at ⟨http://pbpu.unlb.org/pbpu/library/UNOSOM.pdf⟩ (accessed 9 November 2006).
6. UN Security Council, *Report of the Secretary-General to the Security Council on the Protection of Civilians in Armed Conflict*, UN Doc. S/1999/957, 8 September 1999.
7. "UNAIDS Expert Strategy Meeting on HIV/AIDS and Peacekeeping, 11–13 December 2000: Recommendations", available at ⟨http://data.unaids.org/Topics/Security/securityrecommendations_en_doc.htm⟩.
8. UN Security Council, Resolution 1265 (1999), UN Doc. S/RES/1265, 17 September 1999.
9. The proposal has since been transferred to the Special Committee on Peacekeeping Operations of the General Assembly and is still awaiting implementation; see UN Security Council, *Letter Dated 14 February 2000 from the President of the Security Council Addressed to the President of the General Assembly*, UN Doc. S/2000/119, 14 February 2000.
10. John Eriksson, "Synthesis Report", in *The International Response to Conflict and Genocide – Lessons from the Rwanda Experience*, Steering Committee of the Joint Evaluation of Emergency Assistance to Rwanda, March 1996: Chapter 5, Part II, Finding C-6,

recommendation a(ii), available at ⟨http://www.reliefweb.int/library/nordic/book1/pb025g1.html⟩ (accessed 9 November 2006).

11. See, for example, the discussion on a specialized ombudsperson for women brought about by the *Secretary-General's Report on Women, Peace, and Security*, UN Doc. S/2002/1154, 16 October 2002, which had been mandated by Security Council Resolution 1325, 31 October 2000.

12. See, *inter alia*, Florian Hoffmann and Frédéric Mégret, "An Ombudsperson for the United Nations?", *Global Governance*, 11(1), 2005, pp. 43–63.

13. See, *inter alia*, the discussion of UNTAET's budget in the General Assembly's Fifth Committee (see UN Press Release GA/AB/3411, 17 November 2000), and the related *Financing of the United Nations Transitional Administration in East Timor: Report of the Advisory Committee on Administrative and Budgetary Questions* (UN General Assembly, UN Doc. A/55/531, 30 October 2000); see also the East Timor entry of *Amnesty International Report 2001*, ASA 57/005/2000; it should, however, be acknowledged that UNTAET's preparatory work did lead to the eventual creation of the office of the Ombudsman, the national ombudsperson of independent Timor-Leste (see section 27 of the Constitution of the Democratic Republic of Timor-Leste). Hence, ultimately, the United Nations' ombudsperson promotion in East Timor can be seen as not having transcended the rendering of assistance for the establishment of "national human rights institutions".

14. Simon Chesterman, "Kosovo in Limbo: State-Building and 'Substantial Autonomy'", International Peace Academy Report, New York: International Peace Academy, 2001, p. 4.

15. Alexandros Yannis, "The UN as Government in Kosovo", *Global Governance*, 10(1), 2004, p. 68.

16. See Michael J. Jordan, "Five Years after Liberation, UN Officials This Week Are Again Working on a Plan for the Political Status of the Province", *Christian Science Monitor*, 22 September 2004, available at ⟨http://www.csmonitor.com/2004/0922/p01s04-woeu.html⟩ (accessed 9 November 2006).

17. See Julie Mertus, "Improving International Peacebuilding Efforts: The Example of Human Rights Culture in Kosovo", *Global Governance*, 10(3), 2004, p. 333.

18. William O'Neill, *Kosovo: An Unfinished Peace*, Boulder, CO: Lynne Rienner, 2002, p. 52.

19. Yannis, "The UN as Government in Kosovo", p. 67.

20. O'Neill, *Kosovo: An Unfinished Peace*, p. 78.

21. See, for example, the International Crisis Group's Balkans Report No. 74 on *The Policing Gap: Law and Order in the New Kosovo*, Prishtina, 6 August 1999.

22. O'Neill, *Kosovo: An Unfinished Peace*, p. 37.

23. It should be clear, however, that slowness of UNMIK deployment is only one factor that helped bring about the implantation of UÇK/KPC parallel structures and the resulting problems; other, equally important, factors are the similarly slow deployment of CIVPOL, the initial pro-UÇK stance of both the SRSG and KFOR, and the partial integration of UÇK components into "official" structures; see also below.

24. The example that springs to mind is what was, in effect, the unofficial division of the city of Mitrovica along ethnic lines by French KFOR troops, which has turned the city into a potential hot-spot ever since; see, *inter alia*, O'Neill *Kosovo: An Unfinished Peace*, p. 45ff.

25. Ibid., p. 43.

26. See UN Security Council, *Report of the Secretary-General on the United Nations Interim Administration Mission in Kosovo*, Annex 1, UN Doc. S/2004/348, 30 April 2004.

27. O'Neill, *Kosovo: An Unfinished Peace*, p. 102.

28. Ibid., p. 104.
29. See, *inter alia*, O'Neill *Kosovo: An Unfinished Peace*, p. 109; and "Failure to Protect: Anti-Minority Violence in Kosovo, March 2004", *Human Rights Watch*, 16(6) (D), July 2004, p. 22.
30. O'Neill, *Kosovo: An Unfinished Peace*, p. 46.
31. Ibid., p. 119.
32. See Marcus Band, "Institution-Building and Human Rights Protection in Kosovo in Light of UNMIK Legislation", *Nordic Journal of International Law*, 70, 2001, p. 482.
33. *On the Establishment of the Ombudsperson Institution in Kosovo*, UNMIK/REG/2000/38, 30 June 2000.
34. See *Constitutional Framework for Provisional Self-Government*, UNMIK/REG/2001/9, 15 May 2001.
35. *On the Establishment of the Ombudsperson Institution in Kosovo*, Section 3.4.
36. Ibid., Section 4.1.
37. Ibid., Section 8.2(c).
38. See Ombudsperson Institution in Kosovo, *Fourth Annual Report: 2003–2004, addressed to the Special Representative of the Secretary-General of the United Nations*, 12 July 2004, p. 34, available at ⟨http://www.ombudspersonkosovo.org/reports_annual.htm⟩ (accessed 9 November 2006).
39. See OIK, *Fourth Annual Report*, p. 7; see also, in general, Frédéric Mégret and Florian Hoffmann, "The UN as a Human Rights Violator? Some Reflections on the UN's Changing Human Rights Responsibilities", *Human Rights Quarterly*, 25(2), 2003.
40. See Ombudsperson Institution in Kosovo, *Third Annual Report: 2002–2003, addressed to the Special Representative of the Secretary-General of the United Nations*, 10 July 2003, p. 10, available at ⟨http://www.ombudspersonkosovo.org⟩ (accessed 9 November 2006).
41. Ibid.; see also Letter from Human Rights Watch to UN Secretary-General Kofi Annan concerning supporting the OIK, 17 August 2004, available, *inter alia*, at ⟨http://www.ombudspersonkosovo.org/reports_other.htm⟩ (accessed 10 November 2006).
42. See OIK Annual Reports, available at ⟨http://www.ombudspersonkosovo.org⟩ (accessed 10 November 2006).
43. In accordance with Rule 16(3) of the OIK's Rules of Procedure, available at ⟨http://www.ombudspersonkosovo.org⟩.
44. See OIK Special Reports No. 1 (26 April 2001), available at ⟨http://www.ombudspersonkosovo.org/reports_special.htm⟩ (accessed 9 November 2006).
45. See OIK Special Reports No. 3 (29 June 2001) and No. 4 (12 September 2001), available at ⟨http://www.ombudspersonkosovo.org/reports_special.htm⟩ (accessed 9 November 2006).
46. See OIK Special Report No. 5 (29 October 2001), available at ⟨http://www.ombudspersonkosovo.org/reports_special.htm⟩ (accessed 9 November 2006).
47. See OIK Special Reports No. 6 (20 November 2003) and No. 9 (29 June 2004), available at ⟨http://www.ombudspersonkosovo.org/reports_special.htm⟩ (accessed 9 November 2006).
48. See OIK Special Report No. 8 (4 June 2004), available at ⟨http://www.ombudspersonkosovo.org/reports_special.htm⟩ (accessed 9 November 2006).
49. See OIK Special Reports No. 2 (30 May 2001) and No. 7 (5 May 2004), available at ⟨http://www.ombudspersonkosovo.org/reports_special.htm⟩ (accessed 9 November 2006).
50. See "Principles Relating to the Status of National Institutions for the Promotion and Protection of Human Rights" ("Paris Principles"), codified, *inter alia*, in General Assembly Resolution A/RES/48/134, 20 December 1993; see also United Nations Centre for Human Rights, *National Human Rights Institutions: A Handbook on the*

Establishment and Strengthening of National Institutions for the Promotion and Protection of Human Rights, Professional Training Series No. 4 at 4–6, UN Doc. HR/P/PT/4, UN, Sales No. E.95.XIV.2, 1995.

51. UN Security Council, *Report of the Secretary-General to the Security Council on the Protection of Civilians in Armed Conflict*.

52. See Amnesty International, "Serbia and Montenegro (Kosovo): The Legacy of Past Human Rights Abuses", EUR 70/009/2004, 1 April 2004; see also OSCE/UNHCR, *Assessment of the Situation of Ethnic Minorities in Kosovo*, Prishtina, OSCE/UNHCR, 2001, pp. 3–4.

53. Amnesty International, "Serbia and Montenegro (Kosovo): The Legacy of Past Human Rights Abuses", p. 7.

54. See, Kosovo Ombudsperson, Ex officio Registrations No. 8/01/I, Concerning the right to life of V.S. and V.N., 29 January 2002; No. 8/01/II, Concerning the right to life of R.C., 29 January 2002; No. 8/01/IV, Concerning the right to life of S.B., 29 January 2002; and No. 8/01/V, Concerning the right to life of S.A., 29 January 2002; available at ⟨http://www.ombudspersonkosovo.org/reports&dec.htm⟩ (accessed 2 December 2006).

55. See OIK, "The Alleged Lack of Proper Investigation with Regard to the Bombing of the 'Nis Express' Bus", in *Fourth Annual Report*, pp. 63–64.

56. See OIK, "Response Letter from Office of Prime Minister Concerning Public Use of Serbian Language Both Written and Oral", 27 May 2004, available at ⟨http://www.ombudspersonkosovo.org/reports_incoming.htm⟩ (accessed 9 November 2006).

57. See, *inter alia*, OIK, *Fourth Annual Report*, p. 21.

58. See, especially, the successive Annual Reports: most notably in the *Second Annual Report*, p. 4, the *Third Annual Report*, pp. 4 and 8, and the *Fourth Annual Report*, p. 21; see also Leopold von Carlowitz, "Crossing the Boundary from the International to the Domestic Legal Realm: UNMIK Lawmaking and Property Rights in Kosovo", *Global Governance*, 10(3), 2004, pp. 307–331.

59. See OIK, *Fourth Annual Report*, p. 30, and Amnesty International, "Serbia and Montenegro (Kosovo/Kosova) – The March Violence: KFOR and UNMIK's Failure to Protect the Rights of the Minority Communities", EUR 70/016/2004, 8 July 2004.

60. See OIK, *Fourth Annual Report*, p. 30; see also OIK, *Quarterly Information Sheet*, April–June 2004, p. 2, available at ⟨http://www.ombudspersonkosovo.org⟩ (accessed 9 November 2006).

61. OIK, *Fourth Annual Report*, p. 7.

62. UN Security Council, *Report of the Secretary-General on the United Nations Interim Administration Mission in Kosovo*, UN Doc. S/1999/779, 12 July 1999, para. 39.

63. Cited in Miriam Cias, "'Justice Gaps' in Kosovo's Legal System", paper presented at the Graduate Student Workshop, Kokkalis Programme, Kennedy School of Government, Harvard University, 8–9 February 2002, available at ⟨http://www.ksg.harvard.edu/kokkalis/GSW4/CiasPAPER.PDF⟩ (accessed 9 November 2006).

64. Simon Chesterman, "The United Nations as Government: Accountability Mechanisms for Territories under UN Administration", paper presented at the conference "Fighting Corruption in Kosovo: Lessons from the Region", Prishtina, Kosovo, 4–5 March 2002, available at ⟨http://www.ipacademy.org/PDF_Reports/un_as_govt_for_web.pdf⟩ (accessed 9 November 2006), p. 1.

65. O'Neill, *Kosovo: An Unfinished Peace*, p. 75.

66. See "UNMIK Refutes Allegations of Judicial Bias and Lack of Strategy", *UNMIK News*, 25 June 2001.

67. See OIK Special Report No. 3, 29 June 2001.

68. See UNMIK Regulation 1/2000, *On the Kosovo Joint Interim Administrative Structure*, UNMIK/REG/2000/1, 14 January 2000.

69. See, *inter alia*, OIK Special Report No. 4 (12 September 2001), on the shortcomings of the Commission.

70. See UNMIK Regulation 1999/1, *On the Authority of the Interim Administration in Kosovo*, UNMIK/REG/1999/1, as amended by UNMIK/REG/2000/54, 27 September 2000.

71. See OIK, *Fourth Annual Report*, p. 9.

72. Ibid.

73. Most prominently in the case of Italy; see, *inter alia*, Florian Hoffmann, "Report – European Court of Human Rights (2001/2002)", *Annual of German and European Law*, Oxford/New York: Berghahn Books, 2004.

74. See OIK, *Fourth Report*, p. 11; for a not uncritical but, on the whole, much more UNMIK-friendly perspective, see Hansjörg Strohmeyer, "Collapse and Reconstruction of a Judicial System: The United Nations Missions in Kosovo and East Timor", *American Journal of International Law*, 95(1), 2001, pp. 46–63.

75. UNMIK Regulation 47/2000, *On the Status, Privileges and Immunities of KFOR and UNMIK and Their Personnel in Kosovo*, UNMIK/REG/2000/47, 18 August 2000.

76. OIK Special Report No. 1.

77. Letter from SRSG Hans Haekkerup to the OIK on Special Report No. 1, 28 June 2001, available at ⟨http://www.ombudspersonkosovo.org/reports_incoming.htm⟩ (accessed 10 November 2006).

78. OIK, *Fourth Annual Report*, p. 16.

79. OIK, *Third Annual Report*, p. 7.

80. Chesterman, "The United Nations as Government", pp. 2 and 5.

81. OIK, *Fourth Annual Report*, p. 3.

82. See, again, Hoffmann and Mégret, "An Ombudsperson for the United Nations?", p. 60.

12

The vicarious responsibility of the United Nations

Frédéric Mégret

One thing that this book has identified is that some "unintended consequences" of peacekeeping operations are clearly negative and adversely affect not only the operations themselves but the host state and, most importantly, the local population. What I want to argue in this chapter is not only that there should be some accountability for these adverse consequences, but that it is at least partly the United Nations itself *as an institution* that should be accountable. This is what I refer to as the "vicarious" responsibility of the United Nations, and it stands in opposition to, for example, the responsibility of states or of individuals. It is important as a preliminary matter to define, in line with the general framework set by the editors, what one understands by the "unintended consequences" of peace operations for the purposes of UN accountability. In a sense, the Srebrenica massacre and the fact that the United Nations became associated with it through its inaction was (one would hope) an unintended consequence of the failure of the United Nations Protection Force (UNPROFOR). Similarly, the Rwandan genocide could be described at least partly as an unintended consequence of the failure of the United Nations Assistance Mission for Rwanda to halt the rise of Hutu extremism. Indeed, there is a very strong case that the United Nations should feel – and has felt[1] – accountable for such events as the Srebrenica massacre or the Rwandan genocide. Such efforts as have been undertaken by the United Nations in coming to terms with that responsibility[2] are part of the same general movement towards accountability that I am preoccupied with.

Unintended consequences of peacekeeping operations, Aoi, de Coning and Thakur (eds), United Nations University Press, 2007, ISBN 978-92-808-1142-1

This is not, however, the type of issue I will deal with as unintended consequences for which the United Nations should be accountable. In fact, although not intended, failure – even abject failure – is always, if not foreseen, at least contemplated and is part of a larger effort that is itself very much intended. I will understand unintended consequences, on the contrary, not as consequences that result from a failure to fulfil a mandate, but as outcomes that lie in a sense entirely *outside* that mandate. For example, the fact that a peacekeeping operation has an effect on the local economy is completely unrelated to the pursuit of that mission's mandate. More relevant to our purposes, violations of the laws of war or human rights, even though they occur in the course of a mission and the exercise of official duties, are strictly unintended in terms of a mission's mandate. I will be interested principally in such instances of UN abuse, which have become quite common in recent years, be they acts of torture perpetrated by Canadian, Italian or Belgian soldiers in Somalia, the West Africa "sex for aid" scandal or violations of civil liberties by police of the United Nations Interim Administration Mission in Kosovo.

The case for the fact that "someone" or "something" should be accountable for these unintended consequences is a compelling one, from both a legal and a policy perspective. From a legal point of view, it seems that, at least to the extent that they constitute human rights violations, unintended consequences create or should create a right to an "effective remedy" as guaranteed by most international human rights instruments.[3] Of course, not all unintended consequences will be violations of human rights (either because no imaginable right is violated, or because the United Nations is in no position to guarantee such rights in the first place). Nonetheless, human rights obligations are arguably increasingly applicable to the United Nations itself in those "third-generation" peace operations where the United Nations is actively involved in peacebuilding and reconstruction tasks, not to mention situations where the United Nations is in effect the sovereign. Here, it would seem that with added power and the displacement of the traditional sovereign as a provider of remedies come added responsibilities.[4] It is quite clear that those whose rights have been affected in the course of peace operations should not become deprived of that right to an effective remedy merely because the context is one of a UN-mandated operation. In most cases, requiring individuals to turn against their state and look for remedies elsewhere will simply not make sense, either because there is no functioning state to turn to or because, even if there is, it is not interested in providing remedies.

Looking at the issue from the point of view of the United Nations and the law of international organizations (IOs) reveals that it is increasingly accepted that good governance involves a strong measure of accountability. At its most general, the idea that international institutions should be accountable simply reflects the fact that they do not operate in a void, but must be seen as agents that are ultimately answerable to the demands of the society from which they derive their legal existence. As the International Law Association put it, "as a matter of principle, accountability is linked to the authority and power of an IO. Power entails accountability, that is the duty to account for its exercise."[5] In addition, because the United Nations is an institution that has a long history of encouraging states to be accountable in all kinds of ways, there is a particularly clear-cut case that it should itself be accountable. Indeed, as the ILA put it, "[n]o situation should arise where an IO would not be accountable to some authority for an act that might be deemed illegal".[6] Accountability can also be justified from a broader policy perspective. By fostering a culture of respect for the civilian population, it increases the acceptability of a mission. Furthermore, by providing evidence of a commitment to certain standards, it may also inspire local actors to replicate certain features of accountability. Finally, it should be noted that there has certainly been a growing demand for accountability from civilian populations in areas where UN missions are active.[7]

However, the idea that the United Nations should be accountable begs the question: what kind of accountability? Accountability is a term sometimes so wide as to appear porous. There are many ways in which one can be accountable: accountability can be political or it can be legal; it can be collective or it can be individual; it can be *ex ante* or *ex post*; it can be preventive or corrective. The challenge is clearly less to determine that the United Nations should be accountable, and more to determine what accountability means by examining these various options for accountability.

In this chapter I want to address at least one of these dilemmas from the outset, by saying that I will focus on the so-called "vicarious" responsibility of the United Nations. In other words, I am interested in the responsibility of the United Nations *as an institution*. As is well known, individuals may occasionally be held accountable for some unintended negative consequences of peace operations, usually through the operation of domestic or international criminal law, but also through various disciplinary procedures. This is the subject of Chapter 10 in this volume and will therefore not be examined in any detail here. Suffice it to say that penal and disciplinary proceedings, especially when it comes to military personnel, have generally been delegated to troop-contributing states. This is mostly because states insist on retaining such control and because the United Nations does not have the capacity to conduct disciplinary and/or penal proceedings. One insidious effect of this outsourcing, however, apart from the fact that states may sometimes lack energy in pursuing such procedures, is that it entirely circumvents the issue of the United Nations' own partial responsibility. But individual criminal responsibility, for all the attention it has garnered of late, is certainly not exclusive of vicarious responsibility. Both the United Nations (for not providing adequate supervision) and an individual (for actually committing the act) may well be liable simultaneously for the commission of similarly harmful conduct. This is something that the practice of the United Nations is beginning to confirm.[8] Indeed, the fact that the United Nations otherwise considers itself responsible for preventing and detecting abuses in peace operations[9] shows that it cannot claim to be a total stranger to their occurrence.

In fact, there is a very real risk that, by putting the emphasis excessively on individual responsibility at the expense of vicarious responsibility, one neglects the extent to which all individual failure is almost always, in a sense, also an institutional failure. Apart from the case where individual behaviour is entirely unforeseeable (for example a soldier having an entirely unexpected psychotic episode leading him to shoot civilians) or entirely malicious, there will often be ways in which the United Nations as an institution might have better prevented the acts in question. By locating responsibility at the level of the organization, one increases the incentive for that organization to set up policies that will reduce the negative side-effects on the population. In addition, there may be cases where it is simply not possible to trace the origin of an unintended consequence to any individual decision, meaning that vicarious responsibility will be the only channel for accountability.

Although it is difficult to make an abstract assessment of what precise form vicarious accountability should take, one may expect that accountability should adopt certain features. One fairly major trend observable in various areas of governance, for example, is a shift from a "shareholder" view of accountability to one emphasizing the importance of so-called "stakeholders". The ILA, for example, has thrown the net particularly wide by claiming that "[t]he constituency entitled to raise the accountability of IOs consists of all component entities of the international community at large provided their interests or rights have been or may be affected by acts, actions or activities of IOs".[10] This obviously includes private parties. UN accountability in peacekeeping operations should therefore be at least partly for the benefit of those who suffer directly from unintended consequences. An accountability regime that failed that test would probably not stand up to contemporary global governance standards. Another idea that accountability carries with it is a degree of transparency. We would not think that accountability mechanisms operating entirely behind closed doors made the most of what accountability is about: a process of reckoning that involves at least some element of publicity. Finally, we would also probably assume that accountability should be partly legal and "proceduralized", in the sense that an accountability that relied entirely on political whim would appear to be excessively discretionary.

Having said that, the challenge in the case of the United Nations is less to draw up some ideal theory of accountability than it is to ask the question of whether and how the United Nations is (or is not) already accountable. As the ILA concluded after setting out a whole series of "recommended rules and practices" (RRPs) on the accountability of international organizations, these RRPs "may in substance already be incorporated in constituent instruments; they may also be derived from such instruments and from the practice of IOs".[11] The purpose of this chapter, therefore, will be to determine how sometimes dormant or insufficiently understood rules can be used in a way that maximizes accountability, and to see how the United Nations' existing accountability regime stands up to an ideal concept of accountability.

The first type of accountability that comes to mind in the UN context is a sort of broad internal accountability. At its most general, this means that the United Nations should function according to broadly conceived principles of good governance: transparency, democracy, attention to all stakeholders, etc. Constitutionally, the United Nations can be seen as an institution geared towards ensuring a degree of internal accountability through division of power and various checks and balances. In addition to this "internal" system of checks and balances, the United Nations is meant to be accountable to member states. Much UN reform is geared to making the United Nations, and particularly the Secretariat, more accountable in that way.

The effect of this type of accountability on taking into account unintended consequences of peace operations, however, is likely to be only a part of the accountability puzzle. It can only help that the United Nations, as the institution charged with organizing and implementing peace operations, works transparently, in conditions that maximize sensitivity to problems such as unintended consequences. It is because the United Nations as an institution will become aware of such problems that accountability can be improved. It is not inconceivable that state parties would occasionally become interested in the phenomenon of unintended consequences. However, this sort of political accountability is too broad to fully take into account the relatively precise and discrete phenomenon of unintended consequences. Being concerned with policy, it mostly lacks the element of institutional responsiveness that one would associate with full accountability. Moreover, accountability to states misses the point that it is primarily to those affected by unintended consequences that accountability should be owed.

Another way to focus on political accountability, therefore, is to see it as a form of responsiveness to demands for accountability once unintended consequences have arisen. The Secretary-General or key representatives of the United Nations have at times deplored the fact that certain acts were carried out under the UN flag (for example the Secretary-General and the President of the Security Council unambiguously condemned violations of international humanitarian law by UN peacekeepers that occurred in Somalia). This sort of political accountability, however, although it may be a first step to something more concrete, remains relatively symbolic.

It is likely, therefore, that some relatively specific accountability mechanism is required beyond the general governance mechanisms of the United Nations. Some means of legal accountability can be excluded almost *ab initio*. The United Nations, in particular, has immunity from the jurisdiction of domestic courts. This is probably not a privilege one would want to revoke lightly. Immunity from local courts is a good guarantee of the independence of peacekeeping missions. Especially in hostile contexts, there is a real risk that missions would otherwise become the object of judicial harassment. Local courts are therefore not a viable forum for accountability because they would seem to compromise too much of the peacekeeping missions' needs.

However, the United Nations' immunity from jurisdiction is undeniably a privilege, and one that should be seen as entailing certain responsibilities. If anything, it militates in favour of the United Nations' developing accountability mechanisms of its own to make up for the fact that domestic accountability is not an option. On that count, the United Nations' record is mixed to say the least. When it comes to abuses committed by peacekeepers, the United Nations' constant position (and one that obviously has the backing of state parties) has been that disciplining troops is exclusively the responsibility of contributing states. Although there may be very good policy (the need to provide certain guarantees that will entice states to contribute troops) and legal (the absence of a military justice system within the United Nations) reasons for this, the net effect is that the United Nations avoids all kinds of accountability even in situations where abuses are partly traceable to some of its shortcomings (a failure to ensure proper training; a failure to monitor the behaviour of the force in general).

Rather than suggest that the United Nations should take on the exclusive responsibility of dealing with individual abuses itself, which is an impracticable and unlikely solution, I want to explore ways in which the United Nations might be called upon to shoulder part of the blame for unintended consequences that would make sense in relation to its role and responsibilities. I propose to do this is by exploring what mechanisms are already in place and investigating whether they might be suited to the sort of unintended consequences in question.

The United Nations' response to the realization that peace operations occasionally have adverse side-effects has been limited. The only provision that explicitly contemplates that the United Nations should set up some accountability mechanism is Section 29 of the Convention on the Privileges and Immunities of the United Nations, which says that "[t]he United Nations shall make provisions for appropriate modes of settlement of ... disputes arising out of contracts or other disputes of a private law character to which the United Nations is a party". Accordingly, the United Nations has, since the earliest peacekeeping operations, set up mechanisms for reviewing accountability as set out in particular in paragraph 51 of the Model Status-of-Forces Agreement.[12]

The goal of this chapter is to examine the record of these mechanisms from both a substantive and a procedural angle to determine whether and how they might fare more generally as accountability mechanisms for responding to various unintended consequences.

The substantive regime

It is generally recognized that the law relating to the accountability of the United Nations and international organizations in general to third parties is, outside contractual arrangements, "underdeveloped".[13] However, that law does borrow some important features, including some key concepts, from the law of state responsibility (as codified, in particular, by the International Law Commission). It is possible to distinguish between several broad areas where UN "accountability law" is already significantly developed, including (a) the nature of liability, (b) problems of attribution and (c) the issue of the *ratione materiae* (subject matter) scope of liability.

The nature of liability

The liability of the United Nations for the consequences of peacekeeping operations can be defined negatively (by what it excludes) or positively (by what it includes).

Situations where no liability arises

The United Nations' regime of responsibility is a limited one. The idea of "limited liability", in fact, is quite closely premised on the distinction between intended and unintended consequences. The limitation in the idea of limited liability lies in the fact that the United Nations is not responsible for anything covered under (a) the exception of "operational necessity"; (b) acts committed by troops that were unauthorized; and (c) acts performed by peacekeepers off duty.

The exception of "operational necessity"

The exception of operational necessity refers to situations "where damage results from necessary actions taken by a peacekeeping force in the course of carrying out its operations in pursuance of its mandates".[14] In other words, damage naturally expected to occur as a result of the normal pursuit of a peacekeeping operation – damage that is, if not intended, at least clearly foreseen as inevitable – will not trigger the United Nations' responsibility. The rationale for this, as the Secretary-General put it, is based on the "assumption that consensual peacekeeping operations are conducted for the benefit of the country in whose territory they are deployed, and that having expressly or implicitly agreed to the deployment of a peacekeeping operation in its territory, the host country must be deemed to bear the risk of the operation and assume, in part at least, liability for damage arising from such an operation".[15]

It is expected, for example, that, in the course of carrying out a peace operation, some damage will occur to the infrastructure (if only wear and tear) and that some military operations will be launched that may result in damage to property. The United Nations is not responsible for such "ordinary" damage and there is a clear drive on the part of the United Nations to make this as clear as possible. For instance, this is done by including a reference to the principle in Status-of-Forces agreements that would exclude the jurisdiction of claims review boards (see below, "The procedural regime") for such matters.

There may of course be some difficulty in defining what the exact scope of operational necessity is. The Secretary-General has conceded that "[i]t is of course difficult, if not impossible to determine in advance what would constitute 'operational necessity' in any given situation". In the same paragraph, the Secretary-General also insists that such a decision "must remain within the discretionary power of the force commander, who must attempt to strike a balance between the operational necessity of the force and the respect for private property"[16] – which would seem to grant considerable leeway. The Secretary-General, however, has laid out what in his mind are the proper conditions for destruction of property to be covered by operational necessity:

(i)   There must be a good-faith conviction on the part of the force commander that an operational necessity exists;

(ii) The operational need that prompted the action must be strictly necessary and not a matter of mere convenience or expediency. It must also leave

little or no time for the commander to pursue another, less destructive
option;

(iii) The act must be executed in pursuance of an operational plan and not the
result of a rash individual action; and

(iv) The damage caused should be proportional to what is strictly necessary in
order to achieve the operational goal.[17]

Unauthorized and "off-duty" acts

It is not clear whether an unauthorized act committed by troops who
are exercising their duties will engage the United Nations' liability. One
case is known in connection with the First United Nations Emergency
Force (UNEF I), which rejected the idea that it could be responsible for
such acts. In addition, the Model Contribution Agreement between the
United Nations and Participating States Contributing Resources to the
United Nations Peacekeeping Operation anticipates that the United Nations will not be responsible where the harm resulted from "gross negligence or wilful misconduct of the personnel provided by [a] Government".[18] In such a case it is to the contributing state that claims must be
directed. This is particularly the case in situations of combat-related damage that arises in violation of the laws of war and where criminal responsibility is involved.

The United Nations also does not incur responsibility for off-duty acts,
namely acts committed by members of a contingent as private individuals. This is stipulated in the various Status-of-Forces Agreements signed
by the United Nations with host countries. However, what is a strictly off-
duty act may sometimes be difficult to define. As anyone having participated in a peacekeeping mission will know, particularly in a hostile context, there is little off-duty time. Even what peacekeepers do off duty
should be partly the organization's concern. If peacekeepers routinely
abuse local women sexually while taking breaks from the mission's work,
then one would expect that it would fall upon the United Nations to correct that behaviour, especially if national commanding structures are
indifferent or even complicit. In fact, although the United Nations will
deny that it is liable in such situations, it has established a fairly consistent practice of informally indemnifying victims of acts of off-duty peacekeepers (United Nations Forces in Cyprus). The reason liability is not explicitly acknowledged is apparently out of fear that a precedent would be
created that could open the door to considerable liabilities. Although obviously not an international criminal law issue, a formula such as that applicable in cases of command responsibility ("knew or should have known
but failed to act") would seem of some relevance in ascertaining the level
of improper response by the United Nations.

Situations where liability does arise

Conversely, the "liability" part of "limited liability" refers to the fact that the United Nations *is* responsible for all damage that either is caused *ultra vires* or off duty, or is covered by the "operational necessity" exception. More specifically, interpreting the above conditions for invocation of the operational necessity rule *a contrario*, one can conclude that the types of measures that will trigger UN liability are those:

- that are taken in bad faith;
- that are not strictly necessary and are instead only a matter of convenience or expediency;
- that are the result of a rash individual action rather than part of an operational plan; and
- that cause damage that is not proportional to what is strictly necessary in order to achieve the operational goal.

All of these would seem to fall quite squarely in the category of unintended consequences, in the sense that the United Nations cannot have intended soldiers in a peace operation to act outside operational necessity. These are more than mere failures; they are initiatives that expose significant mistakes at best, disregard for the local population and property at worst. An obvious example of acts not covered by the operational necessity exception are violations of the laws of war. Clearly, no amount of operational necessity can make a violation of the laws of war (not to mention a war crime) legal. Indeed, the United Nations has recognized not only that the laws of war apply to it, but that it owes compensation for violations of international humanitarian law committed by peacekeepers.[19] In addition, it is the practice of the United Nations to compensate for both non-consensual occupation and damage to private property that it occupies or that is damaged in the performance of official duties.[20] Such occupation often occurs as a result of failure of the host government to provide adequate locales. In the case of destruction, liability is incurred regardless of whether the property is private or public. The rationale here seems to be that, even when a government is willingly providing property, it does not *a priori* anticipate that use would actually lead to destruction.

Problems of attribution

Perhaps the key difficulty involved in securing UN accountability is the difficulty of apportioning blame under the complex regime whereby troops are contributed by states. When it comes to combat-related activity in particular, the United Nations has a very "either/or" approach. The general principle in international law is that "[c]ontrol over organs and individuals by a subject of law is the basis for attribution of acts or omissions by such organs and individuals to the subject of law exercising such control".[21] On the basis of that principle, the United Nations will accept responsibility only in cases where it has "exclusive command and control"[22] over the troops in question. Since this is a very rare situation, however, it seems very unlikely that the United Nations would ever be considered responsible for violations of the laws of war.

There would seem to be a case, however, for a simultaneous responsibility: even if always in a sense dependent on the contributing state, troops acting under the state flag are also in a way acting under the UN flag, as it were. The fact that they violate the laws of war may in some cases be directly attributable to lack of UN oversight of national contingents or to weaknesses in training. Even when a state is primarily responsible because it has operational control, the United Nations arguably remains bound by an obligation to ensure respect for international humanitarian law, as a result of common Article 1 of the Geneva Conventions.[23] One author has argued that in some cases the "control test" "may even allow for concurrent responsibility because of a limbo status involving an ill-defined form of dual control".[24] Note that the fact that the United Nations is made accountable is certainly not exclusive of state responsibility and, moreover, does not prevent the United Nations from exercising an action against the contributing state.[25] As the Secretary-General put it, "it is precisely because of that element of gross fault or wilful or criminal intent that the organization is justified in seeking recovery from the individual or the troop-contributing state concerned".[26] Similarly, when it comes to compensation paid to the owners of property requisitioned by the United Nations as a result of failure of the relevant state to honour its obligation to provide property, the United Nations can seek reimbursement from that government. In both cases, however, it makes sense that claimants can turn to the United Nations without having to become involved in the complexities of determining who, within a complex allocation of responsibilities set-up, is actually responsible.

The ratione materiae *scope of liability*

The United Nations' approach to liability is mostly focused on "disputes of a private law character to which the United Nations is a party". As the Secretary-General has stressed, the "most commonly encountered of those [are] non-consensual use and occupancy of premises, personal injury and property loss or damage arising from the ordinary operation of the force, and such injury and damage as [a] result [of] combat operations".[27] This would seem relatively distant from the issue of human rights violations or war crimes. A separate regime exists for claims for compensation for death and injury that are not considered "private" claims.[28] Moreover, the proclamation by the Secretary-General of the applicability of international humanitarian law to peacekeepers makes it inevitable, in a context where the United Nations has otherwise been arguing strongly for the need to compensate victims of war crimes, that the United Nations would consider itself liable for such violations. In fact the Secretary-General has said that such applicability "entails the international responsibility of the Organization and its liability in compensation".[29] Whether violations of human rights, for example by civilian or military police in contexts where the United Nations is the administrator of a given territory, also entail liability is less clear, but it is notable that there is a shift from the purely private origins of accountability to a recognition that some element of international public law is involved. It is worth noting, for example, that the Special Representative of the Secretary-General in Kosovo has often, upon referral by the Kosovo Ombudsperson, forwarded human rights complaints to the Kosovo Claims Review Board "for determination as to whether the applicant should be awarded compensation".[30]

The procedural regime

The local claims review boards

The mechanism anticipated by the Model Status-of-Forces Agreement was that a standing claims commission would be set up. The idea of the standing claims commissions was that parties (the United Nations and the host country) would participate on an equal footing. One member would be designated by the Secretary-General, one by the government, and the chairman by both. However, no standing commissions have actually ever been set up. Although the Secretary-General has argued that in itself this is "not an indication that the procedure is inherently unrealistic or ineffective", such a consistent failure to resort to standing claims commissions suggests that this solution has been all but abandoned. There are certainly some cases where standing claims commissions do not seem particularly practicable. As the Secretary-General put it, "in any event, [such commissions] would be problematic in the context of Chapter VII operations where no 'host Government' would be available to participate".[31] Instead, the UN practice has been to set up a local claims review board in each peacekeeping operation, regardless of size. The main difference between a potential claims commission and the review boards is that the boards are composed exclusively of UN staff members (at least three). They tend, therefore, to be a much more "institutional" and internal remedy than what the original claims commission model anticipated. (Although they are sometimes referred to as "local", the boards are also referred to by the United Nations as "internal".) Specifically, review boards owe their mandate to authority delegated by the UN Controller for which they act in an "advisory capacity".[32] It is difficult to assess the value of the review boards' work since their rulings are not made public. However, it is possible to point to several advantages and limitations from what is known of the work of the boards, particularly through its examination by the Secretary-General.

The advantage of local review boards is that they are generally close to where the potential liability-creating incident occurred. Because "[t]he information and documentation relating to the circumstances of a claim are generally located in the field" and because "the personnel of the United Nations operation are most familiar with local factors bearing on the claim", the Secretary-General has described local review boards as a "viable alternative".[33] Furthermore, the mechanism has the advantage of being relatively functional and speedy. Settlements are generally paid in the field.

There are several limitations, however, which should attract the attention of anyone interested in how the United Nations might commit itself to the highest standards of accountability. The main problem (at least the one that the United Nations has devoted most attention to) seems to have been the relative inefficiency of the boards, especially in relation to the increasing scope and complexity of peace operations. Because of shortages of staff, delays are a constant problem. As soon as the amounts claimed exceed a certain amount, the claim has to be referred to Headquarters, which may slow the process substantially. It should also be pointed out that the boards deal not only (or, in fact, even principally) with third-party liability, but with various issues of internal liability and liability vis-à-vis troop-contributing states. Finally, the comparatively greater use of force in Chapter VII operations since the end of the Cold War has often led to an exponential increase in third-party claims.[34] The review boards have often been overwhelmed (one report described the United Nations Transitional Authority in Cambodia as having been "inundated with claims") in a situation where the very persistence of undue delays seems incompatible with the idea of accountability.

In order to speed up the process, adjustments have often been made on a case-by-case basis. One idea is to delegate more authority to review panels so that fewer claims have to be forwarded to Headquarters. The Secretary-General suggested that, instead of having just one review board, each peacekeeping area should have several.[35] However, this has yet to be acted upon. The fact that the United Nations has been slow in honouring compensation awards to its own staff in the past,[36] often because of a lack of cash, does not augur well for what might be an increase in third-party compensation in the context of peace operations. In addition, there may be a number of more severe procedural limitations to the claims review boards, even if they were to work more efficiently. Apart from the relative secrecy that surrounds their work, the fact that the boards are composed exclusively of UN staff raises concerns about their independence and objectivity, a particularly sore point given that the United Nations may be quite reluctant to recognize that it has been involved in human rights abuses.[37] If the strength of a standing commission is its bipartite composition, the weakness of the boards is that, "just and efficient as they may be", these are bodies "in which the Organisation, rightly or wrongly, may be perceived as acting as a judge in its own case". This warrants that, at least "as an option for potential claimants", a procedure "that involves a neutral third party should be retained in the text of the status-of-forces agreement".[38]

The Secretary-General has also suggested that there be a "temporal limitation" to claims. As a result, "stale claims or claims submitted after an unreasonable period of time following the occurrence of the event giving rise to the claim would be excluded from consideration".[39] Time limits to submit claims are a problem when it comes to human rights violations, where claims may be slow to emerge because either the victims are dead or witnesses are too scared to come forward.

Problems linked to the nature of the indemnity

The possibility of lump sum payments to the host state

One idea that has been suggested is for the United Nations to pay a lump sum to the host state, leaving it to that state to then distribute that sum to its nationals "in the manner its sees fit". The idea here is that the government of that state essentially acts on behalf of its nationals by espousing their claims as part of the exercise of its right to diplomatic protection. This mechanism was used in the Democratic Republic of Congo, where the United Nations settled a substantial number of individual claims asserted by non-Congolese nationals by way of global settlement agreements with the relevant states. Such a procedure is supposed to reduce the length of proceedings and to have the advantage that the United Nations is clear about the limit of its liability in a given context.

There are limits to it from an accountability point of view, however. First, as the Secretary-General himself acknowledges, "[t]he choice of a lump-sum settlement as a mode of handling third-party claims is largely dependent on the State's willingness to espouse the claims of its nationals".[40] But there is a very real risk that some states will not be interested.

This might be simply out of disregard for the interests of their citizens. Or it might be because in "collapsed states", for example, no such institution would be ready to launch such a relatively complicated process. Second, there is no guarantee that the lump sum will be equitably and legally distributed. This is especially true in post-conflict scenarios where an element of societal division is generally the rule; it is unclear that it would be open to the United Nations simply to award a settlement to a state either that was not representative of its people or that had engaged in discriminatory behaviour in the past.

Caps on indemnity

Another important limitation, particularly if one has in mind grave violations of human rights or the commission of war crimes, is that there has been a strong effort to limit the amount that the United Nations may be called to pay out. This followed what seems to have been the exponential growth of third-party liability claims directed at the United Nations. For example, in 1997 the Secretary-General estimated that a total of 151 claims were pending in relation to the United Nations Protection Force for some US$28.8 million. In addition to the overall amount of claims being quite considerable, a number of highly publicized individual claims also caused worries in the United Nations. Most notoriously, the government of Bosnia and Herzegovina presented claims totalling US$70.7 million, including about US$43.4 million for damage to roads by UN vehicles, US$18.3 million for damage at Sarajevo airport and about US$2.2 million for damage at Marshal Tito Barracks. As a result, the Secretary-General, at the suggestion of the Advisory Committee on Administrative and Budgetary Questions, produced two reports dealing with the limitation of awards. Although pointing out that "the ceiling of compensation ... should be further studied", the Secretary-General did make a guarded step in the direction of limiting financial liability by pointing to the wide acceptability of such a practice in international law.[41] The idea of such a limitation was then accepted by the Advisory Committee, which recommended it to the General Assembly,[42] which requested that the Secretary-General develop specific measures, including criteria and guidelines, for implementing the principles outlined in his report.[43] Following this request, the Secretary-General has suggested (on the basis of the maximum compensation amounts for military or police observers and members of UN commissions) that the maximum claim for personal injury, death or illness should be US$50,000. Similar, albeit more complex, limits have been suggested for damage to property.[44] The Secretary-General recommended that this cap be made effective by a combination of a General Assembly resolution (giving state party legitimacy), reference in Status-of-Forces Agreements (binding the host state) and terms of reference of the claims review boards (limiting their power).[45]

The limitation is understandable to a degree on the basis of the idea that the receiving state should share some of the burden of the peace operations. In a way, the receiving state "pays" by contributing its infrastructure and by accepting in advance that it will incur damages. In addition, as the Secretary-General pointed out, to the extent that third-party claims are paid by public funds, "lesser amounts may be available to finance additional peacekeeping or other United Nations operations".[46] However, these limitations are also somewhat worrying. As the Secretary-General himself made clear, "[f]inancial limitations on the liability of the Organization, though justified on economic, financial and policy grounds, constitute an exception to the general principle that when tortious liability is engaged, compensation should be paid with a view to redressing the situation and restoring it to what it had been prior to the occurrence of the damage".[47] Indeed, it is not clear that the rules of liability as they exist, specifically the operational necessity principle, do not already adequately limit the United Nations' liability, without needing to also add a cap.

It is a welcome sign in this context that the United Nations has acknowledged that it considers itself fully liable and not bound by any cap in cases of negligence or wilful misconduct. Since these cases probably account for the greater part of the more condemnable unintended consequences, it is reassuring that the United Nations will be in a position to pay whatever full and fair compensation is required.

Conclusion

The mechanism of UN liability in peace operations for acts arising outside operational necessity was not set up with violations of international humanitarian law or of human rights in mind. However, there is no reason to think that it could not conceivably serve that purpose. Although claims review boards have limitations, they are the object of the United Nations' attention and there is a desire to adapt them to the new realities of peace operations. Claims review boards may be only one mechanism of accountability among many (see Chapter 11 on the much more ambitious idea of UN ombudspersons as experienced in Kosovo), but they do provide the prospect of financial compensation to those who have suffered from some unintended consequences of peace operations.

Notes

1. "UN Council Accepts Responsibility in Rwanda Genocide", *Associated Press*, 15 April 2000.

2. *Report of the Independent Enquiry into the Actions of the United Nations during the 1994 Genocide in Rwanda*, Report of the Secretary-General pursuant to General Assembly Resolution 53/35: "The Fall of Srebrenica", UN Doc. A/54/549, presented 15 November 1999.

3. See, generally, D. Shelton, *Remedies in International Human Rights Law*, Oxford: Oxford University Press, 1999.

4. Frédéric Mégret and Florian Hoffmann, "The UN as a Human Rights Violator? Some Reflections on the United Nations Changing Responsibilities", *Human Rights Quarterly*, 25, 2003. Also see, Barbara Harrell-Bond, "Can Humanitarian Work with Refugees Be Humane?", *Human Rights Quarterly*, 24, 2002.

5. International Law Association (ILA), *Accountability of International Organisations, Final Report*, presented at ILA Berlin Conference, 2004, p. 5.

6. Ibid., p. 26.

7. The East Timor and Indonesia Action Network, for example, has publicized many expressions of local discontent at the United Nations Transitional Administration in East Timor on its website (⟨http://www.etan.org/⟩, accessed 10 November 2006).

8. The Kosovo Ombudsperson's practice, for example, shows that the issues of individual criminal responsibility and civil liability, on the one hand, and UN liability, on the other, are not exclusive. See Ombudsperson Institution in Kosovo (OIK), *Registration No. 52/01, Hamdi Rashica against The United Nations Mission in Kosovo (UNMIK)*, 31 October 2001, available at ⟨http://www.ombudspersonkosovo.org/upd_05/rashica.htm⟩ (accessed 10 November 2006).

9. For example, the United Nations is increasingly involved in efforts at investigating sexual exploitation and abuse among peacekeepers, occasionally dismissing civilian staff and ensuring that military staff are expelled from field missions. The Office of Internal Oversight Services, for example, has conducted a "global review of the state of discipline in peacekeeping operations". See *Measures to Strengthen Accountability at the United Nations: Report of the Secretary-General*, UN Doc. A/60/312, 30 August 2005, pp. 15–16.

10. ILA, *Accountability of International Organisations*, p. 5.

11. Ibid., p. 18.

12. United Nations, *Model Status-of-Forces Agreement for Peacekeeping Operations, Report of the Secretary-General*, UN Doc. A/45/594, 9 October 1990.

13. ILA, *Accountability of International Organisations*, p. 21.

14. United Nations, *Financing of the United Nations Protection Force, the United Nations Confidence Restoration Operation in Croatia, the United Nations Preventive Deployment Force and the United Nations Peace Forces headquarters – Administrative and Budgetary Aspects of the Financing of the United Nations Peacekeeping Operations: Financing of the United Nations Peacekeeping Operations*, UN Doc. A/51/389, 20 September 1996, p. 5, para. 13.

15. United Nations, *Administrative and Budgetary Aspects of the Financing of the United Nations Peacekeeping Operations: Financing of the United Nations Peacekeeping Operations: Report of the Secretary-General*, UN Doc. A/51/903, 21 May 1997, p. 5, para. 12.

16. UN Doc. A/51/389, p. 5, para. 14.

17. Ibid.

18. *Model Contribution Agreement between the United Nations and Participating State Contributing Resources to the United Nations Peacekeeping Operation, Annex to Administrative and Budgetary Aspects of the Financing of the United Nations Peacekeeping Operations*, 9 July 1996, UN Doc. A/50/995, p. 6, Article 9.

19. UN Doc. A/51/389, p. 5, para. 16.

20. UN Doc. A/51/903, p. 8, para. 33.

21. ILA, *Accountability of International Organisations*, p. 29.
22. UN Doc. A/51/389, p. 6, para. 17.
23. ILA, *Accountability of International Organisations*, p. 24.
24. R. Murphy, "International Humanitarian Law and Peace Support Operations: Bridging the Gap", *Journal of Conflict Studies*, 23, 2003, p. 173.
25. UN Doc. A/50/995, Annex, para. 9.
26. UN Doc. A/51/903, p. 5, para. 14; see also UN Doc. A/51/389, p. 10, para. 42.
27. UN Doc. A/51/389, p. 3, para. 3.
28. *Review of the Efficiency of the Administrative and Financial Functioning of the United Nations*, UN Doc. A/C.5/49/65, 24 April 1995, p. 13.
29. UN Doc. A/51/389, p. 6, para. 16.
30. See OIK, *Registration No. 52/01, Hamdi Rashica against The United Nations Mission in Kosovo (UNMIK)*, 31 October 2001; *Registration No. 361/01, Shefqet Maliqi against The United Nations Mission in Kosovo (UNMIK)*, 13 March 2002.
31. UN Doc. A/C.5/49/65, para. 17.
32. Administrative instruction, 14 April 1993, UN Doc. ST/AI/149/Rev.4, para. 18.
33. UN Doc. A/51/389, p. 8, para. 30.
34. In particular after the United Nations Operation in Somalia; see UN Doc. A/C.5/49/65, para. 20.
35. UN Doc. A/51/389, p. 8, para. 32.
36. *Report of the Office of Internal Oversight Services*, UN Doc. A/56/381, 19 September 2001, para. 91.
37. See ILA, *Accountability of International Organisations*, p. 39.
38. UN Doc. A/51/903, para. 10.
39. UN Doc. A/51/389, p. 10, para. 40.
40. Ibid., p. 9, para. 37.
41. Ibid., p. 10, para. 39.
42. *Report of the Advisory Committee on Administrative and Budgetary Questions*, UN Doc. A/51/491, 14 October 1996.
43. *Report of the Commissioner-General of the United Nations Relief and Works Agency for Palestine Refugees in the Near East, 1 July 1995–30 June 1996*, UN Doc. A/51/13, 11 October 1996.
44. UN Doc. A/51/903, p. 8, para. 32.
45. Ibid., p. 10, paras 39–41.
46. Ibid., p. 5, para. 12.
47. Ibid., p. 9, para. 37.

13

Conclusion: Can unintended consequences be prevented, contained and managed?

Chiyuki Aoi, Cedric de Coning and Ramesh Thakur

The objective of the preceding chapters was to make a contribution, albeit a modest one, towards enhancing our understanding of the unintended consequences of peace operations on the basis of what improvements can be made to overcome serious negative side-effects. Peace operations are an important instrument in the range of options available to the international community when it attempts to prevent conflict, contain the consequences of conflict or manage peace processes. It is therefore in our collective interest to learn lessons from both our successes and our failures, so as to continuously refine and enhance our capacity to undertake more effective peace operations in future.

It is not sufficient to raise awareness about the fact that peace operations generate unintended consequences. It is also necessary to enhance our capacity to prevent, contain and manage potentially negative unintended consequences by improving our understanding of how they come about and by exploring ways in which we can improve our ability to anticipate and counter them. This concluding chapter is aimed at highlighting the contributions made by the various chapters in this volume towards the goal of offering solutions to managing and preventing unintended consequences. However, if we accept that unintended consequences are a natural outcome of the dynamic nature of complex systems, we also have to recognize that they cannot be avoided altogether. This implies that we should anticipate that, despite peace operations' best efforts to limit their actions to those necessary to achieve a desired outcome, unintended consequences are likely to occur. As this volume

Unintended consequences of peacekeeping operations, Aoi, de Coning and Thakur (eds), United Nations University Press, 2007, ISBN 978-92-808-1142-1

has shown, such unintended consequences should not be ignored because they may be morally unacceptable and/or have a significant impact on the ability of a peace operation to achieve its mandate. So, because unintended consequences are likely to occur and because they must be regarded as important, we have to improve our ability to anticipate such unintended consequences and in some cases take steps to prevent them. In other situations we may have to be satisfied with merely containing and managing the potential negative effects of these unintended consequences. If we manage to contain and manage a situation with some success, the result should be an improvement in the overall effectiveness of peace operations.

This concluding chapter will generalize from the findings of the chapters contained in the volume. It will examine the causes of unintended consequences, namely how unintended consequences come about in a complex system. It will then make recommendations about how to enhance the United Nations' accountability in handling unintended consequences. In this conclusion we will argue that peace operations are not only accountable to the member states that give the United Nations the authority to undertake a peace operation and provide the human and financial resources necessary to carry it out. We will argue that peace operations are also, and primarily, accountable to the people whom the operation is meant to assist.

The causes of unintended consequences

How, and through what processes, do unintended consequences in peace operations come about? The following patterns emerge from the findings of the various chapters contained in this volume.

Permissive environment

Almost all the chapters suggest that the breakdown of law and order, socio-economic infrastructure and social-cultural norms in the prevailing post-conflict condition in which most peace operations operate is fertile ground for unintended consequences to occur. This breakdown means that the natural checks and balances that would in normal circumstances identify, contain and manage potential negative effects are absent. For instance, it is now recognized that sexual and gender-based violence is often part of a conscious strategy to demoralize the opposing side in a conflict. Kent argues that such violence can become institutionalized in post-conflict societies when the conditions that created the violence remain in place. She points out that extreme poverty, lack of economic opportunity, lack of employment and the loss of family and community support networks all account for the vulnerability of women and girls to sexual violence, exploitation and abuse in post-conflict societies, not only by local people but also by international peacekeepers. This would explain, for instance, why human trafficking seems to thrive in post-conflict societies.

Impact on the host system

The demands created by the sudden influx of a large expatriate community add to the complexity of the environment in which peace operations operate. A number of chapters considered and investigated the impact that the imposition of a sudden large expatriate community has on an already fragile host system. The deployment of a peace operation, involving tens of thousands of international civilian, police and military peacekeepers over a relatively short period of time, has various positive and negative effects on the host system. It most cases discussed in this volume the peace operation, humanitarian community and other external actors making up the expatriate community distorted the local economy and stimulated the development of a dual economy. In this dual economy, one served the needs of the expatriate community and the other served the local population. In general, the poorer the host society and the more devastating the damage from the conflict, the greater the impact the peace operation is likely to have on the host system. In most cases the budget of the peace operation is several times that of the GDP of the host system. However, the effect of the operation on the host system will be limited to the portion injected by the peace operation, and the peacekeepers individually, into the host system.

Impact on the local economy

Ammitzboell's research in Afghanistan and Kosovo found evidence that large expatriate communities have a range of unintended economic consequences on their host systems, most of which have a negative effect on the host economy. These effects may range from, but are not limited to, a rise in basic commodity prices, an increase in salary disparities and higher rates of unequal standards of living. Ammitzboell points out that peace operations may have a positive impact on the local economy by creating job opportunities and by increasing or creating a demand for certain services and goods, but cautions that this impact will not necessarily result in the enhancement of local infrastructures or capacities because much of this additional demand is taken up by the international private sector. A large portion of this economic stimulation is linked to the temporary deployment of the peace operation and an influx of international assistance. The positive economic impact that this has in the short term cannot be sustained. As Lee points out, humanitarian assistance in such a context may also give a false sense of relief and distort the local economy, with possible negative unintended consequences. Ammitzboell notes, for instance, how the provision of food assistance allows farmers the opportunity to turn to cash crops. This does not always lead to a desirable result from a food-security perspective, such as with the growing of poppies in Afghanistan.

Impact on the local civil service

Ammitzboell records the effects of the "brain-drain" phenomenon and the "dual public sector syndrome" on the host public sector. Both of these factors contribute to a dysfunctional and unreliable public sector. The perversity of this effect becomes even clearer when we take into consideration that it not only has a negative effect on the local economy, but is in fact directly opposite to the effect the peace operation is supposed to have (the desired consequence) on the local public sector. In most mandates the desired consequence is to build the capacity of the public sector and to support the extension of state control throughout the territory of the host state. Another example would be, as noted by Ammitzboell, the combination of weak local administrative capacity and the inflow of massive aid resulting in an increase in corruption by state officials.

Change in gender roles

Another aspect of the impact that the international community tends to have on a host society is the way in which international assistance programmes empower certain types of individuals, for instance, those with western language and cultural skills. Another category that has tended to be the focus of various types of "empowerment" programmes by international aid organizations over the last decade is women. Women are often given preferential access to jobs, training and other economic and career opportunities. The intended consequence of these programmes is to have a positive impact on development and stability by empowering women to play a more assertive role in their society. The medium- to long-term effects of these initiatives are the subject of various studies, but Koyama and Myrttinen have identified some negative short-term consequences on women. For instance, this preferential treatment, along with their newly gained economic independence and power, can result in resentment against women within families and in society in general. In some cases this may result in an increase in domestic violence. They also point out that, although such programmes may have a short-term and direct impact on the women involved, it takes longer for society to adapt and this may have some unintended consequences. For example, if there is a sudden increase in the employment of women this may affect their traditional roles at home, where women bear the disproportionate share of child-rearing and household work. It may also result in burden-shifting to younger children and the elderly.

Koyama and Myrttinen's research into the Cambodian and Timorese cases touches on the direct link between the deployment of peacekeepers and the influx of aid workers and the growth of the local sex industry. There is also an increase in the number of cases of sexual exploitation and abuse. Furthermore, they note the link between a declining sex industry and the departure, or significant down-sizing, of a peace operation and related humanitarian community.

The impact on troop-contributing countries

Peace operations give rise to a range of opportunities and costs for troop-contributing countries (TCCs), be they financial, social or political. TCCs have responded to these opportunities in varying ways. Some of these opportunities and costs have given rise to unintended consequences, some significant and some not so significant, that were contrary to what is generally expected. For instance, a few chapters suggest that peace operations are considered a "financial opportunity" by both military institutions and individual troops. In Aning's case study of Ghana, financial gains from participation in peace operations for both individuals and the state seem substantial, and Sotomayor's chapter points to similar perceptions in Argentina and Uruguay. Murthy's chapter on India and Pakistan finds, however, that such gains did not constitute a significant effect given the proportionately small number of units participating in peace operations in relation to the overall size of these armies. In more than a few countries examined, participation in peace operations offered some opportunities for corruption to occur. Aning and Sotomayor discuss cases of corruption such as the manipulation of appointments to peace operations (where selection implies significant financial gain for individual soldiers and officers) and the misappropriation of funds received from the United Nations to reimburse countries for some of the costs of their participation in peace operations.

Enhancing our ability to prevent, contain and manage unintended consequences

All of the chapters in this volume noted the importance of institutionalizing accountability in peace operations. In the past the weakness, or lack of clarity, in accountability mechanisms in itself created a "permissive" environment within which unintended negative side-effects went unreported and therefore fell outside the realm of what peace operations should have managed. When they did occur at such a scale that they could not be ignored, they were usually managed as exceptional phenomena that require a temporary, once-off, response.

For instance, Kent, Koyama and Myrttinen's findings indicate that peace operations had not meaningfully anticipated the reality of sexual exploitation and abuse before the late 1990s. It is only half way through the first decade of the twenty-first century that steps to anticipate, prevent and manage sexual violence and abuse in UN peace operations have become institutionalized. Before these latest developments, peace operations rarely addressed enduring violence on women and girls. This was due to a lack of consciousness of the problem, to the severity of the implications of the problem for all concerned and most importantly to a lack of institutional preparedness to identify, contain and manage the problem. In fact, this study finds that peace operations not only have failed to address these unintended consequences, but in some cases may have actually exacerbated them. For instance, there are instances where military, police and civilian peacekeepers are actually among those who exploit such conditions. There are very few examples of UN peace operations identifying, containing and managing unintended consequences outside of the sexual exploitation and abuse realm. Thus, managing unintended consequences is not yet a widely understood and institutionalized phenomenon.

Identifying, containing and managing unintended consequences

In order to improve our ability to plan and manage complex peace operations, we need to improve our understanding of the dynamics of complex systems, including complex social systems. We now know that, whenever we attempt to change something in a complex system, the system responds to our intervention in a number of ways. Some of the responses of the system may be the intended response. However, we also know that it is not possible, in a complex system, to develop a highly specialized agent that can generate only one outcome,[1] and therefore we can expect that the system will respond in other ways that we did not anticipate. All the reactions that fall outside the scope of the response we wanted to elicit are the unintended consequences of our intervention.

This knowledge leads us to the understanding that, in a complex system, unintended consequences should not come as a surprise. Once we realize and accept this fact, it follows that, whenever we plan or undertake action in the complex peace operations context, we have to take into account the potential unintended consequences of our actions. Also, because the system is dynamic, we cannot predict all the ways in which it may respond to our actions. This means that we have to anticipate that, despite our best planning efforts, we will still not be able to foresee all the potential unintended consequences our actions can have. However, through research into past actions and by systematically thinking through the consequences our actions are likely to evoke, we should be able significantly to reduce some of the obvious negative consequences experienced in the past. Anticipating the potential unintended consequences of our actions should become a standard aspect of our planning procedures and processes.

However, if we accept that despite these efforts some unintended consequences will still occur, then we should also establish a monitoring system that can identify when such unintended consequences emerge, so that we can try to contain or counter their potential negative effects. In fact, we need to have such a monitoring and evaluation capacity in place to study whether our intended actions are having their desired effect on the system. An important aspect of such a monitoring system should be the identification of any unintended consequences, especially negative ones. It is vital that those planning peace operations should be alert to potential negative unintended consequences. They should be part of the effort to adapt the plan to make sure the complex system that the peace operation has entered is being adequately dealt with and considered. This aims to ensure that the complex, dynamic system into which the peace operation has entered is responding appropriately to the intervention.

One methodology developed in the context of humanitarian and development assistance for anticipating unintended consequences is the "do no harm" approach.[2] In short, this approach is built on the acknowledgement that aid cannot be provided without becoming part of the wider conflict dynamics. This approach provides a model for planning, continuously monitoring and adjusting the effects of any assistance programme by identifying and downplaying the negative influences while identifying and encouraging the positive influences of the programme. In summary it (a) recognizes that unintended consequences will occur, (b) puts systems in place that will identify the effect the intervention is having (both positive and negative), and (c) steers and refines that effect by countering potential negative effects and encouraging and modulating the positive unintended consequences towards the intended impact. It also (d) states that one needs to understand that intervening in a complex system requires a continuous process of adjustment.

Through planning and monitoring efforts, such as the "do no harm" approach, we are likely to identify unintended consequences that cannot be avoided if we want to continue to pursue a specific course of action. This suggests that we may be faced with situations where we have to take into account and contain the potential negative consequences of our actions with the potential good that those same actions are intended to generate. This predicament is not unknown, and has already been addressed in the context of the "double effect" and Just War theories. We do not intend to repeat these theories in detail, but the principle of double effect is a moral principle for assessing actions that produce side-effect harm. In short, it states that, although actors are responsible for the harmful side-effects that ensue from their actions, actions that produce harmful side-effects are nevertheless permissible provided that: (1) the primary goal of the action is legitimate, (2) the side-effects are not part of the actor's intended goal, (3) the side-effects are not a means to this goal, (4) the actor aims to prevent or minimize the side-effects and (5) no alternative courses of action could have been taken that would have led to fewer or no side-effects.[3]

So there are existing theories available that can assist us in developing practical means for containing and managing unintended consequences when they cannot be avoided altogether. However, we should always be cautious of overestimating our ability to "manage" outcomes in a complex system. A further insight we need to gain from our study of complex systems is that managing the host system, in the sense of controlling it, is impossibly complex. Managing unintended consequences should, in this context, be understood as purposefully interacting with the system with the aim of continuously adjusting our actions to the feedback generated by the system with a view to minimizing any negative unintended consequences the interventions may have caused. When we talk about containing and managing unintended consequences, the emphasis is on being alert to system feedback through institutionalized monitoring and evaluating mechanisms, and constantly adjusting our planning and operations accordingly.

Planning for peace operations can no longer rely on the "fire-and-forget" planning model where a peace operation is mandated and planned, and then perhaps annually reviewed against the original plan. In this model the original plan is revisited only when the situation fundamentally changes. In the complex peace operations context, each action results in the system responding in various ways that will require a range of further actions. The most apt analogy is that of steering a ship. Although the destination is known at the outset, and although it is possible to plan the journey in great detail, the actual voyage requires thousands of route adjustments, some minor and some more significant, to reach the destination. The reality of peace operations is, however, even more complex in that the destination is a very broadly defined desired end state, and the exact journey is unclear beyond the milestones contained in peace agreements. These are typically unrealistic political ideals formed by the need for compromise and mutual assurance, rather than practical reality. Managing complex peace operations necessitates an ongoing planning process that constantly monitors and evaluates the feedback generated by the system so that the peace operation can continuously adjust its programmes or initiate new actions accordingly.

The accountability debate

The attempt to establish clear accountability in peace operations is hampered by two factors. One of them concerns authority, namely, to whom the peace operation is accountable. The second issue concerns the control of the mission.

Hampson and Kihara-Hunt address accountability in the context of the necessity to deal with criminal conduct or breaches of applicable disciplinary codes. This relates to the "control" of the mission issue through the management of the behaviour of individuals and it covers unintended consequences such as sexual exploitation and abuse, corruption and theft. Mégret, on the other hand, addresses authority in the broader sense of unintended consequences caused by the actions or omissions of the mission itself, which covers the kinds of unintended consequences addressed by Ammitzboell (economic consequences), Lee (humanitarian consequences) and Gordon (civil–military coordination consequences). For this category (the question of authority, or to whom a peace operation reports), two models may be relevant, namely the delegation and the participation models.[4] These models capture two separate potential accountability mechanisms. In the delegation model, power is exercised by those who are delegated with the authority to do so, making them accountable to those who delegate the power to them. In the participatory model, those in power are accountable to individuals in the polity. In the international sphere, different perceptions about accountability create tensions and conflicts. Some perceive international organizations, such as the United Nations and the World Bank, as reporting to their member governments (delegation model). Others hold that these organizations' actions should be made accountable directly to the people who are affected by their actions (participation model).

Thus, in the peace operation context, some would argue that a peace operation is accountable to the UN Security Council, the body responsible for establishing and supervising the mission, whereas others would argue that a peace operation should be accountable to its host community, namely the people whom the peace operation is meant to assist. Mégret notes that there is a shift observable in various areas of governance from a "shareholder" view of accountability to one emphasizing the importance of "stakeholders". Ideally, a peace operation should establish a balance between these two models, for neither seems sufficient grounds for accountability by itself. Accountability of the peace operation to the UN Security Council and the UN General Assembly for budgetary matters already exists; however, mechanisms still need to be developed for meaningful host community participatory accountability.

One such mechanism is addressed by Hoffmann, in the form of the ombudsperson model, which provides one example of a mechanism that may empower the local population to submit claims against the peace operation. However, much more can and should be done to develop meaningful accountability towards and by the host community, not just in the context of legal accountability related to some form of wrongdoing. Kent, Koyama and Myrttinen, Hampson and Kihara-Hunt, and Mégret have made a range of practical recommendations for this. Examples are ongoing and proactive political accountability that can come about through a process of consultation and participation in order to seek advice and input from the host community on future plans, as well as to receive and monitor feedback from the community on programmes being undertaken. One obvious question here, however, is who constitutes the host community? One can respond that the host community should be represented through a range of institutions and mechanisms at all levels of society, and should include civil society. In a post-conflict context, which is the condition in which most peace operations find themselves, most of the official institutional positions and mechanisms will be undergoing considerable change in contested circumstances. As a consequence, the peace operation has to be resourceful in ensuring that the mechanisms it is interacting with, or facilitating, reflect the broadest possible representation of popular will and opinion. As Mégret points out, the challenge is no longer to determine whether the United Nations should be accountable; the challenge is now to determine what accountability means by examining the various options for accountability.

The other issue that hampers the establishment of clear accountability in international peace operations concerns the control of the mission. Those who are responsible for the peace operation do not necessarily have effective control over addressing criminal conduct or breaches of applicable disciplinary codes regarding the individuals who are perceived to be its employees.[5] The clearest case in this context is that personnel who are deployed as part of a military contingent to UN peace operations remain under the legal authority of the sending state when it comes

278 CHIYUKI AOI, CEDRIC DE CONING AND RAMESH THAKUR

to criminal and disciplinary issues. Although the conduct of these personnel is also governed by international humanitarian law, international human rights and other bodies of international law, these instruments need
to be applied through the national legal systems of the TCC. Hampson
and Kihara-Hunt also discuss the full spectrum of other categories of
UN peace operations personnel, including Military Observers, UN Civilian Police, international civil servants and international and local UN
staff and the various challenges related to ensuring criminal and disciplinary accountability for them in the peace operations context.

Conclusion

The editors and contributing authors were struck by the absence of literature on, or even remotely related to, the phenomenon of unintended
consequences. Most of the references that were available are anecdotal.
One recommendation is to encourage further research into the unintended consequences of peacekeeping, especially, but not limited to,
those topics generated in this volume. Examples are sexual violence and
abuse, gender inequalities, corruption, distortions of the local economy,
impact on host systems, impact on TCCs and institutional responses by
the United Nations and others.

However, even within the scope of the limited research undertaken
into this topic, and to which this volume is a humble contribution, it
has become clear that unintended consequences are an important yet
neglected subject. It is an important subject because some of the unintended consequences that come about in the context of peace operations are morally and ethically unacceptable, and others can seriously
hamper a mission's capacity to achieve its mandate. In fact, we have seen
that some unintended consequences can bring into doubt the value of
peace operations entirely, and others have brought sending institutions,
such as the United Nations, into disrepute and have been major drivers
for reform and calls for greater accountability within these international
organizations.

Those responsible for the planning, managing and supervision of peace
operations need to recognize that unintended consequences are a natural
consequence of the complex dynamic nature of complex systems. As
such, all peace operations should develop the capacity to identify, contain
and manage unintended consequences. This suggests that the United Nations and other institutions that undertake peace operations need to develop institutional mechanisms for addressing unintended consequences,
and should institutionalize planning and monitoring mechanisms that
will enable them to anticipate and respond to emerging unintended con-

sequences. The overriding message of this book is that we can no longer pretend that these side-effects do not occur or that, when they do, they are exceptional phenomena. Instead, we should bring these unintended consequences under the purview of the daily management processes of the peace operation, so that they can be prevented, contained or managed as part of the day-to-day reality of complex peace operations.

Notes

1. See G. Hardin, "The Cybernetics of Competition", *Perspectives in Biology and Medicine*, 7, Autumn 1963, pp. 79–80.
2. M. B. Anderson, *Do No Harm: How Aid Can Support Peace or War*, London: Lynne Rienner, 1999.
3. See L. Bomann-Larsen and O. Wiggen, eds, *Responsibility in World Business: Managing Harmful Side-effects of Corporate Activity*, Tokyo: United Nations University Press, 2004.
4. For a theorization of these models in the context of international relations, see Ruth W. Grant and Robert O. Keohane, "Accountability and Abuses of Power in World Politics", *American Political Science Review*, 99(1), February 2005, pp. 29–44.
5. Issues concerning the control of power in international relations are discussed in Grant and Keohane, "Accountability and Abuses of Power in World Politics", pp. 37–38.

Index

non-governmental organizations (NGOs) 5, 55; in Afghanistan 118–19; and community engagement in projects 122–3; and employment of local personnel 39; expanding roles in PSOs 110–11; and impartiality 126; in Kosovo 229; post-conflict situations 83; protection 185; and PRTs 116–19; and Rwandan UN mission 103; and SEA allegations 58–60

Norden, Deborah L. 171, 177

North Atlantic Treaty Organization (NATO) 59, 70, 84; Argentine status 177; CIMIC definition 111–12; and Kosovo crisis 96, 204; and UN peacekeeping missions 186, see also Kosovo Force (KFOR)

Norway 166–7, 231

Novicki, Margaret 134

Nowicki, Marek 231–2, 242

Office of UN High Commissioner for Human Rights (OHCHR) 94–5

Omar, Mullah Mohammad 117, 119

Ombudsperson Institution in Kosovo (OIK) 223, 229–34; accountability mechanisms 233–4, 240–1, 244–5; Children's Rights Team (CRT) 232; claims/complaints 261; ethnic tension conditions 234–7; funding/donor states and IOs 229, 231; human rights monitoring 235–6, 241; investigative/jurisdictional powers 230, 240–1, 243, 244–5; mandate 229–30; Non-Discrimination Team (NDT) 232; property rights issues 236; refugees and displaced persons issues 236; sanctioning power 230–1; Special Reports 232–3, 239, 240; UNMIK/KFOR collaboration issues 237–41, 242–3; use patterns 232–3

ombudspersons/ombudspersonship: and accountability 212, 222, 243; investigative/prosecution powers 243; Kosovo lessons 241–5; legal basis 243–4; mandates and funding 243, 244; operational policies 244; theory and practice 221–3; UN-system wide concept 222, 245

Organization of African Unity (African Union) 102

Organization for Security and Co-operation in Europe (OSCE) 70, 226; Office of Democratic Institutions and Human Rights 231

organizational field theory 123, 126

paedophilia 34, 47, 165

Pakistan: and international citizenship 158–9; Islamic solidarity 159; military capabilities 158; mission casualties 157, 162; reimbursement of mission costs 162; UN observer missions 159; UN peace operations 156–7, 166, 186; US relationship 161

peace enforcement (PE) operations 115–16, 195

peace operations personnel: financial benefits 135; participants' allowances 140–1, 162–3, 176, 178; sexual misconduct 164–5

peace operations study: assistance/economical issues overview 73–5; budgets/funding 79, 121–2; coordination/division of roles 97; creation of economic/social problems 76–86; definitions: peacekeeping/peacebuilding 69–70; effects on civil–military relations 187; integrated mission concept 72; interventions 95, 99; light footprint approach 71–2, 86; literature 187; mandates 5, 69, 70, 90, 95, 96–7, 195, 213; and military involvement 95–6, 115; negative consequences 7; neutrality principles 95; participation effects 187; reporting/tracking systems 75; and resource stringency 136–7; staff problems/turnover 75–6; transitional administrations 72, 79–81, 87; unintentional policies 75–6, see also personnel accountability study

Peace Operations (US Army Field Manual) 116

peace support operations (PSOs) 110–11, 196; benefits to participating countries 135; Civil Claims Units 205; doctrines 116; jurisdiction issues 202; planning 275–6

peacekeeping/peacebuilding: civilianizing effects on military 183–7; initiatives 16; and integration debate 114–16; and military interventions 110–11; multidimensional missions 184–5; and organizational theory 123–4; and political legitimization 121; and Special Forces operations 117–18

Peprah, Kwame 148

Perrow, Charles 12

personnel accountability study: accountability/obligations 196, 209, 211, 213, 214–15; ad hoc mechanisms 212;